BORROWING
TO LIVE

JAMES A. JOHNSON METRO SERIES

JAMES A. JOHNSON METRO SERIES

The Metropolitan Policy Program at the Brookings Institution is integrating research and practical experience into a policy agenda for cities and metropolitan areas. By bringing fresh analyses and policy ideas to the public debate, the program hopes to inform key decisionmakers and civic leaders in ways that will spur meaningful change in our nation's communities.

As part of this effort, the James A. Johnson Metro Series aims to introduce new perspectives and policy thinking on current issues and attempts to lay the foundation for longer-term policy reforms. The series examines traditional urban issues, such as neighborhood assets and central city competitiveness, as well as larger metropolitan concerns, such as regional growth, development, and employment patterns. The James A. Johnson Metro Series consists of concise studies and collections of essays designed to appeal to a broad audience. While these studies are formally reviewed, some will not be verified like other research publications. As with all publications, the judgments, conclusions, and recommendations presented in the studies are solely those of the authors and should not be attributed to the trustees, officers, or other staff members of the Institution.

On growth and development

Boomburbs: The Rise of America's Accidental Cities
Robert E. Lang and Jennifer B. LeFurgy

Edgeless Cities: Exploring the Elusive Metropolis
Robert E. Lang

Growth and Convergence in Metropolitan America
Janet Rothenberg Pack

Growth Management and Affordable Housing
Anthony Downs, editor

Laws of the Landscape: How Policies Shape Cities in Europe and America
Pietro S. Nivola

Reflections on Regionalism
Bruce J. Katz, editor

Revisiting Rental Housing: Policies, Programs, and Priorities
Nicolas P. Restinas and Eric S. Belsky, editors

Sunbelt/Frostbelt: Public Policies and Market Forces in Metropolitan Development
Janet Rothenberg Pack, editor

On transportation

Still Stuck in Traffic: Coping with Peak-Hour Traffic Congestion
Anthony Downs

Taking the High Road: A Metropolitan Agenda for Transportation Reform
Bruce Katz and Robert Puentes, editors

On trends

Redefining Urban and Suburban America: Evidence from Census 2000, vol. 1
Bruce Katz and Robert E. Lang, editors

Redefining Urban and Suburban America: Evidence from Census 2000, vol. 2
Alan Berube, Bruce Katz, and Robert E. Lang, editors

On wealth creation

Building Assets, Building Credit: Creating Wealth in Low-Income Communities
Nicolas P. Retsinas and Eric S. Belsky, editors

The Geography of Opportunity: Race and Housing Choice in Metropolitan America
Xavier de Souza Briggs, editor

Low-Income Homeownership: Examining the Unexamined Goal
Nicolas P. Retsinas and Eric S. Belsky, editors

Savings for the Poor: The Hidden Benefits of Electronic Banking
Michael A. Stegman

On other metro issues

Evaluating Gun Policy: Effects on Crime and Violence
Jens Ludwig and Philip J. Cook, editors

BORROWING TO LIVE

Consumer and Mortgage Credit Revisited

NICOLAS P. RETSINAS
ERIC S. BELSKY
Editors

JOINT CENTER FOR HOUSING STUDIES
HARVARD UNIVERSITY
Cambridge, Massachusetts

BROOKINGS INSTITUTION PRESS
Washington, D.C.

Copyright © 2008
THE BROOKINGS INSTITUTION
1775 Massachusetts Avenue, N.W., Washington, D.C. 20036
www.brookings.edu

Library of Congress Cataloging-in-Publication data
Borrowing to live : consumer and mortgage credit revisited / Nicolas P. Retsinas, Eric S. Belsky, editors.
     p.   cm.   — (James A. Johnson metro series)
  Includes bibliographical references and index.
  Summary: "Dissects the current state of consumer and mortgage credit in the United States and helps point the way out of the current impasse"—Provided by publisher.
  ISBN 978-0-8157-7413-6 (pbk. : alk. paper)
  1. Consumer credit—United States. 2. Mortgage loans—United States. I. Retsinas, Nicolas Paul, 1946– II. Belsky, Eric S.
  HG3756.U54B67 2008
  332.70973—dc22   2008038068

1 3 5 7 9 8 6 4 2

The paper used in this publication meets minimum requirements of the
American National Standard for Information Sciences—Permanence of
Paper for Printed Library Materials: ANSI Z39.48-1992.

Typeset in Adobe Garamond

Composition by Circle Graphics
Columbia, Maryland

Printed by R. R. Donnelley
Harrisonburg, Virginia

To

EDWARD M. GRAMLICH

Contents

Acknowledgments

This book is the product of a symposium examining the challenges of improving outcomes for consumers and driving market efficiencies in the consumer credit system, while preserving the choice and access that borrowers with limited financial means and with subpar credit records have enjoyed. The goal of deepening our understanding of national consumer credit issues and exploring how best to formulate a more cogent government response to credit challenges was successfully accomplished, but only with the assistance of several dedicated parties. Principal funding for the symposium was provided by the Ford Foundation, Freddie Mac, and NeighborWorks® America, to whom we are indebted for seeing the value of sponsoring an event dedicated to researching, uncovering, and better understanding the challenges of the credit marketplace. We were fortunate to have worked with an extraordinary group of colleagues, all of whom contributed to making this project such a success. We would especially like to thank George McCarthy and Brandee McHale (formerly) from the Ford Foundation, Edward Golding from Freddie Mac, and Ken Wade from NeighborWorks® America for the formative role they played in shaping the research questions addressed in this book.

In addition, we owe a debt of gratitude to Ellen Seidman of Shorebank International and Michael Barr of the University of Michigan, who gave freely of their time and shared with us ideas that we incorporated into the design of the conference. We also thank the authors of the papers, who presented them at the symposium, and the moderators and discussants, who made the event itself a lively debate and discussion of the issues. In addition to the book's contributors, a group of representatives from the financial services industry and the academic and advocacy communities advised us early in the process and deserve special recognition: Konrad Alt of Promontory Financial Group; Michael Barr of the University of Michigan Law School; Joe Belew of the Consumer Bankers Association; Ray Boshara of the New America Foundation; Sandra Braunstein of the Federal Reserve Board of Governors; Keith Ernst of the Center for Responsible Lending; Edward Golding of Freddie Mac; Edward Gramlich of the University of Michigan; Sharon Hermanson of the AARP Public Policy Institute; Dean Karlan of Yale University; Elizabeth Renuart of the National Consumer Law Center; Kevin Rhein of Wells Fargo; Ellen Seidman of Shore-Bank Corporation; Eldar Shafir of Princeton University; Joseph A. Smith Jr., North Carolina Commissioner of Banks; Michael Staten of the George Washington University Business School; Bonnie Tillen of Standard and Poor's; Peter Tufano of the Harvard Business School; Ken Wade of NeighborWorks® America; and Elizabeth Warren of the Harvard Law School.

Deserving of special recognition is Ren Essene, who managed the development of the symposium. Her diligent efforts and intellectual contributions were vital to the success of this endeavor. We also would like to acknowledge William Apgar for sharing his excellent ideas with us and for his wise guidance at all stages of the initiative. Thanks also to Pamela Baldwin, Elizabeth England, Angela Flynn, Nancy Jennings, Jackie Hernandez, Laurel Gourd, and all of the staff at the Joint Center for Housing Studies for their hard work on the symposium.

Last named here, but first in our hearts, we would like to thank Joan Retsinas and Cynthia Wilson for their support, encouragement, and always sage advice.

Borrowing
to Live

Introduction: Borrowing to Live

NICOLAS P. RETSINAS AND ERIC S. BELSKY

Not so long ago, when poor people desperately needed a loan, they sought out neighborhood sharks—and paid and paid. Or they relied on retailers like car dealers and furniture stores to finance their purchases. Houses were beyond reach. Before the Community Reinvestment Act in 1977 was enacted, deposit-taking banks—the traditional mortgage lenders—often rejected them. These banks would offer thirty-year fixed rate mortgages, generally with 20 percent down payments, to middle- and upper-income Americans. But these borrowers' credit met the lenders' standards: in the jargon, they were "prime" borrowers. The would-be homeowners without stellar credit were "subprime," and mainstream lenders spurned them.

Over the past thirty years, America's entrepreneurial credit industry recognized an opportunity. Subprime borrowers might entail greater risk, but you could compensate for that risk with higher fees and higher interest rates. And people eager to buy homes would pay those fees and interest rates. A new niche industry quickly evolved: subprime lenders. New mortgage banks sprang up. Millions of renters bought homes. Subprime lending soared from nearly none in the early 1990s to 20.1 percent of all originations in 2006.

Poor people were no longer borrowers non grata. Indeed, low-income consumers have been able to borrow easily—critics would say too easily. Lenders were willing, even eager—again, in hindsight, critics would say too eager—to extend credit via a dizzying assortment of products, including no down payment, variable payment, and negative amortization. Credit card companies joined in the frenzy. Just about anybody could get a credit card. If a guardian angel had awakened George Bailey to America in 2000, the kindly banker would have cheered this new world of credit that let many Americans own their homes and buy whatever their hearts desire.

For at least fifteen years, the world of looser credit made many people happy. Low-income renters owned their homes (which some used as ATM machines, spurring a surging market in home equity loans); mortgage brokers received their commissions (paid whether or not the homeowner defaulted); and investors who bought the securitized mortgages earned double-digit returns. And predatory lenders, who profited when borrowers defaulted, crafted a lucrative and nefarious microniche in this niche market.

If George Bailey had awakened to the world of American credit in 2008, he would have been alarmed.

We have learned that too-good-to-be-true deals generally are flawed. They are not good for consumers and are equally toxic for the communities and the nation's financial system. Many homeowners who faced a bump in interest rates could not pay the higher monthly payments because they were allowed to buy homes that stretched their incomes perilously thin, even at the outset. Speculators could easily get credit and then were all too willing to default on their loans when the opportunity to profit from rapid appreciation passed. And a slackening market, with falling home prices, left homeowners and speculators alike unable to recoup their investments or refinance their mortgages when things soured. Homeowners discovered that they owed more than their homes were worth, and many were surprised by the terms of their mortgages, which were often hard to understand. As for the mortgage investors who bought the securitized bundles of subprime mortgages, they watched their net worth drop.

In 2006, when Harvard University's Joint Center for Housing Studies began planning a Symposium on Understanding Consumer Credit, we were, in hindsight, at the apex of housing prosperity, thanks in large measure to a robust subprime industry. We reached out to the Ford Foundation, Freddie Mac, and NeighborWorks® America to help us solicit, organize, and present research on all facets of consumer credit linked to the financing of a home. The symposium was conducted in November 2007 at the Harvard Business School. Two previous symposia with the same sponsors led to two books entitled *Low-Income Homeownership: Examining the Unexamined Goal* (2002) and *Building Assets, Building Credit: Creating Wealth in Low-Income Communities* (2005).

The Center invited researchers to play the role of iconoclasts and statistically probe the effect of consumer credit on borrowers, communities, and our nation. A group of lenders, advocates, and regulators dissected the findings. This book highlights the key papers from that effort.

For America in 2008, credit undergirds everyday life. In our economy most low- and moderate-income people borrow to live on their income. They are not borrowing to keep up with the Joneses; they are borrowing to stay afloat, to keep up with payments for housing, food, transportation, and health care. How they negotiate that credit—whom they borrow from, the terms, the collateral, the conditions—defines our well-being as a nation.

In chapter 1 Belsky, Essene, and Retsinas ("Consumer and Mortgage Credit at the Crossroads") begin the dialogue by tracing the surge in aggregate debt-to-income and debt-service ratios. Today consumers carry more debt than ever and spend more of their income servicing that debt. Borrowers confront a panoply of products, but just as the credit choices have grown more complicated, so too has the potential for wildly unrealistic risk. The paper lays out straightforward ways to assist consumers: counseling, more flexible payment schedules, and insurance products that can mitigate the risks of job loss, disease, and disability.

Cole, Thompson, and Tufano in chapter 2 ("Where Does It Go? Spending by the Financially Constrained") use data from H&R Block to analyze the spending decisions of more than 1.5 million Americans. Not surprisingly, they find that would-be borrowers who cannot borrow from subprime lenders are more likely to spend any tax refunds more quickly and are more likely to spend for necessities.

Sawady and Tescher in chapter 3 ("Financial Decisionmaking Processes of Low-Income Individuals") highlight the emotional context of borrowing. Rationally, based on price and convenience, a given borrower with a set income "should" turn to a traditional bank or credit union, not a subprime lender, and certainly not the local pawnbroker. Yet economics and convenience do not determine all borrowing decisions. Consumers who live in neighborhoods where everybody goes to one subprime lender may follow suit. Indeed, immigrants who distrusted banks in their native lands often distrust banks in this country.

McCoy and Renuart in chapter 4 ("The Legal Infrastructure of Subprime and Nontraditional Home Mortgages") review the pastiche of regulatory paradigms. Banks have gravitated to the more flexible national bank charters, in part to flee state regulation, and the lax regulation of nonbank mortgage lending subsidiaries, coupled with the conflicting mandates of federal banking regulators, has left few private remedies for borrowers.

Bostic, Engel, McCoy, Pennington-Cross, and Wachter in chapter 5 ("The Impact of State Antipredatory Laws: Policy Implications and Insights") discuss the patchwork of antipredatory laws across states. Roughly half the states have passed laws that range from weak to rigorous. Rigorous laws can be designed to restrict predatory loans while preserving, even increasing, the vitality of the subprime market. Weak laws, though, give consumers false confidence that government is protecting them from a predatory loan.

In chapter 6 Barr, Mullainathan, and Shafir ("Behaviorally Informed Home Mortgage Credit Regulation") plumb the role of psychology in consumers' choices. One option, a fixed-rate thirty-year mortgage, with a 20 percent down payment, may be the "best" from an economic vantage. Yet a qualified borrower chooses a variable-rate or a no-down-payment or a negative amortized product. Why? The sheer choice among highly touted, much-advertised products can influence the decision: much as you pick the most-touted, best-placed cereal on the shelves, you may pick the most-touted loan. The authors explore governmental reforms such as better disclosure requirements, mandatory rate-sheet pricing, and bans on yield spread premiums.

In chapter 7 Cutts and Merrill ("Interventions in Mortgage Default: Policies and Practices to Prevent Home Loss and Lower Costs") analyze the true costs of foreclosures. The timeline for foreclosures ranges from 60 days to 120 days, depending on the state. Although housing advocates have argued for longer timelines to give owners more opportunity to forestall the sale, the authors point to the effect of longer delinquencies: more time for the property to deteriorate and lose value, with the concomitant effect on abutting houses. The authors conclude that states could reduce investor costs and reduce foreclosure rates by shortening the statutory timelines.

Finally in chapter 8, Kempson ("Looking beyond Our Shores: Consumer Protection Regulation Lessons from the United Kingdom") comments on self-regulation in the United Kingdom, where banks voluntarily embrace codes of conduct for lending. The sanction for breaking that code is public disclosure, or "name and shame." The author notes the weak oversight of unsecured lending.

This volume offers a window into the new world of consumer credit. The authors reach provocative conclusions, reflecting the desire to balance two goals: protect the consumer and at the same time expand consumer choice. Policymakers who wrestle with the acknowledged limitations of government oversight in this changing marketplace should find the papers useful.

The symposium has stimulated further dialogue. This volume does not provide definitive answers—nobody has discovered a magic-wand solution. But the research points us in the right direction.

1

Consumer and Mortgage Credit at the Crossroads

ERIC S. BELSKY, REN S. ESSENE, AND NICOLAS P. RETSINAS

B y all measures, Americans are awash in debt as never before.[1] While median net wealth grew from $69,465 to $93,001 from 1989 to 2004, it was outpaced by consumer debt, which more than doubled during the same period, from $22,000 to $55,300.[2] By 2004, 76.4 percent of all households reported some form of borrowing; 46.2 percent were carrying a balance on at least one credit card, 48.0 percent on a mortgage loan or line of credit, 39.5 percent on an auto loan or lease, 13.4 percent on a student loan, and 19.3 percent on some other form of borrowing.[3] Undoubtedly, the proportion of Americans who had carried

1. As pointed out in Mote and Nolle (2005), the debt-service ratio shows households' required debt-service payments relative to their disposable income; it therefore measures households' monthly servicing obligation, not other obligations such as rent, auto leases, insurance, and taxes, which are captured in the financial obligations ratio (FOR). Both measures have risen to levels well beyond their historical averages.

2. In 2004 dollars; see Federal Reserve Board (2008c). The Survey of Consumer Finances (SCF), which is conducted every three years, captures the balance sheet, pension, income, and other demographic characteristics of U.S. families, as well as information on the use of financial institutions. See www.federalreserve.gov/pubs/oss/oss2/scfindex.html, where the surveys are listed by year.

3. Federal Reserve Board (2008c). "Mortgage loan or line of credit" is housing debt on principal residences (mortgage, home equity loans, and HELOCs). Other forms of lending include other lines of credit; debt for other residential property (land, residential property other than principal residence, miscellaneous vacation property, and cottage/vacation home); other installment loans (installment loans minus vehicle and education loans); and other debts (loans against pensions, loans against life insurance, margin loans, and miscellaneous loans). The fraction of households with any one of these forms of debt is quite low, and we will not address these forms of debt in this paper. According to the SCF, by 2004 unsecured installment loans, which once were quite common, were being carried by just 9 percent of all households.

debt at some point in their lives is even higher than the point estimate in 2004. In addition, the aggregate debt of the household sector was still climbing at the end of 2007.[4]

As a result, many are finding themselves in a debt trap that they are having difficulty escaping. Starting around 2006, mortgage borrowers who found themselves unable to service their debt were especially hard hit. So too were those who took advantage of low interest rates and bulked up on consumer credit in the early part of this decade, only to find rising interest rates and escalating payments on their variable-rate debt. While problems appeared first and most dramatically with subprime mortgages, they began to spread to unsecured subprime lending and secured prime lending over the course of only a year or two.[5]

Although all measures confirm that debt hit record levels in 2007, different measures paint somewhat different pictures of just how much debt Americans are carrying and the difficulties that they face in servicing that debt. For example, debt-to-income ratios (ratio of amount of debt to income) at both the aggregate and household levels have increased faster than debt-service ratios (ratio of debt payments to income) since 1989. One reason for this growing divergence is that real interest rates fell sharply from 1998 to 2004 and have not come close to returning to the levels of the 1980s and early to mid-1990s.[6] Therefore, it cost less to service an equivalent amount of debt (Dynan, Johnson, and Pence 2003). But renters have consumer debt loads that will take an average of more than five years to pay off and owners' debt loads will take even longer.[7] Therefore, even if a reduction in interest rates was the impetus to take on added debt, households are saddled with it for some time, and those with adjustable rates face the risk of sudden increases in monthly debt payments that can last for a long time.

Other explanations for the rising tide of debt run a wide gamut. Expanded access to credit, particularly mortgage credit, is usually singled out as an important contributor to increasing debt-service ratios. The relaxation of constraints on

4. Federal Reserve Board (2008b). The household sector includes the nonprofit sector because household net wealth is not separately reported.

5. Traditionally, only unsecured lending to individuals or households was considered consumer credit. Households now use home equity to finance consumption and investment, and mortgage debt is the largest single form of debt for most homeowners. It also is a major component of debt burdens and central to the financing decisions of more than half of all households. As a result, we use the term "consumer credit" to refer to secured or unsecured debt held by a consumer.

6. For example, the inflation-adjusted composite effective interest rate on all conventional loans on single-family homes decreased a sharp 239 basis points from 2002 to 2005, to 2.55 percent; it was down 300 basis points in seven years, from a peak of 5.55 percent in 1998; and it was 277 basis points lower than in 1989. Inflation data come from the seasonally adjusted Bureau of Labor Statistics' Consumer Price Index for All Urban Consumers (CPI-U) for All Items, available at (www.bls.gov/cpi). Mortgage rates are the non–seasonally adjusted rates on all conventional single-family mortgages from table 9 of the Monthly Interest Rate Survey of the Federal Housing Finance Board (www.fhfb.gov/Default.aspx?Page=53).

7. From the 2004 Survey of Consumer Finances. In 2004, the average renter with debt had a debt load of $17,000 that would take an estimated sixty-six months to pay off.

maximum permissible debt-to-income ratios also figures prominently. Some argue that the rising cost of such items as housing and education has forced households to borrow more to maintain a fixed standard of living.[8] Others blame the profligate consumer or today's consumer culture for increased consumption and debt.

The implications of the increase in debt range from highly positive to highly negative. On the positive side of the ledger, the aggregate increase in asset holdings between 1989 and 2006 was greater than the aggregate increase in debt. Thus total household net worth grew despite the increases in total debt, until falling home prices in 2007 reduced the value of asset holdings.[9] In addition, several studies have found that growth in consumer credit is associated with growth in consumer spending and is therefore a plus for the economy (Antzoulatos 1996; Bacchetta and Gerlach 1997; McCarthy 1997; Ludvigson 1999). In fact, until the crisis that enveloped credit markets beginning in the summer of 2007, the credit delivery system had been widely viewed as compelling evidence that innovations in the lending industry and the capital markets had led to broader access to lower-cost credit, greater consumption, and more investment in housing than ever before. Now many of those gains are threatened. Underscoring just how fragile the recent gains are turning out to be, the Federal Reserve Board estimates that $600 billion in home equity was lost over the course of 2007 alone.

On the negative side of the ledger, the delivery system has been viewed as allowing—or worse, encouraging—consumers to borrow (either for consumption or to make risky investments) without sufficient understanding of debt products, the exposure to repayment risk, or the risk of negative returns on debt-financed investments. Some also view the credit delivery system as fundamentally flawed, blaming the huge increase in debt and the recent severe credit market disruptions on relaxed terms and lax government oversight. Still other researchers have pointed out that periods of easing credit followed by tightening contribute to periods of overheating in the broader economy and the severity of ensuing recessions (Bernanke, Gertler, and Gilchrist 1996). Others have linked high debt burdens to consumer spending cuts during recessions, which also exacerbate business cycles (King 1994). Last, the rich literature on wealth effects shows that reductions in

8. A recent Federal Reserve report (Dynan and Kohn 2007) states that "the increase in house prices—particularly, but not exclusively, over the past half-dozen years—appears to have played the central role." Some of the increase reflects the increased level and availability of credit to more borrowers, yet the same report concludes that the "democratization of credit" appears to have played only a small role in rising indebtedness. No doubt, the rise in housing assets, accompanied by growth in net worth, has spurred consumer spending while increasing household indebtedness for most Americans. See also Warren and Tyagi (2003).

9. The Flow of Funds shows that aggregate household wealth increased from $32,301.7 billion in 1989 to $55,885.6 billion in 2006 (in 2006 dollars), while the Survey of Consumer Finances reports an increase in average net worth of households from $279,224 in 1989 to $447,041 in 2004 (in 2004 dollars).

credit can cause a drop in spending and lead to a re-pricing of assets, which can amplify business cycles too.

Good or bad, taking on debt entails repayment risk. For millions of Americans each year, some combination of life events and their own choices results in their inability or unwillingness to pay off debts, leading to repossession of vehicles, home foreclosures, and bankruptcy.[10] The number of Americans who filed for nonbusiness bankruptcy grew from 597,965 in 2006 to 822,590 in 2007.[11] In 2006, the number of loans that entered foreclosure was 773,470; in 2007, the number almost doubled, to 1,329,390.[12]

Quite apart from whether the expansion of credit is good or bad from a normative perspective, debate continues on whether the expansion was motivated by consumerism and push marketing or whether it was a rational response to the opening up of new opportunities to invest and smooth consumption over the life cycle. Either way, the rather sudden shift from more sharply restricted credit to wider access and more product choices placed a great deal of importance on the credit decisions of consumers never before confronted with so many options in the credit marketplace. When sharp restrictions on credit returned with violent swiftness in 2007, these same consumers found credit and choices suddenly choked off.

Among the most important attributes of the credit system are those that have the potential to undermine the safety, soundness, and efficiency of mortgage markets and lead to unfair treatment of consumers. Ample evidence has recently accrued that the credit markets violate many essential assumptions regarding the efficient and fair operation of competitive markets. Credit markets require consumers to make increasingly complex decisions about heterogeneous products that require probabilistic judgments. Pricing is not transparent, comparison shopping is costly and difficult, and consumers are prone to make systematic and predictable errors in estimating the true probability of certain events that govern the long-term cost of a loan and their capacity to repay it. In addition, the increasing sophistication with which choices are framed and products are marketed may

10. Interestingly, bankruptcy filers most often cite medical problems as the cause. See Himmelstein and others (2005).

11. The nonbusiness bankruptcy count is from table F-2 of the U.S. Bankruptcy Courts. Cases commenced during the twelve-month period ending December 31, 2006, and 2007 respectively. The FY 2006 figures include most of the filings that were part of the surge in filings prompted by the October 17, 2005, implementation date of the Bankruptcy Abuse Prevention and Consumer Protection Act of 2005 (www.uscourts.gov/bnkrpctystats/bankrupt_f2table_dec2006.xls). The FY 2007 figures can be found at (www.uscourts.gov/Press_Releases/2008/bankrupt_newstat_f2table_dec2007.pdf).

12. Foreclosure numbers for loans that are sixty days delinquent or entering foreclosure equal the four-quarter moving average of non–seasonally adjusted conventional loans serviced, multiplied by the seasonally adjusted rates of delinquencies and foreclosure starts from the Mortgage Bankers Association National Delinquency Survey (www.mbaa.org/ResearchandForecasts/ProductsandSurveys/NationalDelinquencySurvey.htm).

allow suppliers to exploit predictable biases in how consumers make credit decisions to steer them to buy products not on the basis of their initial preferences and clear-eyed calculations of utility, but on the basis of incomplete information and preferences shaped by the suppliers (Essene and Apgar 2007). Those are just the kinds of conditions that can lead to inefficient outcomes.

Equally important, when new products and underwriting standards were being introduced with such blistering speed, it made it difficult for investors to price and for third-party agents to manage risk correctly. Further, it was challenging to manage agency risk and protect consumers and investors in a system in which funding, originating, and servicing was done by so many different agents. Given the higher expected default probabilities of subprime loans, this new form of lending was bound to increase the importance of methods designed to help borrowers avoid credit default or foreclosure without creating greater moral hazard the next time around. Last, the acceptance of higher levels of risk leads to higher rates of loan default given comparable economic conditions. Evidence from loans originated in each of the years from 2005–07 suggests that current models substantially underestimated the risk of nonprime lending. That means that more borrowers are getting into trouble than at any time since the Depression.[13] This places a greater burden on business, public policy, and civic efforts intended to blunt the impact of default on individuals, investors, and (in the case of mortgages) neighboring property owners as well.

Still, few would want to turn back the clock to the days when only prime borrowers could get a loan, sources of funds for loans were restricted mostly to domestic deposit-taking institutions, and loan products met only a small slice of demand for different features. But given the problems that have unfolded in the credit markets, it is likely that changes in credit market practices and regulations will occur in the years ahead. Decisions about how to make those changes will likely be dogged by continuing concerns that the pendulum may swing too far in the direction of tighter standards and fewer choices. Reform efforts may also be confounded by the difficulty in judging which personal credit decisions constitute "errors" and which are caused by intentional misleading of the consumer by the lender. It is especially difficult to make such judgments when consumers' preferences and estimates of utility can vary widely in ways not easily understood. Differences in utilities can result in choices that seem optimal from a consumer's perspective but that appear suboptimal to a more objective observer.

13. Fitch Ratings reported revised subprime default expectations "for the remaining balance of the 2006 and 2007 mortgage pools of 48 percent and 43 percent, respectively. Loss severity expectations are 58 percent for 2006 loans and 64 percent for 2007. The product of the FOF and LS assumptions yields an expected loss (EL) of approximately 28 percent as a percentage of the remaining balance of each vintage. Given that the 2006 vintage remaining balance is smaller, these figures translate into the 21 percent and 26 percent loss expectations, respectively, as a percentage of original balance as cited above" (Bailey, Barberio, and Costello 2008, p. 2).

This chapter briefly explores U.S. consumer debt trends, the reasons advanced for the trends, and their implications. It then traces the evolution of the unbundled capital-market-funded credit system and examines the special challenges, risks, and opportunities that the relatively new and rapidly evolving risk-based pricing system poses for consumers, credit providers, financial intermediaries, regulators, and community groups. Last, it examines how those constituencies can respond and the difficulties that they face in doing so.

Consumer Debt

Consumers have been adding significantly to their debt and a logical first question is to ask why people borrow. There are several different reasons offered, ranging from efforts to smooth consumption over a lifetime as income ebbs and flows, to a necessity to meet basic needs during gaps in income or prolonged periods of low income, to keeping pace with the rising standard of living, to overspending and a desire for instant gratification. Whatever the reasons, both the share of households (especially among minorities in the bottom half of the income distribution) and the amounts of debt they carry has soared. Moreover, a growing share of low-income renters is struggling under significant nonmortgage debt payment burdens, while low-income and minority homeowners are struggling to make their subprime mortgage payments.

Consumer Attitudes

A rich literature explores social attitudes toward and economic and social reasons for borrowing, which, together with the income and spending patterns of households, govern the demand for credit. But effective demand is also critically influenced by the underwriting standards of credit suppliers and by the price and supply of credit.

Many publications and organizations have documented the increase in consumer indebtedness. Hundreds of books (*Surviving Debt, Managing Debt for Dummies,* and *Credit Card Nation,* to name a few) advise consumers how to get out of debt while others seek to understand the causes of indebtedness. Some authors fault consumers for not taking enough personal responsibility and for borrowing to buy things that they do not really need. Others rebuff that claim as an "over-consumption myth," arguing that skyrocketing housing, transportation, and education costs have spurred indebtedness to new heights (Warren and Tyagi 2003; Weller 2006). However, Dynan and Kohn of the Federal Reserve Board conclude that there is little evidence to suggest that households have become increasingly impatient in their desire to consume more or that they are growing less risk averse. While lower interest rates and demographic changes have had a modest impact, they state that "the most important factors behind the rise in debt and the associated decline in savings out of current income have probably been the combination of increasing house prices and financial innovations."[14]

Regardless of the cause, consumers feel the stress and strain of increasing indebtedness. A 2005 poll conducted by the Cambridge Consumer Credit Index indicates that 25 percent of all Americans listed getting out of debt as their top New Year's resolution. In 2004 more respondents (28 percent) said that reducing debt was a greater priority than losing weight or exercising more.[15] A recent survey cosponsored by the Center for American Progress highlights how much the U.S. public recognizes the seriousness of the debt issue: "nearly half describe household debt on items like credit cards, car loans, home mortgages and payday loans as a very serious problem in this country and 82 percent describe it as at least a somewhat serious problem."[16] The study shows that the vast majority (79 percent) believe that it is not just a problem for lower-income families but for middle-income families as well.

If increasing household debt is so stressful, why do consumers borrow? The primary economic reason is to smooth life-cycle consumption and earn a leveraged return from investment. Modern consumption theory is based on the life-cycle framework, which has "roots in the infinite horizon models of Ramsey (1928) and Friedman (1957) and the finite horizon models of Fisher (1930) and Modigliani and Brumberg (1954)."[17] Their models consider how consumers make life-cycle choices and how they allocate time, effort, and money in terms of borrowing, saving, and general consumption. The life-cycle hypothesis considers consumers' current income and predicts that people consume their expected lifetime income smoothly, by borrowing against future earnings during their early working life and consuming saved assets during retirement (Hannsgen 2007). This theory does a reasonably good job of approximating actual behavior.

More recently, the modern consumption model has been compared with real-world data to determine how consumers actually behave. While consumers generally follow the model, they are prone to spend more than predicted and to save less. Courant, Gramlich, and Laitner (1984) and others conclude that the main discrepancy between predicted and actual behavior is that people "underconsume" early and late in their lifetime by failing to borrow against future earnings and not

14. Dynan and Kohn (2007), p. 31.

15. Cambridge Consumer Credit Index, compiled by International Communications Research, from interviews with more than 800 U.S. families (www.icrsurvey.com/Study.aspx?f=Cambridge_Index_0305.html).

16. Greenberg Quinlan Rosner Research, "Public Recognizes Debt as a Fast Growing Problem in U.S.," press release, July 19, 2006 (www.greenbergresearch.com/articles/1711/2094_Debt Survey0406m1.pdf).

17. Browning and Crossley (2001).

saving enough to finance an adequate income in retirement, respectively. People also seem to "overconsume" during their highest-earning years, but the elderly do not consume from their assets as would be expected, particularly from their home equity. Another discrepancy is that consumers generally spend small windfall gains freely, behavior that is inconsistent with the life-cycle model.

Others point to additional shortcomings of the life-cycle model. It does not fully explain consumers' motives in bequeathing wealth to future generations, consider the market imperfections of liquidity constraints, or recognize that it may be difficult to predict future income (Browning and Crossley 2001). Behavioral economists propose a model that builds on the idea that people divide their assets into "mental accounts": current income, current assets, and future income (Thaler 1990). That is consistent with the findings of Courant, Gramlich, and Laitner (1984) and explains the observation that people over-consume during their highest-earning years and spend liberally from small unexpected gains.

A central premise of the life-cycle model is that households accumulate sub-stantial assets for retirement, yet many households have very low levels of accu-mulated wealth.[18] For low-income households, the theory may fall short of describing their allocation of resources and growing level of debt. A recent Brook-ings Institution study showed that borrowing increased for lower-income people as they age and that low-income seniors borrowed more revolving credit than their younger peers, reflecting the difficulty of meeting the cost of living on a fixed income (Fellowes and Mabanta 2007). Clearly, borrowing patterns also reflect efforts by consumers to meet certain social expectations regarding their living stan-dard when current income is insufficient to cover the costs of meeting those expec-tations. As the cost of living increases or standards increase relative to income growth, borrowing becomes greater both in absolute terms and as a share of cur-rent income. Other social reasons to borrow may relate to cultural obligations to extended family or to the community.

Consumer Debt Trends

Debt trends reflect effective demand at different points in time. In other words, it is not just the demand side that matters but the willingness of suppliers to lend under different underwriting tolerances, given the cost and supply of credit. Indeed, several studies show that the intensity of credit constraints (such as will-ingness to lend as measured by surveys) and the size of the credit supply are strongly correlated with consumer credit growth and consumption (Japelli and Pagano 1989; Antzoulatos 1996; Bacchetta and Gerlach 1997; Ludvigson 1999;

18. Hubbard, Skinner, and Zeldes (1994) point to three idiosyncratic risks facing households, including uncertainty about earnings, medical expenses, and length of life; the authors conclude that "expenditure policy, such as the design of social insurance programs, may exert as large an effect on savings behavior as tax policy."

Figure 1-1. *Measures of Household Debt*[a]

Index of debt measures

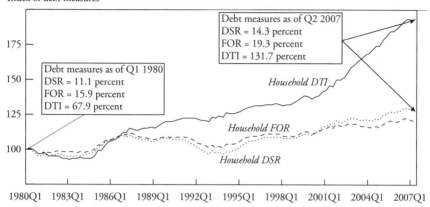

Source: Board of Governors of the Federal Resreve System, *Flow of Funds Accounts of the United States: Flows and Outstandings. Second Quarter 2007*, Z.1 Statistical Release (Washington 2007).
a. All values are as of the first quarter of the year. First quarter 1980 = 100.

Maki 2000). Effective demand has apparently been increasing substantially, fueled by loose underwriting that ended abruptly in 2007.

No matter how it is examined, consumer debt has been growing at a rapid rate, as measured by the Federal Reserve's Flow of Funds. There are three basic measures of consumer debt at the household level, which convey different information:

—household debt-service ratio (DSR)
—household financial obligations ratio (FOR)
—debt-to-income ratio (DTI)

The DSR, which is compiled by the Federal Reserve, is the ratio of the estimated required payments on outstanding mortgage and consumer debt to disposable personal income. It helps analysts understand consumers' ability to service their debt given their current payment schedule. However, the DSR does not include many recurring obligations and it includes minimum debt payments, not actual payments. Understanding those limitations, the Federal Reserve created the FOR, a broader measure of household liabilities (Dynan, Johnson, and Pence 2003). The FOR adds recurring obligations—such as automobile lease payments, rental payments on tenant-occupied property, homeowners' insurance, and property tax payments—to the debt-service ratio. Because the FOR calculates the minimum debt payment required on credit cards, it still understates the total amount of debt held by households.

The third measure, the ratio of total debt to total income, captures the true debt obligations of borrowers. While all three measures have been steadily increasing, overall DTI ratios are up the most sharply (figure 1-1). Aggregate DTI nearly doubled between 1980 and 2007, while the DSR and FOR increased about 25 percent. Still, the DSR reached a record 14.5 percent in the last quarter of 2006, up from around 11 percent thirteen years ago.[19] At the end of 2006, total household FOR also hit a record level, 19.5 percent, due to significant increases in the mortgage payments of homeowners, which rose from 9 percent of aggregate household incomes in 1998 to 11.8 percent in 2006.[20]

Dynan, Johnson, and Pence (2003) point out, however, that rising mortgage FOR does not necessarily mean that existing homeowners are paying more for their debt. Instead, it may reflect the influx of many new owners who had even higher nonmortgage debt obligations as renters. Subtracting the new owners, the FOR of homeowners was reduced by about 1 percentage point at the end of 2003. Given the influx of many more marginal borrowers between 2003 and 2006, it is likely that the effect of these new owners on total homeowner FOR climbed even higher by 2007.

The above measures of debt are aggregate measures of all households. They are not representative of what individual households owe and pay to service their debt, nor do they capture some important trends at the household level. The first such trend is the growing share of households in the lower and lower-middle-income quartiles that have certain debt products (table 1-1). While the Survey of Consumer Finance shows that the share of families with loan balances barely increased in aggregate (from 72.3 percent of all families surveyed in 1989 to 76.4 percent in 2004), the share of those with balances in the lowest income quartile increased from 48.9 percent to 54.7 percent. That increase was driven by dramatic growth in the share of lowest-income households with credit card debt, up from 17.7 percent in 1989 to 30.9 percent in 2004, as well as the share with a mortgage, which doubled, from 8.9 percent to 17.8 percent. Significant growth also is apparent in the share of lower-middle quartile households with debt, which increased from 67.4 percent in 1989 to 76.1 percent in 2004 as the share of those households with a mortgage rose from 30.2 percent to 38.2 percent.

To some degree, any changes in utilization rates or debt-service ratios can be driven by changes in age composition. After all, uses of debt vary by age and the age distribution is changing. However, it does not appear that changes in age composition have played a dominant role; instead, the increasing propensity to take on or carry debt later in life, especially by the baby boom cohort, has been driving

19. Federal Reserve Board, "Household Debt Service and Financial Obligations Ratios" (www.federalreserve.gov/releases/housedebt/default.htm).

20. Homeowner and renter FORs are calculated by applying homeowner and renter shares of payments and income derived from the Survey of Consumer Finances and the Current Population Surveys to the numerator and denominator of the FOR. The homeowner mortgage FOR includes payments on mortgage debt, homeowners' insurance, and property taxes, while the homeowner consumer FOR includes payments on consumer debt and automobile leases.

Table 1-1. *Percentage of Households with Debt, by Type of Debt, Income, and Age*

	Type of debt											
	Auto			Credit card			Mortgage			Any loan or line of credit		
Household	*1989*	*2004*	*Percent change*	*1989*	*2004*	*Percent change*	*1989*	*2004*	*Percent change*	*1989*	*2004*	*Percent change*
All households	34.7	35.6	2.6	39.7	46.2	16.4	39.5	48.0	21.5	72.3	76.4	5.7
Households by income												
Lowest	13.0	14.2	9.2	17.7	30.9	74.6	8.9	17.8	100.0	48.9	54.7	11.9
Lower middle	28.8	33.1	14.9	35.3	48.0	36.0	30.2	38.2	26.5	67.4	76.1	12.9
Upper middle	49.0	48.2	−1.6	53.8	55.6	3.3	46.5	58.6	26.0	81.9	85.3	4.2
Upper	46.9	46.5	−0.9	50.8	50.1	−1.4	70.7	76.0	7.5	89.7	89.2	−0.6
Households by age												
< 35 years old	37.7	41.3	9.5	44.5	47.5	6.7	34.8	37.7	8.3	79.8	79.8	0.0
35–44	50.5	45.5	−9.9	50.5	58.8	16.4	57.9	62.9	8.6	88.6	88.6	0.0
45–54	47.6	39.0	−18.1	49.3	54.1	9.7	58.3	64.7	11.0	85.2	88.4	3.8
55–64	27.7	34.7	25.3	32.9	42.1	28.0	37.0	51.0	37.8	70.8	76.3	7.8
65+	10.3	17.3	68.0	20.0	27.7	38.5	15.4	25.3	64.3	37.8	49.5	31.0

Source: Harvard University, Joint Center for Housing Studies, based on data from the 1989 and 2004 Survey of Consumer Finances.

much of the gain.[21] One good example is the growth in the share of older home-owners with mortgage debt. In 2004, 25.3 percent of homeowners over the age of sixty-five held mortgage debt while only 15.4 percent did so in 1989. For those aged fifty-five to sixty-four, the share was 51 percent in 2004 and only 37 percent in 1989.

Penetration rates of various forms of debt, as suggested by industry measures, imply an even greater expansion of mortgage credit than federal household surveys do. But both point in the same direction: borrowers with spotty credit records found it far easier to get credit in the first half of this decade than in the past, and the relaxation of underwriting constraints on allowable debt-service ratios (and loan-to-value ratios in the case of secured lending) enabled more low-income and lower-middle-income households of all races and ethnicities to borrow and carry debt.

The second trend in household debt patterns is the expanded access of minorities, particularly those in the bottom half of the income distribution, to debt products. The share of lower-income minorities having any kind of debt increased only from 59 percent in 1989 to 63 percent in 2004, but the shares with auto loan, credit card, and mortgage debt all increased sharply, suggesting that more of these households are taking on multiple forms of debt (table 1-2). In 2004, the share of lower-income minorities with mortgage debt was more than 23 percent, up from under 17 percent fifteen years earlier. Over the same period, the share of them with auto loans rose from 16 percent to 23 percent and the share with credit card debt rose the most dramatically, from 24 percent to 39.5 percent.

The third trend is the changing composition of debt in household portfolios. In the aggregate, mortgage debt has become a larger portion of consumer debt holdings and the amount that has increased the fastest. The Federal Reserve Flow of Funds data report that a record 76 percent of all household debt in 2007 was mortgage debt, up from 69 percent in 2001. Housing remains the primary store of wealth for most Americans, constituting one-fifth of total household net wealth. The median wealth of homeowners with annual incomes of less than $20,000 is forty times greater than the median wealth of renters with comparable incomes. However, since the mid-1980s, mortgage debt has grown more rapidly than home values, resulting in a decline in housing wealth as a share of the value of homes.[22] It is well established that housing wealth stimulates consumer spending and being able to tap into home equity easily and at low cost encourages equity borrowing

---

21. SCF data show that the share of age cohorts under forty-five years of age carrying at least one debt has held relatively steady: those under thirty-five, 79.8 percent, and those thirty-five to forty-four, 88.6 percent. For those forty-five to fifty-four, the share with debt increased from 85.2 to 88.4 percent; for those fifty-five to sixty-four, it increased from 70.8 to 76.3 percent. Seniors have seen the greatest increases, from 37.8 to 49.5 percent.

22. Greenspan and Kennedy (2007), figure 2, page 27.

Table 1-2. Percentage of Households with Debt, by Type of Debt, Race, and Income

	Type of debt											
	Auto			Credit card			Mortgage			Any loan or line of credit		
Household	1989	2004	Percent change	1989	2004	Percent change	1989	2004	Percent change	1989	2004	Percent change
Households by race												
White	36.5	37.0	1.4	41.4	46.1	11.4	43.0	51.7	20.2	73.2	77.9	6.4
Minority	29.2	31.7	8.6	34.4	46.5	35.2	28.9	37.3	29.1	69.5	72.3	4.0
Households in the bottom half of the income distribution												
White	23.9	23.9	0.3	28.3	39.3	38.7	21.7	30.4	40.2	58.2	66.7	14.6
Minority	16.3	22.9	40.2	24.2	39.5	63.6	16.8	23.2	38.4	59.0	62.7	6.2

Source: Harvard University, Joint Center for Housing Studies, based on data from the 1989 and 2004 Survey of Consumer Finances.

Figure 1-2. *Mortgage as a Percentage of Debt Obligations and Debt Outstanding*[a]

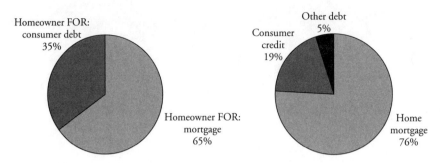

Homeowner financial obligations

Homeowner total debt outstanding

Homeowner FOR: consumer debt 35%

Homeowner FOR: mortgage 65%

Other debt 5%

Consumer credit 19%

Home mortgage 76%

Source: Board of Governors of the Federal Resreve System, *Flow of Funds Accounts of the United States: Flows and Outstandings. Second Quarter 2007*, Z.1 Statistical Release (Washington 2007).
a. Figures are as of the second quarter of 2007.

(Belsky and Prakken 2004).[23] Therefore, while the 1986 change in the tax law encouraged the substitution of mortgage debt for consumer debt, the overall increase in housing wealth has undoubtedly contributed to greater consumer spending and increased levels of overall debt.

While mortgage debt accounts for more than three-quarters of what households owe, as of the second quarter of 2007 it was less than two-thirds of all homeowner financial obligations (figure 1-2). That apparent contradiction arises because most mortgage debt is long-term debt, with payments spread out over the course of decades, whereas most other forms of consumer debt are short-term debt. The enormous run-up in mortgage debt over the last few years lifted the mortgage payment share of total homeowner financial obligations from 59 percent in 2003 to 65 percent in 2007, but it is still shy of the record 68 percent of FOR set in the early 1990s. However, the substitution of mortgage debt for consumer debt has arguably created more room for borrowers to take on more consumer debt.

Despite the substitution of mortgages for other forms of debt, median household nonmortgage debt increased for both owners and renters (table 1-3). Median outstanding nonmortgage debt for owners with such debt increased 30 percent in real terms, from $10,333 to $13,000, between 1989 and 2004. Renters with debt

23. Greenspan and Kennedy (2007) estimate the uses of home equity liquefied through cash-out. Canner, Dynan, and Passmore (2002) show that one-fifth of households used extracted equity to invest in financial assets, real estate, or businesses; one-quarter paid off other debt; one-third used equity for home improvements; and one-sixth bought consumer goods. Bucks, Kennickell, and Moore (2006) report that households mainly used HELOCs for home improvements and debt consolidation.

Table 1-3. *Owner and Renter Nonmortgage Debt, 1989 and 2004*

	Owners			Renters		
Type of debt	1989	2004	Percent change	1989	2004	Percent change
Median nonmortgage debt outstanding (dollars)[a]	10,333	13,000	26	4,428	7,800	76
Median nonmortgage debt monthly payment (dollars)[a]	371	376	1	193	225	17
Median nonmortgage debt monthly payment as percentage of income	7.3	7.1	−2	8.0	8.0	0

Source: Harvard University, Joint Center for Housing Studies, based on data from the 1989 and 2004 Survey of Consumer Finances.

a. Inflation-adjusted 2004 dollars.

had less median debt outstanding than owners, yet their debt grew two and a half times faster, up 76 percent, from $4,428 to $7,800.[24] The same patterns do not hold true, however, for median monthly nonmortgage debt payment as a share of household income. Over the 1990s, income gains and interest rate changes generally offset the impact of additional debt accumulation on required payments. Among renter households, the share of income spent on monthly debt payments remained unchanged between 1989 and 2004. Among owners, the share of income spent on monthly nonmortgage debt payments declined slightly, from 7.3 percent to 7.1 percent, over the same period.

The fourth trend in household debt is the large share of low-income households that are struggling with nonmortgage debt payments so great that it crimps their spending on even basic needs. At the extreme, some are saddled with nonmortgage debt payments that amount to 35 percent or more of their income, creating a severe debt-service ratio burden. Indeed, fully 12 percent of low-income renters and 12 percent of low-income owners struggled with such severe nonmortgage debt burdens. Even more striking, fully 29 percent of low-income renters had a nonmortgage debt-payment-to-income ratio of more than 20 percent.

The fifth trend is the growth in the share of borrowers with subprime loans and lines of credit as well as of borrowers exposed to reset risk. According to Inside Mortgage Finance (2008), the subprime share of all mortgage originations rose from 7 percent in 2002 to 20 percent in 2005 and 2006, only to drop to 8 percent in 2007. Many of the recently originated subprime loans were marketed to

24. For low- and middle-income households, the increase in nonmortgage debt appears to have been even greater, although small sample sizes prohibit drawing firm conclusions from subsets of owners and renters by income.

low-income borrowers and were attractive to them because of initial interest rate discounts. Two years after the peak of subprime lending, th ose discounts started to expire and borrowers are seeing their interest rates and monthly payments rise. According to Credit Suisse (2007), for example, at the end of 2006 almost $500 billion in subprime debt was scheduled to hit a rate reset over the next two years.

The sixth trend is the growth in penalty- and fee-based income as a source of profit for credit suppliers and their financial intermediaries, including loan brokers. For example, credit card companies earn part of their revenue from annual fees or application fees charged to consumers for the use of the card. Other fees are tied to specific types of purchases (currency conversion, balance transfer, and cash advance fees), services (credit protection or insurance), or penalties (late payment and over-limit fees). Overall, credit card fees have been rising steadily. The average late fee in 2005 was $34, with many major issuers charging $39— a 27 percent increase in five years and almost triple the average fee in 1993.[25] Over-limit fees climbed from less than $13 in 1994 to more than $31 on average in 2005.[26] As a result, credit card companies' total revenue from fees increased 18 percent in one year, reaching $24.4 billion in 2004. Consumer Action (2005) reported that CardWeb counted $14.8 billion in penalties (for example, late payment and over-limit fees), $6.1 billion in cash advance fees, and $3.5 billion in annual fees. Similarly, fees on mortgages can be quite high, because borrowers with smaller mortgages or subprime mortgages pay a higher percentage of the loan in fees. Often, they are rolled into the amount borrowed or borrowers are charged a higher interest rate in lieu of payment of upfront fees.

By the end of 2007, it became evident that the forces that drove up the volume of subprime lending could be abruptly reversed. For example, subprime mortgage originations plummeted from around $140 billion in the fourth quarter of 2006 to only $15 billion in the fourth quarter of 2007. Many wonder whether aggressive subprime lending will return, how much loan volume it will produce once the credit markets return to a more normal state, and whether falling home prices and widespread foreclosures will change the composition of household debt.

Milestones in the Evolution of Credit Markets

Existing debt trends are inextricably linked to the evolution of the credit markets over the last ten years, which have created opportunities as well as new tests for businesses, consumers, and policymakers. Most of the developments in consumer

---

25. CardTrak.com, "Tardy Pain," January 17, 2006 (www.cardtrak.com/news/2006/01/17/tardy_pain).

26. CardTrak.com, "Over-Limit Fees," February 6, 2006 (www.cardtrak.com/news/2006/02/06/over_limit_fees).

Figure 1-3. *Nonprime Lending, 2001–07*

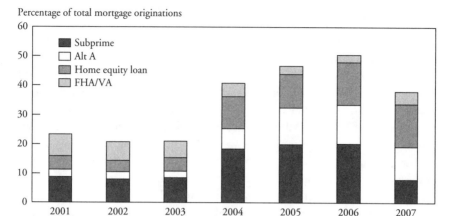

Percentage of total mortgage originations

Source: Inside Mortgage Finance, *The 2008 Mortgage Market Statistical Annual, Volume 1: The Primary Market* (Bethesda, Md. 2008).

credit have occurred across the major forms of credit: mortgages, credit cards, auto loans, installment loans for durable goods, and student loans.[27]

Pricing, Assessing, and Managing Credit Risk

Perhaps the most important of the changes has been the shift from a credit-rationing to a risk-based pricing system. Prior to 1990, the lending industry rationed credit to prime borrowers, using tight underwriting guidelines to assess and control risk. With the new risk-pricing and management tools, subprime lending in the mortgage industry skyrocketed after 2003 (figure 1-3). For several years, far fewer applicants were denied credit; instead, they were offered credit at higher prices intended to reflect the greater risk posed by subprime loans. Although the sudden and dramatic erosion in subprime performance resulted in an equally sudden and dramatic pullback in credit at the end of 2007, it is likely that subprime lending will expand again, though likely on different terms and under different regulations.

As the recent past reveals all too well, risk is not perfectly priced. Some borrowers were charged rates higher than the underlying risk demanded, and others were charged too little. Borrowers most susceptible to being charged a higher rate were those who got loans from brokers who marked them up or charged yield spread premiums beyond the interest rate that the lender demanded. Subprime

27. For brevity's sake, the term "loan" is used here to include lines of credit and "mortgage" is used to include mortgage loans or lines of credit, in both senior and junior lien positions. While open-ended credit is different from closed-ended credit, for our purposes the matters discussed apply to both unless otherwise noted.

lenders also often imposed harsher terms, such as prepayment penalties or higher late fees, ostensibly to contain or compensate for greater risk. On the other hand, the pricing of subprime mortgages did not catch up to the risk layering and lax underwriting that occurred from about 2004 through 2006. As a result, losses on these books of business have been *much* higher than expected.

Subprime lending began to blossom earlier in the auto lending and credit card industries than in the mortgage industry. Auto loan origination totaled an estimated $520 billion in 2004 and the Federal Reserve estimated the total amount of auto loan debt at $840 billion.[28] Although various definitions of what constitutes a subprime auto loan complicate accurate accounting for the sector, available sources estimate that the sector quadrupled in size from 1990 to 2000.[29] Estimates of the growth in subprime credit card lending are harder to come by. In the credit card industry, there is a small subset of secured and subprime credit cards. Secured credit cards usually require a deposit equal to the credit limit on the card (as collateral on the revolving loan), which can be retained by the card issuer if the consumer defaults. Subprime cards are virtually indistinguishable from prime cards except that they have higher fees and interest rates at the outset and lower credit limits; card companies also are less lenient with late or defaulted payments. Subprime cards have been around only for the last five to ten years, and because they are not as profitable as prime cards, fewer card companies offer them. Subprime cards are marketed directly to consumers who have a poor (or no) credit history, those who previously filed for bankruptcy, and even those who may qualify for a prime or unsecured card. With tag lines like "Poor credit OK," card companies can convince some consumers that they may not qualify for a regular card.

Student loans, on the other hand, have generally been available through federal loan programs to all comers at a common price. Yet as the cost of education spirals beyond the federal loan limits and the availability of private student loans grows, risk-based pricing is now being used to price private education debt as well. In fact, private student loan volume is growing much more rapidly than federal student loan volume. If this trend continues, annual private education loan vol-

28. Originations are from www.fi-magazine.com, and total debt outstanding is from the Federal Reserve Statistical Release G.19, estimated at 60 percent of nonrevolving debt; see Federal Reserve Board (2008a). Leedom and Associates (2002) reported that the largest players in the auto finance industry, measured by total auto debt outstanding, are captive finance companies—the financing arm of the automakers—which hold 39 percent of the total auto debt outstanding. Next largest are banks, which hold 30 percent of outstanding auto debt, followed by credit unions, which hold 18 percent, and then independent financing companies, which hold 13 percent. Independent finance companies range from multibillion-dollar corporations, such as CAC and AmeriCredit, with $12 billion in managed auto receivables, to small dealer-financers or "buy-here, pay-here" dealers who may self-finance their own used car loans, which are aimed at those with bad or no credit. Such dealers may have fewer than 300 loans in portfolio. Buy-here, pay-here dealers are a growing force in the industry, with 8.5 to 12 million annual car sales and $80 to $100 billion a year in sales.

29. PIMCO Bonds, "Bond Basics: Asset-Backed Securities," December 2005 (www.pimco.com/LeftNav/Bond+Basics/2005/ABS_Basics.htm).

ume will surpass federal student loan volume within a decade. In 2004–05, lenders provided about $14 billion in private loans, a 734 percent increase from a decade earlier, according to the College Board (Burd 2006). Yet a large number of student loans are currently being deferred. According to the Survey of Consumer Finance, at any given time, payments are not being made on one-quarter to one-half of student loans (Dynan, Johnson, and Pence 2003).

Although the subprime mortgage lending excesses that came to light in 2007 may result in a retreat from some loan products that entail an especially high repayment risk and from lending to borrowers with weak credit records, there is reason to believe that standards and products will not retreat—or not for long—to pre-2000 standards. Enough has been or will be learned to offer credit on a sustained basis to less than prime borrowers.

In addition to the shift to risk-based pricing, a second important change has been the proliferation of credit products and terms. Ten years ago there were far fewer types of auto loans, credit cards, and mortgage products than are commonplace today. For example, most mortgage loans were prime, fixed-rate, self-amortizing loans with no prepayment penalty. Today, hundreds of mortgage loan products are offered to borrowers at multiple price points, with very different fee structures, conditions (including prepayment penalties, mandatory arbitration clauses, and credit life insurance), underwriting requirements (0 down or even 125 percent loan-to-value ratios and housing debt-to-income ratios that far exceed 33 percent), due diligence requirements (including no-income/no-asset loans and low-documentation loans), and amortization schedules (with some loans not starting to amortize until after a set period or, even worse, accruing principal). Comparable developments have taken place in the auto loan, private student loan, and credit card industries. New credit card teaser offers, auto leasing offers, and fees have made it more difficult to compare terms.

A third characteristic of credit markets today is the increasing reliance on statistical credit scores to underwrite loans, to rate publicly traded securities, and to price and service loans. A single number has come to capture the credit quality of borrowers. Decisions regarding pricing, credit rating, and loan approval are based on this score, as are decisions about how to focus limited servicing resources. Increasingly, lenders are also using individual credit lines in credit reports or customized credit scores to aid underwriting decisions. The importance of automated credit information in governing access to and the cost of credit has never been greater. The use of credit scores can be traced back to the 1970s in the case of credit cards, to the mid-1990s in the case of auto loans, and to the 1990s in the case of mortgage loans. In each case, it took a number of years before the majority of loan origination decisions relied on credit scores. This change has removed much, but not all, of the individual discretion of loan officers and brokers in deciding whether to accept or reject an applicant but may not have changed how applicants are treated and their loans are priced.

Originating and Funding Credit Products

The methods by which loans and lines of credit are originated and funded have changed dramatically. The driving force behind the changes has been the rapid growth of the asset-backed securities (ABS) market, which funds many types of loans, particularly subprime and nonstandard loans. The ABS market is made up of consumer credit securities backed by car loans, consumer loans, student loans, and credit card receivables, as well as subprime first-lien and home equity loans and lines of credit (Vink and Thibeault 2007).[30] As a rule of thumb, only subprime mortgage-backed securities are considered part of the ABS market, not mortgage-backed securities (MBS) backed by Alt-A loans that are not guaranteed by Fannie Mae and Freddie Mac or by prime loans. More recently, collateralized debt obligations (CDOs) have emerged as a significant part of the ABS market.

Like subprime lending, the ABS market took off during the 1990s. The birth of the ABS market is usually traced back to 1985, when Sperry Lease Financial Corporation sold securities collateralized by computer leases. That year, total issuance was about $1.2 billion in current dollars. By 2005, the Securities Industry and Financial Markets Association estimated outstanding asset-backed securities totaled $1.955 trillion, including $551 billion in "home equity loan" debt outstanding (including subprime first-lien debt), $357 billion in credit card receivables, $220 billion in auto loans, $153 billion in student loans, and $35 billion in manufactured housing.[31] It is worth noting that Credit Suisse (2007) placed subprime mortgage debt outstanding that was held in securities in 2006 at a higher $825 billion, and valued the Alt-A debt outstanding in the MBS market at $722 billion. Although not considered part of the ABS market, the Alt-A market has driven a significant amount of recent mortgage lending.

Understanding the securities markets is important to understanding the opportunities and challenges that now face consumers, investors, and regulators. The growth of the ABS and Alt-A markets is intertwined with both the surge of subprime and Alt-A lending and the increasing reliance on the less regulated nonbank channel, from loan brokers, finance companies, and independent mortgage banks to private securitization (Apgar, Bendimerad, and Essene 2007). That is because the ability of finance companies and independent mortgage banks to access the capital markets through private securitization has been instrumental to the expansion of Alt-A and subprime lending—remote investors have been more willing to purchase subprime debt than portfolio lenders such as banks and thrifts.

---

30. Choudhry and Fabozzi (2004) note that some mortgage loans other than subprime loans are subsumed under the ABS category labeled "home equity loans." These include certain loans with high loan-to-value ratios (usually over 100 percent), open-ended home equity lines of credit, and loan pools that have been performing poorly.

31. Securities Industry and Financial Markets Association (www.sifma.org/research/pdf/Overall_Outstanding.pdf).

A fifth prominent feature of credit markets, made possible by the deepening of the asset-backed securities market, is the increasing reliance on non-banks to originate and service loans. In some cases, such as payday loans, non-banks fund loans as well. Non-banks include auto finance companies working through auto dealers, mortgage finance companies working through their own retail branches, correspondent lenders, and mortgage brokers. Worth highlighting is the increasing reliance on brokers in the housing finance, auto loan, and installment loan industries and to some extent in the student loan market. Roughly 30 percent of prime and 45 percent of subprime mortgage loans are originated by brokers. Auto loans and leases usually are arranged through dealers acting as brokers for third-party lenders. Many furniture and electronics retailers act as loan brokers as well. This is a logical extension of the retail nature of lending. Using brokers is a less costly way to get to millions of borrowers at the point of product sales than to do so through branch offices that entail large fixed costs for the lender. In addition, it can be more convenient for the borrower.

In an effort to ensure quality and to help student and parent borrowers, higher education financial aid officers traditionally selected their lender and processor partners. Such prescreening may also have provided school financial aid officers with the opportunity to negotiate on behalf of their students better terms in return for higher volumes with lenders. Unfortunately, it has recently come to light that many of the same financial aid officers were receiving kickbacks and perks from the lenders, calling into question whether the officers' decisions regarding student loans were made with the best interests of the students in mind.

A sixth critical development is what has been characterized as a dual market in which low-income and often minority areas are served primarily by one set of institutions, arrangements, and products and higher-income, mostly white areas are served primarily by another.[32] Indeed, low-income and especially minority communities increasingly are being served by lenders that specialize in subprime lending products and use more aggressive marketing and servicing strategies.

In the seventh and final development, the consumer credit lending industry has been consolidated considerably, with increasing use of holding company structures to serve different markets through separate entities under single ownership. In 2005, the top-ten auto loan securities issuers accounted for two-thirds of all auto loan securitizations, while in 2004, the top-ten credit card issuers accounted for about 90 percent of issuances. In the case of mortgage lending, the top twenty-five mortgage lenders in 1990 accounted for 28.4 percent of home mortgage originations but close to 85 percent by 2005 (Inside Mortgage Finance 2005).

---

32. Choudhry and Fabozzi (2004).

The Broad Implications of the New Consumer Credit Marketplace

Taken together, the various developments in the credit markets qualify as transformational. Much of the transformation occurred against a backdrop of the longest bull market in housing on record and a mild recession that ended before some of the more untested loan products were widely used and the largest increases in subprime lending occurred. As the new credit markets are stress-tested in the real world, the fuller implications of those developments have become more apparent. That said, the increase in the national homeownership rate that began in 1993 peaked in 2004, before lending standards were relaxed and consumers snapped up unconventional mortgage products like interest-only and payment-option loans. That suggests that some of the gains that the evolution of the credit system helped bring about in terms of asset building and expanded access to unsecured loans can last if the system in the future is anchored on more conventional loan products and solid underwriting of a borrower's ability to repay a loan. Indeed, most of the recent increase in homeownership and credit card debt occurred before subprime lending began to expand rapidly around 2000.

Capital Market Funding and the Unbundling of Origination and Funding

The opening up of the capital markets to securitized consumer credit allowed U.S. consumers not only to tap into much deeper global capital pools but also to tap into a wider range of investors with a broader range of risk preferences and tolerances. Many have attributed the lower interest rates that consumers have enjoyed in recent years to the integration of global capital and product markets. The downside of these developments, however, may be that the same investors may be too remote from their investments to know their true risk and value. While some information, although less than complete, is available on the loans backing ABS and MBS, the problem is more acute for CDOs. As a result, investors must rely on a limited number of third-party rating agencies that may model risk incorrectly and make markets more vulnerable to disruption. Some analysts initially pointed out that unless the risks come home to roost across a large pool of assets at the same time and at prices that do not cover investors, these disruptions could be contained, because risk in one asset class in one location is divvied up among so many. But when home prices started to soften in a majority of metropolitan areas and many regional economies came under pressure, it became clear that conditions that can lead to major disruptions can arise with stunning speed and with disastrous consequences for credit markets.

The unbundling of loan origination functions once performed by a single financial institution and the increased funding provided by investors in securities backed by consumer credit have created economies of scale and lowered the cost of loan origination and servicing. But those changes also mean that non-banks play a larger role in origination and servicing than in the past. Because non-banks are not subject to the same federal examinations and regulations as deposit-taking institutions, regulation of these entities, including brokers, is the domain of the states. In addition, while agency risk is greater and regulation, examination, and enforcement are more decentralized, investors have reduced legal liability for unfair lending practices because they are not held accountable for the actions of the originator at the point of sale except under narrow circumstances.

The increasing reliance on brokers as a way to lower origination costs and establish a variable cost structure also amplifies agency risk because in most cases the counterparties originating loans are compensated by fees and have little capital at stake. While brokers who wish to maintain their reputation have an incentive not to defraud lenders or do poor underwriting, it is a difficult system to police. Moreover, because lenders rely on brokers for business and market share, they must compete for brokers' business. This is a classic collective action problem in which lenders may be better served by moving away from such heavy reliance on brokers, but no single lender will take unilateral action because of the potential loss of market share.

To compete for brokers' business, lenders offer incentives, including yield spread premiums for mortgage loans and markups for auto loans (and even in some instances for student loans) that brokers may retain as a source of income. That in turn creates an incentive for brokers to maximize fees and costs to borrowers and may result in intentional discrimination or disparate outcomes for borrowers. Indeed, several cases have been brought and settled out of court against auto and mortgage lenders for singling out protected classes for different treatment. Further, it is problematic that brokers are compensated per transaction and not the basis of how long borrowers continue to make timely payments on the loans that the broker closes.

Subprime Lending, Automated Underwriting, and Product Proliferation

Risk-based pricing based on credit scores drove an enormous expansion of subprime mortgage credit to low-income and minority households.[33] But automated underwriting and credit scores were used extensively in the prime mortgage market as well and led to a significant expansion of prime credit to previously underserved markets (Courchane, Surette, and Zorn 2002).[34] Unfortunately, no good data are available on the incidence of subprime credit cards or auto loans by the income, race, or ethnicity of borrowers. Therefore, it remains unclear how much

33. While subprime lending did expand access to credit, the high rates of defaults and foreclosures caused the subprime market to all but shut down in 2006. Thus the recent surge in access may have been a temporary aberration unless, and until, the subprime market revives.

34. Using more powerful risk assessment tools to expand borrower access to prime credit appears to be a far more sustainable method of reaching additional borrowers than doing so through opening up access to subprime credit, especially when the subprime credit carries variable rates or other risks for later payment shocks.

the use of automated underwriting has contributed to the large increase since 1989 in the share of especially low-income and minority households that have carried these forms of debt.

Of course, lending to borrowers with a higher predicted probability of default is riskier for borrowers as well as lenders. Subprime loans are more concentrated in the lower credit score categories, and lenders used no- or low-documentation loans to help borrowers (including speculators) step around underwriting standards that they may not have met (Golding, Green, and McManus 2007), resulting in higher risk. Further, a higher proportion of riskier subprime borrowers and borrowers with riskier mortgage products get into trouble than prime borrowers faced with similar economic hardships. For example, in 2006 the serious delinquency rate was 0.78 percent on fixed-rate prime mortgages, 5.45 percent on fixed-rate subprime mortgages, and 7.99 percent on adjustable-rate subprime mortgages.[35]

The implications are significant, especially when subprime mortgages are geographically concentrated in low-income and minority communities. More households will end up in default or in foreclosure, households that fail to repay loans will face higher future borrowing costs or may be precluded from borrowing, and negative externalities will affect the community as well (Apgar and Duda 2005). Many of the borrowers and products are just now being stress-tested, and higher-than-expected investor losses have been seen, leading to a pullback in credit for a wider group of borrowers. A case in point is that the worst-performing book of mortgage business was originated in 2006, a year in which a high proportion of subprime loans were issued that were not rigorously underwritten, often did not have verified incomes, and had risky loan features like adjustable interest rates with deep initial discounts. Just six months later, 6.1 percent of subprime loans from 2006 were in default, compared with 1.7 percent of subprime loans originated in 2003; after nine months, the default rate for 2006 loans was 7.5 percent, compared with 2.6 percent for 2003 loans.[36] Finally, as over a half million home loans entered foreclosure in the first quarter of 2008 alone, the share of all loans entering foreclosure reached a record high since data were first reported in 1979.[37]

More generally, the risk-based pricing system and the dual market structure create the potential for discrimination against protected classes on the basis of

---

35. "Serious delinquency" is defined here as the sum of loans sixty or more days late and started in foreclosure; the numbers are weighted averages from the Mortgage Bankers Association National Delinquency Survey (www.mbaa.org/ResearchandForecasts/ProductsandSurveys/NationalDelinquencySurvey.htm).

36. Data provided by First American CoreLogic, LoanPerformance (www.loanperformance.com).

37. From the Mortgage Bankers Association, National Delinquency Survey (www.mbaa.org/ResearchandForecasts/ProductsandSurveys/NationalDelinquencySurvey.htm).

price or features. Under the credit-rationing system, discrimination and unfair treatment almost exclusively took the form of discouraging or denying loan applicants. Now, consumers can be the victims of discrimination or unfair treatment without ever having been denied a loan. It was easier to detect discrimination when a common set of underwriting rules was embraced, with only small deviations, by all lenders. It is far more difficult to detect discrimination when lenders underwrite using very different rules, a wide range of prices based on the experience of their own loan portfolios, and particular loan conditions and terms. Patterns of unfair or discriminatory treatment with respect to price, fees, terms, and conditions must be detected in the complicated context of an industry that has yet to agree on common practices and prices. In addition, the important question arises of whether a geographically segmented and differentiated strategy for originating and servicing loans in underserved markets constitutes unfair treatment in and of itself. In other words, it is conceivable that every borrower is treated the same by a particular subprime lender, but the fact that the borrower ended up with a specific subprime lender who treats all borrowers unfairly may result in unfair treatment.

Last but certainly not least, the proliferation of products has profound implications for the experience of consumers in the marketplace as well as their access to capital. On one hand, it has provided consumers with a wider range of choices to meet their credit needs and manage their financial affairs. On the other, it has significantly complicated credit product choices that are inherently difficult to make. It makes it harder for consumers to divine which products they should be able to qualify for and what the lowest possible cost should be. To do so, they must incur steep search costs. It also makes it difficult for consumers to compare products because loans have subtly different features that are difficult to value separately (such as a lower late fee or the option to prepay a mortgage loan). That leaves consumers vulnerable to making missteps and to being treated unfairly.

Consumer Behavior and Market Outcomes

Perfectly competitive markets rest on the assumption that consumers have fixed preferences and act rationally on the basis of perfect, complete information to maximize their utilities through exchange (McFadden 2006). These and other strict conditions required of perfectly competitive markets are seldom met completely in the real world. In the case of credit markets, consumers lack perfect information on prices and product features and have preferences that are malleable and subject to influence by marketing and the framing of choices. In addition, they must make decisions under uncertainty that involve judging the probability of future events. Experimental evidence suggests that in making those decisions, people are prone to making certain errors.

Imperfect Information and Lack of Price Transparency

With a few possible exceptions, it is difficult for consumers to gather enough information on the prices of credit products to make informed choices. The explosion of credit products with different rates, fees, terms, and conditions makes comparison shopping extremely difficult. While the Schumer Box was imposed on purveyors of credit cards to facilitate the comparison of credit card offers, there is no comparable requirement of suppliers of auto and mortgage loans. While mortgage and auto loan brokers have detailed information on the prices and products offered by multiple lenders, they seldom share that information with borrowers. Instead, they suggest a product to the borrower and often charge markups or yield spread premiums that consumers are unaware of. Lacking information on potential competitive bids from other lenders and hard pressed to value individual loan terms and features, borrowers often rely on the advice of their brokers. Altogether, there is a striking lack of transparency in pricing, especially in the mortgage, installment loan, and auto loan markets.

For subprime borrowers, gathering information is made a great deal harder by the fact that it is not until after a loan application has been underwritten that borrowers know the actual price that they will be charged and loan features that they will qualify for. Further, lender rate sheets are not widely disseminated, and even if consumers know their credit rating, it is unclear to consumers what risk grade they will be assigned by any particular lender because most firms use proprietary scoring models and modify their pricing depending on the features of the loan.

Cognitive Biases in Decisionmaking

Behavioral economists have explored consumers' cognitive biases regarding consumer and credit decisions. Their robust findings show that those biases come into play when consumers make decisions under uncertainty that require them to guess the probability of future events and give relative weights to present and future utilities. Most people have little information on which to base probabilistic assessments of the likelihood of idiosyncratic events like death, divorce, the rate of wealth accumulation, changes in income, consumption demands, and moves from one home to another, or of future exogenous events like interest rate changes, recessions, house price changes, and changes in tax and other laws and regulations. In reviewing a wide body of literature on behavioral economics, Laibson and Zeckhauser (1998) conclude that biases are more likely to appear when decisions involve risk and uncertainty, when multidimensional goods are involved that are difficult to compare, and when "some of the dimensions are not readily priced." Credit products have all of those features, and a study of a national lender that works through a broker network provides empirical confirmation that such features lead to consumer confusion (Woodward

2003). Consumers who were presented with a single mortgage payment measure made more optimal choices than those who were not. Furthermore, consumers paid more on average for complex mortgage products because the individual price components were difficult to discern and fairly value. Consumers are stymied because it is hard to value all the terms and conditions of a loan, and that makes it difficult to compare total loan costs.

One common bias is to overweight the present and discount the future—so-called hyperbolic discounting. In other words, consumers have a tendency to prefer smaller payoffs now to larger payoffs in the future and to give less weight to the probability of certain negative future events than to present satisfaction. That means that consequences that may occur in the future have less bearing on present decisions than do immediate consequences. Hyperbolic discounting has been used to explain why consumers tend to borrow so much at high interest rates (Harris and Laibson 2001; Gabaix and others 2006). It is viewed as a result of other psychological tendencies, such as problems with commitment and self-control and the desire for instant gratification.

Another critical and well-documented bias is optimism about the future—believing that one's own chance of experiencing a bad event is less than the average person's chance.[38] When combined with hyperbolic discounting, optimism bias can lead consumers to take on risky loan products even if they have a general idea about events that would make it difficult or impossible for them to repay their debts. It almost certainly helps explain why consumers recently flocked to products that entail higher repayment risk, such as interest-only mortgage loans, adjustable-rate loans, and payment-option mortgages.[39] The record default rates on such loans in 2007 suggests significant risk taking on the part of consumers and deep discounting of future probabilities of events like interest payment shocks and house price declines.

In the context of credit, a particular cognitive bias that has great force is the tendency for most people to err on the low side when equating annual percentage rates to monthly payments. Nearly everyone assumes that the APR associated with a monthly payment is lower than it actually is. By one estimate, the underestimate can be much as several hundred basis points on average (Stango and Zinman 2006). That leaves consumers vulnerable to offers that tout low monthly payments but have high interest rates.

A large class of additional cognitive biases results from the common use of heuristics or "rules of thumb" when assigning probabilities to future events and

38. Jolls (1998) provides a summary of the research on optimism bias and how it influences a range of product choices.
39. As Epstein (2006) points out, however, it does less well in explaining why nearly half of credit card borrowers pay off their balances each month.

making complicated decisions.[40] Faced with complex decisions, consumers often resort to fairly predictable shortcuts to make processing information more manageable. Gabaix and others (2006) point out that the use of heuristics makes sense when there are information processing costs and diminishing marginal returns to search. Nevertheless, the use of heuristics often leads to errors in judgment. One common bias is to anchor final answers to a problem at an initial starting point, guess, or salient feature. This bias accounts for the tendency for consumers to negotiate prices from arbitrary starting points dictated by suppliers, such as the manufacturer's suggested retail price or dealer invoice in the case of automobiles. The anchoring heuristic leads to judgments that are unduly influenced by the starting point. Thus, if the guess about the starting point is wrong, judgments based on it will be erroneous as well.

While errors in credit decisions are more common in the presence than the absence of processing deficiencies, such as innumeracy (Peters and others 2006) or an inaccurate estimate of one's own credit score (Courchane, Surette, and Zorn 2004), these errors are common even in the absence of such deficiencies. Take, for example, the results of a study of business school students at the University of Chicago in which they were asked to pick the best way to finance a furniture purchase (Shu 2003). Participants, who reviewed various loan payment schedules, came to no agreement on the best option. While a discounted present value calculation of the loan options would have identified the best option, these business school students used a variety of simpler heuristics, including minimizing the total undiscounted loan payments and minimizing the length of the loan term. That reveals that often incorrect rules of thumb are used even among groups that have a more sophisticated understanding of economics and finance than the general population. Similarly, Epstein (2006) concludes that "most students who take probability theory find many of its results strongly counterintuitive, only to be baffled by the mathematical formulas that promise some clarity . . . persons who make logical errors in calculation are likely to make inconsistent judgments about their preferences, and to do so in ways that can hurt them in both the short and long run."[41]

40. Tversky and Kahneman (1974, 1981) and Kahneman and Tversky (1979) were the first to point that out and formalize their observations, but since their early work on the subject a large body of experimental literature has confirmed and extended their initial findings, expounding on the implications of decisionmaking errors for market operations and outcomes. Several excellent review articles have been written; see, for example, Laibson and Zeckhauser (1998) and Fundenberg (2006). Further, paying attention to how consumers actually make decisions rather than assuming that they make them in rational ways, without error, has spawned an entire field of behavioral economics that focuses on how economic decisions are shaped by situational factors, social influences, and cognitive processes. These developments have led to a richer understanding of markets.

41. Epstein (2006, p. 113). The tendency for consumers to make systematic errors in judgment is further underscored by a recent controlled experiment conducted by a large U.S. bank in which two credit card options were presented to consumers (Agarwal and others 2006). Only one was clearly optimal for any given consumer. Fully 40 percent of consumers in the trial picked the option that

Framing, Marketing Social Influences, and the Malleability of Choices

The study of behavioral economics has also produced considerable experimental evidence that the framing of choices has a significant influence on consumer preferences and decisions. As a result, credit suppliers can exploit known cognitive biases to achieve desired outcomes. Glaeser (2004) neatly summed this up by stating that market outcomes "will reflect the interaction of interested suppliers of influence and consumers who then respond to that influence."[42] As Gabaix and Laibson (2006) bluntly noted, "when consumers make mistakes, firms will try to exploit those mistakes."[43] Indeed, the authors find evidence that even competitive markets will not always induce firms to reveal information that would make markets more efficient because firms have an incentive to keep information from consumers, as when the equilibrium price reflects a cross-subsidy from naïve to sophisticated consumers. Understanding how framing and social influences shape credit decisions, therefore, is essential to fully appreciating the challenges inherent in today's consumer credit marketplace and what to do about them.

A recent experiment conducted by a lender in South Africa provides the most compelling evidence that framing matters in credit decisions (Bertrand, Mullainathan, and Shafir 2006). The lender sent letters offering incumbent clients short-term loans at randomly chosen interest rates; embedded in the offers were randomized psychological features. The features were selected to test the influence of specific types of frames and cues that were shown in the lab to have a powerful influence on behavior but that from a normative perspective should have no impact whatsoever on the decision to take out a loan.[44] While the interest rate offered in letters sent at random to potential customers did significantly affect loan take-up, the experiment confirmed the importance of framing. Many of the psychological features embedded in the offer letters, along with interest rates, had a

---

did not minimize their net costs. However, the same experiment also revealed that an error correction process exists, so that over time only a small fraction of those that made a mistake stuck with their initial choice. While that is a promising finding, at least in the context of credit cards, such initial errors can have more lasting consequences in credit markets, where switching is more costly or impossible. Switching is often more costly in mortgage and auto lending markets, and it may be prohibited or heavily discouraged by prepayment penalties.

42. Glaeser (2004, p. 408).

43. Gabaix and Laibson (2006, p. 505). They go on to show that suppliers may intentionally shroud information to maximize profits even in perfectly competitive markets with costless advertising and even though it results in allocational inefficiencies. Examples include shrouding of information about the add-on costs of ink replacement cartridges for printers and of the fees associated with bank accounts.

44. Types of frames and cues tested include the description of the offer (inclusion of a single example of an interest rate and monthly payment or of several examples of terms and rates), whether the rates of a competitor were included in the offer, whether the offer was framed as a gain or loss, whether the gain or loss was expressed as an absolute amount or a percentage, subtle features like inclusion of photos, and suggestions about possible uses of the funds.

significant influence on take-up rates. The average effect of the features was equivalent to a 50-basis-point difference in interest rates.

Some features had strikingly large effects while others had little or no effect. Consistent with other studies,[45] this study found remarkably that the use of a simple description of a single offer rather than of multiple terms and rates had the same effect on credit demand as dropping the interest rate offered by fully 2.3 percentage points. The implication is that credit offers that are simple and not confused by the presentation of alternatives will increase take-up. As Kahneman and Tversky's prospect theory predicted and consistent with other experimental evidence (Thaler 1980), whether the identical offer was framed as a gain or loss also had an inordinate influence on whether a consumer took out a loan.[46] Framing the offer as a loss (a missed opportunity) increased the take-up rate of the loan.

The strong cognitive bias toward underestimating annual percentage rates leaves borrowers vulnerable to sales pitches that stress monthly payments and provides an incentive for lenders to obfuscate the underlying interest rate. One study found that biased households paid several hundred basis points more for loans than those that were unbiased, even after the analysis controlled for loan type and borrower characteristics (Stango and Zimmerman 2006).[47] Indeed, it is now common knowledge that borrowers focus on monthly payments, which typically are highlighted in print ads while annual percentage rates are relegated to the fine print.

Optimism and hyperbolic discounting leave consumers vulnerable to a series of market pitches that emphasize present gratification and deemphasize long-term costs and risks. To the extent that products are designed specifically to appeal to consumers' focus on current rewards and their discounting of future risks, consumers' biases can also result in greater market penetration even if prices are high. Consumers are attracted to sales pitches that promise no money down and no payments for some period of time. To presume that people have the ability to accurately assess the average risk of certain loan features, like adjustable rates or future modifications of loan terms in the case of credit cards, is a large leap of faith.

Another framing decision that has a large influence on the type of product and the lender that a consumer chooses is how quick, predictable, and easy it is to qualify for a loan. Groundbreaking research conducted by Fannie Mae showed that mortgage customers fear rejection and place a premium on a high probability of

45. See, for example, Iyengar and Lepper (2000).

46. Prospect theory contends that consumers first code a choice as implying a gain or a loss from a reference point and then evaluate it (Kahneman and Tversky 1979). Losses loom larger than gains for most consumers. Thus, suggesting that not choosing an option will result in a loss or a disadvantage is more apt to spur consumers to action than suggesting that choosing it will result in a gain or an advantage.

47. They also found that those effects were larger for consumers who went to finance companies for a loan than for those who went to banks.

getting approved.[48] Firms that offer an easy yes have an advantage over those that adhere to more stringent standards and are more thorough in verifying information. That bias may permit lenders to compete on the basis of ease of approval rather than price. Indeed, just the convenience provided by an easy application and fast decisionmaking process may have strong appeal, quite apart from assuaging applicants' fears of rejection. Several public health studies show that the convenience of being close to a clinic and having a map that marks the location of a clinic can strongly influence positive responses to a public health campaign. That suggests that lenders that reach out to borrowers where they live, work, or pray to offer a fast and easy application process would have the upper hand in competing for customers.

The Challenges of Paternalism

While it is tempting to search for solutions to the many problems that consumers face in a marketplace described by McFadden (2006) as a "contest," no clear agreement exists on whether a consumer's credit choices should be second-guessed. Some argue that consumers' choices reveal their preferences, while others counter that households may not express their preferences optimally for a host of reasons that should be cause for concern because of the resulting welfare losses (Campbell 2006). Furthermore, it may be difficult to come up with a normative yardstick for measuring any solutions. While there is a way to compare the long-term costs of a loan under various scenarios of the course of future events, a consumer's ultimate goal may not be to lower the long-term cost but to minimize initial payments, even if the cost of doing so is added risk of higher long-term payments or payment shocks. Although the tendency of many consumers to underweight the future may strike many observers as foolish, from another perspective it can be seen as a legitimate preference. Just as many people may rail against the diet or exercise habits of others but not attempt to dictate such highly personal decisions, many believe that individuals' discounting preferences are their own and should not be faulted. The problem arises when consumers of credit do not understand their own preferences, or if marketing and framing lead consumers to hold preferences that they might not otherwise have and that diminish their utility.

There often is a presumption that the behavior of low-income households is in some sense nonrational. However, rationality is itself subjective and depends on context. The choices people make when they are poor, out of cash, and have limited options may appear less than rational to those who have steady incomes that exceed their expenses.

Sunstein and Thaler (2003) made a strong case that in many situations, the choices of consumers are inevitably influenced by the entities that frame their

---

48. Yin (2003) quotes Vada Hill, formerly a marketing director at the Fannie Mae Foundation.

choices, like businesses, governments, and nonprofits. Therefore it is preferable for business owners, public officials, and representatives of nonprofits to be deliberate about and fully conscious of how they frame choices rather than ignore how they do it or fail to recognize the consequences. Surely, all of marketing is an effort to influence behavior and, judging by the sums spent on it, it has an effect. Sunstein and Thaler provide many examples of how default rules, framing effects, and starting points shape consumer behavior. They consider, as a simple example, the choice of which type of food to place at the start of a cafeteria line, which influences the take-up rate of food. Only one type can be at the start of the line. Placement may be random, or it may be intended to maximize firm profits or encourage more healthful eating. Paternalistic judgments about what is best for the consumer sometimes prevail, whether or not the path that leads to maximum consumer welfare is known.

The Efficacy of Credit Market Regulations

While it is not the purpose of this paper to describe in detail the complex set of regulations that govern credit transactions and the financial institutions that engage in them, some broad-brush observations are useful to help explain concerns about the compliance costs and effectiveness of current policy in protecting consumers and securing the safety and soundness of the financial system.[49]

Federal laws and elements of the Uniform Commercial Code, which has been adopted by nearly all states, influence all credit transactions regardless of how and where the financial institutions are chartered. Antidiscrimination laws, laws banning unfair and deceptive business practices, and laws demanding certain consumer disclosures fall under this rubric.[50] Others laws and regulations depend to an important extent on the type of financial intermediary and on how and where they were chartered. Deposit-taking institutions are subject to the Community Reinvestment Act (CRA) because they receive federal deposit insurance. CRA places an affirmative obligation on banks and thrifts to meet the credit needs of all segments of their communities, including low- and moderate-income neighborhoods and individuals. In addition, even when chartered at the state level and whether chartered as a thrift or bank, deposit-taking institutions are subject to regular examination by federal regulators.[51]

---

49. Further details on the regulation of the financial system are provided in chapter 4 in this volume by Patricia McCoy and Elizabeth Renuart.

50. These include the Equal Credit Opportunity Act, Federal Credit Reporting Act, Fair Debt Collection Practices Act, Credit Repair Organization Act, Financial Modernization Act, Truth in Lending Act, Fair Housing Act, Home Owners Equity and Protection Act, Real Estate Settlement and Procedures Act, and Home Equity Consumer Loan Act.

51. However, whether they are part of a bank holding company, state bank or thrift, national bank or thrift, or credit union determines which regulatory agency or agencies oversee their activi-

Yet in 2004, CRA-regulated institutions originated just 26 percent of loans inside their assessment areas.[52]

Although some non-banks fall in the orbit of federal examiners because they are part of a bank holding company regulated by the Federal Reserve, most are examined by state regulators, if at all. Fannie Mae and Freddie Mac, the large government-sponsored housing enterprises, are separately regulated by the Office of Federal Housing Enterprise Oversight and the Department of Housing and Urban Development (HUD). The securities markets and the investment banks that serve them are regulated mostly by the Securities and Exchange Commission (SEC), the National Association of Securities Dealers (NASD), and the listing requirements of the exchanges on which they are registered. Only the SEC and NASD have self-policing aspects.[53] Thus, the type of financial institution and where the institution is chartered largely determine the nature and intensity of regulations, examinations, and enforcement that it faces. Meanwhile, the Federal Trade Commission is charged with enforcing laws that ban unfair and deceptive business practices, but it lacks the authority to give examinations.

In addition to variations in regulations that stem from the type of financial institution and where it is chartered, there are some variations based on type of credit. Mortgage and associated real estate transactions are the most regulated of credit transactions at both the federal and state levels and even, to some degree, at the local level. While state laws intended to regulate the offering of these products are too numerous and rapidly changing to recount here, some federal examples are worth noting.

With respect to mortgages, the Home Mortgage Disclosure Act (HMDA) is unique in the level of public disclosure of lending activities that it requires of loan originators and the Home Ownership and Equity Protection Act (HOEPA) is unique in the federal restrictions that it places on the terms of mortgages and the heightened public disclosures that it demands. The Real Estate Settlement Practices Act (RESPA) is unique in the disclosure of fees that it requires at real estate settlements, while the Fair Housing Act places additional bans on discrimination in underwriting and granting mortgage credit. The Alternative Mortgage Transactions Parity Act (AMTPA) is unique in its preemption of state laws banning certain mortgage terms and practices. With respect to credit cards, the enactment of the 1988 Fair Credit and Charge Card Act with the well-known Schumer Box is unique in the consumer disclosures that it demands of credit card issuers. Last,

---

ties. State-chartered banks and thrifts along with nonbank financial institutions and intermediaries (including finance companies, mortgage banks, loan brokers, appraisers, and insurers) are state regulated and may be licensed or examined by the state.

52. Apgar, Bendimerad, and Essene (2007, p. 54).

53. Freeman (2000) refers to forms of regulation like the SEC as audited self-regulation since the federal government appoints the SEC's commissioners and deputizes it to promulgate and enforce laws and rules of conduct.

only ten categories of debt are excluded from discharge under the Bankruptcy Code 523 (one is federal student loan debt).[54]

Finding General Fault with the Regulatory Scheme

The tangle of regulations governing credit transactions and financial intermediaries is the subject of much criticism. Not surprisingly, one of the most common criticisms is that the cost of complying with various financial, fair-housing, and credit regulations is great and has not been measured against its benefits (Jackson 2005). Another is that regulations may have unintended consequences, such as discouraging competition, increasing the cost of credit, and preventing lenders from offering products that consumers might otherwise demand (Staten 2007).

While few view the present regulatory system as perfect, many view it as sufficient because it bans discrimination, demands reasonable disclosure, gathers and disseminates certain public information on critical lending activities that can be used to highlight apparent problems, and prohibits unfair and deceptive lending practices. Vocal critics, however, have found multiple faults with the present regulatory system. Many of their criticisms have gained more traction since some of the problems in the subprime mortgage market came to light in 2007, and many have special cogency because of the proliferation of credit products and the reliance of consumer credit on the capital markets. Only some of the most significant and general of the many criticisms leveled against the system are discussed here.

The sheer variation in regulation, examination, and enforcement in the consumer credit system is a major source of complaint for both industry groups and consumer advocates. Many businesses take the position that it makes operating across state lines difficult and argue for federal preemption of state laws. Although some would welcome more federal preemptions, a vast difference of opinion exists over whether they should be aimed at lowering the bar, thereby bypassing the more rigorous state standards that exist in some states, or raising it to a federal standard based on the toughest state standards. Consumer advocates take the view that state efforts have afforded consumers at least some consumer protections in some states, although they criticize states for lax oversight of many market players that are not regulated under the federal banking system. Consumer advocates take a range of positions, from fighting for more state resources for regulation to applying a minimum federal standard based on more rigorous existing state standards but allowing states to exceed the minimum federal standard. A case in point is the debate over whether to preempt state predatory lending laws and if so, through what specific provisions.

---

54. For a short summary of recent case law related to student loan debt during bankruptcy, go to (www.coheao.org/resource/data/telesem0203/ZaunHandout.doc).

Regardless of the view that one takes of specific regulations and compliance with and enforcement of them, financial institutions can exploit any unevenness of regulation. For example, the opportunity to work through financial institutions that do not have to comply with the Community Reinvestment Act may have encouraged banks to acquire finance companies as affiliates rather than make them operating subsidiaries. At a minimum, unevenness has played a part in the shifting of market share from banks and thrifts subject to CRA to their nonbank counterparts. In addition, even among federal banking regulators, some bestow greater flexibility on lenders than others do. The Office of the Comptroller of the Currency has been especially aggressive in asserting the powers of national banks, so a national charter bestows the greatest flexibility. However, with that extra power comes arguably the most extensive examination regimen of all. The Office of Thrift Supervision has been similarly aggressive, and some argue that the two regulators are in competition to woo financial institutions to their charters by offering ever greater powers. It also is clear that the variation in regulations can alter the nature of credit supply and delivery itself. For example, when risk-based capital standards were applied to banks and thrifts, the market moved more toward capital market funding to replace banks with other investors not subject to such requirements.

In addition, state examination and licensing of financial institutions is highly uneven. As a result, in states with weak examination and enforcement regimens, the Federal Trade Commission is left to combat unfair and deceptive lending practices, yet it lacks the authority and resources to examine institutions for violations. State-by-state variation leaves some consumers with minimal protection. Regardless of whether state or federal agencies are involved in detecting violations of credit law, the sheer number of financial intermediaries engaged in auto, installment, and mortgage loans makes it difficult to examine each of them. While developing licensing standards for brokers would not be that costly, periodic examination would not be easy or cheap. The chairman of the Federal Reserve Board even listed uniform enforcement as a major concern in testimony before Congress: "The recent problems in subprime lending have underscored the need for better disclosure and new rules but also for more uniform enforcement in the fragmented structure of brokers and lenders."[55]

Another general complaint with the present system is that it relies too heavily on consumers to detect discrimination and unfair or deceptive business practices as well as on the presumption that consumers can adequately protect themselves if they have enough information about the costs and risks of credit products. It appears that even if consumers have enough information, they are still prone to

55. Edmund L. Andrews, "Accord Seen on Revising Mortgage Rules," *New York Times,* September 19, 2007 (www.nytimes.com/2007/09/21/business/21home.html).

cognitive biases that lead to judgment errors and they remain vulnerable to manipulation through framing and marketing.

Finding Fault with the Regulation of Capital Markets and Intermediaries

The unbundling of loan functions, reliance on the capital markets to fund mortgages, and the paucity of regulations governing the sale of asset-backed securities have also led to some fundamental public policy concerns. With so many loans sold into the secondary market, it matters whether investors or the financial intermediaries that package and sell loans as securities are liable for any misdeeds that occur at the point of loan origination. At present, "the holder in due course" doctrine of the Uniform Commercial Code allows purchasers of securities backed by loans to avoid liability for the misdeeds of the loan originators except under narrow circumstances—for example, if a loan contract itself is illegal or a product purchased on credit was defective and the seller does not indemnify the consumer for the product. Lack of assignee liability is a first concern that has led to accusations that consumers have insufficient recourse if they are mistreated by the lender that initially made their loan or by their broker. Increasing the rights of borrowers to present claims that would offset or reduce the borrower's liability would indeed have an impact on the pricing and rating of such securities. The ability of the market to quantify and rate (or price) a possible reduction in payments and recoveries remains to be seen.

A second concern with the system for originating and funding loans through the capital markets is the way in which loan originators and lenders are compensated, as detailed earlier. Lawsuits brought against auto and mortgage lenders and the settlements in those cases underscore the potential to abuse the system and charge certain customers higher prices. In the case of auto loan brokers, the victims were protected classes; therefore the practice was actionable. But in cases in which a protected class is not at issue—such as low-income households not mistreated on the basis of race, religion, national origin, age, or gender—brokers' practices are not actionable unless they are unfair, deceptive, or fraudulent. Others argue that the system as currently configured works adequately and that what critics view as unfair treatment of customers is instead just compensation to brokers for the extra time and effort that it takes to reach out to markets that are more difficult or costly to serve.

A third concern is the lack of serious licensing standards for loan brokers in many states. Because limited broker capital is at risk and evidence shows that broker-originated loans perform much more poorly on average than those originated through other means, the spotlight is on brokers. In response, some states have taken action to beef up their licensing and registration requirements. Related to this problem is the lack of a fiduciary obligation on the part of the broker to the customer. In July of 2008, a federal law strengthening existing state-operated mortgage originator licensing and registration systems was passed. It requires the Department of Housing and Urban Development to set up systems in states that do not participate and federal banking regulators to set up systems for firms that are insured by the Federal Deposit Insurance Corporation. Whether this will quiet critics or prove effective remains to be seen.

A fourth concern is the effectiveness of the tools used to assess the credit risk associated with securities backed by consumer credit, such as credit card receivables, auto loans, and subprime mortgage loans.[56] Investors rely heavily on a handful of rating agencies to affirm the credit quality of ABS, MBS, and CDOs. The experience in 2007 with the performance of subprime mortgages has underscored the fact that the ratings of these agencies systematically underestimated risk. Agencies have been faulted for not focusing enough on attributes other than the credit quality of the borrower, including vulnerability to payment shocks, the features of the loans themselves, the conditions under which the loans were originated, and the strength and track records of the counterparties involved. In defense of the rating agencies, investments are by nature risky and returns are guaranteed only on inflation-adjusted federal bonds. Rating agencies spell out those risks and the lack of certainty in their ratings through exhaustive disclosures. Nonetheless, the power of rating agencies and their limited government oversight have become important issues.[57]

56. Reliance on credit scores raises several other concerns regarding this system. First, the laws governing the capture of consumer credit information take effect only if firms decide to voluntarily supply it. Many payments, such as for utilities and rent, are not supplied, even though they may be the only regular payments certain consumers make. In addition, payments on payday and subprime loans sometimes are not reported to the standard national credit repositories. Hence, some consumers do not have credit scores at all while others have scores that may not reflect a positive payment history that demonstrates their willingness and ability to pay for housing. Second, discrimination laws require only that underwriting decisions that result in disparate treatment of protected classes meet a business necessity test. There is no requirement that lenders demonstrate that they made an effort to try alternative model specifications in their automated underwriting to reduce as much as possible the correlation of rejection decisions with protected classes. Third, there is reason to suspect that borrowers may be charged higher rates in part because of past inefficiencies and sloppiness on the part of subprime lenders. After all, if all the costs of using poor underwriting and risk management practices are passed along in the form of higher rates and fees, then lenders have no motivation to do anything about them unless market competition or investors force them. Hence, what appear to be reasonable loan prices may instead be a form of institutionalized mistreatment. Fourth, the federal credit reporting system is based on the premise that a consumer will know when to suspect that he or she has been unfairly treated or has been given an incorrect credit score. But it is harder and harder for a consumer to do that. It is tough to judge whether the price and terms received on a loan are warranted because there are no readily available benchmarks on which to judge them. In addition, consumers are not apt to understand whether their credit score is warranted given their past history because the scoring methods themselves are proprietary.

57. In addition, Regulation AB (which governs disclosure requirements) is often criticized as too lenient. Although new requirements that will significantly expand existing requirements went into effect on January 1, 2006, many changes that had been called for did not make it into the revised rule.

Finding Fault with the Regulation and Marketing of Credit Products

Given all that has been learned about the potential for confusion, error, manipulation, and mistreatment (especially in the new world of multiple products with complex features and price points, often distributed through different channels), it is no wonder that many criticisms of the regulatory system focus on inadequate efforts to inform and protect consumers. As Durkin (2007) points out, information availability is highly significant in promoting competitive conditions and the efficient functioning of markets; accordingly, reducing consumers' search costs through disclosures became a central element of consumer protection policy. A first major criticism is that consumer-lending disclosures are inadequate both in scope and content. While both TILA and RESPA were enacted to remove informational barriers to consumer search, they may not have kept pace with the market's transformation, particularly with the deployment of risk-based pricing (McCoy 2006).[58] One of the greatest barriers is that the federal disclosure laws do not ensure that consumers receive information in time to help them compare prices. Except for high-cost refinance home mortgages, TILA does not require that lenders reveal binding prices until closing, and subprime lenders are permitted to advertise their best rates without disclosing that the consumer may not qualify for that rate. To help consumers comparison-shop, McCoy (2007) argues for changes in advertising, price quotes, and variable-rate disclosures. Durkin, however, points out that the central conceptual issue is what constitutes the cost of credit. He went further to frame the debate as the need to balance the "laudable search for exactitude, completeness, consistency and comparability" against the difficulty that consumers have in understanding all the necessary concepts, while at the same time ensuring reasonable ease of compliance with regulations.

Another major concern related to disclosure is the general practice of shrouding information—intentionally withholding information so that consumers have more difficulty properly valuing and assessing products. A classic example is withholding information on the cost of replacement ink cartridges when a consumer purchases a printer. The pricing of credit products also often involves shrouding of potential and known costs. Gabaix and Laibson (2006) suggests that short of outlawing ignorance or banning misleading but not false advertis-

---

58. McCoy (2006) argues that advertising should be both prominent and bold and include the range of APRs and a warning that those with weak credit will not qualify for the best price; that lenders should be required to provide firm price quotes before they require payment of nonrefundable fees; and that there should be additional variable-rate disclosures. The author recommends that the following aspects of a variable-rate loan should be clearly disclosed: the fact that it is an adjustable-rate mortgage (ARM); the number of months or years until the rate resets; the maximum interest rate and monthly principal and interest for the actual loan; the earliest date on which the loan could become fully indexed and the maximum interest and monthly payment on that date; and the maximum amount and timing of any prepayment penalty.

ing, there are four types of possible but imperfect regulations to deal with shrouding:
—compelling, complete, and easy-to-understand disclosures
—using warning labels to alert consumers to look out for shrouded costs
—imposing caps on the costs of shrouded attributes
—reducing barriers to entry

They cautioned, however, that "even if good theoretical arguments exist for shrouding regulation, such regulations put us on a slippery slope that may produce great unintended consequences."[59]

Even if disclosures were improved, it is an open question whether they could overcome many consumers' general lack of financial literacy and susceptibility to being steered to particular products, the complexity of the concepts involved in making choices about the future, and the difficulty of comparison shopping in a world with so many product choices. Finally, disclosures do not help consumers make choices among alternative forms of debt. The Schumer Box, for example, arguably helps consumers compare credit card products, but it surely does not help them decide whether they should get a payday loan or a home equity loan instead. Is it therefore sensible to believe that a disclosure-based regime can bring meaningful benefits?

Given concerns over the judgment of even those consumers who are equipped with the best and most binding of disclosures provided early enough in the process, another major criticism of the regulation of credit products is that it does not, except in a handful of state laws, place enough curbs on abusive lending practices or on predatory credit products. Many are lobbying for changes in federal and state laws in order to either restrict certain practices or impose some form of "suitability" standard. Most such proposals aim to restrict the use of loan features that expose borrowers to large repayment risks and to curb the ability of lenders to lend without regard for the capacity of a borrower to repay, without verification of income and assets, and without examining whether refinancing benefits the borrower. Opponents fear that specific prohibitions will limit credit while ill-defined prohibitions, such as a suitability standard, will lead to confusion, add to costs, limit credit availability, and stifle innovation.

Other observers fault the contract terms found in certain consumer credit products that place the debtor at a disadvantage, including contracts that allow credit card issuers to change at their discretion many of the terms and fees associated with the product, contracts that contain mandatory arbitration clauses, and those that permit credit card issuers to treat a default on another lender's credit card as a universal default on all lenders. Although consumers always have the option to pay off their debts or roll them over to another lender if terms are changed, doing so can still create a situation in which initial offers are changed

---

59. Gabaix and Laibson (2006, p. 531).

in ways that consumers cannot predict but must incur transaction and search costs to avoid. Furthermore, the practice of universal default, whereby consumers' failure to pay a debt to one lender triggers higher charges on all of their credit cards, is viewed as unfair. There have been calls to limit the ways in which terms and fees can be changed and to prohibit universal default and mandatory arbitration provisions. Jackson (2007) suggests markup rules and duties of best execution, which both govern the extent to which securities firms can mark up the price of securities and impose obligations on firms. To that end, the author suggests that originators should be required to keep contemporaneous records of the market value of originations to assist regulators in their supervisory efforts.

Regulation of Market Behavior

Regulations are viewed by many as a blunt instrument that should be used judiciously and cautiously. Still, most economists argue that regulation of market behavior is a legitimate method of correcting market failures, ensuring competition, and protecting consumers from unfair, deceptive, and discriminatory treatment. As previously described, some authorities view the set of regulations that have evolved to achieve those goals as sufficient while others find them lacking. Yet reforms are clearly necessary given the recent credit crisis that has roiled the capital markets. Many actions at the federal level have been proposed, such as requiring national licensing of brokers, adopting a "reasonable ability to pay" standard for underwriting and a minimum standard for assignee liability, allowing cram-downs (forced reductions by a bankruptcy court in the principal that a petitioner owes over the objections of lenders) of mortgage debt in bankruptcy, prohibiting certain terms, reforming consumer disclosures, more actively regulating the advertising of loan terms, and undertaking the wholesale overhaul of the financial regulatory system (up to and including greatly expanding the regulatory authority and reach of the Federal Reserve and eliminating the Office of Thrift Supervision). In the first half of 2008, the Treasury Department issued an extensive report calling for an overhaul of federal regulation of financial institutions. Meanwhile, the Federal Reserve issued much tougher rules governing high-cost loans and imposed rules on a new class of loans called higher-cost with the bar set lower as to which loans are covered. The rule covers all financial institutions regardless of which agency or level of government supervises them. Congress passed and the president also signed a bill that requires broader and tougher licensing and registration standards for mortgage originators. Ultimately which issues will actually result in the passage of additional new laws or the promulgation of substantially revised regulations is difficult to divine. But times of crises and media attention provide the conditions most likely to break political logjams and lead to meaningful action.

Eleven Legal and Regulatory Levers

There are at least eleven legal and regulatory levers that those who wish to press for particular reforms can use to address perceived weaknesses in the present regulatory system.

—*Strengthen examination and enforcement mechanisms.* A major reform in this area would be to expand the types of financial institutions that are examined by state and especially by federal regulators on a regular basis. Many believe that federal examination is desirable. Although the Federal Reserve has some flexibility in deciding whether and how to examine some of the subsidiaries of bank holding companies, broadening the federal role would require new legislation and could be seen as usurping states' rights. On the enforcement side, additional resources to explore and pursue alleged violations of existing law would be an obvious means to strengthen consumer protections.

—*Increase public disclosures on lending activities.* At present, the principal public disclosure law on lending activities is the Home Mortgage Disclosure Act, which provides for detailed information on the mortgage lending activities of almost all firms that originate mortgages. Information is reported for all mortgage loans for which an application is received, including whether it was accepted or rejected, the race or ethnicity of the applicant, the applicant's income, the mortgage amount, whether the property is intended for owner-occupancy, when an originated loan is sold and how, and the annual percentage rate for loans if it is above a certain spread relative to the interest rates on Treasuries of comparable maturities.[60] Initially during the 1980s, HMDA data were used to plead the case that lenders were redlining communities, and the data appear to have played a role in the achievement of Community Reinvestment Act agreements in which banks pledged to lend to community groups and in low- and moderate-income communities. The public release of the information had an even greater impact in the 1990s, when information was provided on applications and the characteristics of applicants in addition to information on accepted loans and borrowers. It led to a landmark study conducted by the Federal Reserve Bank of Boston that strongly suggested that lenders were discriminating against minorities. While the study sparked an intense scholarly debate over the validity of its findings, it sent a chill through the lending community, which feared that the perception of discrimination would negatively affect business and lead to lawsuits with the potential for large settlements. It is likely that the very public nature of the debate was an important factor in the dramatic increase in efforts by prime lenders to reach out to low-income and minority communities, paving the way for later efforts by subprime lending specialists. No comparable law governs credit cards, installment loans, or automobile loans, and the passage of such laws could have a similarly

---

60. While information on race and ethnicity is requested, it is not required and is missing from a significant fraction of all loan records.

illuminating and important influence on those forms of lending. In addition, the public disclosure requirements associated with offering consumer credit–backed securities for public sale could be strengthened in a variety of ways to give investors a better understanding of the risks and features of the pooled loans that back the securities that they are purchasing, as well as the conditions under which the loans were originated and sold.

—*Better inform consumers through consumer lending disclosures.* As noted, consumer lending disclosures are the source of some controversy. There is evidence that the form that disclosures currently take is often unhelpful or insufficient to give consumers enough information to make appropriate choices and easily compare products. Indeed, not as much attention has been paid to figuring out the best way to communicate the necessary information as has been paid in the area of food and drug disclosures. In addition to truth-in-lending disclosures, which are required of all lenders, there are the Schumer Box disclosures required of credit card companies, the Home Ownership and Equity Protection Act disclosures required of high-cost mortgage lenders, and the Real Estate Settlement Practices Act disclosures required of lenders in home sales. Of those, the Schumer Box is an example of an effort to help consumers compare products through a common method of displaying information on the many separate terms and fees that go into a credit card contract. Although it does not cover all possible product features and many elements can be modified later at the lender's discretion, it could serve as an example for consumer purchases in the areas of mortgage, automobile, and installment credit. The features of the Schumer Box itself could also be improved and expanded. Finally, the regulations that govern the time between when good faith estimates are made and when the actual interest rate and loan fees must be locked in and revealed to borrowers could be strengthened.

—*De-bias consumers better through disclosures.* This step links most specifically to the rich literature that has developed around behavioral law and economics. As elaborated by Jolls and Sunstein (2005), the idea is to use the law to help correct cognitive biases and consumer myopia by steering consumers in "more rational directions" and "by reducing or even eliminating their bounded rationality." The authors contrast this approach with efforts to use the law merely to inform consumers or block private choices by banning certain products. They make a compelling case that a cognitive bias like optimism can render even information that is perfectly communicated through disclosure ineffective in steering consumers away from taking on debt with undue risks. For example, even if debtors understand the risks associated with an adjustable rate or interest-only loan (which they may not, given current TILA disclosures), they can still pick a product that is riskier than the one that they would pick if they did not discount their own risk relative to the average risk. To counteract such biases, laws and regulations could require that other cognitive biases be used to steer consumers away from decisions that are unduly influenced by their biases. For example, they suggest making sure that disclosures frame the risks associated with products as potential losses rather than potential gains (to take advantage of the cognitive bias toward loss aversion) and that the disclosure gives concrete examples of worst-case outcomes to countervail consumers' optimism bias (due to the availability heuristic in which people's prediction of the frequency of an event tends to be based on how readily they can call it to mind).

As Jolls and Sunstein (2005) put it, "In the consumer safety context, de-biasing through the availability heuristic would focus on putting at the consumers' cognitive disposal the prospect of negative outcomes from use, or at least unsafe use, of a particular product . . . on pain of administrative penalties or tort liability . . . to provide a truthful account of consequences that resulted from a particular harm-producing use of the product, rather than simply providing a generalized warning or statement that fails to harness availability."[61] While de-biasing sounds promising, the experience with safety warnings on drugs suggests that it may face an uphill climb in steering consumers to the proper products. Certain drug and tobacco safety warnings often highlight dreadful outcomes that are specifically called out, even in television ads. Yet consumers still use the products. Nonetheless, it is difficult to argue that consumers would not be served by spelling out for them, as a matter of law, the various serious consequences of failing to repay debts and of the specific magnitudes of the worst-case scenario rate resets that may befall them through the loan products that they selected.

—*Prohibit certain products, practices, rates, or contract terms.* When a loan practice or product can leave large shares of borrowers vulnerable to unfair treatment or default even in the absence of unfair treatment, what action can be taken? A natural reaction is to consider whether the practices or product features should be banned outright, allowed to be combined with only certain other features when offered, or banned for use by some groups of borrowers, such as those with low credit scores. Restricting specific practices and product features offered in the mortgage market is an issue that has been actively debated in Congress and in state legislatures since the turn of this century.

—*Establish broad suitability standards.* Suitability standards have the advantage of not banning certain practices and product features outright and of not having to anticipate the next product or practice that could create big problems. However, they leave room for interpretation and later standard setting by regulators that may introduce considerable uncertainty in lending. Any ambiguity can end up reflected in higher prices for and a lower supply of consumer credit.

—*Create an affirmative obligation to meet certain lending standards.* The most noteworthy affirmative obligation is the Community Reinvestment Act, which requires deposit-taking institutions to meet the credit needs of low- and

61. Jolls and Sunstein (2005, pp. 13–14).

moderate-income communities. If they do not, they may receive a low grade that could tarnish their reputation and they may have their applications for mergers and acquisitions conditioned or rejected. There is ample evidence that over time CRA has resulted in more mortgage credit being extended to low-income communities. However, it is unclear how much of its impact derives from the teeth in the law (conditioning or rejecting mergers and acquisitions) and how much from the public grading of institutions. Nevertheless, it is worth considering whether other financial institutions should be placed under similar obligations and whether the public release of information used to grade institutions should apply to forms of credit besides mortgages and small business loans.

—Expand legal standing to bring a case and stiffen penalties. For a willful violator, misbehavior in the market is discouraged only to the extent that significant penalties are imposed for such behavior and a number of entities have standing to bring legal action. A logical way to bring about greater compliance, therefore, is to modify credit laws so that more parties can bring suits and penalties are more severe. Indeed, Ayres and Braithwaite (1992) argue that the government could do far more to expand the right of public interest groups and associations to file suits and get engaged perhaps more directly in monitoring compliance with laws. McCoy (2007) contends that borrowers should be granted a private right of action to sue if they feel that they have been a victim of predatory or abusive lending practices or if they relied on false advertising in choosing a credit product. However, there also is some evidence that compliance falls once a law exceeds an optimal level of stringency (Viscusi and Zeckhauser 1979).

—Strengthen debtor remedies. Debtors can file for bankruptcy as a way to seek relief from repayment. They also have certain rights when creditors seek remedies against them, such as by garnishing their wages. In addition, debtors are protected when they purchase products that have defects that the creditor is unwilling to make right or when a contract violates the Uniform Commercial Code's unconscionable contract provision. Strengthening the remedies available to debtors is one way to discourage lenders from certain practices that are not in the debtor's best interest. Perhaps the most critical issue in terms of debtor remedies (beyond those implied by the standing to bring legal action and the stiffness of penalties) is the very limited conditions under which consumers can seek recourse from holders in due course. The most often discussed enhancement to existing debtor remedies, therefore, is to expand greatly the conditions under which assignees can be held liable even if they purchased a loan or security in good faith. That is especially important because it would provide a more powerful incentive for assignees to manage agency risk in the system and choose their partners and loan products wisely. It is also important because brokers, who operate at the point of sale and are responsible for originating such a large portion of home and auto loans, often

do not have deep pockets. Imposition of assignee liability would have far-reaching consequences. Those opposed to assignee liability fear that it will result in shutting down credit markets unless liability is narrowly defined and capped at a reasonable amount.

—*Weaken creditor remedies.* Creditors generally have a number of remedies at their disposal. Weakening any of them, but especially those that are used more often, would have the effect of making lenders more cautious about how they lend. As with strengthening debtor remedies, however, doing so could have chilling effects on the flow of credit. A weakening of remedies that is sometimes imposed in a crisis is a temporary state ban on home foreclosures. Other efforts to weaken creditor remedies have made it more difficult for lenders to place liens on assets or to garnish wages under certain conditions. Blocking creditor remedies may also increase moral hazard by making borrowers less willing to repay loans in the future in the belief that government regulations will thwart lenders' efforts to collect.

—*Focus on remedies like imposing licensing standards and sanctions for violating standards.* An often-heard complaint is that some states either lack licensing standards for important parties to a transaction or have standards that are too lax. Beefing up licensing standards, perhaps by creating federal requirements, and creating meaningful sanctions if they are violated are ways to address those concerns. Standards for licensing loan brokers are most often singled out for improvement and were included in the federal law passed in the summer of 2008.

Issues to Consider

Deciding how to regulate demands enormous wisdom and foresight. Often laws are passed and regulations promulgated with imperfect information about costs and possible unintended consequences. Even when the urgency of a problem renders efforts to obtain perfect information impractical, several considerations ought to come into play in assessing the relative merits of pursuing different avenues to achieve policy goals.

A first consideration is how much an approach restricts consumer choices. Approaches that preserve consumer choice have strong appeal. Still, the public may have a compelling reason to restrict choice—for example, the choice to drink and drive or to purchase cheaper paint that contains lead. In that respect, untested efforts to better inform and de-bias consumers hold promise. A second consideration is how costly it is to comply with a requirement. Approaches that have higher compliance costs for the average firm have less appeal. A third consideration is how much uncertainty an approach creates regarding the cost of complying or not complying with the law. Approaches that reduce uncertainty are desirable because they allow businesses to calculate their costs better. Thus, assignee or other liabilities, if imposed, should have some cap so that the cost of noncompliance is known and the risk is priced into interest rate charges. A fourth consideration is the externalities that changes in regulation may create. Those that create positive externalities (such as averting home foreclosures that are costly to neighbors) have more appeal than those that create negative externalities. A fifth consideration is unintended consequences of a regulation. Those that have the potential to restrict the flow of credit to previous borrowers, for example, can exacerbate problems, at least initially, unless a bridge is built to help them out. A sixth and critical consideration is likely welfare effects. It is important to do some kind of welfare analysis of both potential gains and potential losses to different types of consumers and different types of firms. A seventh and also critical consideration is whether a change is likely to achieve the desired outcome. There is a concern, for example, that consumer disclosures may not be effective unless they are improved and that de-biasing consumers through better disclosures may not be effective because the process has not yet been adequately tested.

Beyond Individual Levers

The current debate hinges on specific reforms and interventions that could make markets safer and more efficient while protecting consumers and preserving broad access to credit. But the current regulatory system raises even larger issues about the philosophy and approach to consumer regulation in the United States. In addition to fundamental issues already raised that relate to the decentralization and federalism of the U.S. regulatory system, other issues worth exploring concern how the public and private sectors can work together to arrive at a regulatory system that achieves its objectives most intelligently and at the least cost.

Freeman (2000) suggests four models of public-private interdependence in regulation. One is *standard setting,* the adoption of rules developed mostly or entirely by private parties and adopted by the government. An example is the standard setting of the American Society for Testing and Engineering. A variant is to rely on panels of experts to propose standards, as do the Office of Safety and Health Administration, the Environmental Protection Agency, and the Food and Drug Administration.

Another model is *voluntary self-regulation,* which occurs when professional and trade associations, for example, set standards and impose them on their members or pressure their members to abide by them. Usually, self-regulation takes the form of recommended management practices and internal accountability standards, not standards for marketing practices or product offerings. Examples include the ISO and the Chemical Manufacturers Association Responsible Care Program. A third model is *audited self-regulation.* In this model, Congress deputizes organizations to promulgate and enforce rules of conducts and laws; examples are the SEC and NASD. The final model is *negotiated rule making,* seen, for example, when an agency convenes stakeholders and a facilitator to come up with consensus-based rules under federal guidelines. This is seldom used, in part because the rules of engagement allow parties to break off the negotiation at any time and for the agency not to promulgate the consensus reached.

Only the second and third models appear to have been used in the regulation of consumer credit. The prospects for using the other two have not been much explored, and only audited self-regulation has been used extensively in the financial markets. That suggests that there is reason to consider whether more heavy reliance on standard setting, voluntary self-regulation, and negotiated rule making might make sense.

Ayres and Braithwaite (1992), building on Nonet and Selznick (1978), argue for an entirely new way of thinking about regulation that is "responsive" to industry structure. It is based on the normative view that regulation is most effective when it balances the diverse objectives of industry associations, regulated firms, and public interest groups. They call for greater delegation of regulation to public interest groups and the regulated firms themselves. To avoid capture of the regulators by the regulated, they advocate for an enforcement pyramid that creates credible threats of costly enforcement actions if responsive regulations fail—that is, if self-regulation is not properly constituted or executed. However, they also argue for an interventionist state that enforces the participation rights of, and provides resources to, less powerful groups in negotiating regulations, such as public interest groups and trade associations that represent weak competitors. They offer the Trade Practices Commission in Australia as their principal example of an entity formed to create responsive regulations. The commission switched from being an enforcer of strict rules to being a facilitator of deregulation and self-regulation. In the process, the government ensured a place at the table for less powerful parties and granted them significant influence.

Trumbull (2007) points out that prevailing societal views about access to credit and the means for overcoming economic exclusion play a role in how different countries shape credit regulations. He points out that in the United Kingdom the prevailing view is that entrepreneurship is the way for the poor to overcome social and economic exclusion. In contrast, France has greater concern about the transfer of wealth from the poor to the rich through credit contracts. The United Kingdom's model of self-regulation grew from dissatisfaction with government regulations. In 1991 growing political pressure led three trade associations to develop the Banking Code, to which all retail banks, building societies, and credit card issuers are signatories.[62] The code, which covers unsecured consumer credit, features a monitoring body (the Standards Board) that includes executives from the three sponsoring trade associations, but a majority of members, including the chair, are independent. Signatories are required to submit an annual statement of

---

62. A Finance and Leasing Association Code also exists, which covers finance companies that offer consumer and auto finance, but its signatories cover only about 30 percent of lending (Kempson 2007).

compliance, and the Standards Board monitors compliance through on-site examinations similar to the exams that a government regulator would conduct. Serious infractions are referred to the disciplinary committee, which can require companies to compensate consumers, publicly announce violations to pressure firms to change their practices, and expel signatories. Furthermore, every three years the Banking Code undergoes revision through a process led by an independent reviewer; thus far, the majority of the reviewer's recommendations have been adopted by the sponsoring organizations. The code is viewed as both strong and flexible enough to prevent consumer credit from being brought fully under the control of the rigorous Financial Services and Markets Act of 2000, as was mortgage credit, which was subject to a much weaker and heavily criticized Mortgage Code. The Banking Code suggests that effective self-regulation is possible in the consumer credit sphere.

Beyond Regulation: Other Strategies to Improve Market Outcomes

In addition to possible modifications to the regulation of consumer credit markets, a wide range of possible and promising actions could be taken by the private, civic, and public sectors to improve market outcomes. These actions can be grouped into actions that help consumers once they are in trouble, help consumers stay out of trouble without directly steering their product choices, and help consumers stay out of trouble by steering them to the right choice. But first, it is worth examining what gets borrowers into trouble in the first place.

Borrowers experience financial difficulty in repaying their loans primarily because of life events such as a reduction in income or an illness that forces them to spend much more than they had budgeted on critical medical care. These are sometimes referred to as trigger events. Factors more endogenous to debt behaviors are responsible for difficulties when consumers take on too much debt relative to their regular budgets and incomes, either knowingly or because they overestimate their future wealth or income; when they must pay unanticipated or rising costs or late fees; when universal default drives up their payments to other creditors when they miss making payments to one creditor; and when their loan payment resets because the interest rate changes, an initial discount offer expires, or an interest-only period expires.

Increasing debt payments become a problem mostly when interest rates rise or when especially steep discounts on initial rates expire. Taking on too much debt relative to regular income becomes a problem especially during periods of lax underwriting or rapidly rising costs that exceed income gains. Budget shocks like large medical bills happen with some predictability in the aggregate but with considerable unpredictability in the lives of most individuals. Income shocks are likely to increase around periods of recession or national job loss, but they also occur with some aggregate predictability from death, injury, and divorce; again, however,

Table 1-4. *Reasons for Delinquency among All Delinquent Borrowers*
Percent

Reason	2001–05	2006
Unemployment or curtailment of income	42.8	36.3
Illness or death in the family	22.9	25.0
Excessive obligations	11.1	13.6
Marital difficulties	7.9	6.0
Property problem or casualty loss	1.7	2.8
Extreme hardship	2.8	0.9
Inability to sell or rent property	1.3	1.4
Employment transfer or military service	0.9	0.6
All other reasons	8.7	13.3

Source: Cutts (2007). Data cover period from 2001 to 2006; 2006 data exclude delinquent loans in Louisiana and Mississippi resulting from hurricane effects.

they occur with considerable unpredictability in an individual life. Difficulties refinancing a mortgage, of course, occur during periods of falling home prices (which in turn occur most often after periods of overbuilding, overheating of house prices, and recession).

An indication of the relative weight of these factors is offered by data for 2006 and average data for 2001–05 from Freddie Mac (see table 1-4). These data plainly show that unemployment or other income curtailment is the principal reason that borrowers, or at least borrowers of prime mortgage credit, default on their loans. They also show that excessive debt payments were a greater problem in 2006 than they were on average over the previous five years. Although data are not available, it is likely that income curtailment was a significantly more important driver of defaults around 2001–02 than during 2003–05. During periods when the national unemployment rate is increasing, as it was in and around the 2001 recession, it is logical to expect job loss to trigger more defaults than during other periods. It also is likely that excessive debt payments will be a greater problem in the years ahead as a result of the risk layering, subprime lending, and use of discounted teaser rates in recent years. Still, among prime mortgage borrowers, excessive obligations accounted for only about 14 percent of all reasons for default in 2006.

Helping Consumers in Trouble

Once consumers get into trouble, it is difficult to help them. Yet the likelihood of that occurring given any set of macroeconomic circumstances has increased as a result of the higher debt burden that the typical American faces today than in the past; the opening up of credit to borrowers with previous repayment difficulties; and the use of credit products that entail greater repayment risk (such as increasing use of adjustable debt tied to short-term interest rates, the recent widespread adoption of interest-only and payment-option mortgage loans, and the use of aggressive teaser discounts).

Elliehausen, Lundquist, and Staten (2003) examine the impact of one-on-one credit counseling delivered to 14,000 clients by five member agencies of the National Foundation for Credit Counseling and finds that one-on-one counseling had a positive impact on borrower behavior over an extended period. Borrowers who received financial counseling improved their credit profile, and there was a measured reduction in delinquency. The study suggests that early interventions that help consumers understand their options and the implications of defaulting on all or some of their debts are important.[63] Consumers need to understand the pros and cons of filing for different forms of bankruptcy and their eligibility to do so. They may also benefit from financial counseling in which counselors help them work with lenders to modify loan terms, extend payments, refinance or consolidate their debts, or sell their property. In a recent survey of 1,003 Americans conducted by Princeton Survey Research Associates International (PSRAI), more than one-third of respondents said that they had received professional financial advice of some kind.[64]

Currently, the nonprofit sector provides most counseling while the government and foundations often subsidize it. With their support, counseling agencies test ways to work out loans pooled into securities, and some provide blended subsidized and market-rate debt to reach out to more borrowers wanting to refinance to pay off old debts and remain current on new ones. The cost of counseling remains an issue, especially during times of macroeconomic stress, when the demand for counseling can easily exceed supply. It is promising, therefore, that more and more studies are finding that such counseling leads to lower credit costs and that it is in the best interest of businesses to fund, if not provide, assistance themselves. But having such studies in hand is a far cry from getting businesses or government to cover the costs.

The most common form of debt held by households is mortgage debt, and the loss of a home due to nonpayment is both traumatizing for the household involved and full of potential negative externalities for nearby neighbors and the economy as a whole (Apgar and Duda 2005). Given such impacts, it is important to single out possible strategies for saving homes at risk of foreclosure.

The securitization of debt poses special challenges, because the permissible terms for working out credit often are spelled out in the servicing agreement developed at the time that the credit was pooled, securitized, and sold. Those terms vary considerably and often are not designed with enough forethought about

---

63. Hirad and Zorn (2001) also find that certain forms of counseling, after controlling for a variety of factors, have a measurable impact on reducing mortgage delinquencies.

64. Princeton Survey Research Associates International (PSRAI) conducted the Financial Literacy Survey on behalf of the National Foundation for Credit Counseling (NFCC) in 2007.

whether they serve the ultimate interests of the investors in the securities. Once the securities are issued, the agreement remains in force and the only way to get released from it is to have the debt repaid or completely written off and sold out of the pool. Thus, moving forward, financial intermediaries need to put more thought into the terms of servicing agreements so that sensible workouts are feasible. In the meantime, government agencies and civic organizations can try to identify securities governed by more or less liberal agreements and work with servicers to try to achieve the best outcome for the lender and the borrower. Another option for these agencies is to negotiate to buy a loan out of a pool, effectively refinancing and helping borrowers. That has been done by the Ohio and Massachusetts housing finance agencies in the case of failing mortgage loans.

The economic concept of SwapRent is another way to help keep mortgage borrowers in their home, avert foreclosures, and avoid distressing investors in residential mortgage–backed securities (RMBS) or related collateralized debt obligations. While maintaining legal ownership, owners become renters of their own houses for a period of time, trading the appreciation benefits—or downside depreciation risk—for a discounted rate.[65]

Helping Consumers to Stay out of Trouble and Make Better and More Informed Credit Choices

Much more promising and satisfying than remedies to help consumers get out of serious debt are actions and strategies that prevent them from getting into trouble in the first place. Strategies could include financial education to help consumers make better choices, savings incentives and options for creating a financial safety net, and insurance and debt protection products to cover the risks that often drive default. The approach around which nearly all interested parties will usually rally is financial education designed to help consumers make smarter choices that leave them less vulnerable to debt repayment problems and that get them to live within their means. Lusardi (2007) argues that widespread financial illiteracy needs to be addressed and suggests a range of remedies, including requiring education through a "financial driver's license" program, providing incentives like a government-funded savings accounts for children, and de-biasing information. Many worry whether education alone can do the trick, especially when costs of some key items, like health care, health insurance, housing, and education spiral higher and incomes, especially in the bottom half of the income distribution, grow so slowly.

Moreover, two major questions remain: what kind of counseling works, and whether it is cost effective. Sawady and Tescher (2007) question whether a classroom-based financial education curriculum is the best way to maximize economic benefits for consumers or whether promoting guidance and coaching is a

65. See www.swaprent.com.

better way to help consumers navigate the increasingly complex choices in the world of financial services. In addition, it is not evident that broad counseling is the most cost-effective use of resources, and cost-effectiveness is difficult to measure. Others advocate providing financial education that targets "teachable moments," such as specific credit and financial decisions, through the civic sector with government and philanthropic support. To address such concerns, some credit counseling agencies are deploying cost-efficient strategies, such as telephone or web-based counseling. Yet, the question of who should pay for these services remains elusive, even as bankruptcy law now requires financial counseling for filers (Fay, Hurst, and White 2002).

It remains to be seen whether broad financial education is sufficient to overcome both push-marketing tactics and consumers' cognitive biases when it comes to sales efforts that focus on "quick and easy" credit (Essene and Apgar 2007). As seen, choosing credit products is so complex that it is arguably better to offer advice than to expect consumers to become expert enough to understand their options and the ramifications of their credit choices. People often seek professional investment advice, and professional credit advice may be just as crucial.

Thus, while this issue need not be reduced to a choice between providing training for financial literacy and counseling on one hand and providing advice on the other, there are compelling reasons to focus added attention on advice. But what should govern the nature of the advice offered and how should the advice be delivered? Advice can be delivered through telephone hotlines, individual meetings with a credit adviser, or Internet websites. While it would be possible also to hold small-group sessions, the individualized nature of the decision would place that option at the bottom of the list of delivery mechanisms likely to be effective.

But the fundamental question of how to offer advice—what factors to take into account, how to sort products, and how to communicate advice—is far from having a uniform or single answer. It is striking that so much attention is paid to investing choices and so little to the liabilities side of a mainstream consumer's balance sheet. This is an area of great promise, where research, pilot experiments, and an organized effort by those committed to improving the outcomes of credit consumers are all essential to success. If the history with the provision of homeownership counseling is any guide, however, it is clear that this will not be an easy task. Getting agreement on the content of the curriculum and how to deliver it has been elusive in homeownership counseling, despite determined efforts to reach agreement.

Another avenue with real promise for preventing consumers from getting into trouble is to provide better incentives and options for saving. Helping people to save before they borrow so that they have a cushion to fall back on in the event of trouble and helping to engender in them the habit of saving—so that they trade off some spending for greater security—are real options. Tufano and

Schneider (2007) review the many ways that government, the private sector, and NGOs can support consumer saving and place the alternatives on a spectrum, with compelling people to save at one end and generating excitement about saving at the other. An example of forced saving is the United Kingdom's Child Trust Fund account, which sets aside 250 pounds for every British child born after September 1, 2002, with vendors providing a range of account types. At the other extreme, lottery-linked saving (in which savers are entered into lotteries) or a physical collectible (in which achievement of each progressive savings goal earns the saver a collectible item until the set is complete and all the goals are met) that allows consumers to track their progress can create excitement about saving.

In between are programs that make it difficult not to save (by setting default options to saving and bundling saving with other transactions), that make it easier to save (by allowing saving through channels other than just banks and thrifts), that provide incentives to save, and that leverage social networks to support saving. Private lenders have been especially active in developing innovative programs that bundle saving with other services. For example, the Bank of America's Keep the Change program rounds up the amount of a debit card deduction and deposits the change into a savings account with a matching component.

For at least a subset of consumers, bundling rental housing assistance with counseling on credit and saving strategies and implementing other initiatives to promote saving are an effective option. At any given time, about a quarter of all eligible renters receive some form of government rental assistance, while an even larger share receives such assistance or lives in homes managed by mission-driven nonprofit organizations. That provides an opportunity for outreach, building on the renters' current relationship with their subsidy providers or nonprofit landlord. Counseling these renters on credit and saving options could pay rich dividends in the form of fewer renter households with low credit scores, fewer uninformed credit consumers, and fewer households without a cushion of savings. While little attention has been paid to the credit consumption of renters receiving assistance and those served by nonprofit housing providers, efforts to promote saving among them have formally begun, thanks to a federal program called Family Self-Sufficiency (FSS). Although it is still a small-scale program, its aim is to allow those with increasing incomes to take 30 percent of the increase and place it in a savings account rather than plow it back into housing payments. Evaluations of the program suggest that FSS encourages greater work effort and homeownership, although the success of homeowners aided through the program has not been tracked. Promising as this approach is, it would fail to reach renters who do not live in subsidized or nonprofit-managed housing and homeowners who may be in equal need of counseling and encouragement to save.

Another approach to helping consumers stay out of trouble is to have them take out more and better insurance against risks over which they have little control but that have well-established actuarial frequencies of occurrence, such as layoffs, unexpected and uninsured medical expenses, disability, and death of a family member (Belsky, Case, and Smith 2007). Indeed, products are now available to insure borrowers against such all-too-common risks; such products are offered by insurers, through brokers, or, in the case of debt cancellation products, by banks. However, issues have been raised about how such products work out in practice, in terms of broker compensation, marketing practices, and pricing, all of which may not serve customers well. In addition, the products cover only a subset of the events that make it difficult for borrowers to repay their bills, such as divorce, job loss for reasons other than layoff, or declining house prices. The first two of these are difficult to insure against because they create moral hazard and the risk that borrowers will game the system to escape the obligation to repay their debts to others. Meanwhile, efforts to develop products to help people insure against house price declines have only begun to be introduced. Still, insuring the borrower has appeal because it helps consumers avoid the higher interest rates they will be charged by lenders if their credit score is lower and the stress of trying to work out or work off debts that they cannot repay. Because it also indemnifies lenders, it appeals to business as well. This is an area where much work is needed to explore the market potential of products, regulatory reforms, regulations that may better protect consumers, and debt cancellation products offered by banks, on which there are almost no studies and no public disclosures.

Creating Better Choices for Consumers

Other efforts could prevent consumers from taking on credit products that they do not understand and that expose them to greater risks than they can manage. Building a third-party adviser system, supported with automated tools for consumers and counselors, is one idea. Another idea, building on behavioral economics, is to change the default settings of current choices in the marketplace to encourage the least risky products.

Having a knowledgeable financial adviser's objective opinion could prove useful at shopping time, as these advisers evaluate, compare, and provide information on specific loan products. In fact, brokers often provide financial advice to inform consumers and help them make better credit choices. On the other hand, when brokers' compensation (both revealed to the consumer and embedded in the mortgage interest rate or other components of the overall mortgage cost) is linked to the sale of particular mortgage products, brokers have an incentive to sell the products that maximize their earnings. A flat-fee mortgage broker system, operating under the guidelines of a trusted adviser network—a network of advisers certified by trusted third parties as acting competently and in the interests of consumers—could provide unbiased advice to the consumer that decouples compensation from the push marketing of specific products. The system would encourage mortgage advisers to compete by offering superior customer service and higher-quality advice. However, the challenges of selling the concept of "fairness," building brand awareness, and having a meaningful impact are real, and regulatory advantages may be required to develop such a system (Apgar and Essene 2007). Promoting the development and licensing of third-party objective advisers and developing automated decision support tools for advisers and consumers is one way to steer consumers toward better choices.

Changing the default settings of current choices in the marketplace to encourage "good loans" with the least risky terms may help consumers stay out of trouble.[66] Requiring consumers to make an affirmative choice or to "opt out" of the least risky product may help consumers counter their tendency toward hyperbolic discounting and support the default setting. Barr, Mullainathan, and Shafir (2007) point out that some opt-outs may be too weak to withstand market pressures and may work only when they are closely aligned with market incentives. The authors caution that the take-up of a program depends on many factors, as "options are construed, elaborated, and contextually interpreted in ways that are both systematic and consequential."[67]

Conclusion

Consumer and mortgage credit plays a vital role in fueling economic growth, smoothing consumption over the life cycle, and creating opportunities to invest in tangible assets and human capital. Although credit has the potential to bring many benefits, it also has created serious problems. For example, it can propagate business cycles if credit standards and practices become so relaxed that a period of credit tightening follows. The nation is now living out this lesson. Furthermore, the evolution of the consumer credit system presents a remarkable number of challenges to the efficient operation of credit markets and to the protection of consumers.

In striving to retain access to credit while better informing and protecting consumers, it is well to understand these challenges, the consumer behaviors and cognitive biases that give rise to them, the range of potential regulatory responses to issues of public concern, considerations that influence estimates of the relative value of the responses, and the many means to improve the credit markets besides regulation. Striking the right balance between free choice, access to credit, and innovation, on one hand, and consumer protection and market efficiency, on the other, is a daunting but necessary task.

66. Essene and Apgar (2007, p. 41).
67. Barr, Mullainathan, and Shafir (2007, p. 29).

References

Agarwal, Sumit, and others. 2006. "Do Consumers Choose the Right Credit Contracts?" Working Paper 2006-11. Federal Reserve Bank of Chicago.

Antzoulatos, Angelos A. 1996. "Consumer Credit and Consumption Forecasts." *International Journal of Forecasting* 12, no. 4 (December): 439–53.

Apgar, William C., Amal Bendimerad, and Ren Essene. 2007. *Mortgage Market Channels and Fair Lending: An Analysis of HMDA Data.* Harvard University, Joint Center for Housing Studies (JCHS) (www.jchs.harvard.edu/publications/finance/mm07-2_mortgage_market_channels.pdf).

Apgar, William C., and Mark Duda. 2005. *Collateral Damage: The Municipal Impact of Today's Mortgage Foreclosure Boom.* A report prepared for the Homeownership Preservation Foundation, Minneapolis, Minn. (www.995hope.org/content/pdf/Apgar_Duda_Study_Short_Version.pdf).

Apgar, William, and Ren Essene. 2007. "Helping Consumers Make Better Mortgage Choices." Paper outline presented at the Understanding Consumer Credit Symposium, Boston, Mass., November 28–29.

Ayres, Ian, and John Braithwaite. 1992. *Responsive Regulation: Transcending the Deregulation Debate.* Oxford University Press.

Bacchetta, Philippe, and Stefan Gerlach. 1997. "Consumption and Credit Constraints: International Evidence." *Journal of Monetary Economics* 40, no. 2: 207–38.

Bailey, Grant, Vincent Barberio, and Glenn Costello. 2008. "Revised Loss Expectations for 2006 and 2007 Subprime Vintage Collateral." Fitch Ratings, Structured Finance.

Barr, Michael, Sendhil Mullainathan, and Eldar Shafir. 2007. "Behaviorally Informed Credit Regulation." Paper presented at the Understanding Consumer Credit Symposium, Boston, Mass., November 28–29.

Belsky, Eric, Karl E. Case, and Susan J. Smith. 2007. "Identifying, Managing and Mitigating Risks to Borrowers in Changing Mortgage and Consumer Credit Markets." Paper presented at the Understanding Consumer Credit Symposium, Boston, Mass., November 28–29.

Belsky, Eric, and Joel Prakken. 2004. *Housing Wealth Effects: Housing's Impact on Wealth Accumulation, Wealth Distribution and Consumer Spending.* Chicago: National Association of Realtors.

Bernanke, Ben, Mark Gertler, and Simon Gilchrist. 1996. "The Financial Accelerator and the Flight to Quality." *Review of Economics and Statistics* 78, no. 1 (February): 1–15.

Bertrand, Marianne, Sendhil Mullainathan, and Eldar Shafir. 2006. "Behavioral Economics and Marketing in Aid of Decision Making among the Poor." *Journal of Public Policy and Marketing* 25, no. 1: 8–23.

Browning, Martin, and Thomas F. Crossley. 2001. "The Life-Cycle Model of Consumption and Saving." *Journal of Economic Perspectives* 15, no. 3: 3–22.

Bucks, Brian K., Arthur B. Kennickell, and Kevin B. Moore. 2006. "Recent Changes in U.S. Family Finances: Evidence from the 2001 and 2004 Survey." *Federal Reserve Bulletin* 92 (March): A1–A38.

Burd, Stephen. 2006. "As the Volume of Private Loans Soars, Students Feel the Pinch." *Chronicle of Higher Education* (http://chronicle.com/free/v53/i05/05a02001.htm).

Campbell, John. 2006. "Household Finance." *Journal of Finance* 61, no. 4: 1553–604.

Canner, Glenn, Karen Dynan, and Wayne Passmore. 2002. "Mortgage Refinancing in 2001 and Early 2002." *Federal Reserve Bulletin* 88 (December): 469–81.

Choudhry, Moorad, and Frank J. Fabozzi. 2004. *The Handbook of European Structured Financial Products.* Hoboken, N.J.: John Wiley and Sons.

Courant, Paul, Edward Gramlich, and John Laitner. 1984. "A Dynamic Microeconomic Estimate of the Life-Cycle Model." In *Retirement and Economic Behavior,* edited by H. Aaron and G. Burtless, pp. 279–309. Brookings.

Courchane, Marsha J., Brian J. Surette, and Peter M. Zorn. 2004. "Subprime Borrowers: Mortgage Transitions and Outcomes." *Journal of Real Estate Finance and Economics* 29, no. 4: 365–92.

Cutts, Amy Crews. 2007. "Housing and Mortgage Market Outlook." Presentation at the Fourth Annual Five Star Mortgage Servicing Default Conference, Dallas, Texas, September 10.

Credit Suisse. 2007. "Mortgage Liquidity du Jour: Underestimated No More." March 12.

Durkin, Thomas. 2007. "Should Consumer Credit Disclosures Be Updated?" Paper presented at the Understanding Consumer Credit Symposium, Boston, Mass., November 28–29.

Dynan, Karen E., and Donald L. Kohn. 2007. "The Rise in U.S. Household Indebtedness: Causes and Consequences." Federal Reserve Board, Finance and Economics Discussion Series 2007-37. Washington: Board of Governors of the Federal Reserve System.

Dynan, Karen, Kathleen Johnson, and Karen Pence. 2003. "Recent Changes to a Measure of U.S. Household Debt Service." *Federal Reserve Bulletin* 89 (October): 417–26.

Elliehausen, Gregory E., Christopher Lundquist, and Michael E. Staten. 2003. "Impact of Credit Counseling on Subsequent Borrower Credit Usage and Payment Behavior." Paper presented at Seeds of Growth—Sustainable Community Development: What Works, What Doesn't and Why? Federal Reserve System Community Affairs Research Conference, Washington, D.C., March 27–28 (www.chicagofed.org/cedric/files/2003_conf_paper_session1_staten.pdf).

Epstein, Richard A. 2006. "Behavioral Economics: Human Errors and Market Corrections." *University of Chicago Law Review* 73, no. 1: 111–32.

Essene, Ren, and William Apgar. 2007. *Understanding Mortgage Markets: Creating Good Mortgage Options for All Americans.* Harvard University, Joint Center for Housing Studies (www.jchs.harvard.edu/publications/finance/mm07-1_mortgage_market_behavior.pdf).

Fay, Scott, Erik Hurst, and Michelle J. White. 2002. "The Household Bankruptcy Decision." *American Economic Review* 92, no. 3: 706–18 (www.jstor.org/pss/3083362).

FI-Magazine.com. "F&I Research: 2005 Finances" (www.fi-magazine.com/t_inside.cfm?action=statistics#).

Federal Reserve Board. 2008a. "Federal Reserve Statistical Release G.19: Consumer Credit" (www.federalreserve.gov/releases/g19/Current/).

———. 2008b. "Flow of Funds Accounts of the United States" (www.federalreserve.gov/releases/z1/current).

———. 2008c. "Survey of Consumer Finances" (www.federalreserve.gov/pubs/oss/oss2/scfindex.html).

Fellowes, Matt, and Mia Mabanta. 2007. *Borrowing to Get Ahead, and Behind: The Credit Boom and Bust in Lower-Income Markets.* Brookings Metropolitan Policy Program.

Fisher, Irving. 1930. *The Theory of Interest.* New York: Macmillan Company.

Freeman, Jody. 2000. "The Private Role in Public Governance." *New York University Law Review* 75, no. 3: 543–675.

Friedman, Milton. 1957. *A Theory of the Consumption Function.* Princeton University Press.

Fundenberg, Drew. 2006. "Advancing beyond Advances in Behavioral Economics." *Journal of Economic Literature* 44, no. 3: 694–711.

Gabaix, Xavier, and Laibson, David. 2006. "Shrouded Attributes, Consumer Myopia, and Information Suppression in Competitive Markets." *Quarterly Journal of Economics* 121, no. 2: 505–40.

Gabaix, Xavier, and others. 2006. "Costly Information Acquisition: Experimental Analysis of a Boundedly Rational Model." *American Economic Review* 96, no. 4: 1043–68.

Garner, Alan C. 1996. "Can Measures of the Consumer Debt Burden Reliably Predict an Economic Slowdown?" Federal Reserve Bank of Kansas City, *Economic Review* (Quarter 4): 63–76.

Glaeser, Edward. 2004. "Psychology and the Market." *American Economic Review Papers and Proceedings* 94, no. 2: 408–13.

Greenspan, Alan, and James Kennedy. 2007. "Sources and Uses of Equity Extracted from Homes." Federal Reserve Board, Finance and Economics Discussion Series 2007-20. Washington: Board of Governors of the Federal Reserve System.

Hannsgen, Greg. 2007. "A Random Walk Down Maple Lane? A Critique of Neoclassical Consumption Theory with Reference to Housing Wealth." *Review of Political Economy* 19, no. 1: 1–20.

Harris, Christopher, and David Laibson. 2001. "Dynamic Choices of Hyperbolic Consumers." *Econometrica* 69, no. 4: 935–57.

Himmelstein, David U., and others. 2005. "Illness and Injury as Contributors to Bankruptcy." Health Affairs MarketWatch.

Hirad, Abdighani, and Peter Zorn. 2001. "A Little Knowledge Is a Good Thing: Empirical Evidence of the Effectiveness of Pre-Purchase Homeownership Counseling." Working Paper LIHO-01.4. Harvard University, Joint Center for Housing Studies (www.jchs.harvard.edu/publications/homeownership/liho01-4.pdf).

Hubbard, R. Glenn, Jonathan Skinner, and Stephen P. Zeldes. 1994. "Expanding the Life-Cycle Model: Precautionary Saving and Public Policy." In *Papers and Proceedings of the Hundred and Sixth Annual Meeting of the American Economic Association, American Economic Review* 84, no. 2: 178–79.

Inside Mortgage Finance Publications. 2008. *The 2008 Mortgage Market Statistical Annual, Volume 1: The Primary Market.* Bethesda, Md.

Iyengar, Sheena S., and Mark Lepper. 2000. "When Choice Is Demotivating: Can One Desire too Much of a Good Thing?" *Journal of Personality and Social Psychology* 79: 995–1006.

Jackson, Howell. 2005. *Variation in the Intensity of Financial Regulation: Preliminary Evidence and Potential Implications.* Harvard Law School Discussion Paper No. 521.

———. 2007. "Enlisting Market Mechanisms to Police the Origination of Home Mortgages." Paper presented at the Understanding Consumer Credit Symposium, Boston, Mass., November 28–29.

Japelli, Tullio, and Marco Pagano. 1989. "Consumption and Capital Market Imperfections: An International Comparison." *American Economic Review* 79, no. 5: 1088–105.

Jolls, Christine. 1998. "Behavioral Economic Analysis of Redistributive Legal Rules in Symposium: The Legal Implications of Psychology: Human Behavior, Behavioral Economics, and the Law." *Vanderbilt Law Review* 51, no. 6: 1653–677.

Jolls, Christine, and Cass Sunstein. 2005. *Debiasing through Law.* Working Paper 11738. Cambridge, Mass.: National Bureau of Economic Research.

Kahneman, Daniel, and Amos Tversky. 1979. "Prospect Theory: An Analysis of Decisions under Risk." *Econometrica* 47, no. 2: 263–91.

Kempson, Elaine. 2007. "Looking beyond Our Shores: Consumer Protection Regulation Lessons from the UK." Paper presented at the Understanding Consumer Credit Symposium, Boston, Mass., November 28–29.

King, Mervyn A. 1994. "Debt Deflation: Theory and Evidence." *European Economic Review* 38, nos. 3–4: 419–45.

Laibson, David, and Richard Zeckhauser. 1998. "Amos Tversky and the Ascent of Behavioral Economics." *Journal of Risk and Uncertainty* 16: 7–47.

Leedom and Associates, LLC. 2002. "Analysis of the Buy Here-Pay Here Capitalization Market," December. Sarasota, Fla.: Leedom and Associates (www.twentygroups.com/index.php).

Ludvigson, Sydney. 1999. "Consumption and Credit: A Model of Time-Varying Liquidity Constraints." *Review of Economics and Statistics* 81, no. 3: 434–47.

Lusardi, Annamaria. 2007. "Financial Literacy: An Essential Tool for Informed Consumer Choice?" Paper presented at the Understanding Consumer Credit Symposium, Boston, Mass., November 28–29.

Maki, Dean M. 2000. "The Growth of Consumer Credit and the Household Debt Service Burden." Federal Reserve Board, Finance and Economics Discussion Series 2000-12. Washington: Board of Governors of the Federal Reserve System.

McCarthy, Jonathan. 1997. "Debt, Delinquencies, and Consumer Spending." *Current Issues in Economics and Finance* 3 (February): 1–6.

McCoy, Patricia A. 2006. Testimony before Hearings by the Board of Governors of the Federal Reserve System on Home Equity Loans, Atlanta, Georgia, July 11 (www.federalreserve.gov/SECRS/2007/July/20070724/OP-1253/OP-1253_40_1.pdf).

———. 2007. "Rethinking Disclosure in a World of Risk-Based Pricing." *Harvard Law Journal* 44, no. 1: 123–66.

McFadden, Daniel. 2006. "Free Markets and Fettered Consumers." *American Economic Review* 96, no. 1: 5–29.

Modigliani, Franco, and Richard E. Brumberg, 1954. "Utility Analysis and the Consumption Function: An Interpretation of Cross Section Data." In *Post-Keynesian Economics,* edited by Kenneth K. Kurihara. Rutgers University Press.

Mote, Larry, and Daniel E. Nolle. 2005. "Special Studies—Rising Household Debt: A Long-Run View." *Quarterly Journal* 24 (March): 41–55 (www.occ.treas.gov/qj/qj24-1/3-Special Studies.pdf).

Nonet, Philipe, and Philip Selznick. 1978. *Law and Society in Transitions: Toward Responsive Law.* New York: Harper and Row.

Peters, Ellen, and others. 2006. "Numeracy and Decision Making." *Psychological Science* 17, no. 5: 407–13.

Quercia, Roberto G., Michael A. Stegman, and Walter R. Davis. 2005. "The Impact of Predatory Loan Terms on Subprime Foreclosures: The Special Case of Prepayment Penalties and Balloon Payments." Center for Community Capitalism, Kenan Institute for Private Enterprise, University of North Carolina at Chapel Hill (www.kenan-flagler.unc.edu/assets/documents/foreclosurepaper.pdf).

Ramsey, Frank P. 1928. "A Mathematical Theory of Saving." *Economic Journal* 38, no. 152: 543–59.

Retsinas, Nicolas, and Eric Belsky, eds. 2002. *Low-Income Homeownership: Examining the Unexamined Goal.* Brookings and Joint Center for Housing Studies.

———. 2005. *Building Assets, Building Credit: Creating Wealth in Low-Income Communities.* Brookings and Joint Center for Housing Studies.

Sawady, Edna, and Jennifer Tescher. 2007. "Financial Decision Making Processes of Low-Income Individuals." Paper presented at the Understanding Consumer Credit Symposium, Boston, Mass., November 28–29.

Shu, Suzanne. 2003. "Choosing for the Long Run: Making Tradeoffs in Multiperiod Borrowing." Working Paper. University of Chicago.

Stango, Victor, and Jonathan Zinman. 2006. "How a Cognitive Bias Shapes Competition: Evidence from Consumer Credit Markets." Dartmouth College, Tuck School of Business (http://ssrn.com/abstract=928956).

Staten, Michael. 2007. "The Impact of Credit Price and Term Regulations on Credit Supply." Paper presented at the Understanding Consumer Credit Symposium, Boston, Mass., November 28–29.

Sunstein, Cass R., and Richard H. Thaler. April 2003. "Libertarian Paternalism is Not an Oxymoron." Working Paper 03-2. AEI-Brookings Joint Center for Regulatory Studies, Washington, D.C. A similar paper with the same name was later published in *University of Chicago Law Review* 70, no. 4: 1159–1202.

Thaler, Richard H. 1980. "Toward a Positive Theory of Consumer Choice." *Journal of Economic Behavior and Organization* 1, no. 1: 39–60.

———. 1990. "Anomalies: Saving, Fungibility, and Mental Accounts." *Journal of Economic Perspectives* 4, no. 1: 193–205.

Trumbull, Gunnar. 2007. "Consumer Protection in French and British Credit Markets." Paper presented at the Understanding Consumer Credit Symposium, Boston, Mass., November 28–29.

Tufano, Peter, and Daniel Schneider. 2007. "Using Financial Innovation to Support Savers: From Coercion to Excitement." Paper presented at the Understanding Consumer Credit Symposium, Boston, Mass., November 28–29.

Tversky, Amos, and Daniel Kahneman. 1974. "Judgment under Uncertainty: Heuristics and Biases." *Science* 185, no. 4157: 1124–131.

———. 1981. "The Framing of Decisions and the Psychology of Choice." *Science* 211: 453–58.

Vink, Dennis, and Andre Thibeault. 2007. "ABS, MBS and CDO Compared: An Empirical Analysis." Munich Personal Research Papers in Economics (RePEc) Archive Paper 5028 (http://mpra.ub.uni-muenchen.de/5028/).

Viscusi, Kip, and Richard Zeckhauser. 1979. "Optimal Standards with Incomplete Enforcement." *Public Policy* 27, no. 4: 437–56.

Warren, Elizabeth, and Amelia Warren Tyagi. 2003. *The Two-Income Trap: Why Middle Class Mothers and Fathers Are Going Broke.* New York: Basic Books.

Weller, Christian E. 2006. *Drowning in Debt: America's Middle Class Falls Deeper in Debt as Income Growth Slows and Costs Climb.* Washington: Center for American Progress.

Woodward, Susan. 2003. *Consumer Confusion in the Mortgage Market.* Palo Alto, Calif.: Sand Hill Econometrics.

Yin, Sandra. 2003. "The Title Wave That Isn't." *American Demographics* (October 1) (http://findarticles.com/p/articles/mi_m4021/is_8_25/ai_108538941/pg_2).

2

Where Does It Go? Spending by the Financially Constrained

SHAWN COLE, JOHN THOMPSON, AND PETER TUFANO

Despite widespread interest by academics, businesspeople, and policy-makers, little is known about the financial behavior of low-income individuals, particularly the unbanked and underbanked. We examine the spending patterns of low- and moderate-income (LMI) households using a new database and focus on differences in spending as a function of consumers' credit constraints. Our work leverages a unique and proprietary data set of spending information on more than 1.5 million individuals to shed light on important questions at the intersection of consumer credit and consumer spending: Do credit-constrained consumers spend money more quickly than less constrained consumers? Do they spend the money in different manners (card-based merchant transactions versus cash ATM withdrawals)? Finally, do credit-constrained consumers have different spending patterns than the less constrained—do they buy different goods and services?

The authors thank David Hussong at H&R Block for excellent research support, and Eric Belsky, Ren Essene, Annamaria Lusardi, Chuck Muckenfuss, John Campbell, Daniel Schneider, and participants at the JCHS Symposium for helpful comments. Cole and Tufano thank the Division of Research of the Harvard Business School for financial support. The views in this chapter do not represent those of the H&R Block Corporation. No personally identifiable information about Emerald Card holders was shared with the authors of this study.

We answer these questions by analyzing data from H&R Block Bank, a subsidiary of the nation's largest commercial tax preparer,[1] on how 1,543,553 individuals spent their tax refunds in 2007. Tax refunds represent a substantial source of liquidity for the American population: in aggregate, in the 2007 tax season, the IRS paid out $233.7 billion in refunds to 103.5 million taxpayers for an average refund of $2,259.[2] Many of Block's clients are LMI individuals, who are eligible for and claim the federal earned income tax credit (EITC), among other refunds and credits. These tax refunds represent material payments for low-income filers. Nationwide, among families with adjusted gross incomes of less than $30,000, 84 percent received refunds.[3] The average refund size for this group was $1,617. For those filers with positive adjusted gross income (AGI), the refund was worth an average of about 6.5 weeks of AGI. The numbers for Block clients are similar: about 57.4 percent of Block clients have AGIs of $30,000 or less and about 88 percent of them receive refunds. The average refund payment received in our sample, net of tax preparation fees and financing charges, is approximately $2,700.

Tax preparers like Block not only process returns but also offer customers additional services, including savings, payment, and credit products. Some of these services reduce the time a client must wait to receive her tax refund. As a benchmark, for households without bank accounts, the standard method to receive a refund is to wait for a paper check from the IRS to arrive in the mail and then cash the check. This process can take up to eight weeks. We study several related products available to Block customers in 2007 that permitted them to accelerate receipt of funds: some enabled clients to receive refunds days or weeks before they might have otherwise received them,[4] and one allowed clients to receive a loan as early as October 15, three months before the earliest date taxes could have been filed. Importantly, each product was offered together with an "Emerald Card," a stored value card that can be used for PIN and signature-based purchases and ATM withdrawals, and which leaves an electronic record that enables us to observe consumer transactions.

---

1. See Tufano and Schneider (2004) and Rose, Schneider, and Tufano (2006) for additional background on H&R Block. Throughout this chapter, we refer to H&R Block rather than to the various Block divisions or subsidiaries, such as H&R Block Bank or the firm's tax preparation division.

2. Summary data for tax year 2006 (data are typically filed in the winter of the following year). www.irs.gov/taxstats/article/0,,id=96629,00.html (January 20, 2008).

3. Detailed data for tax year 2005 (the most recent year available); see www.irs.gov/taxstats/indtaxstats/article/0,,id=96981,00.html, Table 3.3 (January 20, 2008). In tax year 2005, approximately 50 percent of filers had AGIs of $30,000 or below.

4. Technically, none of the products speeds up the payment of the refund by the IRS or state taxing authorities. Instead, these products either support the payment of speedier electronic refunds or involve a loan to the taxpayer.

We use the variation in settlement and loan products to identify credit constraints and the Emerald Card transaction data to track spending. We find that (1) more credit-constrained or impatient consumers spend their funds a bit faster than others; (2) the method of transaction (merchant versus ATM) does not vary between the more and less credit-constrained; and (3) more credit-constrained people spend a greater fraction of their merchant purchases on apparent day-to-day necessities such as grocery store and gasoline purchases.

We believe our findings are important for three reasons. First, unlike most earlier studies on spending of tax refunds or rebates, our transaction-level data can precisely indicate how fast and where funds are spent. In the context of current discussions about using tax rebates as economic stimulus, our findings and methods should be of interest to policymakers who seek to understand how the monies will pulse through the economy. Second, there are heated discussions about the costs and benefits of short-term lending to LMI. Recent research focuses on one type of this lending (payday lending) to study the ultimate, but necessarily indirect, effect of this lending.[5] We can examine the direct use of the borrowed funds to understand more about credit constraints. Finally, unlike most earlier studies of either tax refunds or credit, we do not study only a few people or a small representative sample. Rather, our large database allows us to study how more than $3.6 billion was spent in a relatively short time by 1.5 million LMI families, nearly 1.5 percent of all refund recipients nationally.

In this chapter we review the existing literature on spending and credit constraints. and then offer details on Block's various loans and settlement products that reveal credit constraints or impatience. Next, we describe the database of transaction records and baseline data on the various spending metrics: speed of spending, mode of spending (cash versus merchant), and merchant category. We analyze spending patterns for the most "impatient" spending, which occurs before the client could have received money without the loan or settlement product. We then study how behavior varies by degree of credit constraint. Finally, we conclude and discuss implications of our findings and future extensions of this work.

Related Work

As a study of spending patterns related to tax refunds, our work relates to extant research on the planned and actual use of tax refunds. Tax refunds, in particular the EITC, are an important public policy tool, redistributing income to support low-income families. The EITC is a refundable tax credit, supplementing the income of low-income families with children.[6] A relatively large literature has

---

5. See Morse (2006), Skiba and Tobacman (2007), and Melzer (2007).
6. See, for example, Hotz and Scholz (2003).

developed around the EITC. Although much attention has focused on the effects of the EITC on labor supply,[7] a parallel literature examines the effect of refunds (or tax rebates) on the marginal propensity to consume and save as well as the type of consumption supported by tax refunds. Scholars have taken two main approaches to this question.

First, several studies use qualitative methods or small-sample surveys to collect data directly from tax filers on the use of refunds. Some of these studies are specifically geared toward understanding the use of refunds (Olson and Davis 1994; Romich and Weisner 2000; Smeeding, Ross, and O'Conner 2000; Schneider and Tufano 2006). Others collect these data almost incidentally while assessing the effect on savings of interventions designed to offer bank accounts at tax time (Beverly, Tescher, and Marzahl 2000; Rhine and others 2005; Beverly, Schneider, and Tufano 2006). A recurrent finding of this literature is that filers report valuing the lump sum disbursement of refunds because it functions as a forced savings mechanism (Olson and Davis 1994; Romich and Weisner 2000).

Despite these intentions to save, a large share of refunds appears to be used for consumption. Across studies, most respondents report planning to spend their refunds or use them to pay off debt (Beverly, Tescher, and Marzahl 2000; Romich and Weisner 2000; Rhine and others 2005; Schneider and Tufano 2006). Low-income tax refund recipients put particular emphasis on plans to purchase clothing or school supplies, to maintain or purchase cars, to pay for groceries, and to catch up on credit card debt and late bills (Romich and Weisner 2000; Smeeding, Ross, and O'Conner 2000; Beverly, Schneider, and Tufano 2006).

Although these studies have added substantially to our knowledge of how EITC funds are used, they are limited in important ways. First, each study (except Schneider and Tufano [2006], who study a municipal EITC) relies on data collected from filers at Volunteer Income Tax Assistance (VITA) sites. VITA's free tax preparation is a useful service for many low-income filers, but it reaches only a tiny share of EITC filers, about 2 percent in 2004 (Kneebone 2007). This raises serious questions about the representativeness of the data used in the literature. Second, these studies examine only planned refund use, not how the funds were actually used. Social desirability response bias, intervening events between the time of interview and the time of use, and perhaps some wishful thinking on the part of respondents may make these data less than reliable.

---

7. Most work has focused on calculating the take-up rate or the drivers of take-up for the EITC (Scholz 1990, 1994; Liebman 1996; Hill and others 1999; GAO 2001; IRS 2002; Blumenthal, Erard, and Ho 2005; Caputo 2006; Kopczuk and Pop-Eleches 2007), estimating the effect of the EITC on marriage and fertility decisions (see, for example, Ellwood, 2000; Baughman and Dickert-Conlin 2003; Dickert-Conlin and Houser 2002), and examining how the EITC shapes labor market activity (see, for example, Eissa and Liebman 1996; Ellwood 2000). Also see Hotz and Scholz (2003) and Eissa and Hoynes (2006) for reviews of the literature.

A second group of studies has taken a different methodological approach to studying the use of the EITC and other tax refunds. These collect data for spending patterns after the refund is received and use broadly representative samples, remedying some of the problems with the first group of studies. One set of these studies uses custom-designed surveys to assess the effect of tax refunds on consumption. Using data from the Michigan Survey of Consumers to examine the effect of the 2001 Economic Growth and Tax Relief Reconciliation Act (EGTRRA) tax rebates (Shapiro and Slemrod 2003) and the effect of the Jobs and Growth Tax Relief Reconciliation Act (JGTRRA) (Coronado, Lupton, and Sheiner 2005), the researchers find that about 20 percent of respondents planned to spend most of their rebates, 45 percent planned to use most of the rebate to pay down debt, and between 27 percent and 37 percent planned to save most of the funds. Liquidity constraints proxied by income levels did little to predict the use of the funds.

Taking a different tactic, Barr and Dokko (2006) survey low-income respondents in Detroit, Michigan, about their use of EITC funds and find that about half spent the entire refund, 10 percent saved the entire refund, and the remainder allocated some to savings and some to spending. Those spending their refund tended to pay down debt, with smaller shares buying appliances or vehicles or paying for education. Barr and Dokko (2006) segment their respondents by self-reported refund anticipation loan (RAL) receipt or no RAL and find that those taking RALs were more likely to spend all their refund (54 percent) than those without RALs (46 percent) and were also more likely to purchase appliances— 27 percent versus 19 percent.

A related set of studies uses standard consumer surveys such as the Consumer Expenditure Survey (CEX) to estimate how tax policy affects consumption (Souleles 1999, 2002; Barrow and McGranahan 2000; Johnson, Parker, and Souleles 2006;). More specifically, several of these studies attempt to assess if, contrary to the permanent income hypothesis, spending increases in response to an expected change in income (Souleles 1999, 2002; Johnson, Parker, and Souleles 2006). A related study by Stephens (2003) examines changes in consumption patterns around the receipt of Social Security payments.

Data from the CEX appear to indicate that tax refund and rebate recipients do increase their spending. Souleles (1999) examines CEX data from 1980 to 1991 and finds that households increase their spending, particularly on durable goods, around the time of refund receipt. Most of these funds (between one-third and two-thirds) are spent within the quarter, and more liquidity-constrained households spend more of their refunds. Investigating a similar question using data from President Ronald Reagan's 1981 tax cut, Souleles (2002) finds similar results, though he uncovers less evidence for the role of liquidity constraints. Drawing on a unique supplement to the CEX on the timing of refund receipt, Johnson, Parker, and Souleles (2006) estimate that recipients spent between 20 and 40 percent of funds within the three-month survey period surrounding receipt and as much as two-thirds within a six-month period as recipients spent more on clothing, health care, and food in particular. Proxying for liquidity constraints using income and assets, Johnson, Parker, and Souleles (2006) find a significant positive effect on spending. Focusing on low-income refund recipients and the disposition of EITC funds in particular, Barrow and McGranahan (2000) find that spending increased by about 3 percent on nondurables and by about 9 percent on durables during February, the modal month of EITC receipt. Further, these funds were spent fairly quickly, with about one-fifth used within the first month of receipt.

Compared to these studies, our Emerald Card database contains accurate and extensive data on spending by many individuals. It circumvents the limitations of the qualitative and small-sample literature on the EITC by using data from a commercial tax preparer rather than VITA sites and collects extremely precise retrospective data on refund disposition rather than planned use. Additionally we look at the specific disposition of refund dollars rather than the total effect of refund receipt on spending. Given evidence of mental accounting among consumers, it is an advantage to see how these particular funds are used.

We exploit differences in credit constraints or liquidity to understand spending patterns, and thus our work also relates to a large body of work on credit constraints, payment types, and household decisions. Several papers examining whether liquidity or credit constraints affect consumption decisions use a host of measures of credit or liquidity constraints, including savings (Hayashi 1985), asset to income ratios (Zeldes 1989), homeownership (Runkle 1991), denial of access to credit (Jappelli, Pischke, and Souleles 1998), timing of the receipt of paychecks (Stephens 2006), bankruptcy (Filer and Fisher 2007), and changes of credit card credit limits (Gross and Souleles 2002; Soman and Cheema 2002).

The research closest in spirit to our work is Agarwal, Lin, and Souleles (2007). They study the 2001 federal tax rebate to households by examining credit card spending in the wake of these rebates, and like us, attempt to identify consumers with different levels of credit constraints. Our work differs from that of Agarwal, Lin, and Souleles in at least four ways. First, they study a one-time windfall and we examine tax refunds that are an annual part of family cash flows. The average size of the refund in our sample is much larger than the rebate they study. Second, they evaluate general spending patterns or, more precisely, credit card transactions, which are not directly linked to the tax refund. In contrast, we observe all the transactions used to spend down the refund. Even though money is fungible in practice, our approach may more accurately capture the effect on spending if consumers engage in some type of mental accounting (Thaler 1980, 1985). A disadvantage of our method is that we do not observe how consumers' non–Emerald

Card spending adjusts to the refund.[8] Third, Agarwal, Lin, and Souleles use age and credit limits set by credit card companies as proxies for credit constraints; we use the revealed choices of loan products to identify differences in credit constraints or liquidity. Finally, their sample is restricted to individuals that possess credit cards; our sample includes numerous households with little or no access to financial services and who therefore opt to use the Emerald Card.

The Emerald Card: A Window into Spending Behavior

The Emerald Card serves as a debit card, allowing Block clients to withdraw money from most ATMs or to purchase goods and services (without transaction fees) from any merchant honoring Mastercard. It is particularly valuable to unbanked or underbanked households, and Block estimated that about 60 percent of clients opting for the Emerald Card were unbanked. Customers could also withdraw some or all of their balance at most banks. We therefore observe precisely how and when clients spend their money.

The Emerald Card is a stored value card, meaning that it is loaded with a certain amount of cash, which is withdrawn (and possibly replenished) over time. In most cases, the Emerald Card was initially "loaded" with the client's tax refund (minus processing and financing charges) or the proceeds of the tax refund loan. Customers could add more funds or "reload" the cards through direct deposit from their employer or at various retail locations (such as Wal-Mart, Radio Shack, and others) that serve as "reload centers." With the ability to reload, the card could serve as a permanent payments transaction account. The card by itself offers no credit either explicitly or as a courtesy overdraft.[9] The card also carried consumer protections and capabilities that made it the equivalent of a checking account, with the exception of paper checks and no ability to overdraw the account. Like most checking accounts, funds on the Emerald Card did not earn interest, and like most ATM cards, various fees are charged for its use.[10] During the period in

8. A further complication is that spending may vary depending on the payment mode used (cash, check, credit card, debit card, stored value card). See, for example, Hirschman (1979), Feinberg (1986), and Prelec and Simester (2001). These studies tend to find different behaviors (more spending or a willingness to pay more) when credit cards are used instead of cash. The Emerald Card is not a credit card, though, and may not behave the same as a credit card.

9. A debit account with "courtesy overdraft" would allow a consumer to exceed the available balance, but the consumer would be charged a fee (often $25 to $30) and required to remediate the overdraft quickly.

10. The fee schedule for the Emerald Card includes $0 for card acquisition; $0 for merchant purchase (either signature, PIN, or PIN with cash back); $1.50 per ATM withdrawal (plus fees charged by ATM owner); $15 for "over-the counter" withdrawals at a bank (up to $9,999); $2.50 for each live-agent customer service call (two free calls per month); and a $2.50 monthly fee (waived for the first three months if any subsequent deposits are made or if the balance is $0).

review, the average Emerald Card user paid approximately $12–$14 in card fees related to receiving and using the refund proceeds. Were clients to have cashed a $2,700 refund check at a check casher, they would likely have incurred fees of 2 to 3 percent (or $54 to $81), far more than the card fees (Tufano and Schneider 2004). Block priced the card competitively to be attractive to consumers by offering lower prices and reduced financing charges for some products if the client took the Emerald Card before the beginning of the tax season, Block publicly announced a goal of opening 1 million Emerald Card accounts; it exceeded that number considerably; our sample includes over 1.4 million cardholders.

For each card we observe the transactions that add or subtract value from the balance, gaining insight into the breakdown of merchant versus ATM transactions and the nature of the merchant transactions. In contrast to household or consumer surveys, which may suffer from recall biases and measurement errors, these commercial financial records give a precise accounting of the behavior of each Emerald Card consumer.

Loan and Settlement Options: Revealing Credit Constraints

Although Block is unique among tax preparers in offering a quasi-bank account to its customers, many commercial preparers (in conjunction with banking partners) make credit available to their customers at tax time. We use the endogenous decision by the refund recipient on refund settlement or loans to identify their credit constraints or impatience.

All the individuals in our sample could have received a refund check or direct deposit from the IRS at some point in the winter of 2007 with no additional fees (beyond the cost of tax preparation.) The length of time from filing until refund receipt varies with the type of filing (paper or electronic) and method of refund disbursement (check or direct deposit.) An electronically filed return with a refund directly deposited into the client's existing bank account can be received in as little as eight days (or fifteen days if a check is mailed.) A paper-filed return with a cash refund check issued by the IRS can take up to eight weeks (perhaps a week less, if directly deposited.)

Block offers several products to accelerate the payment of cash to filers expecting refunds.[11] Table 2-1 summarizes these products. Our measure of impatience or credit constraint is the amount of time they choose to accelerate this receipt relative to their tax filing date. At the least-constrained end of the spectrum are customers who choose to wait until the IRS processes their return and issues a refund: those choosing the refund anticipation check (RAC) settlement option. For a

---

11. Block also made available several savings products to consumers, including a high-yield savings account and an IRA product; in some locations it also made savings bonds available to clients. We do not have data on the use of these products in this study.

Table 2-1. *Products*[a]

Product	Date available	Time from application to disbursal of money	Cost	Description
Instant money anticipation loan (IMAL)	October 15	Same day	Finance charge (36 percent APR)	Loan made before taxes can be calculated
Instant refund anticipation loan (IRAL)	On filing	Same day	$29.95 + $20 + finance charge (36 percent APR)	Loan made after taxes calculated
Refund anticipation loan (RAL)	On filing	1-2 days	$29.95 + finance charge (36 percent APR)	Loan made after taxes calculated
Refund anticipation check (RAC)	On filing	8-15 days	$29.95	Bank account opened on behalf of client; electronic refund from IRS received; client paid by paper check
Direct deposit	On filing	8 days-7 weeks	None	Requires bank account
Paper check mailed from IRS	On filing	15 days-8 weeks	Check cashing fees	

a. Table describes the range of products available to Block tax filers. Filers may use more than one product. For example, the IMAL is typically smaller than the total antici-pated refund, so an IMAL client may also apply for and receive a RAC or a RAL. If the client does not use an Emerald Card or receives a paper check from the IRS and does not have a bank account, he or she would incur check cashing fees, typically up to 3 percent of the value of the check.

$29.95 fee, Block (and its partners) facilitates the electronic deposit of the refund into an account, providing the filer with funds once the IRS has deposited the refund into the account, usually eight to fifteen days after filing. RAC users can also have their tax preparation fees deducted from their refund rather than paying these fees before receiving their refund. This product is particularly valuable to households without bank accounts—who were hence unable to request direct deposit—and therefore have to wait seven to eight weeks to receive a paper check. In our sample, RAC users exhibit the lowest level of impatience or credit constraints, receiving money between T + 8 to T + 15, where T is the date of tax filing, and paying $29.95 to speed up access to cash by five to seven weeks. Note that a RAC is not a loan; no funds are disbursed until the refund is received from the IRS. (Unfortunately, clients who elect to simply receive direct deposit or a refund check from the IRS are not in our database because they typically do not receive an Emerald Card.)

Clients electing a classic RAL borrow to receive funds even earlier than RAC clients. Block arranges for the client to get a short-term unsecured loan from its partner bank, HSBC, to the client for an amount less than the anticipated refund. The refund effectively serves as collateral for the loan. Clients choosing a RAL return a day after filing to collect their funds (T + 1). A classic RAL requires payment of a $29.95 administrative fee plus a finance charge of 36 percent APR. Thus a $2,500 loan would incur a total cost of $56; a $3,000 RAL would incur a total cost of $62.14.[12]

An instant refund anticipation loan (IRAL) is similar to a RAL, except that the client receives a loan on the same day (T) rather than returning the next day. Once a loan is approved, the proceeds are available in the Emerald Card within approximately 2 hours. Fees for IRALs are higher than for RALs; in particular, customers pay an additional fixed charge of $20 on top of the RAL charges to get money one day sooner than if they had used a RAL. Customers who request IRALs were subject to credit scoring; those with weak credit might receive less than the amount of IRAL they sought. This partial loan is known as a partial IRAL or PIRAL. Throughout this chapter we categorize IRAL and PIRAL clients together.

An instant money advance loan (IMAL) is a loan product offered before the tax season starts, available as early as October 15. Clients produce pay stubs and other information from which Block and HSBC calculate the estimated tax refund and advance a portion of the estimated refund. This product requires credit approval. The IMAL user obtains funds considerably before tax preparation; without an IMAL the customer would have had to wait until at least early January

---

12. Block set its rates to make it attractive to use the Emerald Card. Without the card the financing charge would have been closer to 60 percent than the 36 percent for Emerald Card users for both RALs and IRALs.

before the necessary W-2 forms were available, and most likely would not receive a refund before January 15, even if she had filed electronically as quickly as possible. Thus, an IMAL enables a client to receive funds as early as $T - 90$. If the loan proceeds are loaded onto an Emerald Card, the only fee for the IMAL is the 36 percent APR financing charge. (If taken as a paper check, an additional $25 is charged.)[13]

The fees on these products must be understood in contrast to the fees available elsewhere for small dollar unsecured lending. For example, Skiba and Tobacman (2007) report that the typical payday lender charges 18 percent of the value of a paycheck for two weeks of credit. Payday lenders typically would not lend as much as lent in these loans, but were they to do so a client with a $2,500 loan would pay fees of $375 for each two-week period. In contrast, the Block financing charge of 36 percent APR taken over a comparable two-week period for a $2,500 loan would be about $35, excluding the fixed administrative fees. Block's early season (IMAL) fees were also reportedly lower than those charged by competitors (see Wu and Fox [2006] and Tufano, Roy, and Ekins [2007]).

In functional terms, the RAL, IRAL, and IMAL are loan products because they allow filers to receive cash more quickly than the IRS processes would otherwise permit. Through their selection of these products—and the fees they are willing to pay—clients reveal their "impatience" to receive money or their credit constraints. Products that offer money earlier or more quickly are more expensive than those that offer money later or more slowly. We therefore rank clients' level of credit constraint as greatest for those who choose an IMAL, who demand money soonest (although the fees for IMALs are arguably less than for other loans). For in-season loans, we rank credit constraints as greatest for those who choose an IRAL, a RAL, and finally a RAC, each of which demands greater immediacy, and the customer pays additional fees for this immediacy. This variation drives our analysis. We use the term "credit constraints" to reflect the source of variation revealed by the settlement and loan choices. We think that the choice of this credit reflects the lack of other lower-cost credit alternatives. Another view is that the loan choices reflect differences in liquidity (or cash flow) constraints or impatience or a combination of these factors.[14] Whatever the label, revealed loan and settlement choices reflect real differences among households' willingness and ability to trade present consumption for future consumption. For the sake of exposition, we use the term "credit constraints" throughout this chapter.

---

13. See www.consumerfed.org/pdfs/Paystub_RALs_Report_Final112906.pdf (January 27, 2008).

14. Truly impatient households could have adjusted withholdings or claimed advance EITC to reduce taxes withheld and thus the refunds payable at tax time. The households in our study may be those who are using excess withholding as a commitment device in the long run, but loans as a means to accelerate this forced saving in the short run.

Sound theoretical reasons support the belief that expansion of access to consumer credit is beneficial; for example, it facilitates intertemporal consumption substitution, allows the purchase of consumer durables, and smooths short-run consumption when the consumer is hit with negative shocks. The literature on credit constraints (as well as paycheck receipt) finds that money made available by relaxing credit or liquidity constraints is generally spent, and spent relatively quickly. We therefore expect tax settlement products to result in spending. Findings by Agarwal, Liu, and Souleles (2007) suggest that the 2001 tax rebate led to more spending by the credit-constrained. If this were to hold in our sample, we would expect to see greater spending—or more rapid spending—among the most credit-constrained. Finally, using CEX data, Souleles (1999) found that consumption of food and nondurables increased for the most constrained refund recipients as measured by their liquid wealth normalized by earnings. With our finer data, we can look for a similar result.

Data and Methodology

We studied 1.544 million clients of H&R Block who obtained an Emerald Card between October 2006 and April 2007. These individuals are slightly less than 10 percent of the 15.9 million U.S. retail clients served by the firm in that tax season and 37 percent of its 4.2 million loan clients.[15] These individuals are spread throughout the entire United States.

The underlying transaction data show the zip code of the Emerald Card user, her transactions, and the form of loan or settlement project selected by the filer. Transaction and loan data are obviously proprietary, and the research team was not given direct access to any confidential customer information. Instead, we submitted database queries that were executed by Block staff. We have indirect access to the following data: the initial load date of the card; the settlement or credit products used (for example, RAC, RAL, IRAL, or IMAL); the client's zip code; and detailed transaction information about how the client used the card. We observe reloads, cash withdrawals (from an ATM or via a bank teller), and details of merchant purchases. We have transaction data from the date of card loading (starting as early as November 1, 2006, for an IMAL) through October 13, 2007, which would include transactions six months after the close of tax season. We also had access to an aggregated database containing information at the zip code level. Although Block has tax return data for each Emerald Card holder, we were not given even indirect access to these data.

Consumers could choose more than one of the loan products. For example, a customer could take out an IMAL in November followed by a RAL in January.

15. See http://media.corporate-ir.net/media_files/irol/76/76888/ShareholderMtg090607 Presentation.pdf (January 27, 2008).

Table 2-2. *Sample Size*[a]

Group	Product	Number of clients	Average refund (dollars)
1	RAC only	128,697	1,983
2	RAL only	451,110	2,220
3	IRAL only	412,487	2,192
4	IMAL only	47,907	2,040
5	IMAL and RAC	57,283	2,092
6	IMAL and RAL or IMAL and IRAL	446,069	2,813

a. Table lists the range of products available to Block tax filers, sorted approximately in the order of revealed credit constraint. See table 2-1 for a description of the various products.

We rank their relative degree of credit constraint by looking at the set of products they chose. Table 2-2 gives the sample size and the average total amount loaded on the card from the tax refund. We have data on more than 1.41 million Block customers who took out loans and 128,697 who expedited their refunds through the RAC product.

We map credit constraints to the choice of products. Those clients who sought only an RAC were the most patient, willing to wait a week or two for their money. Next are RAL users, who sought funds within a few days of filing, then IRAL users, who sought their money the same day. The most impatient were those taking out IMALs, who sought to accelerate their funds by a few months. People taking out IMALs in conjunction with other loan products were ranked as a function of the other product, with IMAL/IRAL users considered the most credit constrained.

Although we do not have access to filer-level data, we can broadly characterize the population in our sample, which is disproportionately drawn from LMI families. Tufano and Schneider (2004) report that 58 percent of H&R Block's retail tax clients in 2004 had adjusted gross incomes of less than $30,000. Rose, Schneider, and Tufano (2006) report that Block serves one-third of all households with this level of income. No figures on the demographics of IMAL and RAC users have been published, but some studies have looked at RAL users. RAL purchasers tend to have lower educational attainments (30 percent of respondents without a high school degree had purchased a RAL versus 23 percent of those who graduated from high school, 12 percent of those who had graduated from college, and 18 percent overall) and lower incomes (25 percent of those with household income of less than $50,000 reported purchasing a RAL). In addition, respondents with children were more likely to have purchased a RAL (26 percent). Larger shares of African Americans (28 percent) and Latinos (21 percent) than whites (17 percent) purchased a RAL (Wu and Fox 2005). We are confident that our sample largely represents LMI Americans. Within this group, however, we observe different settlement and loan choices.

Before we analyze spending patterns, we note four important caveats. First, we cannot observe the individual characteristics of people selecting these products. Product choice is clearly endogenous and could be related to unobservable characteristics such as wealth, income, and family structure, among others. We use loan and settlement activity as a proxy for credit constraints, which are likely to be the product of more fundamental family economics, alternative credit options, and financial literacy. A further complication is that the IMAL product is typically obtained before the end of the year; the RAC, RAL, and IRAL products are obtained at the time of tax filing. Observed IMAL behavior may therefore vary from the behavior of RAC, RAL, and IRAL clients not only because the clients are particularly impatient but also because clients choosing this product use the proceeds for holiday shopping.

Second, we cannot observe spending patterns of those people who did not use the Emerald Card product. We suspect that these people are the least credit constrained and are banked. Therefore our findings apply to a sample of those who are predominantly credit constrained and unbanked. We observe only approved loans, not loan applications. The approval rate for these products, however, is quite high: roughly 84 percent for a RAL and 94 percent for an IRAL. (IRAL approval rates are typically 60–65 percent, but HSBC offered through Block a "guaranteed approval" product during the tax season of our analysis and hence the high approval rate). Our sample therefore omits some individuals who were not approved for a loan product; these are presumably the most credit constrained. Furthermore, some people seeking RALs or IRALs might have been turned down and taken RACs instead, which would tend to reduce any differences we observe.

A third caveat is that research cited earlier has shown that spending patterns depend on the type of transaction medium used (credit card versus cash). Our spending data relate to a form that has not been well studied (prepaid cards) but may not represent either cash or credit card patterns. In addition, we observe only card activity, which may not represent all spending. Given the economy-wide move to consumers' using debit cards for spending, however, this payment medium is a relevant and important one to study.[16]

Finally, we can observe the spending from the Emerald Card, but not other spending by these customers. Customers might engage in some sort of mental accounting in which they use the proceeds from their Emerald Card differently than the monies regularly received. Even so, we can interpret our results in the context of existing survey work on spending from the EITC refunds, as referenced earlier. At a minimum our results provide new and additional data on how EITC monies are spent.

---

16. Industry sources note that the number of debit card transactions exceeded the number of credit card transactions for the first time in 2006. See www.creditunions.com/home/articles/template.asp?article_id=2183 (January 20, 2008).

Table 2-3. *Speed of Spend-Down*[a]

Item	All	RAC	RAL	IRAL	IMAL
Average life of account (days)	68	72	61	56	82
Share (percent) of accounts empty after					
Same day	3	4	5	3	1
One week	18	20	22	23	10
Two weeks	29	30	35	38	17
One month	46	48	53	58	31
Two months	63	63	69	73	52
Three months	73	72	76	79	68

a. The average life of an account is calculated as the number of days after account opening that the account balance falls to less than $5. To minimize truncation bias, calculations are conducted on accounts for which at least six months of data are available (this includes all accounts opened on or before April 15, 2007). Similarly, the "share of accounts empty" is the percentage of accounts whose balance first dropped below $5 by the indicated time period. See table 2-1 for a description of the various products.

Baseline Spending Patterns

Our fundamental research strategy is to study the differences in spending among the different groups of consumers as defined by their self-revealed impatience. Before looking at these differences, we first report the aggregate data on the three key spending measures: spend-down; means of spending; and merchant activity.

Speed of spend-down can be measured in a wide variety of ways, but broadly one can look at spending per unit of time (for example, average spending per day) or the time to reach a certain level of spending (time to spend-down). Given that earlier work on EITC refunds has focused on spend-down speeds (Beverly, Schneider, and Tufano 2006), we present the latter formulation. We analyze the speed at which the clients spend down the balance, measured by the amount of time until the Emerald Card's balances are exhausted. For this test, we define a card as exhausted by the first date the balance falls below $5 (For reference, the average initial load is $2,353—parts of the refund not loaded onto the card include tax preparation fees or money saved in one of Block's saving or IRA products). Spend-down is therefore slower if a consumer debits the card less or reloads the card with additional funds. Table 2-3 indicates the speed at which the card balances are exhausted. Cards are rarely exhausted entirely on their first day. Immediate depletion can be easily achieved by visiting nearly any bank, which, for a small fee (about $15) would provide the entire balance in cash to the customer. Rather, cards tend to stay active for longer, with 27 percent having a balance of more than $5 after three months.

A second spending measure is the way in which *funds are removed* from the Emerald Card. A customer can take out cash at an ATM or use the card at a merchant location. We do not have information about the uses for cash taken out from ATMs, but it may be that the primary use of this cash is to pay bills where

Table 2-4. *How Refunds Are Spent*[a]

Method of spending	Total expenditure (millions of dollars)	Share of total expenditure (percent)
ATM/cash out	2,560	56.4
Merchant	1,880	41.3
Other/miscellaneous	105	2.3

a. Total expenditures from balances on the Emerald Card for the sample period (November 1, 2006-October 13, 2007). "Other/miscellaneous" includes fees.

MasterCard is not accepted, which would include rent, which the literature suggests is an important use of the EITC (Smeeding, Ross, and O'Conner 2000). Client surveys by Block in 2005 suggest that RAL users planned to use their loans to pay bills, loans, and rent. Cash withdrawals could, however, also be used for a variety of other purposes. Table 2-4 gives the amount spent from Emerald Cards in our sample by method of spending. The majority (56 percent) is taken out either as ATM withdrawals or as withdrawals from banks, 41 percent is spent at merchants on goods and services, and the balance is spent on miscellaneous charges such as fees.

A third measure of spending is to observe the merchants at which the card is used. A merchant category code is assigned to each Emerald Card purchase. The data have 614 codes: some merchants (for example, airlines and hotels) have their own code, but most are assigned to categories such as "Carpentry," "Discount Stores," or "Eating Places, Restaurants." To facilitate analysis, we aggregate these 614 codes into 28 broader categories. Table 2-5 shows the disaggregated codes and our groupings of them.

Table 2-6 lists the top 10 categories of merchant expenditures, which account for 85 percent of all merchant activity. The second column gives the amount spent on Emerald Cards in the indicated category, and the third column gives the share of total expenditures for that category. For reference, data from the 2006 CEX are given in the final column, which indicates the share of nonhousing expenditure a family with one parent and at least one child, earning $35,491, would have spent on the indicated categories. Although some categories are roughly in line with CEX figures (for example, entertainment and health), Emerald Card clients spend proportionately less of their refunds on groceries and less on transport, utilities, and restaurants compared to routine expenditures by roughly comparable Americans. (However, we again note that we do not observe how cash is spent.)

In broad terms, the spending patterns do not immediately suggest profligacy: the biggest single merchant class is grocery stores,[17] followed by automobile

---

17. We can identify the merchant, but not the exact purchase. For example, within grocery stores we cannot tell the spending on food versus household supplies, tobacco, or in some states, alcohol.

Table 2-5. *Examples of Merchant Category Codes*[a]

Bin	Merchant category	Merchant type
Auto	Automobiles and vehicles	Motor vehicle supplies and new parts
Business	Business	Construction materials
Business	Business services	Computer maintenance, repair, and services
Business	Transportation	Courier services
Clothing	Miscellaneous stores	Sewing, needlework, fabric, and piece goods stores
Consumer	Miscellaneous stores	Catalog merchant
Direct marketing	Miscellaneous stores	Direct selling establishments and door-to-door selling
Discount	Personal service providers	Discount stores
Donations	Professional services	Political organizations
Durables	Business	Durable goods
Education	Professional services	Colleges, universities, and professional schools
Entertainment	Amusement and entertainment	Motion picture theaters
Entertainment	Personal service providers	Photographic studios
Entertainment	Service providers	Trailer parks and campgrounds
Financial	Service providers	Financial institutions—merchandise and services
Groceries	Retail stores	Grocery stores and supermarkets
Health	Professional services	Medical services and health practitioners
Housing	Business	Hardware stores
Housing	Contracted services	Carpenters
Legal	Professional services	Legal services and attorneys
Luxuries	Clothing stores	Furriers and fur shops
Luxuries	Miscellaneous stores	Jewelry stores and silverware stores
Miscellaneous	Professional services	Intragovernment purchases, government only
Necessities	Clothing stores	Clothing and accessories stores for men and boys
Necessities	Professional services	Child care services
Pawn	Miscellaneous stores	Pawnshops
Remittance	Utilities	Wire transfer and money orders
Restaurant	Miscellaneous stores	Eating establishments and restaurants
Retail	Retail stores	Department stores
Services	Publishing services	Miscellaneous publishing and printing
Taxes	Professional services	Tax payments
Travel	Airlines	Airlines such as United Airlines[b]
Travel	Automobile rentals	Car rental agencies such as Hertz
Travel	Hotels and motels	Lodging, such as Holiday Inn Express
Unidentified	Not given	Not given
Utilities	Miscellaneous stores	Fuel dealers—fuel oil, wood, coal, liquefied petroleum gas (LPG)
Vice	Personal service providers	Dating and escort services
Vice	Retail stores	Package stores—beer, wine, and liquor

a. "Bin" indicates the authors' taxonomy; the authors narrowed the merchant category codes into twenty-seven specific product bins. Examples of the raw data are given in the second and third columns.

b. Airlines, hotels, and car rental agencies typically have their own code.

Table 2-6. *How Consumers Spend Their Credit*[a]

Category	Total expenditure (millions of dollars)	Share (percent)	CEX data (percent)
Groceries	466.0	25	14
Transportation	223.0	12	25
Discount stores	180.0	10	
Entertainment	156.0	8	9
Necessities	125.0	7	
Utilities	122.0	6	15
Durable goods	106.0	6	
Restaurants	103.0	5	10
Retail	64.7	3	
Health	48.3	3	6
All other	284.5	15	
Total	1,878.5		

a. The first two columns give the amount and share spent by all Emerald Card holders in the top ten categories of expenditure. (For a list of categories, see table 2-5.) For comparison, the third column gives estimates from the 2006 Consumer Expenditure Survey of the share of nonhousing expenditures of a single-parent household with at least one child, earning $35,491, for the indicated categories.

expenses (including gas). Together, these two items account for 37 percent of all merchant expenditures. If we add necessities, utilities, and health, these categories account for 53 percent of all merchant spending. Only "Entertainment" and "Restaurants" are clearly discretionary items, but together they constitute only 13 percent of merchant expenditures. Durable purchases such as appliances tend to fall into three categories: durable goods, discount stores, and retail. They therefore account for at most 19 percent of total Emerald Card expenditure.

Spending Patterns and Credit Constraints

The settlement or credit option chosen by the customer is our measure of credit constraints or impatience. Based on the evidence from earlier related studies, one might posit the following relationships:

—*Rate of Spending:* Credit-constrained individuals might spend their money faster, because the decision to pay fees to receive cash sooner than otherwise might indicate a need or desire for quick money.

—*Mode of Spending:* Credit-constrained individuals might spend more of their money in the form of cash, to the extent that we interpret cash purchases as representing the payment of rent, housing expenses, repayment of debt, and so on that cannot easily be done in a merchant transaction and which are more "necessities" than luxuries.

—*Merchant Spending:* Credit-constrained individuals might spend more of their merchant dollars for "necessities" such as groceries and auto expenses, and

Table 2-7. *Does Method of Spending Vary with Credit Constraints?*[a]

Percent of expenditure

Method of spending	RAC only	RAL only	IRAL only	IMAL only	IMAL and RAC	IMAL and RAL
ATM/cash out	55	60	61	55	52	56
Merchant	42	38	37	42	45	42
Other/miscellaneous	2	2	2	3	2	2

a. Presents the percent of Emerald Card value spent in ATM/cash transactions, merchant transactions, and others, for clients choosing different refund products. The "RAC only" column represents those most patient (or least constrained) clients; the "IMAL and RAL" column represents those most impatient or constrained. Table 2-4 gives the unconditional means. See table 2-1 for a description of the various products.

less on entertainment and eating out. An alternative hypothesis is that they may be impatient to spend on more pleasurable activities.

The next tables indicate how these measures vary by product choice of the client. The clearest comparisons are between those choosing a RAC, a RAL, or an IRAL because they are offered at the same time (when the client files taxes) and each involves a single payment to the client. To avoid problems with censoring, we look at accounts opened before April 1, 2007, meaning we observe at least six months of data for each account. We also report the spending patterns for pre-tax-season IMAL users, many of whom also used another settlement or loan product at the time of tax filing. For these clients, we would expect a similar ordering with respect to the tax-time product usage.

More constrained clients spend money more rapidly, as indicated by the second through fourth columns of table 2-3. The speed of spend-down indicates that IRAL customers drain their accounts the most quickly, followed by RAL and then RAC customers. The differences are statistically significant, but not very large: for example, after three months, 28 percent of those choosing a RAC maintain a balance greater than $5 against 24 percent of those choosing a RAL and 21 percent of those choosing an IRAL.

Among IMAL users, the relative speed of spend-down is not as clearly related to their tax-time product usage. One seemingly odd finding is that clients who took out only IMALs and were therefore among the most constrained had more funds left on their Emerald Cards after one to three months than did those clients who used a tax-time settlement or loan product. This may be explained by the fact that IMAL clients typically received a loan with a value equal to a portion of their refund in the pre-season, and thus enjoyed further deposits when the refund was settled. However, within the IMAL users who also took out a tax-season loan, the ordering of spend-down is not clearly related to the immediacy of cash flow delivered by the loan.

With respect to the cash/merchant split, we find that the various groups withdraw funds in similar ways. Table 2-7 gives the share of spent balances that are withdrawn as cash, used to pay fees or send transfers, or spent at merchants by revealed constraint levels. We find little support for the hypothesis that more constrained households withdraw a larger share of funds in the form of cash. The share withdrawn in cash increases with our measure of credit constraint for households choosing one of three similar products (RAC versus RAL versus IRAL), but those choosing IMALs withdraw less in cash than those choosing RALs or IRALs. This could reflect the conjecture that IMALs are more likely to be used for end of year holiday spending, some of which can be done at merchants accepting MasterCard. However, even among IMAL users, the percentage withdrawn in cash does not increase with the level of revealed credit constraint.

To test how spending varies across groups as a function of their revealed credit constraints, we compare expenditures of six groups identified in table 2-2. To control for unobserved heterogeneity attributable to geographic location, we compare client types within the same zip code to each other. These geographic zip code fixed effects would jointly capture demographic differences across zip codes as well as differing costs of living. We estimate the following equation:

$$(1) \qquad \text{share}_{g,i,z} = a_z + \beta_2 * (\text{RAL}_z) + \beta_3 (\text{IRAL}_z) + \beta_4 (\text{IMAL}_z)$$
$$+ \beta_5 * (\text{IMAL\_RAC}_z) + \beta_6 * (\text{IMAL\_RAL}_z) + \varepsilon,$$

where $\text{share}_{g,i,z}$ is the percentage of spending on merchant category i of product group g in zip code z; a is a zip code fixed effect, RAC users are the omitted category, and the other variables are dummy indicators of which product group of table 2-2 the client falls into.

Table 2-8 reports results for the ten largest expenditure categories. For reference, the unconditional share (averaged across all types in all zip codes) of spending in these categories for RAC clients is given in column 1. Columns 2–6 report point estimates and standard errors for the coefficients to $\beta_2 - \beta_6$. Each coefficient can be interpreted as the average difference, relative to RAC clients in the same zip code, in the share of expenditure that particular group spends on the given merchant category. For example, the coefficient of -0.014 for RAL for the automobile and transport category indicates that RAL clients spent a 1.4 percentage point smaller share of their expenditure on this category than do RAC households. Similarly, clients purchasing both IMAL and RAL spent a 2.9 percentage point smaller share of their income on automobiles and transport than RAC clients.

Several patterns stand out. First, compared to RAC clients, more constrained clients spend substantially greater shares of their refunds at grocery stores. For example, IMAL clients spend approximately 20 percent (or 5 percentage points) more on groceries than RAC clients. The more constrained spend more on utilities and less on automobiles and transportation. The extremely constrained (columns 5 and 6) spend substantially less on durable goods and restaurants, but somewhat more on necessities and more at discount stores. Finally, compared

Table 2-8. *Do Consumption Bundles Vary with Credit Constraints?*[a]

	Average share	Difference from RAC clients				
		RAL only	IRAL only	IMAL only	IMAL and RAC	IMAL and RAL
Category	1	2	3	4	5	6
Automobile and transport	0.134	−0.014*** (0.002)	−0.006*** (0.002)	−0.008*** (0.002)	−0.026*** (0.002)	−0.029*** (0.002)
Discount stores	0.092	0.001 (0.001)	−0.002* (0.001)	0.000 (0.001)	0.006*** (0.001)	0.010*** (0.001)
Durable goods	0.044	0.008*** (0.001)	0.002* (0.001)	−0.020*** (0.001)	−0.013*** (0.001)	−0.006*** (0.001)
Entertainment	0.080	0.002** (0.001)	0.005*** (0.001)	−0.001 (0.001)	0.001 (0.001)	0.000 (0.001)
Groceries	0.263	0.001 (0.002)	0.010*** (0.002)	0.051*** (0.002)	0.050*** (0.002)	0.049*** (0.002)
Health	0.027	−0.001 (0.001)	−0.002*** (0.001)	−0.004*** (0.001)	0.000 (0.001)	−0.002*** (0.001)
Necessities	0.059	0.000 (0.001)	−0.005*** (0.001)	−0.002 (0.001)	0.009*** (0.001)	0.001 (0.001)
Restaurants	0.057	−0.007*** (0.001)	0.006*** (0.001)	0.006*** (0.001)	−0.004*** (0.001)	−0.010*** (0.001)
Retail	0.035	0.000 (0.001)	−0.002*** (0.001)	0.000 (0.001)	0.006*** (0.001)	0.001 (0.001)
Utilities	0.063	0.004*** (0.001)	0.000 (0.001)	0.007*** (0.001)	0.002* (0.001)	0.007*** (0.001)

*Significant at 10%; **significant at 5%; ***significant at 1%.

a. Column 1 reports the average share (across zip codes) of expenditure by RAC clients, for the ten categories that accounted for more than 2.5 percent of RAC expenditure. Columns 2–6 report the difference between the indicated client type and RAC clients. For example, the coefficient of −0.014 for RAL for the automobile and transport category indicates that RAL clients spent a 1.4 percentage point smaller share of their expenditure on this category than did RAC households. Similarly, clients purchasing both the IMAL and RAL spent a 2.9 percentage point smaller share of their income on automobiles and transit than RAC clients did. Standard errors (in parentheses) are clustered at the zip code level. See table 2-1 for a description of the various products.

to RAC clients, more constrained households spend a smaller share on health and housing.

The Most Impatient Spending

Instead of borrowing with a RAL, IRAL, or IMAL or speeding up their refund using a RAC, tax customers could have waited to get their refunds. The cost of their impatience is reflected in the fees they pay to accelerate the receipt of funds. The benefit of this acceleration is reflected in the immediate consumption made possible with the loan product. Spending in the first few days of receiving the card may therefore provide the most accurate picture of the motives behind the consumer's decision to borrow, because later spending could have been supported had the customer waited to receive her refund.

To explore consumption patterns immediately following the receipt refunds, we look at the spending patterns in the first day, first week, and first thirty days that the Emerald Card is active for three categories of customers. Table 2-9 lists the results, which are striking. Grocery expenditures account for 25 percent of overall spending of Emerald Card holders. However, on the first day clients receive their card, groceries account for 30 percent of expenditures of RAC clients, 36 percent of RAL clients, and 41 percent of IMAL clients. These differences are less pronounced when one examines the longer windows of one week and one month, yet they still persist. One reason why grocery store purchases may be so predominant on the first day is that grocery purchases tend to be more frequent than other purchases.[18] Yet, when one considers that the marginal benefit of these particular loans is to support spending in the relatively short window until refunds would have otherwise been received, the results are still meaningful.

One posited reason for borrowing is to purchase durable goods that provide a stream of consumption; however, IMAL clients spend a significantly smaller share of their refunds in the first month on durable goods; this pattern also holds for the first day and first week for discount and retail stores. Most of the other spending patterns are broadly similar across groups for the time periods considered. These relationships reinforce the notion that severely credit-constrained consumers are likely to spend much of their money at grocery stores, not purchasing durables.

Conclusions and Further Research

This chapter describes preliminary data on spending patterns of 1.5 million refund recipients, all of whom used either a loan or a settlement product to access refund money faster than the IRS processes would have otherwise allowed. Our

---

18. We thank Annamaria Lusardi for this interpretation.

Table 2-9. *Spending Immediately after Receipt of Funds*[a]
Percent

Category	First day			First three days			First month		
	RAC	IRAL	IMAL	RAC	IRAL	IMAL	RAC	IRAL	IMAL
Groceries	30	36	41	25	29	34	20	25	29
Transportation	7	6	6	8	8	7	10	10	9
Discount stores	15	14	11	13	12	10	10	10	10
Entertainment	7	8	8	8	9	9	9	9	9
Necessities	1	1	1	2	2	2	3	2	2
Utilities	7	7	7	8	8	8	8	8	8
Durable goods	10	7	4	10	8	4	8	6	4
Restaurants	2	3	4	3	4	5	5	6	6
Retail	4	4	4	4	4	4	4	3	4
Health	1	0	0	1	1	0	2	1	1
All other	17	14	14	19	17	17	23	20	19

a. Table reports the share of Emerald Card spending for the indicated product category and time period. For example, for RAC users, groceries make up 30 percent (on average) of all spending incurred in the first day of purchases. For IMAL users, 41 cents of each dollar spent in the first day is spent on groceries. See table 2-1 for a description of the various products.

results should inform the view of policymakers, financial service professionals, scholars, and consumer advocates.

Policymakers may be intrigued by our confirmation of earlier findings that document the fairly rapid speed of spending of refunds, which is relevant for thinking about the economic stimulus impact of tax refunds and rebates. Furthermore, the details about how refunds are spent offer insight into the importance of the EITC program. In particular, the conclusion that a material fraction of funds is used to pay for necessities suggests that the program is central to the lives of the poor. Finally, academics and policymakers may be intrigued by the potential to use a stored value card platform to distribute funds, which enables the analysis of spending patterns without expensive and imprecise surveying and without fees associated with check cashing.

Businesspeople and consumer advocates have sometimes been in opposing camps with respect to their feelings about tax refund loan products. The data we report are fairly sobering, because they show these loans seem to be used to obtain necessities, especially funds spent in the first few days of the loans. Consumer advocates who seek to ban these products should consider how a ban would affect households' ability to consume. Similarly, businesses that are pricing and marketing these products should be mindful that the products are not a luxury for their users.

These groups, and academics, can learn considerably more from the spending data we used. This chapter reports preliminary findings, but our hope is to link this information with richer data, either at the individual or the zip code level, to better understand the demand for loan products and the differential relationships among credit constraints, spending, and savings.

References

Agarwal, Sumit, Chunlin Liu, and Nicholas Souleles. 2007. "The Reaction of Consumer Spending and Debt to Tax Rebates." *Journal of Political Economy* 115, no. 6 (December): 986–1019.

Barr, Michael S., and Jane K. Dokko. 2006. "Tax Filing Experiences and Withholding Preferences of Low- and Moderate-Income Households: Preliminary Evidence from a New Survey." Paper presented at the IRS Research Conference, Georgetown University Law School, July 14–15.

Barrow, Lisa, and Leslie M. McGranahan. 2000. "The Effects of the Earned Income Credit on the Seasonality of Household Expenditures." *National Tax Journal* 53, no. 4: 1211–243.

Baughman, Reagan, and Stacy Dickert-Conlin. 2003. "Did Expanding the EITC Promote Motherhood?" *American Economic Review* 93, no. 2: 247–51.

Beverly, Sondra, Daniel Schneider, and Peter Tufano. 2006. "Splitting Tax Refunds and Building Savings: An Empirical Test." In *Tax Policy and the Economy,* vol. 20, edited by James M. Poterba, pp. 111–62. MIT Press.

Beverly, Sondra, Jennifer Tescher, and David Marzahl. 2000. *Linking Tax Refunds and Low-Cost Bank Accounts.* Center for Social Development, George Warren Brown School of Social Work, Washington University, St. Louis.

Blumenthal, Marsha, Brian Erard, and Chih-chin Ho. 2005. "Effects of the Earned Income Tax Credit on Income and Welfare." *National Tax Journal* 57, no. 2: 189–213.

Caputo, Richard. 2006. "The Earned Income Tax Credit: A Study of Eligible Participants versus Non-Participants." *Journal of Sociology and Social Welfare* 33, no. 1: 9–29.

Coronado, Julia Lynn, Joseph Lupton, and Louise Sheiner. 2005. "The Household Spending Response to the 2003 Tax Cut: Evidence from Survey Data." Finance and Economics Discussion Series. Washington: Federal Reserve Board Division of Research and Statistics and Monetary Affairs.

Dickert-Conlin, Stacy, and Scott Houser. 2002. "EITC and Marriage." *National Tax Journal* 55, no. 1: 25–40.

Eissa, Nada, and Hilary Hoynes. 2006. "Behavioral Responses to Taxes: Lessons from the EITC and Labor Supply." In *Tax Policy and the Economy,* vol. 20, edited by James M. Poterba, pp. 74–110. MIT Press.

Eissa, Nada, and Jeffery Liebman. 1996. "Labor Supply Response to the Earned Income Tax Credit." *Quarterly Journal of Economics* 111, no. 2: 605–37.

Ellwood, David. 2000. "The Impact of the Earned Income Tax Credit and Social Policy Reforms on Work, Marriage, and Living Arrangements." *National Tax Journal* 53, no. 4: 1063–106.

Feinberg, Richard. 1986. "Credit Cards as Spending Facilitating Stimuli: A Conditioning Interpretation." *Journal of Consumer Research* 13, no. 3: 348–56.

Filer, Larry, and Jonathan Fisher. 2007. "Do Liquidity Constraints Generate Excess Sensitivity in Consumption? New Evidence from a Sample of Post-Bankruptcy Households." *Journal of Macroeconomics* 29, no. 4: 790–805.

Government Accountability Office (GAO). 2001. "Earned Income Tax Credit Eligibility and Participation." Letter to Representative William J. Coyne, ranking minority member, Subcommittee on Oversight, House Committee on Ways and Means, 107 Cong. 1 sess., GAO-02-290R (December 14).

Gross, David, and Nicholas Souleles. 2002. "Do Liquidity Constraints and Interest Rates Matter for Consumer Behavior? Evidence from Credit Card Data." *Quarterly Journal of Economics* 117, no. 1: 149–85.

Hayashi, Fumio. 1985. "The Effect of Liquidity Constraints on Consumption: A Cross Sectional Analysis." *Quarterly Journal of Economics* 100, no. 1: 183–206.

Hill, Carolyn, and others. 1999. "EITC Eligibility, Participation and Compliance Rates for AFDC Households: Evidence from the California Caseload." Working Paper 102. Joint Center for Poverty Research, Northwestern University and University of Chicago.

Hirschman, Elizabeth. 1979. "Differences in Consumer Purchase Behavior by Credit Card Payment System." *Journal of Consumer Research* 6, no. 1: 58–66.

Hotz, V. Joseph, and John Karl Scholz. 2003. "The Earned Income Tax Credit." In *Means-Tested Transfer Programs in the United States,* edited by Robert Moffit. University of Chicago Press.

Internal Revenue Service. 2002. *Participation in the Earned Income Tax Credit Program for Tax Year 1996.* Fiscal Year 2001 Research Project 12.26. IRS, Small Business and Self-Employed (January 31).

Jappelli, Tullio, Jorn-Steffen Pischke, and Nicholas Souleles. 1998. "Testing for Liquidity in Euler Equations with Complementary Data Sources." *Review of Economics and Statistics* 80, no. 2: 251–62.

Johnson, David, Jonathan Parker, and Nicholas Souleles. 2006. "Household Expenditure and the Income Tax Rebates of 2001." *American Economic Review* 96, no. 5: 1589–610.

Kneebone, Elizabeth. 2007. "A Local Ladder for Low-Income Workers: Recent Trends in the Earned Income Tax Credit." Metropolitan Policy Program, Brookings.

Kopczuk, Wojciech, and Cristian Pop-Eleches. 2007. "Electronic Filing, Tax Preparers and Participation in the Earned Income Tax Credit." *Journal of Public Economics* 91, nos. 7–8: 1351–367.

Liebman, Jeffrey. 1996. "The Impact of the Earned Income Tax Credit on Labor Supply and Taxpayer Compliance." Ph.D. dissertation, Harvard University.

Melzer, Brian. 2007. "The Real Costs of Credit Access: Evidence from the Payday Lending Market." Ph.D. dissertation, University of Chicago.

Morse, Adair. 2006. "Payday Lenders: Heroes or Villains?" Ph.D. dissertation, University of Chicago.

Olson, Lynn, and Audrey Davis. 1994. "The Earned Income Tax Credit: Views from the Street Level." Evanston, Ill.: Center for Urban Affairs and Policy Research, Northwestern University.

Prelec, Drazen, and Duncan Simester. 2001. "Always Leave Home without It: A Further Investigation of the Credit Card Effect on Willingness to Pay." *Marketing Letters* 12, no. 1 (February): 5–12.

Rhine, Sherrie L. W., and others. 2005. "Householder Response to the Earned Income Tax Credit: Path of Sustenance or Road to Asset Building." Federal Reserve Bank of New York.

Romich, Jennifer, and Thomas Weisner. 2000. "How Families View and Use the EITC: Advance Payment versus Lump Sum Delivery." *National Tax Journal* 53, no. 4: 1245–266.

Rose, David, Daniel Schneider, and Peter Tufano. 2006. "H&R Block's Refund Anticipation Loan: Perilous Profits at the Bottom of the Pyramid." In *Business Solutions for Reaching the Poor,* edited by K. Rangan and J. Quelch. New York: Jossey-Bass.

Runkle, David. 1991. "Liquidity Constraints and the Permanent Income Hypothesis." *Journal of Monetary Economics* 27, no. 1: 73–98.

Schneider, Daniel, and Peter Tufano. 2006. "The San Francisco Working Families Credit: Analysis of Program Applicants." Report to SFWorks and the City of San Francisco.

Scholz, John Karl. 1990. "The Participation Rate of the Earned Income Tax Credit." Institute for Research on Poverty, University of Wisconsin-Madison.

———. 1994. "The Earned Income Tax Credit: Participation, Compliance, and Antipoverty Effectiveness." *National Tax Journal* 47, no. 1: 63–87.

Shapiro, Matthew, and Joel Slemrod. 2003. "Consumer Response to Tax Rebates." *American Economic Review* 93, no. 1: 381–96.

Skiba, Paige, and Jeremy Tobacman. 2007. "Measuring the Individual-Level Effects of Access to Credit: Evidence from Payday Loans." Vanderbilt Law School and Oxford University.

Smeeding, Timothy, Katherine Ross, and Michael O'Conner. 2000. "The EITC: Expectation, Knowledge, Use, and Economic and Social Mobility." *National Tax Journal* 53, no. 4: 1187–209.

Soman, Dilip, and Amar Cheema. 2002. "The Effect of Credit on Spending Decisions: The Role of the Credit Limit and Credibility." *Marketing Science* 21, no. 1: 32–53.

Souleles, Nicholas. 1999. "The Response of Household Consumption to Income Tax Refunds." *American Economic Review* 89, no. 4: 847–958.

———. 2002. "Consumer Response to the Reagan Tax Cuts." *Journal of Public Economics* 85, no. 1: 99–120.

Stephens, Melvin. 2003. " '3rd of tha Month': Do Social Security Recipients Smooth Consumption between Checks?" *American Economic Review* 93, no. 1: 406–22.

———. 2006. "Paycheque Receipt and the Timing of Consumption." *Economic Journal* 116, no. 513: 680–701.

Thaler, Richard. 1980. "Towards a Positive Theory of Consumer Choice." *Journal of Economic Behavior and Organization* 1, no. 1 (March): 39–60.

———. 1985. "Mental Accounting and Consumer Choice." *Marketing Science* 4, no. 3: 199–214.

Tufano, Peter, and Daniel Schneider. 2004. "H&R Block and Everyday Financial Services." HBS Case 205-013. Harvard Business School Publishing.

Tufano, Peter, Arijit Roy, and Emily McClintock Ekins. 2007. "H&R Block 2006." HBS Case 307-091. Harvard Business School Publishing.

Wu, Chi Chi, and Jean Ann Fox. 2005. "Still a Bad Deal: Beware Quick Tax Refund Loans." Boston: Consumer Federation of America and the National Consumer Law Center.

———. 2006. "Pay Stub and Holiday RALs: Faster, Costlier, Riskier in the Race to the Bottom." Boston: Consumer Federation of America and the National Consumer Law Center.

Zeldes, Stephen. 1989. "Consumption and Liquidity Constraints: An Empirical Investigation." *Journal of Political Economy* 97, no. 2: 305–46.

3

Financial Decisionmaking Processes of Low-Income Individuals

EDNA R. SAWADY AND JENNIFER TESCHER

In *The End of Poverty,* Jeffrey Sachs describes the poor as "ready to act, both individually and collectively . . . hard working . . . [and having] a very realistic idea about their conditions and how to improve them, not a mystical acceptance of their fate."[1] This description differs markedly from the stereotypical portrayal of low-income individuals as reluctant workers and irrational consumers. By judging various choices as irrational, observers who are not themselves poor invoke the traditional notion of rationality, which assumes that individuals make choices that maximize economic utility. Examples of perceived irrationality abound, particularly when it comes to basic financial decisions. For instance, some wonder why lower-income consumers choose to cash their paychecks for a fee when they could open a bank account instead and have the funds deposited electronically. Similarly, others question why immigrants would use a higher-priced money transfer service when a growing number of banks offer free or reduced-cost transfers via a bank account. This thinking reflects how difficult it is for a casual observer to understand the lives and circumstances of low-income individuals. Further

The authors would like to acknowledge Alex Baker, Sarah Cohen, Lynn Edwards, Steve Kutner, and Pat Sachs for their contributions to this chapter. We also want to thank the two financial institutions whose proprietary research forms the basis of this work for allowing us to share the insights we developed together.
    1. Sachs (2005, p. 317).

confirming their diagnosis of "irrationality," these same observers often suggest financial education as the cure.

The field of behavioral economics has emerged as a response to the traditional view of rationality, focusing on choices that may not seem rational. Behavioral economists and psychologists have shown that people weighing options employ heuristics and are subject to a range of cognitive influences. Their insights can be useful in structuring financial products that encourage low-income individuals to make what society considers the optimal choice. Still, behavioral economics does not help us understand how financial services firms might design broader experiences that would be effective in reaching this customer segment.

Recent research in economics seeks to model seemingly "irrational" economic decisions in the context of self-imposed cultural norms. Economist Roland Fryer has developed a model to describe how individuals in a minority community may reduce investment in high-return human interaction outside the cultural group in favor of in-group interactions because of the potential loss of status in the minority community.[2] This behavior, which Fryer links to the phenomenon of social sanctions for "acting white," can help explain how context may drive decisions that appear irrational in objective economic terms.

Acknowledging the importance of context, we turn to anthropology for further insights into the financial decisionmaking processes of low-income individuals. Anthropological views of culture and cognition are helping reveal how cultural, social, and experiential factors influence the decisions of consumers with shared experiences. This field emphasizes in-depth examination of social context and its influence on behavior, and relies heavily on ethnographic research techniques. To anthropologists, rationality is the ability to make decisions that are logical within a given context.

After a review of the literature and discussion of the construct of reasoning systems, we describe the ethnographic study undertaken to infer the reasoning of low-income consumers. Then we show how understanding this reasoning system can help financial institutions design products and services to meet market needs and desires. We conclude by discussing the broader implications of a reasoning systems approach.

Literature Review

In the past several decades, anthropology has proved increasingly useful to students of consumer behavior in complex industrialized societies. Even though consumer decisions in modern economies are often considered the province of economics or psychology, these disciplines, with their emphasis on understanding

---

2. Fryer (2007).

individual actions, are not particularly good at illuminating how culture affects consumer decisionmaking. In response, researchers have turned to the ethnographic tools developed in anthropology to provide rich detail about individual motivations, preferences, and strategies that are difficult to observe in laboratory settings. Anthropology does not lay claim to the universal conclusions of psychology or economics, but it can offer us insights into the salient cognitive drivers among groups with shared experiences.

Within the broad discipline of anthropology, cultural anthropology seeks to "describe the standards and principles by which people perceive their world, by which they define their objectives in relation to it, and by which they select from the material, intellectual, and social resources available to them in order to accomplish their objectives."[3] Two strands in cultural anthropology are most relevant to the current analysis: symbolic anthropology and cognitive anthropology.

Symbolic anthropology is concerned with culture as the shared understandings and beliefs of individuals. Culture is mediated through symbols that individuals assign meaning to and interpret in order to arrive at actions and thoughts that are "sensible" in terms of their system of understanding. At a deeper level, they represent the embedded norms that unconsciously shape our actions and beliefs, what Geertz describes as common sense: "Common sense is not what the mind . . . spontaneously apprehends; it is what the mind filled with presuppositions . . . concludes."[4]

Symbolic anthropology and its methodological tools have found wide application in the behavior of modern consumers in industrialized countries.[5] The body of research Arnold and Thompson describe as consumer culture theory seeks to illuminate "the symbolic, embodied, and experiential aspects of acquisition behaviors and the socio-cultural complexities of exchange behaviors and relationships."[6] This research concerns itself with an array of phenomena, including the overlapping cultural, sociohistorical, and institutional factors that influence consumption behaviors and the ways in which consumers use products to define and express themselves.

Similarly, cognitive anthropology focuses on the part of culture that "consists of the shared aspects of the structure of cognitive representations held by the individual members of that culture."[7] Cognitive anthropology considers the "interdependence of cognition, emotion, and motivation" in the production of these representations and how they guide decisionmaking.[8] One concept anthropologists have developed to understand this interdependence is the "schema," a "set of rules

3. Goodenough (1969, p. 329).
4. Geertz (2000, p. 84).
5. Goulding (1999).
6. Arnould and Thompson (2005, p. 871).
7. Romney and Moore (1998).
8. Garro (1998, p. 324).

or strategies for imposing order on experience."[9] This framework allows anthropologists to follow individuals' cognitive processes as a rational process without focusing on whether decisions are correct according to outside normative criteria.

In recent years, researchers have considered what cognitive anthropology can tell us about how consumers make decisions in the marketplace. Tadajewski and Wagner-Tsukamoto argue that contextual approaches are especially useful for understanding different facets of consumer experience. Contextual knowledge, they argue, guides both the set of choices facing individuals in the marketplace and the resources they choose to access.[10]

Rather than being a substitute for psychological and economic decision models, these anthropological perspectives complement them. Anthropological tools can offer unique insights into the context in which low-income consumers make financial decisions and can allow us to deduce the "rationality" of their actions.

Analysis

We are mindful of theory, yet this chapter is grounded in the results of proprietary market research conducted on behalf of two different U.S. financial services firms—a large bank with a multistate footprint and a midsized credit union serving a regional market—to help them better reach and serve lower-income consumers. Both research efforts sought to identify the key drivers of decisionmaking among lower-income consumers, and then to test a series of product, marketing, branch delivery, and customer service concepts developed in response to those drivers. The research involved both qualitative and quantitative methods.

Both projects focused mostly on households earning less than $50,000 a year. The qualitative, ethnographic work was conducted in a predominantly African American community, although the resulting concepts were tested in broad surveys that included consumers of varying ethnicities. Prospective customers were recruited to help design the concepts to be tested. Although we are confident in the validity of our findings, it is important to note that they reflect our sponsors' areas of interest and are intended to be illustrative rather than comprehensive.

Inferring the Reasoning System of Low-Income Consumers of Financial Services

The term "reasoning system," which we use extensively, refers to the interconnected core beliefs that guide individuals, sometimes unconsciously, in making decisions. It is adapted from the concept of "cultural common sense" advocated by Geertz and also recalls the concept of a schema discussed by Rice. Keeping with the various anthropological perspectives, we see rationality as the process of making decisions that are sensible, or logical, within a given reasoning system.

9. Rice (1980, p. 153).
10. Tadajewski and Wagner-Tsukamoto (2006).

This "common sense" reflects social and physical realities and has shared meaning within the culture. Underlying it are deeply rooted and highly persistent perceptions, beliefs, and attitudes shaped by circumstances and experiences that govern decisionmaking. Underlying beliefs are tacit, accessed intuitively by members of the group, and rarely understood beyond group boundaries. Because it is often hard for people to articulate their fundamental beliefs in reply to a direct question, we used ethnographic inquiries to infer the reasoning system that governs financial decisionmaking of low-income individuals.

Working with a team of ethnographers, we systematically observed people in relevant circumstances and conducted in-depth interviews to understand their everyday lives and everyday influences on their financial decisionmaking. We interacted with twenty-seven people, all residents of a low- to moderate-income neighborhood. Twenty were users of nonbank check-cashing services, and seven were new customers of the bank-based check-cashing program. Interviews ranged from a single, one-hour discussion to multiple discussions that took a few hours. We recruited people through bank personnel, through intercepts at check-cashing locations, and through the social networks of people we interviewed. Interviews took place in homes, libraries, and shopping malls—all at the interviewees' suggestions. Ethnographic techniques revealed a broad range of shared beliefs. Both observation and interviewing helped us understand different perspectives on financial issues and ultimately infer a shared reasoning system.

We observed and discussed:
1. What people say they do.
2. What people actually do.
3. What people think or believe other people do.
4. How people's behavior is influenced by others.

Using the framework in figure 3-1, we gathered extensive qualitative data reflecting a broad range of collective experiences, common emotional needs, and shared responses to prevailing circumstances. We organized these data and the corresponding insights according to our interpretation of the reasoning system construct. We looked at shared experiences and prevailing circumstances as the context that creates the foundation of the reasoning system. We then represented the inferred reasoning system as an intersection of common emotional needs and the response patterns that emerged over time. The context we describe helped us see the "internal logic" that low-income consumers use in making financial decisions.

Our analysis suggests that the context of shared experiences shapes the reasoning system of low-income individuals in profound ways.

Poverty leads to short-term focus. We observed poverty to be accompanied by constantly changing and frequently unpredictable circumstances. Incomes fluctuate, permanent assets are few, jobs change, work availability often changes, family structures change, money comes and goes. Within this context, it is not

Figure 3-1. *Reasoning System Development Framework*

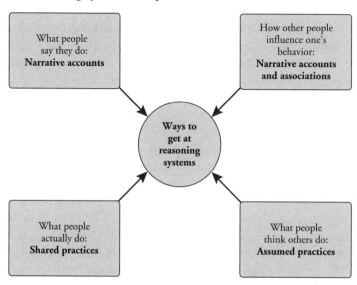

surprising that short-term focus prevails. Long-term thinking anchored in the need for achievement does occur, but it requires deliberate effort. People live paycheck to paycheck, confronting job insecurity and housing instability. Having cash in hand is comforting. Convenience is bought at a premium. Investing in long-term financial actions is difficult, even when their value is understood and desired.

A history of exclusion leads to mistrust. Trust emerged as central issue in low-income people's lives. Decades of exclusion from the mainstream, by either ethnicity or class, have engendered deep distrust of mainstream practices. This attitude is generalized to all large institutions, which are predominantly in the mainstream, and to government agencies. It is hardly surprising that within this context, trust is fragile and self-protection is crucial. Consumers strongly emphasize intangibles such as respect, trust, safety, security, and a sense of belonging. Subtle manifestations of disrespect, frequently unintended, are perceived as messages of exclusion—an attitude that mainstream organizations in turn often see as overreaction to simple procedural matters. When people believe an institution is breaking an agreement with them—as is the case with "hidden fees" or an inadvertently overdrawn account—they feel a promise has been broken. Their trust is compromised and they may bail out of the system.

Community and family networks facilitate access to resources. Social networks play a crucial role in the lives of people of moderate means. The role of such networks in everyday life goes well beyond the emotional support they supply across all economic strata. Low-income households rely on community and family networks for survival. Close personal connections and strong trust within an expanded network offer flexible access to resources, including financial resources. In this world, people take care of each other and regularly exchange favors.

Prevailing financial practices present an overwhelming range of options. Broadly speaking, people meet their financial services needs by tapping into one of two worlds. One is the informal cash economy that is familiar and comfortable and is an integral part of the community. Social networks include check cashers and fringe lenders. People are acutely aware of the relatively high fees and the stigma they evoke, yet they are willing to pay the price to avoid possible rejection and disrespectful treatment. The other is the formal financial services system. It is a different world, one that conjures an image of stability and upward mobility and therefore presents a positive aspiration. Yet there is an emotional price to pay here—many are confused by practices they don't understand, and others feel rejected. Some try to penetrate that world; some of those give up following negative experiences; others give up without trying. Some function in both worlds simultaneously.

The qualitative data reveal that shared emotional needs form a crucial dimension of the financial reasoning system of low-income individuals. Over and over, people we interviewed about their financial decisions stressed their need for belonging, respect, trust, and achievement.

The feeling of *belonging* is deeply rooted in the collective mind-set of low-income consumers and determines their level of comfort in any situation. As it relates to financial services, many low-income people believe that banks are not for them but for "people with money." The banking practice of "selling up" when the customer has barely enough money to get by, or offering products that clearly do not fit the customer's needs, contributes to the sense of alienation from the formal financial system—the feeling that "banks are not for me . . . they make me feel poor."

The primacy of *respect* in the emotional lives of low-income people came across as interviewees gave many examples of being disrespected, with always showing visible annoyance. They spoke of bank personnel "rolling the eyes when I ask a question" and of waiting in line longer than "real customers" did. From responses to indirect questions, we learned that "caring" is the basis for respect within the social network. The formal financial system is often perceived as not caring, which feels disrespectful.

Within the community, *trust* is robust; within formal financial institutions, it is tenuous. As one interviewee commented, "They don't have your back." Social capital theory elucidates this dichotomy, distinguishing between two types of trust: within-group trust and generalized trust. Within-group trust is that within immediate networks such as family and friends. In these narrow networks, social capital lowers transaction costs between agents and increases the strength of repeated interactions.[11] In Putnam's formulation, this is "bonding" social capital.

---

11. Fedderke and Luiz (1999).

Although good for strengthening specific reciprocal relationships, it may have negative effects on overall economic prosperity: social capital theory predicts it will correlate negatively with generalized trust, that is, the capacity and willingness to trust those outside the immediate network.[12] Generalized trust is associated with "bridging" social capital. Individuals who possess high levels of generalized trust are more likely to have faith in those unlike them and optimism about the reliability of these agents, key elements for successful interactions between low-income individuals and financial services providers who are perceived as outsiders. Higher levels of generalized trust have been associated with more highly developed financial markets, including a propensity to use checks, seek formal lending, and invest in the stock market.[13]

The universal need to *achieve* was apparent as people verbalized their financial aspirations. They want to use checks and have savings; they want to understand credit; they want to buy a home and take care of their children's future. They were very proud of attaining a course certificate.

Further analysis of the data shows that the reasoning system of low-income individuals reveals common response patterns. These patterns emerge over time to address emotional and practical needs. The major response patterns we encountered are as follows:

Low-income communities frequently *pool resources* to maximize them. Anchored in strong social networks and the collective mind-set of low-income individuals, this practice is at the core of collective assets and casual lending with relaxed reciprocity. Buying a house or a car for an extended family member is common. Borrowing money from friends and family is common. One's word is trusted. Formal contracts are rare. People will pay back borrowed money when they can. The network will continue to lend even before it is paid back.

The need for *explicit attention to navigation* and the requirements for navigation aids are typical among those who feel overwhelmed by the complexities of everyday living. To optimize financial decisions, one must be able to maneuver through formal and informal entities and compare competing offers within and across providers. The rampant confusion among underbanked consumers about mainstream institutions and their products and policies leads to feelings of not belonging. Identification requirements are interpreted as discrimination; overdraft fees are perceived as betrayal. We heard prospective customers say, "Banks are not for me," "Banks discriminate," and "Banks make me feel poor." When they feel this way, they may prefer a simple and familiar solution, even if it costs more. They appreciate help in navigating the complexities of both systems.

Low-income communities show a deep sense of *loyalty* that arises from the belief that a community-based safety net exists in which exchanges are not

12. Putnam (2000).
13. Guiso, Sapienza, and Zingales (2004, p. 527).

Figure 3-2. *The Inferred Reasoning System with Illustrative Service Concepts*

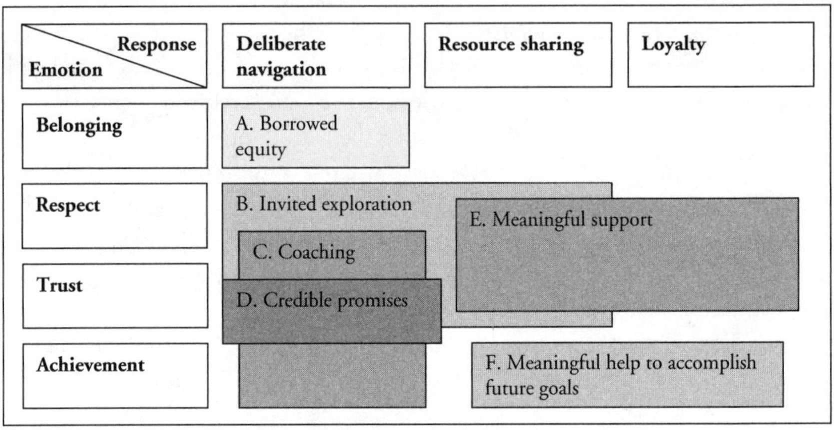

Emotion / Response	Deliberate navigation	Resource sharing	Loyalty
Belonging	A. Borrowed equity		
Respect	B. Invited exploration	E. Meaningful support	
	C. Coaching		
Trust	D. Credible promises		
Achievement		F. Meaningful help to accomplish future goals	

explicitly tracked. They trust that over the long run things will even out; at the end "things will work out." Thus, long-term relationships tend to be more loyal. Longevity may be tracked over multiple generations. The partners in a long-term relationship expect preferential treatment, bordering on entitlement. It is this aspect of reasoning that helps explain why a frustrated consumer, upon being rejected for a loan, might exclaim, "But my grandfather banked with you!"

Service Concepts That Emerge from the Inferred Reasoning System

One critical challenge of serving the financial needs of low-income consumers is to develop a customer experience that is relevant, culturally sensitive, and consistent with their values and beliefs. To that end, we used the reasoning system to define relevant service concepts. Figure 3-2 depicts the emotional needs and the response patterns identified in the ethnographic research and the service concepts derived from that framework.

The service concepts shown are examples and illustrations rather than an exhaustive list. They demonstrate how financial services firms can acknowledge the emotions and typical responses of lower-income consumers to reach and serve them.

The service concepts derived from the inferred reasoning system include the following:

Borrowed Equity (A). Anchored in the Belonging-Navigation space. Refers to using credible agents from within the social network to help with and encourage exploration and to create receptivity. Examples include referrals from satisfied clients to friends and family or use of credible or familiar locations to increase receptivity. Challenges include gaining cooperation from agents without damaging their credibility in the social network.

Invited Exploration (B). Mostly anchored in the Respect and Trust spaces, yet incorporating Navigation and Resource Sharing elements. Achieved through encouraging and enabling exploration in a culturally appropriate manner. Examples include issuing personal invitations (respect), providing transportation (resource sharing), including friends and family (small groups for cultural support), using "touch and feel" experiences to increase familiarity and sense of control (navigation), and building trust by staying true to the stated intent (that is, exploration, not sales). Additional navigation elements include explaining operations and addressing safety and concerns.

Coaching (C). Firmly anchored in Navigation and spanning Respect, Trust, and Achievement needs. The self-respect that comes from the sense of "mastery" creates a positive mind-set that, in turn, enables Trust to develop. Clear, direct, and consistent communications are crucial. Mastery of a situation (immediate or longer term) is equally crucial. Sincere appreciation of customers and their business is vital.

Credible Promise (D). Resides in the Navigation-Trust intersection. It has to do with clear and simple requirements, clearly spelled out "rules of the game," and simple, direct, and familiar terms. No assumptions should be made; everything should be explicit. A perceived break of trust is a danger; it usually results from different assumptions that have led to different interpretations of a situation. Example: overdraft at an ATM. Client assumption: "The bank will tell me if I have money to withdraw." Bank assumption: "The client wants credit and will pay for it." Client interpretation of resulting fee: "Banks are sneaky and should not be trusted." Bank interpretation: "Client is irresponsible."

Meaningful Support in the Immediate and Medium Term (E). Meaningful help is perceived as a sign of respect. Practical help is needed and appreciated as a form of resource sharing. Examples include providing transportation and supporting school-related activities, sports, and family gatherings. Help must be given in a courteous, culturally appropriate manner. There is an interesting conceptual progression from Resource Sharing (that is, "because you have resources") to Loyalty ("because I stuck with you"); both spaces are relevant.

Assistance with Financial Issues Promoting Longer-Term Goals (F). This appeals to the Achievement need and builds on a future orientation. Help can come in various forms and intensities, from help with credit-score issues to credit repair to building assets. This concept, too, can cover anything from Resource Sharing ("because you can") to Loyalty ("because I earned it").

Translating Concepts into Tactics

To bring this work to life, we translated the reasoning system and the emerging service concepts into tactics. For the bank, we talked with bank employees, customers, and people from the community to suggest possible practical applications linked to the building blocks of the reasoning system; the result was a list of 43 customer experience statements. The employee and community discussions also yielded a few pricing and convenience statements that did not emerge from the conceptual construct, and we included them in the research because of their importance in financial decisionmaking. This list is by no means comprehensive; it is just one possible manifestation of the underlying service concepts.

We then tested the validity and importance of the various statements through a survey of 760 respondents whose household income was under $50,000 and who cashed at least one check at a place other than a bank or credit union in the six months before the survey date. Participants were asked to indicate the importance of the 43 experiences to them (on a 7-point scale, with 4 being neutral) in the context of choosing a place to cash checks. Table 3-1 lists the survey statements, ranked by the mean importance score. The percentage change from neutral is also shown. Our client used these data in combination with other findings to inform branch practices and operating procedures.

In a subsequent analysis of the data, we assigned a description of the underlying need each statement addresses. Ethnographic practice, with its emphasis on context, enables deeper understanding of emotional needs. For example, we interpreted multiple locations and proximity to home as signs of respect. This interpretation was based on interviewees' emotionally charged comments such as "Real customers can go to any branch they want, but I can use only some branches," or "My neighbors can use the branch next to home, but we need to go far away." In contrast, interviewees referred to availability of additional services as pure convenience.

A few findings emerge from the results:

—All tactics were rated above neutral, which suggests that the reasoning system construct can be useful for deriving customer experience tactics.

—Tactics that addressed emotional needs, particularly respect and belonging, ranked higher in importance than those addressing practical needs.

—With the exception of check-cashing rates (which ranked 14 out of 43), all other tactics related to pricing and convenience—most of which did *not* emerge directly from the reasoning system construct—ranked in the bottom half.

In a second study, this time in partnership with a credit union, we confirmed the relevance of elements from the reasoning system through interviews and small group discussions. We then exposed a set of experience statements related to respect and navigation to quantitative validation across four ethnic groups. This was part of a web-enabled survey of 295 respondents, mostly with household income of $50,000 or less. All respondents were un- or underbanked (that is, they used nonbank providers for financial services either exclusively or in addition to a bank relationship) and represented four ethnicities. The results were reweighted to reflect the income and ethnicity characteristics of the target population. We found both respect and navigation to be of utmost importance across the four

Table 3-1. *Importance of Experience Elements*

	How important to you is it that:	Underlying need	Mean importance	Percent change from neutral
1	My information is kept confidential	Trust	6.36	58.9
2	Respect is shown in every employee interaction	Respect	6.33	58.2
3	The location feels safe	Belonging	6.24	56.1
4	Customer service is hassle-free	Respect	6.22	55.5
5	Services are delivered quickly	Respect	6.2	54.9
6	Employee interactions are warm and friendly	Respect	6.16	54.1
7	I do not need to worry about rejection	Belonging	6.15	53.8
8	Employee interactions feel comfortable	Belonging	6.13	53.3
9	I trust the check casher	Trust	6.1	52.4
10	There are many locations	Respect	6.06	51.6
11	There are clearly stated terms	Navigation	6.06	51.6
12	Employees make every effort to satisfy me	Respect	6.04	51.0
13	I understand what is expected	Navigation	6.03	50.8
14	Check services have competitive rates	Pricing	6.02	50.6
15	Locations are open a lot of hours	Respect	6.02	50.4
16	Locations are close to home	Respect	5.97	49.1
17	I don't need to wait too long	Respect	5.93	48.2
18	Provider follows up after a problem	Navigation	5.82	45.5
19	Account set-up is fast	Respect	5.82	45.5
20	Provider has good reputation	Belonging	5.82	45.4
21	In the physical space signs are clear	Navigation	5.77	44.3
22	Help with financial issues	Navigation	5.77	44.2
23	Maximum amount charged on check services	Pricing	5.74	43.5
24	Never disappoint me	Trust	5.72	43.1
25	Parking	Convenience	5.62	40.5
26	Trust brand name	Trust	5.61	40.2
27	Offer bill payment service	Convenience	5.54	38.6
28	Location close to work	Convenience	5.47	36.7
29	Not have one-time set-up fee	Pricing	5.46	36.4
30	Apologize if long waiting time	Respect	5.41	35.2
31	Offer money orders	Convenience	5.39	34.7
32	Have a loyalty program	Loyalty	5.37	34.3
33	Offer option to put cash on a card	Convenience	5.18	29.5
34	Loyal get special treatment	Respect	4.98	24.5
35	Can buy stamps and bus pass; send faxes	Convenience	4.98	24.4
36	Can get on website	Navigation	4.97	24.3
37	Furnishings are nice	Respect	4.94	23.6
38	Offer wire transfer service	Convenience	4.91	22.7
39	Provide educational brochures	Resource sharing	4.78	19.6
40	Employees willing to bend the rules	Respect	4.77	19.3
41	Employees know me	Respect	4.75	18.7
42	Offer educational classes	Resource sharing	4.58	14.5
43	Offer payday loans	Convenience	4.32	8.0

Figure 3-3. *Respect Tactics*

Percent change from neutral point

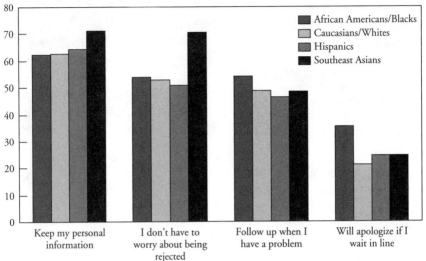

ethnic groups, further emphasizing their centrality in the reasoning system of low-income consumers.

Figure 3-3 demonstrates this finding as it relates to respect. We tested a series of respect-related tactics to determine their appeal to individuals of different ethnic groups. We found that individuals assigned a high degree of importance to the respect-related tactics consistently across ethnicities. It is interesting that the Asian group was even more sensitized to respect-related tactics than the other groups.

Similarly, figure 3-4 shows that help with navigation is crucial for all four ethnicities. As with figure 3-3, the high importance assigned to navigation-related tactics held consistent across ethnicities, with the Asian group assigning it the highest scores.

Implications

Discussions about "banking the unbanked" tend to focus on the same few solutions. Reducing or eliminating fees is usually at the top of the list, followed by the need for more bank branches in lower-income communities and financial education. In other words, solutions tend to focus first on price and convenience and then on strategies to provide consumers with better information so they will make the "right" decision.

The results of the research presented here demonstrate something far broader is at work. The emotional core of the reasoning system and the response patterns that developed in tandem drive decisionmaking that may be economically less

Figure 3-4. *Navigation Tactics*

Percent change from neutral point

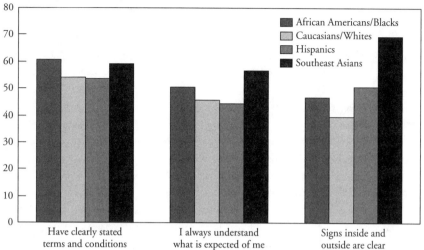

than optimal, or "irrational," but makes perfect sense within the shared belief system. The reasoning system this chapter describes suggests ways to reach people of modest means on their terms, thus serving them more effectively. We believe this reasoning system is a rich source of strategies and tactics for financial institutions and policymakers alike.

Business Implications

Financial services providers aspiring to reach and serve people of modest means need to be mindful of the implicit messages embedded in the various elements of the customer experience—from the way products are designed to the way branches operate to the style of frontline staff as they interact with consumers. Low-income consumers may read disrespect into situations where none was intended, from the location of a branch to the speed of one teller line versus another. Similarly, although financial institutions often seek to project an air of seriousness and stability to signal that they are safe places to keep money, low-income individuals may see that atmosphere as a sign that they do not belong at the bank.

Belonging and respect can be communicated in subtle yet powerful ways. A no-minimum-balance requirement, for example, sends a message of belonging and of open doors. Evening and weekend operating hours convey respect for customers' schedules. Frontline staffers who believe that low-income customers can be profitable customers will unconsciously communicate these beliefs through tone of voice and other nonverbal cues. Clear and open communication that explicitly describes adverse consequences of consumer actions will build trust if used consistently over time. Another important insight is that people, not brands, are the major differentiator in low-income consumers' eyes. The relationship with a teller or other bank personnel is a more significant factor in creating loyalty to a bank because it helps establish trust and a sense of belonging. An anthropological approach suggests banks need to think differently about how they staff, train, and script branch personnel, customizing the tenor of the interactions to better nurture budding customer relationships.

To ensure effective interaction with people of modest means, the response patterns discussed in this chapter should be acknowledged and incorporated into the customer experience. Although financial services providers may intuitively understand the emotional needs of belonging, respect, and trust, the concepts of resource sharing and navigation and the particular meaning of loyalty are much less understood, and their importance is therefore underestimated. Resource sharing can be acknowledged through offers of family accounts—accounts where members of an extended family can save together, run a transaction account together, and qualify for credit based on their combined debt capacity. Longevity of relationships should be acknowledged and rewarded because it is the basis for loyalty among low-income consumers. Potentially the meaning of longevity could be expanded to include repeat transactions, although this definition of loyalty may not be intuitive to this customer segment and should therefore be explicitly described.

The need for good navigation tools goes well beyond formal disclosures. Easy-to-understand information about how a product works and how it can be useful are important; clear warnings about negative consequences of customers' actions are crucial. Banks are well situated to provide the kind of coaching and navigational help that consumers need. Banks sometimes feel uncomfortable providing financial education directly to consumers for fear that consumers will perceive them to be biased toward selling rather than imparting objective information. Coaching, however, suggests a different kind of relationship between banker and consumer, one that harkens back to an earlier era when consumers routinely sought guidance from bankers. Although we cannot turn back the clock, we can find ways to communicate important information to consumers more simply and clearly and at more points in the life cycle of each product.

The short-term focus of lower-income consumers and their reliance on social networks also suggest important implications. Short-term focus should be respectfully acknowledged as an outcome of people's very hectic and volatile lives. Structuring rewards to be earned over relatively short periods is a practice that should be relatively easy to implement. A more difficult practice that could be very powerful is structuring a loan product to allow frequent small payments instead of the all-or-nothing monthly payment that is expected with most loans. The success of "friends and family" promotions in reaching this customer base underscores the importance of following social networks. Retailers use this practice extensively to increase consumers' comfort and sense of belonging, but it is underused by financial services providers.

Policy Guidance

Government initiatives have tended to focus on account design or on incentives to encourage financial institutions to increase lending to low-income borrowers or to maintain bank branches in economically distressed neighborhoods. These initiatives may address drivers such as price and access, but they do not speak to the emotions that drive behavior. Successfully serving people of modest means requires considering both sets of drivers. Opening a new bank branch in a low-income community can be good, for instance, but not if customers are uncomfortable interacting with the bank.

It is impossible to mandate positive customer interactions that are grounded in the various elements of the reasoning system, yet it is feasible to track and evaluate the outcomes of such interactions. The service test in the Community Reinvestment Act is a natural mechanism for encouraging such outcomes. Rather than judging service by level of effort such as number of branches or hours of financial education or specific product design, service should be judged by outcomes such as the extent to which previously unbanked consumers use mainstream products.

Financial literacy is a national priority. This research suggests that the financial lives of low-income consumers are driven by what makes sense within their reasoning system, even if it has adverse financial impact on them in the long run. Classroom-based financial education that typically feels paternalistic and a curriculum that requires a long-term orientation may not be the best way to give consumers the tools they need to maximize economic benefits. We suggest shifting the funding focus from "education" to programs promoting guidance and coaching. Consumers need guidance in navigating the increasingly complex world of financial services choices. They need a coach who will help identify opportunities for positive financial outcomes and caution against financial pitfalls.

Finally, our findings confirm the need for strong consumer protection laws. Predatory financial services providers have been quite successful in understanding the emotional drivers of low-income consumers and manipulating them for financial gain. Financial education and public awareness campaigns are not a substitute for a regulatory framework that protects consumers while promoting innovation.

Conclusion

As research for this chapter shows, "rationality" is a complicated construct. What is rational depends on context and culture. We believe it is important for financial institutions and policymakers to consider the context of shared experiences in which low-income people operate, and acknowledge the influence of such experiences on the way people make decisions. In developing programs to support low-income consumers, it is helpful to realize that short-term focus and mistrust of financial institutions are deeply rooted in poverty and in a history of exclusion. Such elements should therefore be respectfully acknowledged rather than fought within the program structure. It is equally helpful to realize that emotional drivers of behavior such as trust, respect, and a feeling of belonging are likely to be as strong as or stronger than economic drivers among low-income communities. Although decisions individuals make in this context may not seem rational from a strictly economic perspective, they may make perfect sense in terms of one's comfort level and willingness to engage with the financial institution.

The framework presented in this chapter gives financial services firms a foundation for creating innovative tactics to reach low-income consumers. What isn't clear is just how pervasive the findings are among different subsegments. This research looked across ethnic groups, but not across income or other strata. For instance, is the duration of poverty important, such that families entrenched in poverty are more likely to subscribe to the reasoning system described here than others? Do elements of the reasoning system persist when people move out of poverty? Further exploration and testing may reveal additional insights and uncover other tactical applications.

The framework we discuss may give readers a reason to wonder whether "banking the unbanked" in ways that resonate with consumers is even possible. Can economic benefits be maximized within a reasoning system so heavily influenced by strong emotional needs and unique coping patterns? We believe it is possible, although not easy. It requires acute sensitivity to all elements of the reasoning system and clever use of enabling practices such as social networks and financial coaches to bridge the two worlds.

References

Arnould, E. J., and C. J. Thompson. 2005. "Consumer Culture Theory (CCT): Twenty Years of Research." *Journal of Consumer Research* 31, no. 4: 868–82.

Fedderke, J., R. De Kadt, and J. Luiz. 1999. "Economic Growth and Social Capital: A Critical Reflection." *Theory and Society* 28, no. 5: 709–45.

Fryer, Roland G. 2007. "A Model of Social Interactions and Endogenous Poverty Traps." *Rationality and Society* 19, no 3: 335–66 (www.economics.harvard.edu/faculty/fryer/files/cultural_capital_final.pdf).

Garro, L. C. 1998. "On the Rationality of Decisionmaking Studies. Part 1: Decision Models of Treatment Choice." *Medical Anthropology Quarterly* 12, no. 3: 319–40.

Geertz, C. 2000. *Local Knowledge: Further Essays in Interpretive Anthropology.* 3rd ed. New York: Basic Books.

Goodenough, W. H. 1969. "Frontiers of Cultural Anthropology: Social Organization." *Proceedings of the American Philosophical Society* 113, no. 5: 329–35.

Goulding, C. 1999. "Consumer Research, Interpretive Paradigms, and Methodological Ambiguities." *European Journal of Marketing* 33, nos. 9–10: 859–73.

Guiso, L., P. Sapienza, and L. Zingales. 2004. "The Role of Social Capital in Financial Development." *American Economic Review* 94, no. 3: 526–56.

Putnam, R. 2000. *Bowling Alone: The Collapse and Revival of American Community.* New York: Simon and Schuster.

Rice, G. E. 1980. "On Cultural Schemata." *American Ethnologist* 7, no. 1: 152–71.

Romney, A. K., and C. C. Moore. 1998. "Toward a Theory of Culture as Shared Cognitive Structures." *Ethos* 26, no. 3: 314–37.

Sachs, J. D. 2005. *The End of Poverty: Economic Possibilities for Our Time.* New York: Penguin Press.

Tadajewski, M., and S. Wagner-Tsukamoto. 2006. "Anthropology and Consumer Research: Qualitative Insights into Green Consumer Behavior." *Qualitative Market Research* 9, no. 1: 8–25.

4

The Legal Infrastructure of Subprime and Nontraditional Home Mortgages

PATRICIA A. MCCOY AND ELIZABETH RENUART

W e are at a crossroads. The regulatory landscape of mortgages, through decades of deregulation, crass competition for charters, and aggressive concentration of federal power at the expense of state laws protecting local citizens, failed to curb abuses in the mortgage market in any meaningful way. The subprime crisis was the direct result of not policing the market, resulting in skyrocketing foreclosures, falling homeownership rates, lost municipal tax revenues, vacant buildings, and distress to the economy as a whole. The persistent nature of these problems strongly suggests that proper reregulation of mortgage loans, with a strong federal floor augmented by state regulation, is necessary to stabilize the economy and make homeownership sustainable.

In this chapter, we offer a critical analysis of the legal landscape of residential mortgage lending and explain how federal law abdicated regulation of the subprime market.[1] In the loan origination market, federal deregulation and preemption of state law combined to produce a system of dual regulation of home

1. We use the term "subprime" to refer to home mortgage loans that carry higher interest rates, points, or fees when compared with loans extended to the best-qualified borrowers (also known as "prime" borrowers). Although the subprime market was designed for borrowers with impaired credit, lenders also frequently made subprime loans to unsuspecting borrowers who could have qualified for the best-rate prime mortgages. See, for example, Rick Brooks and Ruth Simon, "Subprime Debacle Traps Even Very Credit-Worthy," *Wall Street Journal,* December 3, 2007, p. A1. Accordingly, our definition of subprime loans turns on the high-cost nature of those loans, not on the borrowers' credit profiles.

mortgages that precipitated a race to the bottom in mortgage-lending standards. In the process, numerous aggrieved borrowers were left with little or no recourse for abusive lending practices. This laissez-faire state of residential mortgage law, the disastrous marketing of faulty mortgages that contain multiple layers of risk, and declining property values combined to produce the worst fore-closure crisis in the United States since the Great Depression.

The Evolving Legal Architecture of the Residential Mortgage-Origination Market

Today, federal disclosure law forms the main regulatory paradigm for overseeing residential mortgage credit. That was not always the case, however. Until 1980, state and federal laws regulated the substantive terms of mortgage loans. This reg-ulation included maximum caps on interest rates, otherwise known as usury laws, and restrictions on other loan terms and practices. In this section, we chronicle how federal disclosure laws came to displace the extensive former regime of state regulation.

Legal Developments Preceding the Emergence of the Subprime Market

Modern consumer credit transactions in the United States are regulated (or not) by an overlapping set of state and federal laws, which are riddled with exceptions and undermined by federal banking agency preemption. These complexities and loopholes did not always exist. Indeed, across-the-board usury caps reigned in state law until the twentieth century. In response to a surge in high-cost "salary" lend-ing and loan sharking in the early 1900s, states began to pass "specialty" usury laws, each of which addressed a specific loan product (for example, a small loan, a retail installment sales finance contract, or revolving credit). These laws were exceptions to the states' general usury caps. They permitted lending at higher rates and fees and regulated some noninterest aspects of the transactions.[2]

2. Peterson (2003, pp. 843–44, 862–63); Drysdale and Keest (2000, pp. 618–21). The state usury caps were modeled on the Statute of Anne, passed in England in 1713, which set a maximum interest rate of 5 percent per annum. See also Renuart and Keest (2005, sections 2.2.1, 2.2.2).
    Throughout the twentieth century, states used a variety of techniques to regulate consumer credit, generally for the protection of borrowers. These included limitations on attorneys' fees, credit insur-ance premiums, "service charges," appraisal fees, commitment fees, and other charges that a creditor might impose. Moreover, many of these laws were (and are) unrelated to direct limitations on the interest rate or other charges that can be assessed by a creditor. For example, state credit statutes fre-quently render unenforceable some particularly one-sided contract clauses such as waivers of a bor-rower's legal rights, confessions of judgment, or wage assignments. Other restrictions make the consumer debt easier to repay. For example, a special usury law might grant the lender the right to collect a higher interest rate than the general usury law, but might also require that the rate be fixed and the loan repaid in equal monthly installments over a minimum period of time. See Renuart and Keest (2005, section 1.3) and Saunders and Cohen (2004, p. 4), who note that "[w]hile one could describe this scheme as 'piecemeal,' it led to relatively comprehensive protection for consumers."

Mortgage lending, for the most part, remained under the auspices of state general usury laws until 1933. Only national banks had the option of selecting the higher of a federal rate or the maximum allowed under state law, giving them "most favored lender" status.[3] Credit tightening exacerbated by events leading up to and following the 1929 stock market collapse, however, created a national housing crisis that required a national solution.[4]

Presidents Hoover and Roosevelt faced high foreclosure rates, a housing industry "still flat on its face . . . two million men unemployed in the construction industry, and properties falling apart for lack of money to pay for repairs."[5] As a result, Congress passed the Home Owners' Loan Act in 1933 to help distressed homeowners by refinancing their short-term, renewal mortgages with new fifteen-year amortizing loans that carried annual interest rates of no more than 6 percent.[6] Federally chartered "savings and loan" associations, the vehicles for making these loans, were born.[7]

One year later, at the behest of President Roosevelt, his cabinet, and others, Congress quickly adopted the National Housing Act.[8] Among other things, this law created the Federal Housing Administration (FHA) and the FHA-insured mortgage loan program. For the first time, a federal law created usury and credit regulation that applied to participating lenders, regardless of how and where they were chartered. The program limited annual interest rates to 5 percent and gave the administrator discretion to raise the cap to 6 percent. It also imposed maximum loan amounts, established loan-to-value ratios and underwriting criteria based on borrowers' ability to repay, required appraisals, and specified that mortgage liens be in first position.[9]

---

3. 12 U.S.C. § 85. The federal rate is 1 percent above the discount rate on ninety-day commercial paper in effect at the federal reserve bank in the district where the institution is located. For example, the discount rate on ninety-day "AA" financial paper was 5.48 percent on September 7, 2007; adding 1 percent resulted in a rate of 6.48 percent (Federal Reserve Release 2007). Because state laws routinely contained strict usury caps until 1980, national banks operated under a solid usury regime that does not exist today.

4. Federal Housing Administration (1959, p. 2); Peterson (2003, pp. 862–63).

5. Federal Housing Administration (1959, p. 2). By 1933, nonfarm foreclosures had reached 252,400 and housing starts had plummeted to less than a tenth of the 1925 record of 937,000.

6. Pub. L. No. 73-43, 48 Stat. 128; Mansfield (2000, pp. 479–80). A significant portion of the mortgage loans outstanding during the period from 1925 to 1929 were nonamortizing or partially amortizing loans. See also Willen (2007, p. 5).

7. Federal credit unions came into existence in 1934 when Congress created the National Credit Union Administration. Deeming a deposit insurance fund critical, Congress passed the Federal Deposit Insurance Act in 1933.

8. June 27, 1934, ch. 847, 48 Stat. 1246, codified at 12 U.S.C. §§ 1701 et seq. The bill was introduced on May 14, 1934, and was passed and signed by the president on June 27, 1934.

9. Federal Housing Administration (1959, pp. 5, 10). In 1935 alone, the FHA insured 23,400 mortgages totaling $94 million.

Toward the end of World War II, the Servicemen's Readjustment Act of 1944 (better known as the "G.I. Bill") gave the Veterans' Administration (today, the U.S. Department of Veterans Affairs, or VA) authority to begin a mortgage insurance program similar to that of the FHA.[10] The VA could guarantee $2,000 of home mortgage debt owed by an individual who had served in the armed forces at an interest rate of 4 percent. These agencies were later allowed to set the maximum interest rates on insured mortgage loans, an authorization that lasted until 1983 for FHA loans and until 1992 for VA loans. After those dates, Congress repealed this authority and effectively eliminated rate caps on those loans.[11]

In the 1960s, Congress concerned itself with two serious problems consumers faced when shopping for credit: (1) the nonstandardized methods of computing interest, which resulted in apples-to-oranges comparisons of rates; and (2) the fact that, because of the additional fees charged in connection with credit, rates alone did not reflect the full cost of credit. After several years of hearings, Congress passed the Truth in Lending Act (TILA) in 1968 to "assure a meaningful disclosure of credit terms" so that consumers could comparison shop and avoid expensive and abusive credit.[12] TILA did not regulate or restrict the terms of credit. Instead, Congress created a disclosure regime to complement the existing substantive credit regulation embodied in state law. Congress explicitly deferred to and expected the states to substantively regulate consumer credit.[13]

The late 1970s and early 1980s were watershed years for usury law. Efforts were under way in the states to pass uniform consumer credit codes that would consolidate all or parts of their diverse usury laws and make credit regulation more uniform from state to state.[14] In 1978, however, the Supreme Court bypassed the

---

10. Pub. L. No. 78-346, §§ 500, 501, 58 Stat. 284, 291–92.

11. FHA, 12 U.S.C. § 1709(b)(5); VA, 38 U.S.C. § 3745 and 38 C.F.R. § 36.4311. "In addition to being controlled by agency-dictated rate ceilings, FHA and VA loans were also subject to state interest rate caps between 1958 and 1979, unless a state's usury provision specifically exempted such mortgages from the state's usury laws. Thus from the inception of these two loan programs until 1979, the interest rate that lenders could charge for FHA and VA loans was effectively capped at whichever was the lowest rate, the VA/FHA rate or the state usury rate" (Mansfield 2000, pp. 483–84).

12. 15 U.S.C. § 1601(a). See generally Keest (1995, pp. 360–61).

13. When TILA was enacted, it was adopted against a background of widespread state credit regulation. Most states still had usury limitations (U.S. House of Representatives, Subcommittee on Consumer Affairs 1967, p. 139). TILA's drafters never thought that its disclosure rules would be sufficient to fix all the problems with consumer credit. As Robertson testified, "I do not think this bill is going to cover all of the abuses in the credit field. . . . It is merely a start in the right direction" (1967, p. 133). For its part, the Senate Banking Committee sought to "encourage as much state legislation in this area as is possible so that the federal law will no longer be necessary" (U.S. Senate Committee on Banking and Currency 1967, p. 8). Renuart and Thompson (2008, p. 186–87).

14. Renuart and Keest (2005, section 2.3.3.10). The Uniform Consumer Credit Code (UCCC) was meant to consolidate the various specialty usury laws into one set of comprehensive provisions covering consumer credit. Versions of the 1968 and 1974 editions were adopted in about eleven states. This effort at uniformity failed, in part, because of federal preemption.

uniform laws process by deciding the case of *Marquette National Bank of Min-neapolis* v. *First of Omaha Service Corp.*[15] In *Marquette*, the Court gave national banks the right to take their most favored lender status across state lines and pre-empt the usury law of the borrower's home state. As a result, national banks could establish their headquarters in states with high usury limits—or none at all—and charge the high interest rates permitted by the bank's home state to borrowers located in any other state. The holding, which came to be known as the "expor-tation doctrine," subsequently transformed the credit marketplace.

Emboldened in part by this decision, South Dakota and Delaware decided to attract the lending industry as part of their economic development strategy and repealed their usury caps. The states wanted to "provide [their] citizens with the jobs and benefits a large national credit card operation [could] provide (attracted by the ability to export limitless credit card rates to other states)."[16] It worked. South Dakota's tax revenues from banks went from $3.2 million in 1980 to almost $27.2 million in 1987, with the comparable figures for Delaware rising from $2.4 million to almost $40 million.[17] This strategy weakened the resolve of states that wished to retain consumer credit protections because their local banks argued that having to comply with such laws put them at a competitive dis-advantage with out-of-state banks.

Simultaneously, conventional mortgage interest rates began to rise dramati-cally, from 7.38 percent a year in 1972 to 9.63 percent in 1978 (the year of the *Marquette* ruling) to 13.77 percent in 1980.[18] These rates exceeded many state usury ceilings, severely restricting mortgage lending in some states. In response to this crisis, Congress passed the Depository Institutions Deregulation and Mone-tary Control Act (DIDMCA) in 1980.[19] This law affected state usury caps in two significant ways. First, it abolished all interest ceilings for first-lien mortgages on residences and mobile homes. The law defined "interest" restrictions to include both periodic rate caps and the costs included in the TILA annual percentage rate, thus broadening the scope of the preemption.[20] Second, it extended the most

15. 439 U.S. 299 (1978). Although the case involved credit card lending, the core of the hold-ing was not limited to any credit product type.

16. *Independent Community Bankers' Ass'n of South Dakota* v. *Board of Governors, Federal Reserve Sys.,* 838 F.2d 969, 975 (8th Cir. 1988). The ruling also notes that South Dakota repealed its usury cap and holds that South Dakota cannot protect its state banks against out-of-state holding compa-nies that purchase in-state banks by restricting their location to one office.

17. "Small Is Usurious (Bank Credit Card Business Transferred to States Having No Interest Ceilings)," *Economist,* July 2, 1988, p. 26.

18. Federal Reserve Statistical Release (FRB 2007). These rates reached their peak in 1981 with an annual average rate of 16.63 percent.

19. Pub. L. No. 96-221, tit. v, 95 Stat. 164.

20. 12 U.S.C. § 1735f-7a; S. Rep. No. 96-368 at 19, reprinted in 1980 U.S.C.C.A.N. 236. According to TILA, the annual percentage rate is defined to include both the interest that will be earned over the loan term and certain costs associated with the loan, such as origination and broker fees, points, and other closing costs (15 U.S.C. § 1605).

favored lender status conferred on national banks to the other types of depository institutions. This expansion meant that most depository institutions could select which of the two available rates—the one based on the federal discount rate or the applicable state rate—they wished to use in any given transaction of any type.[21] Just as important, these institutions could take advantage of the *Marquette* decision and export their home state's rates to sister states.

Another congressional override of state consumer credit laws occurred in 1982 with the enactment of the Alternative Mortgage Transaction Parity Act (AMTPA).[22] This law addressed the structure of mortgage loans by trumping state laws that restricted variable-rate terms, balloon payments, and negative amortization. Its preemptive effects are available to virtually all types of residential lenders. The law covers all "alternative" loans, both first and subordinate lien loans, but not fully amortizing fixed-rate loans.[23]

Congress' immediate motivation for enacting DIDMCA and AMTPA was to revive thrift lenders and the mortgage market, which had both plunged into crisis with the rampant inflation of the late 1970s. Ultimately, however, both statutes had other far-reaching structural effects. By liberalizing the permissible features of loan products and facilitating differential pricing according to risk, the DIDMCA and AMTPA set the legal stage for the emergence of the subprime mortgage market a decade later.

Congress allowed the states to opt out of this DIDMCA provision by April 1, 1983. Fourteen states originally opted out, although not all chose to maintain their usury caps (Renuart and Keest 2003, section 3.9.4.1).

21. Federal savings and loan associations, 12 U.S.C. §§ 1463(g); federal credit unions, 1785(g); and state-chartered banks and savings banks, 1831d(a). Under federal law, states still have the ability to opt out of the most favored lender preemption.

As states relaxed or removed their usury caps, these depositories could make loans with liberal or no rate restrictions. In addition, in the early 1980s many states also enacted "parity" or "wild-card" laws. The purpose of these laws was to put state banks on equal footing with their federal bank counterparts (Renuart and Keest 2005, section 3.14.1). Today, nearly every state has enacted some form of parity provision (Schroeder 2003, p. 202).

22. 12 U.S.C. § 3801 et seq. A handful of states opted out of federal preemption under AMTPA (Renuart and Keest 2005, sections 3.10.1, 3.10.2 at n. 679).

23. Alternative mortgage loans include (1) loans in which the finance charge or interest rate can be adjusted or renegotiated; (2) loans that have fixed rates but implicitly permit rate adjustments by having the debt mature at the end of an interval shorter than the term of the amortization schedule ("balloon" loans); and (3) loans involving any similar type of rate, method of determining return, term, repayment, or other variation not common to traditional fixed-rate, fixed-term transactions (12 U.S.C. § 3802). The Office of Thrift Supervision (OTS), the agency with the authority to enact AMTPA regulations that govern nondepository lenders, repealed AMTPA preemption as it related to prepayment penalties and late fees in 2003 (12 C.F.R. § 560.210, amended by OTS (2002)). In support of its decision, the agency stated: "OTS believes that laws on prepayment penalties and late charges are a key component in states' regulation of predatory lending. Because these laws reflect each state legislature's judgment, after due consideration, about appropriate consumer protections applicable to state-chartered lenders, OTS will not construe its authority under AMTPA to frustrate these state efforts where another less intrusive construction of AMTPA is permissible."

The Rise of the Subprime Market and Re-Regulation

Today's home mortgage market bears little resemblance to its predecessors. Before the advent of securitization, lenders underwrote their loan applications by hand and held most of their home mortgages in portfolio. Given the risks of holding such long-term assets, lenders rationed credit and extended loans only to borrowers with perfect or nearly perfect credit, the so-called prime customers.[24] Customers with weaker credit—including numerous minorities—were shut out of the home mortgage market altogether.

Four developments changed this state of affairs and laid the groundwork for the emergence of the subprime market. Deregulation was the first of these developments. Federal deregulation permitted lenders to charge a "risk premium" to less creditworthy borrowers in the form of higher interest rates and fees. Equally as important, deregulation allowed lenders to market new and more complex types of mortgage products, including adjustable-rate mortgages and loans with balloon payments and negative amortization, which expanded the pool of eligible borrowers and helped lenders control for interest-rate risk.[25]

Deregulation dismantled legal obstacles to the subprime market, but other innovations, mainly technological in nature, helped to bring that market to life. Previously, the mortgage market had labored under a number of challenges that made lenders wary of making loans to consumers with blemished credit. Lenders lacked sophisticated and reliable models for evaluating default risk. In addition, lenders raised capital for mortgages regionally, not nationally or internationally, which led to regional imbalances and credit crunches. Finally, the mortgage market lacked a well-established mechanism for diversifying the heightened risks of subprime loans through the capital markets. In a few short years, however, a series of innovations solved these problems and paved the way for the subprime market.

Transformation of the Residential Mortgage Market

In the 1970s and 1980s, technological advances revolutionized residential mortgage lending. For example, *statistical credit scoring models* and *automated underwriting* enabled pricing of disparate credit risks and allowed people who had previously been deemed unqualified for loans to get credit. Before the advent of these technologies, underwriters analyzed residential loan applications manually, drawing on personal experience, intuition, and strict underwriting standards. With the introduction of the new tools, analysts concluded that traditional underwriting requirements such as a 20 percent down payment, two to three months of expenses in savings, continuous employment for one to two years, stellar credit records, low debt ratios, and full documentation could be relaxed

24. Stiglitz and Weiss (1981, pp. 394–97); Munnell and others (1996, pp. 25–53); Engel and McCoy (2002a, pp. 1271–273).

25. See also Engel and McCoy (2002a, p. 1275).

without significantly boosting default rates. Eventually, the automated technologies caught on and gave lenders confidence to offer home loans with reduced down payments or piggyback loans, lower savings requirements, higher debt-to-income ratios, stated income underwriting, and liberal employment standards.[26]

The second innovation was *securitization,* which made capital markets financing available to originators to lend while allowing them to spread the risk of long-term mortgages among secondary market investors. Securitization consists of bundling loans, selling them to a trust, and carving the cash flows from the mortgages into bonds sold to investors that are backed by the collateral underlying the mortgages. This new technology, which was the brainchild of Salomon Brothers' Lewis Ranieri, became commonplace in the prime market in the 1980s once Freddie Mac and Fannie Mae embraced it. The Secondary Mortgage Market Enhancement Act (SMMEA) of 1984 made it easier for private entities to issue private mortgage-backed securities and for banks and thrifts to buy these securities.[27] Subsequently, once statistical modeling and automated underwriting gave mortgage professionals the confidence to price subprime loans, securitization expanded to the subprime market in the early 1990s.[28]

Securitization paved the way for the emergence of subprime lending in several critical respects. First, it solved the "term mismatch" problem of lenders, who previously had been forced to hold most mortgages in portfolio and thus borrow short and lend long. With securitization, lenders could sell their mortgages to investors for cash and get them off their books. At the same time, securitization sliced and diced the added risk of subprime mortgages into ever finer strips and spread it among millions of investors, who were arguably better able to diversify that risk than lenders. Securitization also relieved lenders of any need to maintain deep capital reserves. Instead, in a continual cycle, lenders could make a batch of loans, collect up-front fees from the borrowers, securitize the loans, and then plow

26. Fannie Mae, Freddie Mac, and private lenders all adopted the flexible lending standards afforded by automated underwriting (Gates, Perry, and Zorn 2002); U.S. Census Bureau 2002); Belsky and Calder (2004, p. 8); Belsky and Retsinas (2005).

27. Codified in scattered sections of the United States Code at 12 U.S.C. §§ 24, 105, 1464(c)(1)(R), 1757(15); 15 U.S.C. §§ 77r-1(a), (c), 78c(a)(41), 78g(g), 78h(a), 78k(d)(1). Among other things, SMMEA exempted "mortgage-related securities" from registration under state blue sky laws (subject to state opt-out); authorized shelf registration for these securities; amended the margin requirements to permit bona fide delayed delivery of these securities; preempted state investment laws that would otherwise block state-chartered financial institutions, pension funds, and insurance companies from investing in these securities (also subject to state opt-out); and expanded the powers of federal chartered banks, credit unions, and thrift institutions to hold mortgage-backed securities as assets. See also Pittman (1989); Shenker and Colletta (1991, pp. 1386–388); Gambro and Leichtner (1997, pp. 140–41, 153–54, 167–68).

28. Ranieri (1996) and Engel and McCoy (2007, pp. 2045–048; 2007b, pp. 1273–274). For a more detailed description of the process of securitization, see Engel and McCoy (2007, pp. 2045–063).

the cash proceeds into a new set of loans, which in turn would be securitized. Finally, securitization injected huge sums of capital into lenders from investors who were hungry for higher returns. This capital markets finance tool opened the door for a new breed of nonbank subprime lender, who was thinly capitalized, free from federal banking regulation, and indifferent to the reputational concerns of banks and thrifts.[29]

New government incentives to lend to low- and moderate-income borrowers were the last development leading to the rise of the subprime market. Federal legislation that established affordable housing goals for Fannie Mae and Freddie Mac, consisting of quotas for loan purchases from low- and moderate-income households and high-minority or low-income census tracts, pushed both government-sponsored entities (GSEs) into wholesale purchases of subprime mortgage-backed securities.[30] Similarly, the Community Reinvestment Act (CRA) of 1977 (and subsequent amendments) rewarded federally insured banks and thrifts for originating or buying mortgages to minority and lower income borrowers.[31] Meanwhile, President George W. Bush promoted expanded home ownership for the working class through his Ownership Society initiative, aided by the American Dream Downpayment Act of 2003,[32] which authorized subsidies to 40,000 low-income households per year to cover down payments and closing costs. The legacy of historical discrimination against blacks and Hispanics guaranteed pent-up demand for these new loans.

As these developments converged, subprime mortgages experienced meteoric growth from 1994 through 2006. In 1994, subprime mortgage originations were only a drop in the bucket, totaling $35 billion and accounting for only five percent of total new mortgages that year. By 2005, subprime originations had soared to $625 million and made up fully one-fifth of total mortgage originations. Subprime originations declined in 2006 to $600 billion and dropped precipitously in 2007 to $191 billion.[33]

---

29. Engel and McCoy (2007, pp. 2045, 2056–057; 2002b, p. 1274).

30. In recent years, Fannie Mae and Freddie Mac helped meet their affordable housing goals by purchasing AAA-rated subprime mortgage bonds. See, for example, Fannie Mae (2007, p. 8), which states "approximately 2 percent of [Fannie Mae's] single-family mortgage credit book of business as of both March 31, 2007 and December 31, 2006 consisted of private-label mortgage-related securities backed by subprime mortgage loans and, to a lesser extent, resecuritizations of private-label mortgage-related securities backed by subprime mortgage loans." According to the Office of Federal Housing Enterprise Oversight (OFHEO 2007), the investment portfolios of the two GSEs together contained $170 billion in private-label subprime mortgage-backed securities as of September 2007.

31. Engel and McCoy (2002a; 2002b, pp. 1276–277). See also Federal Financial Institutions Examination Council (2001), which explains the conditions under which mortgage-backed securities receive CRA credit.

32. 42 U.S.C. § 12821. See generally "Fact Sheet: America's Ownership Society: Expanding Opportunities Increasing Homeownership" (www.whitehouse.gov/news/releases/2004/08/2004 0809-9.html).

33. Gramlich (2007a, p. 6); Inside Mortgage Finance (2008, vol. I, p. 4).

Predatory Lending Concerns and Partial Re-Regulation

Early in the emergence of the subprime mortgage market, concerns surfaced about lending abuses. These concerns spurred Congress into action, and in 1994, Congress passed the Home Ownership and Equity Protection Act (HOEPA), which prohibits certain predatory lending practices in the costliest subprime loans. HOEPA applies only to "high-cost" refinance loans, which the statute defines as refinance mortgages that exceed either of the following two thresholds: (1) where the annual percentage rate (APR) at closing exceeds the yield on the comparable Treasury security plus eight (ten) percent for first-lien (junior-lien) loans; or (2) where total points and fees exceed the greater of eight percent of the total loan amount or $400 (indexed annually).[34]

HOEPA regulates terms and practices for nonpurchase loans that qualify as high-cost loans. For those loans, among other things, HOEPA and its implementing regulations restrict or ban the following: balloon clauses, loans without regard to the borrowers' ability to pay, negative amortization, increased interest rates after default, prepayment penalties, due-on-demand clauses, payments to home improvement contractors, and early refinancings. In addition, lenders who make HOEPA loans must provide special truth in lending disclosures to loan applicants in advance of closing. Lenders that violate HOEPA and their assignees are liable to borrowers for violations of the act.[35]

HOEPA's narrow coverage has proved to be a serious Achilles' heel. Lenders discovered that they could evade HOEPA's triggers by switching to adjustable-rate mortgages (ARMs) featuring teaser rates with low initial APRs. As a result, even though the Federal Reserve Board lowered HOEPA's triggers effective in 2002, HOEPA still applied to only one percent of all subprime home loans.[36]

In the years following HOEPA's passage in 1994, allegations of predatory lending continued to mount.[37] The majority of states stepped into the breach, enacting antipredatory lending statutes of their own. Most of these state statutes were patterned after HOEPA and had lower triggers, more stringent loan restrictions, or both. By the beginning of 2007, twenty-nine states and the District of Columbia had "mini-HOEPA" laws. Some of these states—along with other states—also had older provisions on their books restricting prepayment penalties and sometimes balloon terms. In addition, other states that eschewed mini-HOEPA laws implemented alternative approaches to predatory lending, such as broker

---

34. 15 U.S.C. § 1602(aa)(1)–(4); 12 C.F.R. § 226.32(a)(1), (b)(1). In 2007 the dollar trigger equaled $561 (72 *Fed. Reg.* 44032, August 7, 2007).

35. 15 U.S.C. § 1640(a); 12 C.F.R. §§ 226.32, 226.34. HOEPA's assignee liability provisions are broad and holders of HOEPA loans are "subject to all claims and defenses . . . that could be raised against the original lender" (15 U.S.C. § 1641(d)(1)).

36. Gramlich (2007a, p. 28).

37. For a partial list of adjudications, settlements, and consent orders in cases alleging predatory subprime mortgages, see Engel and McCoy (2007, pp. 2063–065, n. 121).

certification, licensing statutes, disclosure laws, or state banking regulations. State antipredatory lending laws of one type or another became so widespread that by the start of 2007, only six states—Arizona, Delaware, Montana, North Dakota, Oregon, and South Dakota—did not regulate any of the subprime loan terms generating the greatest concern, namely prepayment penalties, balloon clauses, or mandatory arbitration clauses.[38]

Backlash: Preemption Rulings by Federal Banking Regulators

The states that enacted antipredatory lending laws did not legislate in a vacuum. Instead, they instituted their laws against a background of federal preemption that suspended the effect of those state laws for certain loan products and lenders. Recall that DIDMCA, for example, nullified interest caps by states on first-lien mortgages on residential structures and mobile homes and conferred most favored lender status on state banks, thrifts, and credit unions, thereby allowing them to export their home-state usury laws to other states for junior-lien and other types of loans. AMTPA overturned state restrictions on adjustable-rate, balloon-term, and negative-amortization loans. In addition to these two congressional statutes, beginning in the mid-1990s, the OTS issued scores of opinion letters and several sets of regulations asserting federal preemption of state laws that restrict residential mortgages for federal savings associations. OTS preemption solidified in 1996 when the OTS adopted a sweeping preemption regulation.[39]

The OTS regulations predated the modern state antipredatory lending laws. Starting in 1999, as more and more states adopted those laws, national banks and their mortgage-lending subsidiaries lobbied their federal regulator, the Office of the Comptroller of the Currency (OCC), to afford them the same relief as federal thrifts. Eager to accommodate its regulated entities and to encourage state banks to convert their charters to federal charters, the OCC issued its now-famous 2004 regulation that was virtually identical to the preemption regulation adopted by the OTS. In retrospect, it is apparent that both agencies conferred broad federal preemption on the institutions that they regulate in order to win more charters to their supervisory fold.[40]

Collectively, these pronouncements permit national banks and federal saving associations to ignore a whole host of state credit protection laws.[41] Certain types

38. Bostic and others (2008, pp. 49, 55–58).

39. 12 C.F.R. § 560.2.

40. Office of the Comptroller of the Currency (2004b), codified at 12 C.F.R. §§ 34.3 (mortgage lending) and 7.4008 (general lending). See also Wilmarth (2004a, p. 37). In contrast, state-chartered banks, credit unions, and independent nondepository lenders do not have the same support in the law to claim broad preemption of state law (Renuart and Keest 2003, sections 3.6, 3.7).

41. For example, these institutions can make mortgage loans without regard to state laws relating to:

(1) licensing, registration, or reporting by creditors;

of state laws are enforceable against federal savings associations and national banks, but only if they incidentally affect the exercise of the institutions' powers. In addition, state agencies have no right to enforce even applicable state laws, such as state lending discrimination laws, against these institutions. Arguably, such visitorial powers vest solely in the OTS and the OCC.[42] Furthermore, before 2008, neither of these federal agencies replaced the preempted state laws with any comparable, binding consumer protection regulations of its own, thus creating a consumer protection vacuum for federally chartered banks and thrifts. In their most controversial move, which was upheld by the Supreme Court,[43] the agencies extended bank preemption privileges to the operating subsidiaries of these depositories.

The cloak of federal preemption helped boost the attractiveness of being owned by (or merging with) a federally chartered depository institution, in comparison with remaining an independent nonbank lender. Moreover, the justification for limiting the benefits of federal preemption to depository institutions and their operating subsidiaries proved to be elastic and easily manipulated. Recently, both

---

(2) the ability of a creditor to require or obtain insurance for collateral or other credit enhancement or risk mitigant;

(3) loan-to-value ratios;

(4) the terms of credit, including the schedule for repayment of principal and interest, amortization of loans, balance, payments due, minimum payments, term to maturity of the loan, or the ability to call the loan due and payable upon the passage of time or a specified event external to the loan;

(5) escrow or similar accounts;

(6) security property;

(7) access to and use of credit reports;

(8) disclosure and advertising requirements in credit application forms, credit solicitations, billing statement, credit contracts, or other related documents;

(9) disbursements and repayments;

(10) rates of interest;

(11) the aggregate amount of funds that can be loaned upon the security of real estate; processing, origination, servicing, sale, or purchase of, investment in, or participation in mortgages;

(12) due-on-sale clauses, with some exceptions; and

(13) covenants and restrictions that must be contained in a lease to make it qualify as acceptable security for a real estate loan.

For discussion of these rules and their consequences, see also Wilmarth (2004b, pp. 233–36); Renuart and Keest (2005, sections 3.4.6.1, 3.4.6.2, 3.5.3); and Peterson (2007, pp. 70–72).

42. 12 U.S.C. § 484, 12 C.F.R. § 7.4000 (OCC visitorial powers) and *Fidelity Fed. Sav. & Loan Ass'n* v. *de la Cuesta,* 458 U.S. 141 (1982). OTS regulations cover saving associations from cradle to grave. The courts retain power to enforce applicable law when cases are filed by private litigants, however.

Areas of state law that are not preempted include contract, tort, criminal, homestead, rights to collect debts, property, taxation, and zoning laws. The agencies, however, reserve the right to decide, on a selective and ad hoc basis, that these and any other state laws are preempted.

43. *Watters* v. *Wachovia Bank, N.A.,* 127 S. Ct. 1559, 1564 (2007). See OTS, 12 C.F.R. § 559.3(h); OCC, 12 C.F.R. § 7.4006; Wilmarth (2004b, pp. 306–11, 353–56). Frank Alexander (1993) correctly forecast this development more than a decade before the OCC adopted its preemption rule.

agencies opined that mere agents or independent contractors of these depositories, in certain circumstances, are entitled to preempt state registration and licensing laws.[44] Consequently, the paramount question of what law, if any, applies to the four corners of any given consumer credit contract is difficult to discern.

Taken together, these federal preemption statutes and rules create major loopholes in the applicability and enforcement of state antipredatory laws and credit regulation. The most important loophole exempts federally chartered banks and thrifts from state provisions and supervision. Specifically, federal savings associations, national banks, and their nonbank lending subsidiaries are free from state antipredatory lending laws under federal banking regulators' interpretations of the Home Owners' Loan Act and the National Bank Act, respectively.[45] In addition, some states, such as Georgia, have parity or wild-card laws that exempt state-chartered banks and thrifts and their subsidiaries from state antipredatory lending laws to the same extent as national banks and federal thrifts. In those states, antipredatory lending laws apply only to independent nondepository mortgage lenders. These independent lenders originated less than half—45.7 percent—of higher-cost mortgages made in 2006.[46] Even in regulated states, the degree of regulation applying to independent nondepository mortgage lenders depends on the strength and coverage of a particular state's law. Finally, DIDMCA and AMTPA relieve even independent lenders from state restrictions on usury and adjustable-rate, negative amortization, and balloon clauses—except in "plain vanilla," fixed-rate, fully amortizing mortgages.

Dual Regulation of the Home Mortgage Market

As our discussion of federal preemption suggests, the mortgage-lending industry operates under a dual regulatory structure that varies according to the entity. Depository institutions are regulated under federal banking laws, and a subset

44. OCC, 66 *Fed. Reg.* 28593 (May 23, 2001); OTS Letter P-2004-7 (October 25, 2004), available at www.ots.treas.gov/docs/5/560404.pdf). The increased attractiveness of the federal depository charter may explain the fact that from 2004—when the OCC unveiled its preemption rule—to 2006, the total market share of higher-priced residential mortgages made by independent mortgage companies shrank from 50.6 to 45.7 percent. Over the same time period, the total market share of higher-priced residential mortgages originated by depository institutions and their subsidiaries and affiliates grew from 49.4 percent in 2004 to 54.3 percent in 2006 (Avery, Brevoort, and Canner 2007, pp. A88–A89); see also Wilmarth (2004b, pp. 358–59). In a similar vein, from 2004 to 2007, the percentage of total U.S. commercial banking assets held by national banks (including their shares in mortgage lending subsidiaries) grew 19 percent, from 57 to 68 percent (OCC 2004a, p. 7; OCC 2007, p. 9).

45. See, for example, OCC (2003), available at *Fed. Reg.* 46264 (August 5, 2003) for the OCC preemption of Georgia law and OTS Letter (2003), available at www.ots.treas.gov/docs/5/56306.pdf for the OTS preemption of New Mexico law.

46. Avery, Brevoort, and Canner (2007, pp. A88–A89). For examples of state wild-card laws, see Ga. Code Ann. §7-6A-12; Johnson (1995).

of those institutions—namely, federally chartered depositories and their subsidiaries—claim that they are exempt from state antipredatory lending and credit laws by virtue of federal regulation. In contrast, independent nondepository mortgage lenders escape most federal banking regulation but must comply with state laws, except for state provisions preempted by DIDMCA and AMTPA. Only state-chartered banks and thrifts in some states (a dwindling group) are subject to both sets of laws.

Under the dual system of regulation, depository institutions are subject to a variety of federal examinations, including fair lending, CRA, and safety and soundness assessments. Independent lenders are not subject to these examinations. Similarly, banks and thrifts must comply with other CRA provisions, including reporting requirements and merger review. Federally insured depository institutions must also meet minimum risk-based capital requirements and reserve requirements, unlike their independent nondepository counterparts.

The parallel regulatory universe that consists of federally chartered banks and thrifts and their mortgage-lending subsidiaries had serious implications for consumer protections for loans made by those lenders. Because of federal preemption, the only antipredatory lending provisions that national banks and federally chartered thrifts had to obey were HOEPA and agency guidances on subprime and nontraditional mortgage lending. Of these, HOEPA has an extremely narrow scope.[47] Meanwhile, the guidances lack the binding effect of rules and their substantive content is not as strict as the stronger state laws. In the main, the guidances are enforced through federal bank examinations, backed by the possibility of agency enforcement. For mortgage-lending affiliates of banks and thrifts, however, federal examinations were sparse to nonexistent through 2006. This creates a significant loophole, because these lightly regulated lending subsidiaries accounted for one-quarter of all subprime originations in 2006.[48] The OCC was also demonstrably lax with respect to enforcement actions against national banks. The public record reveals only a handful of OCC actions against national banks—mostly small institutions—for violations of consumer protection laws. Left untouched were some of the largest national bank franchises—including Citibank

47. Board of Governors of the Federal Reserve System and others (1999); Federal Deposit Insurance Corporation (2007); OCC and others (2001, 2006, 2007). Of course, these lenders, like all lenders, are subject to prosecution in cases of fraud. Lenders are also subject to the Federal Trade Commission Act, 15 U.S.C. §§ 41-58, which prohibits unfair and deceptive acts and practices (UDAPs). Federal banking regulators, though, did not adopt rules to define and punish UDAP violations by mortgage lenders until July 2008 and then primarily only for higher-priced loans (73 *Fed. Reg.* 44522, July 30, 2008). Furthermore, those rules do not take effect until October 1, 2009.

For 2006, covered lenders reported only making 15,172 HOEPA loans nationwide, which accounted for less than 0.1 percent of all originations of mortgage refinancings and home improvement loans nationwide (Avery, Brevoort, and Canner 2007, p. 22 and table 4).

48. Avery, Brevoort, and Canner (2007, table 9). The late Federal Reserve governor Ned Gramlich stressed in his book on subprime lending that the Federal Reserve almost never examined mortgage lending affiliates of banks (Gramlich 2007b, pp. 8–9).

and Fleet Bank—that were subject to enforcement action by other state or federal agencies for alleged predatory lending violations.[49] The OCC's inaction, coupled with ineffectual examinations and guidances, epitomized the breakdown in federal regulation that fueled the subprime crisis.

All this would have been of less concern if borrowers could privately pursue federally chartered depository institutions and their mortgage-lending subsidiaries. But the guidances provided no private relief to borrowers from those institutions, either in the form of private rights of action or defenses to collection or foreclosure, unless those borrowers had HOEPA loans. Instead, the vast majority of injured borrowers with home mortgages from national banks, federal thrifts, or their subsidiaries could only turn to federal call centers—which have a policy of not intervening on behalf of customers—for help. These poorly staffed call centers stop with lamely advising consumers that "[i]f your case involves [a factual or contractual dispute between the bank and the customer], we will suggest that you consult an attorney for assistance."[50]

This unlevel playing field left lenders and borrowers alike dissatisfied. Although national banks, federal savings associations, and their lending subsidiaries enjoy federal preemption, they nevertheless complain that independent lenders are free from federal examinations and the strictures of CRA. In response, independent lenders protest that they are handicapped vis-à-vis lenders who have federal preemption because they must comply with a patchwork of differing and sometimes demanding state laws. Meanwhile, borrowers with loans from federally chartered depository institutions or from lenders in lightly regulated or unregulated states lacked protection against predatory lending practices and foreclosures. In late 2007, matters came to a head after mounting subprime foreclosures threw the capital markets into a tailspin. The House of Representatives passed a federal antipredatory lending bill, Senator Christopher Dodd (D-Conn.), chairman of the Senate Committee on Banking, Housing, and Urban Affairs, introduced an even stronger bill, and the Federal Reserve finally adopted a subprime mortgage rule.[51]

Consequences of Deregulation and Preemption

The past quarter century has revealed the effects of federal deregulation on the mortgage market and homeowners. First, mortgage lenders, whether configured as banking institutions or finance companies, could charge any interest rate and specify fees in unlimited amounts when originating mortgage loans, opening the floodgates to predatory lenders that imposed high rates and fees. Second, home

49. Engel and McCoy (2008, pp. 2063–065, n. 121); Wilmarth (2004b, pp. 353–57); and Wilmarth (2007, pp. 14–16).

50. U.S. Government Accountability Office (GAO; 2006b, pp. 8–9, 23–25) and Wilmarth (2007, pp. 17–19).

51. H.R. 3915; S. 2452; 73 *Fed. Reg.* 44522 (July 30, 2008).

equity debt grew significantly after 1983 because, in part, it was marketed to pay off other debts, thus shifting both non-mortgage-secured and unsecured debt into home-secured debt. Third, the DIDMCA created an economic incentive for lenders to engage in loan flipping, which injured borrowers who sought to tap their home equity. Under that statute, lenders can avoid state usury laws that govern second-lien home equity loans and lines of credit by refinancing the original mortgage and taking first-lien position. In this way, the lenders qualify for DIDMCA's interest preemption and earn higher fees on the larger loan principal. Fourth, although banks and savings and loan associations dominated the mortgage origination market in 1982 (compared to nondepository finance companies), these roles had been reversed by 1996.[52] This change is significant because finance companies, whether stand-alone companies or affiliates of banks, are credited with a substantial portion of predatory lending.

Explosive Growth of Adjustable-Rate Mortgages

The growth of ARM products can be tied directly to the passage of AMTPA because it paved the way for lenders to make these loans without regard to consumer protections under state law. Just from 2001 to 2006, the dollar volume of ARMs grew from $355 billion to $1.3 trillion. The percentage of ARM loans (not including interest-only ARMs) originated from 1998 to 2004 increased from 32 percent to almost 55 percent. In recent years, lenders sold nontraditional ARMs in increasing numbers. These products include 2/28 or 3/27 ARMs (many with starter rates for two or three years, followed by conversion to the fully indexed rate); interest-only ARMs (permitting interest-only payments for a set period of time during which the rate may fluctuate, resulting in rising payments); option-payment ARMs (offering up to four payment options, including minimum and interest-only payments, which, if chosen, result in negative amortization and rising principal); and 40-year ARMs (in which payments are calculated based on a 40-year payment term but the loan terminates in 30 years, resulting in a final large balloon payment).[53]

These nontraditional ARMs are so complex that even savvy borrowers have difficulty understanding the risks that they present. Worse yet, subprime lenders

52. Kennickell, Starr-McCluer, and Sundén (1997, p. 20); OTS (2002, pp. 60542–0545, n. 14); 67 *Fed. Reg.* 60545 n. 14 (September 26, 2002). Flipping is the practice whereby lenders refinance homeowners from one loan to another without providing any real net benefit to the borrower. Instead, the refinance increases revenues to brokers and lenders and strips equity from the home. OTS (2002, pp. 60542–0548, n. 35).

The proportion of families borrowing through mortgage loans grew between 1989 and 1995 and the median amount of mortgage debt outstanding rose almost 30 percent (Kennickell, Starr-McCluer, and Sundén 1997, pp. 16–17). The share of households using nonmortgage installment borrowing declined in the same period, suggesting a substitution of borrowing via mortgage loans, among others. See also Mansfield (2000, pp. 522–26, 539–51).

53. Avery, Brevoort, and Canner (2007, pp. 8–9); Cagan (2006, pp. 24–27); Duncan (2006, p. 18); Inside Mortgage Finance (2007, vol. I, p. 4); Schloemer and others (2006, p. 46).

peddled many of these loans to borrowers who not only did not understand them but had little chance of avoiding default. These nontraditional mortgages were offered "by more lenders to a wider spectrum of borrowers who [might] not otherwise qualify for more traditional mortgage loans and [might] not fully understand the associated risks." Many of these products were underwritten with less stringent income and asset verification requirements ("reduced documentation") and were often combined with simultaneous second-lien loans, leaving borrowers with little or no equity. Indeed, federal banking agencies were sufficiently alarmed about the increased risk that these products posed to financial institutions that they issued guidelines in 2006 addressing risk management and safety and soundness concerns. As well they should have, given that these controversial "exotic" ARMs had exploded in just three years, with dollar volume rising from $205 billion in 2004 to $775 billion in 2006.[54]

The risks associated with these loans are evident from the increased foreclosure rates (and loss of homes to homeowners). Between 1998 and 2003, the foreclosure risk of these ARMs was 62 to 123 percent higher than that of fixed-rate mortgages.[55] Balloon loans posed a foreclosure risk ranging between 14.1 and 85.9 percent higher than loans without this feature.

By late 2006, the first wave of the risky ARMs made from 2004 through 2006 came due to reset and the house of cards collapsed. Housing prices declined on a national basis for the first time since the Great Depression, sharply in some markets, and distressed borrowers discovered that they had limited options. Rising interest rates, stricter underwriting, and harsh prepayment penalties made it difficult to refinance, while falling real estate values made it hard for delinquent borrowers to sell their homes. Defaults soared and so did foreclosures. In July 2008, Treasury Secretary Henry Paulson projected 4 million foreclosure starts in total for calendar years 2007 and 2008. The previous fall, the U.S. Congress Joint Economic Committee predicted that subprime foreclosures would directly destroy $71 billion in housing wealth and another $32 billion in housing wealth because of the spillover effect of those foreclosures on surrounding properties. The Joint Committee further forecast that states and cities would lose more than $917 million in property tax revenues brought on by subprime foreclosures.[56]

State Responses to Federal Preemption

Another result of federal preemption has been the process state legislatures have undertaken to reconsider what role, if any, usury statutes should play in a modern economy. Many states chose one of two paths. They repealed their general

54. Interagency Guidance (2006, p. 17); Inside Mortgage Finance (2007, vol. I, p. 6). Fishbein and Woodall (2006, pp. 19–21) arqued that these loans are "toxic" and describe the payment shock that can await consumers who hold these loans.

55. Schloemer and others (2006, p. 21).

56. U.S. Department of the Treasury (2008); U.S. Congress Joint Economic Committee (2007).

usury ceilings completely (or for particular types of credit) or they modified their interest ceilings to permit them to fluctuate with some published market rate. A smaller group of states retained their usury ceilings embodied in lending laws, criminal codes, or state constitutions.

Many states in both groups replaced or augmented their traditional usury laws with newer types of credit regulation in the form of state mini-HOEPA laws. For both groups of states, however, the legal landscape now prevents them from enforcing these laws against national banks, federal savings associations, and their mortgage-lending subsidiaries.

These developments heralded the rise of the philosophy that disclosure is a "market-perfecting" mechanism and preferable to any regulation of the terms and conditions of credit in a market economy. TILA, as the primary federal disclosure law, now shoulders most of the consumer protection load. This means that the consumer credit marketplace is governed almost exclusively by disclosure rules. Unfortunately, though not surprisingly, the provision of information about proposed credit terms did not control unscrupulous or greedy market forces. Not only are the mandated disclosures woefully inadequate, but consumers operate on an unequal playing field in relation to mortgage brokers and lenders. Contracts are not negotiated (consumers must take it or leave it), information asymmetries benefit industry players, and fraudulent marketing techniques lure potential borrowers into the trap. Subprime mortgage lending did not exist before 1980. Instead, its gestation and birth occurred in the current deregulated environment.[57]

Business Models in the Current Environment

The vast majority of consumer credit lenders are either depository or nondepository institutions. Depository lenders, which include banks, savings associations, credit unions, and industrial loan banks,[58] accept deposits from their customers and lend money to the public, or, in the case of credit unions, to their members.

---

57. Edwards (2005, p. 204); Engel and McCoy (2002a, pp. 1272–273, 1280–283, 1299); Peterson (2003, p. 881); U.S. Government Accountability Office (2006a, p. 6).

58. Industrial loan companies (ILCs) or industrial banks are state-chartered and state-regulated financial institutions. ILCs have active charters in seven states—California, Colorado, Hawaii, Indiana, Minnesota, Nevada, and Utah. Federal law treats an ILC the same as any other state-chartered bank, with one important exception—an industrial bank can be owned by a commercial enterprise that does not thereby become a bank holding company. Because ILCs are creatures of state law, state law generally applies to most of their activities. In addition, the state in which they are chartered will determine whether ILCs are different from a bank in any functional manner. For most purposes, ILCs can function as banks. Like other state-chartered banks, ILCs may be eligible for Federal Deposit Insurance Corporation (FDIC) insurance (although the FDIC placed a temporary moratorium on ILC deposit insurance applications by holding companies engaged in commerce that expired in January 2008 (Federal Deposit Insurance Corporation 2007). This insurance is useful—an insured state bank, including an ILC, is entitled to interest rate exportation and most favored lender status to the same extent as a national bank (Renuart and Keest 2003, section 3.7A 2007 Supp.).

Table 4-1. *Who Is in Charge*

Type of lender	Primary supervisor(s)[a]
National bank (and its nonbank operating subsidiaries)	Office of the Comptroller of the Currency (OCC)
Federal savings association, federal savings bank (and their nonbank operating subsidiaries)	Office of Thrift Supervision (OTS)
Federal credit union	National Credit Union Administration (NCUA)
State bank, state savings bank, or industrial loan bank	State Banking Commissioner, Federal Reserve Board (if a member of the Federal Reserve System) or Federal Deposit Insurance Corporation (FDIC) (if not a member of the Federal Reserve System)
State savings association	State S&L Commissioner and the OTS
State credit union	State credit union administrator and National Credit Union Share Insurance Fund, if insured
Finance companies, other lenders	State financial institution agencies

a. The Federal Reserve Board also supervises bank holding companies and the nonbank sister affiliates of banks. Following the passage in 1994 of the Interstate Banking and Branching Efficiency Act, the FDIC, the Federal Reserve Board, and state banking supervisors entered into cooperative agreements that address examinations of state-chartered banks with out-of-state branches. Accordingly, state banking supervisors may examine state-chartered banks in their states, sometimes including branches located in other states. However, the state bank's primary federal supervisor, either the FDIC or the Federal Reserve Board, can and does conduct its own examinations, generally in alternate years.

Federal law primarily controls the creation and operation of national banks, federal savings associations, and federal credit unions. Their chartering laws are, respectively, the National Bank Act, the Home Owners' Loan Act, and the Federal Credit Union Act. State law primarily governs the creation and some operations of state-chartered banks, credit unions, and industrial loan companies. Every state has a banking law, but extensive federal safety and soundness regulation applies to most state-chartered depositories because almost all of them subscribe to federal deposit insurance, either from the FDIC or the National Credit Union Administration (NCUA).

Nondepository lenders include mortgage finance companies, retailers, convenience lenders, payday and auto title lenders, and pawnbrokers. These businesses are primarily regulated under state law, apart from businesses that are subsidiaries of federally chartered banks or thrifts. Table 4-1 presents the supervisors and the supervised in the consumer credit market.

Given the legal environment we described earlier in this chapter, lenders consider several factors when deciding on a structural business model. Initially, the lender must decide whether to incorporate as a depository or nondepository.[59] If

59. A bank charter has a "franchise" value. For example:
   (1) the bank chartering process erects high barriers to new entrants and dampens competition by making expansion by banks and thrifts subject to government approval;

the choice is to become a depository, other questions arise: Which type of charter (federal or state) and which banking supervisor are preferable, and where should the institution locate its headquarters? If the choice is to become a nondepository, the next question becomes in which state or states should the lender incorporate and do business?

The banking system consists of two parallel tracks for banks and thrifts—those that operate under federal charters and those that operate under state charters. Depository institutions can choose to be chartered primarily by a federal or a state agency. Entry controls exist, however, that are designed to keep out risky enterprises and manage competition for existing banks. The type of bank powers, the extent of preemption rights available to a depository institution, and the legal infrastructure under which it will operate flow from this choice.[60]

When deciding on a depository versus a nondepository charter, a lender considers several factors. Banks must abide by risk-based capital and reserve requirements that are much more stringent than asset rules or bonding requirements under state lender licensing laws.[61] For nondepositories, fees for licensing and examination are invariably lower and any examinations are generally more lenient and less frequent.[62] By using bank holding companies and operating subsidiaries, depository institutions can expand into products that are off-limits to banks and thrifts themselves, diversify risk and smooth revenues through multiple lines of business, isolate activities presenting increased risk in nonbank subsidiaries, and utilize certain tax advantages. Finally, banks and thrifts can convert their charters without permission or conditions from their current regulator, as long as they receive permission from the new chartering agency. This permits depositories to

---

(2) the charter provides access to federal deposit insurance, which confers a unique competitive advantage in attracting customers;

(3) federal deposit insurance allows banks and thrifts to acquire deposits inexpensively because insured depositors do not receive high interest payments for the use of their money;

(4) possession of a charter gives banks access to the Federal Reserve's payment system, critical to the quick and efficient movement of money;

(5) insured depository institutions can access the Federal Reserve's discount window for short-term liquidity shortfalls; and

(6) a bank charter is critical if U.S. banks are to obtain banking privileges in many foreign countries (McCoy 2000, § 3.02[2]).

60. McCoy (2000, chapter 3) discusses the history of the dual banking system and the choices among charters.

61. All banks, thrifts, and credit unions must hold approximately 10 percent of their transaction accounts in reserve with a federal reserve bank or similar institution. McCoy (2000, § 11.05). All insured depository institutions are further subject to minimum risk-based capital requirements. McCoy (2000, § 6.03).

62. The federal banking agencies must conduct a "full-scope," on-site examination of each insured depository institution every twelve or eighteen months (12 U.S.C. § 1820(d)(1)). The Federal Deposit Insurance Act makes no mention of examinations of operating subsidiaries. Although OCC regulations do call for examinations of operating subsidiaries, they do not specify their frequency or scope (12 C.F.R. § 5.34(e)(3)). The Federal Reserve rarely, if ever, examined nonbank sister affiliate mortgage lenders of banks (Gramlich 2007a, pp. 8–9).

escape an inhospitable regulator. The ease of conversion is tempered, though, by high transaction costs.

Several questions must be answered when one chooses a particular bank supervisor.[63] Which supervisory agency offers ease and predictability of success in obtaining a charter? Which agency charges more for the chartering process, annual assessments, and examination costs? Who is toughest in the examination process? Which legal regime promises the broadest bank powers and ability to preempt state law? Finally, which charter provides the fewest restrictions to interstate branching? In the realm of mortgage banking, of all these factors, federal preemption is the most significant incentive to select a federal charter and be supervised by either the OCC or the OTS.[64]

Implications for Consumers and the Rule of Law

As we have shown, consumers take the biggest hit when well-established credit protections are repealed. Deregulation and preemption allow businesses to select not only the most favorable regulator but also which set of laws apply to them, an unprecedented shift in the consumer credit market. In addition, constitutional questions arise about our republican form of government and the sovereign role of the state in matters historically within their control. The implications of these changes are profound and merit the most careful attention by federal and state elected officials. We address these issues in the paragraphs that follow.

Banks and thrifts want to operate using a national business and legal platform. A fair generalization at this point in time—depositories and their related companies are either very large or very small. Only a small percentage of all banks are not part of a bank holding company. Large banks and their holding companies want to operate at a national level and do not want to deal with the differences among fifty sets of state law. They want federal preemption or deregulation, whichever helps them to achieve this goal.[65] Managers of banks who were queasy

63. McCoy discusses these factors in *Banking Law Manual* (2000, § 3.02[3](b)).

64. Wilmarth (2004a, p. 37). In our view, the OTS holds the lead in the preemption race, although the OCC is a close second. The national bank charter, however, offers broader powers than the charter for federal savings associations.

The OCC charges the highest fees, which helps explain its incentives to offset its cost structure by offering institutions broad federal preemption. It has a reputation for tough examinations of national banks, but not of their operating subsidiaries.

65. 69 *Fed. Reg.* 1904, 1908 (January 13, 2004) observes that "[f]or national banks . . . the ability to operate under uniform standards of operation and supervision is fundamental to the character of their national charter." Peterson (2005, p. 8) argues that "current efforts to preempt state law have little or nothing to do with federalism in general or in uniformity in particular, but are, in fact, simply efforts to deregulate."

Total U.S. commercial bank assets in 2005 exceeded $8.9 trillion. Independent banks that are not part of a bank holding company accounted for only about $212 billion, or roughly 2 percent, of this total (Report on the Condition of the U.S. Banking Industry, June 2007, p. B12).

about the trends we describe might have felt that they had no choice but to ride along with the rest.

Federal banking regulators are engaged in a race for charters. The OCC and the OTS have jockeyed over the last twelve years to make the charters and legal regimes for their institutions more desirable than each other's. The FDIC has been under pressure to keep state-chartered banks competitive by entering this race.[66] Both the OCC and the OTS pay for their operations from the chartering, annual, and examination fees they receive from their constituents, the federally chartered banks and thrifts. More and bigger is better. One way each positions itself to be more attractive is to expand activity powers and the preemption of state laws, which translates to deregulation. The bottom line: charter competition is the name of the game until and unless Congress creates a unitary chartering and supervisory system or curbs unilateral agency preemption orders.

Independent finance companies are likely to migrate into operating subsidiaries. State-licensed finance companies and lenders (other than lending subsidiaries of national banks and federal thrifts) are subject to the full panoply of state and federal law that applies to their business. These companies experience a cost disadvantage vis-à-vis banks because they must comply with state consumer protection laws. Moreover, if they conduct business in other states, they likely need to be licensed in each state. Their compliance costs rise when they enter into business in each state, particularly when they expand into many or all states. Over time, these companies are likely to sell themselves to bank holding companies, which will align them as operating subsidiaries of national banks. This reaction to the banking preemption regulations is already well under way.[67] Consequently, the recent state efforts to regulate predatory lending practices out of the market, described elsewhere in this chapter, will fall in the face of federal preemption.

---

66. Federal Deposit Insurance Corporation (2005, p. 60019) notes that the Financial Services Roundtable, a trade association for financial services companies, petitioned the FDIC to issue rules expanding the preemption powers of state-chartered banks so as to reach parity with national banks.

67. In 2004 and 2005 alone, JP Morgan Chase, HSBC, and Bank of Montreal (Harris Trust) switched from state to national bank charters (Wilmarth 2007, pp. 11–12). In 2007, another seven state banks made the same switch (Hopkins 2008). See also Finance Commission of Texas and Credit Union Commission of Texas (2006, p. 26), which reports that between January 16, 2003, and December 14, 2005, the Texas Consumer Credit Commissioner received cancellation notices for 47 licenses from companies specifically claiming federal preemption as operating subsidiaries of national banks. At least three large banks and their operating subsidiaries relinquished their licenses and sued their former state regulators when the regulators balked: National City Bank of Indiana, Wachovia Bank, and Wells Fargo Bank. See *Nat'l City Bank of Indiana* v. *Turnbaugh*, 463 F.3d 325 (4th Cir. 2006); *Wachovia Bank, N.A.* v. *Burke*, 414 F.3d 305 (2d Cir. 2005); *Wachovia Bank, N.A.* v. *Watters*, 431 F.3d 556 (6th Cir. 2005), aff'd, 127 S. Ct. 1559 (2007); *Wells Fargo Bank, N.A.* v. *Boutris*, 419 F.3d 949 (9th Cir. 2005). See also H&R Block, Inc. (2006, p. 3), which reports that the OTS approved the charter of the H&R Block Bank in March 2006 and states that "we will realign certain segments of our business to reflect a new management reporting structure."

Operating subsidiaries and affiliates can be loose cannons. In general, operating subsidiaries and affiliates of banks are rarely examined, in contrast with banks themselves, for safety and soundness. Among other things, Congress tied the hands of the Federal Reserve System in examining sister mortgage-lending affiliates of banks in the Gramm-Leach-Bliley Act of 1999 (also known as the Financial Modernization Act of 1999). The Federal Reserve cannot examine those lenders unless their activities could have a materially adverse effect on the safety and soundness of any of their sister bank or thrift affiliates, based on set criteria. Instead, to the fullest extent possible, the Federal Reserve is supposed to use bank and thrift examination reports prepared by other state and federal banking regulators.[68] In addition, banks and thrifts need not include their mortgage-lending subsidiaries in their CRA examinations.

Because of concerns about the reputational risks of banks, regulators generally prefer that the subprime activities of a bank be pushed into a subsidiary. Nonbank subsidiaries are less sensitive to reputation than the parent banks. Although examiners may be worried about safety and soundness, the failure of the subsidiary is not nearly as momentous as the failure of the parent bank. Regulators often supported higher fee-generating activities by subsidiaries and their parents on the grounds that increased revenues enhanced the continued solvency of these institutions.

The federal banking agencies are not consumer protection agencies. The OCC, the OTS, the FRB, and the FDIC are primarily concerned with bank safety and soundness, not with consumer protection. The laws that create and authorize these agencies say virtually nothing about consumer protection. Federal UDAP standards that apply to federal depository institutions are, however, embodied in the Federal Trade Commission Act.[69] Nevertheless, the consumer has no legal right to enforce those provisions. Similarly, other consumer protection rules or guidances that the OCC and the OTS might issue are unenforceable by consumers.[70] The OCC's own enforcement record has been "undistinguished."

68. Pub. L. No. 106-102, § 111 (codified at 12 U.S.C. § 1844(c)(2)(C)–(D)).

69. The Federal Trade Commission Act requires the FRB (for banks), the OTS (for saving associations), and the NCUA (for federal credit unions) to prescribe regulations defining UDAPs (15 U.S.C. § 57a(f)). These same agencies must also adopt regulations for these institutions that are "substantially similar" to regulations prohibiting acts or practices issued by the Federal Trade Commission (FTC) within 60 days after the FTC rules take effect. The FTC has issued several regulations that address particular unfair or deceptive practices. The FRB and the OTS applied some of the FTC rules related to lending activities to banks and savings associations (FRB, 12 C.F.R. part 227; OTS, 12 C.F.R. part 535). The OCC recognizes that it has no authority to define unfair or deceptive practices (69 *Fed. Reg.* 1904, 1911, n. 55, January 13, 2004).

70. Wilmarth (2007, pp. 14–15). The OCC included a single antipredatory lending provision in its broad preemption regulations of 2004 (12 C.F.R. §§ 7.4008(b), 34.3(b)). The rule prohibits national banks from making a loan based predominantly on the value of any collateral without regard to the borrower's ability to repay. The OTS published a request for public input on how it could use its authority to address UDAPs perpetrated by federal savings associations (OTS (2007)).

In 1994, Congress required the FRB to prohibit acts or practices in connection with mortgage loans that the Board finds to be unfair or deceptive. Congress specifically flagged mortgage refinancings that are associated with abusive lending practices or are not in the interest of the borrower as areas of concern.[71] In 2001, the Board used this authority to prohibit a narrow set of early refinancings of HOEPA loans and to forbid structuring a loan as open-ended in order to evade HOEPA. Only after subprime abuses triggered a full-blown economic crisis, however, did the Board amend its rules to prohibit UDAPs in other parts of the mortgage market.[72]

Preemption of state consumer credit and protection laws by depository institutions can result in the "Wild West." Where state law is displaced, a vacuum arises unless there is federal law on point to replace that loss. In the area of consumer credit, there is little federal regulation beyond the disclosure rules. In these circumstances, the contract alone controls the lender–consumer relationship. Consequently, the "law" becomes the terms listed in the contract. The lenders write the contracts, which are contracts of adhesion, meaning that the consumer cannot negotiate the printed terms. If we return primarily to the law of the contract, we return to the notion of *caveat emptor*—let the buyer beware—because no one is protecting the consumer.

State attorneys general and law enforcement agencies can only observe on the sidelines. Finally, given the visitorial powers of the OCC and the OTS, state law enforcement over federally chartered depository institutions and their mortgage-lending subsidiaries has dried up. With respect to those institutions, state attorneys general and state banking commissioners are impotent.

Conclusion

In sum, the history of subprime and nontraditional mortgage loans is a story of failure and rank indifference by the federal government. The seeds of this crisis were planted in the late 1970s and early 1980s, when Congress and the Supreme Court deregulated state usury caps on residential mortgages, thereby removing legal obstacles to the rise of the subprime market. A quarter-century later, once the subprime market had matured, rampant abuses in that market compelled a majority of the states to enact mini-HOEPA laws that regulate the terms of high-cost mortgages, but not their price. Instead of welcoming supervision by the states, however, federal banking regulators greeted the state laws with hostility. In a series of federal preemption rulings, the OCC and the OTS excused national banks and federal thrifts and their nonbank mortgage-lending subsidiaries from complying

---

71. 15 U.S.C. § 1639(1)(2).

72. 73 *Fed. Reg.* 44522 (July 30, 2008). The Board's 2001 rules appeared at Board of Governors of the Federal Reserve System (2001).

with the state laws. As a result, as long as lenders who enjoyed preemption complied with arcane federal disclosure laws, they could lend with impunity and pass off recklessly underwritten loans to unsuspecting investors through securitization. Only three short years after the OCC's preemption rule greased a race to the bottom for recklessly underwritten subprime and nontraditional loans, the U.S. economy plunged into crisis.

The dialectic of federal deregulation, state reregulation, and federal preemption has produced a dual system of regulation in which increasing numbers of aggrieved borrowers are stripped of defenses to foreclosure. This same dialectic explains why major lenders have flocked to federal preemption under the national bank and federal savings association umbrellas.

References

Alexander, Frank S. 1993. "Federal Intervention in Real Estate Finance: Preemption and Federal Common Law." *North Carolina Law Review* 71, no. 293: 300–70.

Avery, Robert B., Kenneth P. Brevoort, and Glenn B. Canner. 2007. "The 2006 HMDA Data." *Federal Reserve Bulletin* A73 (www.federalreserve.gov/pubs/bulletin/2007/pdf/hmda 06draft.pdf).

Belsky, Eric S., and Allegra Calder. 2004. "Credit Matters: Low-Income Asset Building Challenges in a Dual Financial Service System." Working Paper BABC 04-1. Harvard Joint Center for Housing Studies (JCHS).

Belsky, Eric S., and Nicolas P. Retsinas. 2005. "New Paths to Building Assets for the Poor." In *Building Assets, Building Credit: Creating Wealth in Low-Income Communities.* Brookings.

Board of Governors of the Federal Reserve System. 2001. "Truth in Lending." *Federal Register* 66, no. 245 (December 20): 65604–5622.

Board of Governors of the Federal Reserve System and others. 1999. "Interagency Guidance on Subprime Lending" (www.federalreserve.gov/boarddocs/srletters/1999/sr9906a1.pdf).

Bostic, Raphael W., and others. 2008. "State and Local Anti-Predatory Lending Laws: The Effect of Legal Enforcement Mechanisms." *Journal of Economics and Business* 60, nos. 1–2: 47–66.

Cagan, Christopher L. 2006. "Mortgage Payment Reset: The Rumor and the Reality." (www.firstamres.com/pdf/MPR_White_Paper_FINAL.pdf).

Drysdale, Lynn, and Kathleen E. Keest. 2000. "The Two-Tiered Consumer Financial Services Marketplace: The Fringe Banking System and Its Challenge to Current Thinking about the Role of Usury Laws in Today's Society." *South Carolina Law Review* 51, no. 3: 589–669.

Duncan, Doug. 2006. "Market Outlook: MBA Nonprime Conference" (www.mortgage bankers.org/ProfessionalDevelopment/UpcomingConferencesandEvents/Presentationsfrom PastConferencesandEvents/Non-PrimeLendingandAlternativeProductsConference.htm).

Edwards, Matthew A. 2005. "Empirical and Behavioral Critiques of Mandatory Disclosure: Socioeconomics and the Quest for Truth in Lending." *Cornell Journal of Law and Public Policy* 14 (Summer): 199–249.

Engel, Kathleen C., and Patricia A. McCoy. 2002a. "A Tale of Three Markets: The Law and Economics of Predatory Lending." *Texas Law Review* 80, no. 6: 1255–381.

———. 2002b. "The CRA Implications of Predatory Lending." *Fordham Urban Law Journal* 29 (April): 1571–605.

———. 2007. "Turning a Blind Eye: Wall Street Finance of Predatory Lending." *Fordham Law Review* 75 (March): 2039–103.

———. 2008. "From Credit Denial to Predatory Lending: The Challenge of Sustaining Minority Homeownership." In *Segregation: The Rising Costs for America,* edited by James H. Carr and Nandinee K. Kutty, pp. 81–123. New York: Routledge.

Fannie Mae (Federal National Mortgage Association). 2007. "Form 12b-25 for the Period Ended March 31, 2007" (www.fanniemae.com/media/pdf/newsreleases/12b25may 2007.pdf).

Federal Deposit Insurance Corporation (FDIC). 2007. "Moratorium on Certain Industrial Bank Applications and Notices." *Federal Register* 72, no. 23 (February 5): 5290–294.

Federal Deposit Insurance Corporation and others. 2007. "Statement on Loss Mitigation Strategies for Servicers of Residential Mortgages" (www.federalreserve.gov/newsevents/press/bcreg/bcreg20070904a1.pdf).

Federal Financial Institutions Examination Council. 2001. "Community Reinvestment Act; Interagency Questions and Answers regarding Community Reinvestment." *Federal Register* 66, no. 134 (July 12): 36620–6653.

Federal Housing Administration (FHA). 1959. *The FHA Story in Summary* (www.hud.gov/local/or/working/fha25year.pdf).

Federal Reserve Release. "Commercial Paper Rates and Outstanding" (www.federalreserve.gov/releases/cp [September 10, 2007]).

Federal Reserve Statistical Release. "H.15 Selected Interest Rates, Historical Data, Conventional Mortgages, Annual Rates" (www.federalreserve.gov/releases/h15/data.htm [September 13, 2007]).

Finance Commission of Texas and Credit Union Commission of Texas. 2006. "Legislative Report: Preemption of Financial Services Study" (www.fc.state.tx.us/Studies/preemption.pdf).

Fishbein, Allen J., and Patrick Woodall. 2006. "Exotic or Toxic? An Examination of the Non-Traditional Mortgage Market for Consumers and Lenders." Washington: Consumer Federation of America (www.consumerfed.org/pdfs/Exotic_Toxic_Mortgage_Report0506.pdf).

Gambro, Michael S., and Scott Leichtner. 1997. "Selected Legal Issues Affecting Securitization." *North Carolina Banking Institute* 1 (March): 131–68.

Gates, Susan Wharton, Vanessa Gail Perry, and Peter M. Zorn. 2002. "Automated Underwriting in Mortgage Lending: Good News for the Underserved?" *Housing Policy Debate* 13, no. 2: 369–91.

Gramlich, Edward M. 2007a. *Subprime Mortgages: America's Latest Boom and Bust.* Washington: Urban Institute.

———. 2007b. "Boom and Busts, The Case of Subprime Mortgages." Speech given at symposium, "Housing, Housing Finance, and Monetary Policy." Sponsored by the Federal Reserve Bank of Kansas City, Jackson Hole, Wyoming, August 31 (www.kansascityfed.org/publicat/sympos/2007/pdf/2007.09.04.gramlich.pdf).

H&R Block, Inc. 2006. "Form 10-K and Annual Report" (www.sec.gov/Archives/edgar/data/12659/000095013706007517/c04679e10vk.htm).

Hopkins, Cheyenne. 2008. "OCC Surplus Said to Prompt First Fee Cut in Years." *American Banker* 173, no. 21 (January 31): 3.

Inside Mortgage Finance. 2007. *The 2007 Mortgage Market Statistical Annual.* Bethesda, Md.

———. 2008. *The 2008 Mortgage Market Statistical Annual.* Bethesda, Md.

Johnson, Christian A. 1995. "Wild Card Statutes, Parity, and National Banks—The Renascence of State Banking Powers." *Loyola University Chicago Law Journal* 26, no. 3: 351–79.

Kaper, Stacy. 2007. "A Door Closes, and Mortgage Reform Takes Shape." *American Banker* 172, no. 154 (August 10): 1.

Keest, Kathleen E. 1995. "Whither Now? Truth in Lending in Transition—Again." *Consumer Finance Law Quarterly Report* 49 (Fall): 360–67.

Kennickell, Arthur B., Martha Starr-McCluer, and Annika E. Sundén. 1997. "Family Finances in the U.S.: Recent Evidence from the Survey of Consumer Finances." *Federal Reserve Bulletin* (January): 1–24.

Mansfield, Cathy Lesser. 2000. "The Road to Subprime 'HEL' Was Paved with Good Congressional Intentions: Usury Deregulation and the Subprime Home Equity Market." *South Carolina Law Review* 51 (Spring): 473–587.

McCoy, Patricia A. 2000. *Banking Law Manual: Federal Regulation of Financial Holding Companies, Banks and Thrifts.* 2nd ed. and cumulative supplements. Newark, N.J.: Lexis.

Munnell, Alicia H., and others. 1996. "Mortgage Lending in Boston: Interpreting HMDA Data." *American Economic Review* 86, no. 1: 25–53.

Office of the Comptroller of the Currency (OCC). 2003. "Preemption Determination and Order." *Federal Register* 68, no. 150 (August 5): 46264–6281.

———. 2004a. *Annual Report, Fiscal Year 2004* (www.occ.treas.gov/annrpt/annual.htm).

———. 2004b. "Bank Activities and Operations; Real Estate Lending and Appraisals." *Federal Register* 69, no. 8 (January 13): 1904–918.

———. 2007. *Annual Report, Fiscal Year 2007* (www.occ.treas.gov/annrpt/annual.htm).

Office of the Comptroller of the Currency and others. 2001. "Expanded Guidance for Subprime Lending Programs." Supervision and Regulation (SR) Letter 01-4 (GEN) (www.federalreserve.gov/boarddocs/srletters/2001/sr0104a1.pdf).

———. 2006. "Interagency Guidance on Nontraditional Mortgage Product Risks" (September 29) (www.federalreserve.gov/newsevents/press/bcreg/bcreg20060929a1.pdf).

———. 2007. "Statement on Subprime Mortgage Lending." (July 24) (www.federalreserve.gov/newsevents/press/bcreg/bcreg20070629a1.pdf).

Office of Federal Housing Enterprise Oversight (OFHEO). 2007. "OFHEO Director James B. Lockhart Commends GSEs on Implementation of Subprime Mortgage Lending Guidance" (September 10) (www.ofheo.gov/NewsRoom_Print.aspx?ID=382).

Office of Thrift Supervision (OTS). 2002. "Alternative Mortgage Transaction Parity Act; Preemption." *Federal Register* 67, no. 187 (September 26): 60542–0555.

———. 2007. "Unfair or Deceptive Acts or Practices." *Federal Register* 72, no. 150 (August 6): 43570–3576.

Peterson, Christopher L. 2003. "Truth, Understanding, and High-Cost Consumer Credit: The Historical Context of the Truth in Lending Act." *Florida Law Review* 55 (July): 807–903.

———. 2005. "Federalism and Predatory Lending: Unmasking the Deregulatory Agenda." *Temple Law Review* 78 (Spring): 1–98.

Pittman, Edward L. 1989. "Economic and Regulatory Developments Affecting Mortgage Related Securities." *Notre Dame Law Review* 64, no. 4: 497–551.

Ranieri, Lewis S. 1996. "The Origins of Securitization, Sources of its Growth, and Its Future Potential." In *A Primer on Securitization,* edited by Leon T. Kendall and Michael J. Fishman, pp. 31–44. MIT Press.

Renuart, Elizabeth, and Kathleen E. Keest. 2005. 3rd ed. and 2007 Supplement. *The Cost of Credit: Regulation, Preemption, and Industry Abuses.* Boston: National Consumer Law Center.

Renuart, Elizabeth, and Diane E. Thompson. 2008. "The Truth, the Whole Truth, and Nothing but the Truth: Fulfilling the Promise of Truth in Lending." *Yale Journal on Regulation* 25, no. 2: 181–245.

"Report on the Condition of the U.S. Banking Industry." 2007. *Federal Reserve Bulletin* (June): B7–B12.

Saunders, Margot, and Alys Cohen. 2004. "Federal Regulation of Consumer Credit: The Cause or the Cure for Predatory Lending." Working Paper Series BABC 04-21. Harvard Joint Center for Housing Studies (JCHS) (www.jchs.harvard.edu/publications/finance/babc/babc_04-21.pdf).

Schloemer, Ellen, and others. 2006. "Losing Ground: Foreclosures in the Subprime Market and Their Cost to Homeowners." Durham, N.C.: Center for Responsible Lending (www.responsiblelending.org/pdfs/foreclosure-paper-report-2-17.pdf).

Schroeder, John J. 2003. " 'Duel' Banking System? State Bank Parity Laws: An Examination of Regulatory Practice, Constitutional Issues, and Philosophical Questions." *Indiana Law Review* 36, no. 1: 197–222.

Shenker, Joseph C., and Anthony J. Colletta. 1991. "Asset Securitization: Evolution, Current Issues and New Frontiers." *Texas Law Review* 69 (May): 1369–429.

Stiglitz, Joseph E., and Andrew Weiss. 1981. "Credit Rationing in Markets with Imperfect Information." *American Economic Review* 71, no. 3: 393–410.

U.S. Census Bureau. 2002. *American Housing Survey for the United States: 2001.* Series H150/01. Current Housing Reports. Government Printing Office (www.census.gov/prod/2002pubs/h150-01.pdf).

U.S. Congress Joint Economic Committee. 2007. "The Subprime Lending Crisis: The Economic Impact on Wealth, Property Values and Tax Revenues, and How We Got Here" (http://jec.senate.gov/index.cfm?FuseAction=Reports.Reports&ContentRecord_id=c6627bb2-7e9c-9af9-7ac7-32b94d398d27&Region_id=&Issue_id=).

U.S. Department of the Treasury. 2008. "Remarks by Secretary Henry M. Paulson Jr. on U.S. Housing Market before FDIC's Forum on Mortgage Lending to Low and Moderate Income Households." Press Release HP-1070 (July 8) (http://www.treasury.gov/press/releases/hp1070.htm).

U.S. Government Accountability Office (GAO). 2006a. *Credit Cards: Increased Complexity in Rates and Fees Heightens Need for More Effective Disclosure to Consumers.* GAO-06-929 (www.gao.gov/new.items/d06929.pdf).

———. 2006b. *OCC Consumer Assistance: Process Is Similar to That of Other Regulators but Could Be Improved by Enhanced Outreach.* GAO-06-293 (www.gao.gov/new.items/d06293.pdf).

U.S. House of Representatives. Subcommittee on Consumer Affairs of the House Committee on Banking and Commerce. 1967. Consumer Credit Protection Act: Hearings before the Subcommittee on Consumer Affairs of the House Committee on Banking and Commerce on H.R. 11601. 90 Cong. 1 sess.

U.S. Senate Committee on Banking and Currency. 1967. "Truth in Lending 1967." Report No. 90-392. 90 Cong. 1 sess.

Wilmarth, Arthur E., Jr. 2004a. "Testimony of Arthur E. Wilmarth Jr. before the Committee on Banking, Housing, and Urban Affairs." U.S. Senate, 108 Cong. 2 sess. (April 7).

———. 2004b. "The OCC's Preemption Rules Exceed the Agency's Authority and Present a Serious Threat to the Dual Banking System." *Annual Review of Banking and Finance Law* 23, no. 1: 225–364.

———. 2007. "Written Testimony of Arthur E. Wilmarth Jr., Hearing on 'Credit Card Practices: Current Consumer and Regulatory Issues' before the Subcommittee on Financial Institutions and Consumer Credit of the Committee on Financial Services." U.S. House of Representatives, 110 Cong. 1 sess. (April 26).

5

The Impact of State Antipredatory Lending Laws: Policy Implications and Insights

RAPHAEL W. BOSTIC, KATHLEEN C. ENGEL,
PATRICIA A. MCCOY, ANTHONY PENNINGTON-CROSS,
AND SUSAN M. WACHTER

The subprime mortgage market, which consists of high-cost loans designed for borrowers with weak credit,[1] has grown tremendously over the past ten years. Between 1993 and 2005, the subprime market experienced an average annual growth rate of 26 percent.[2] As this market emerged, so did allegations that subprime loans contained predatory features or were the result of predatory sales practices.[3] In the worst cases, brokers deceived borrowers about the meaning of loan terms or falsely promised to assist them in obtaining future refinance loans

---

1. Different definitions exist for the term "subprime loans." Some limit the term's meaning to nonconforming mortgages made to borrowers with impaired or nonexistent credit. Over time, however, this definition has proven unsatisfactory, given the growing evidence that large proportions of high-cost mortgages went to borrowers with credit scores high enough to qualify for prime loans. See, for example, Rick Brooks and Ruth Simon, "Subprime Debacle Traps Even Very Credit-Worthy," *Wall Street Journal*, December 3, 2007, p. A1. More recent definitions have tended to focus on the high-cost structure of subprime loans, without regard to the borrowers' characteristics.

2. Gramlich (2007a, p. 2). See also John Waggoner, "Subprime Woes Could Spill Over into Other Sectors," *USA Today*, March 16, 2007, p. 4B.

3. Although predatory lending is hard to define with precision, generally it is concentrated in the subprime market and involves excessive prices in view of the borrowers' risk or lending without regard to borrowers' ability to repay. Engel and McCoy (2007, pp. 2043–045) define predatory lending as a syndrome of loan terms or practices involving one or more of the following features: (1) loans structured to result in seriously disproportionate net harm to borrowers, (2) rent seeking, (3) illegal fraud or deception, (4) other information asymmetries favoring brokers or lenders, (5) mandatory arbitration clauses, (6) lending discrimination, and (7) servicing abuses.

with better terms. In other situations, borrowers entered into loans with low teaser rates, not aware how high their monthly payments could go when their interest rates reset.[4]

Many policymakers across the country agree that subprime loans are an important vehicle for making credit available to consumers; however, concerns about abuses in the subprime market have led the federal government and most states to enact laws that place limits on subprime lending. The federal government led the way with the *Home Ownership Equity Protection Act* (HOEPA), which was enacted in 1994.[5] A growing number of states followed suit, passing laws modeled on HOEPA (known as "mini-HOEPA laws"). Today, well over half the states have antipredatory lending statutes of one kind or another.[6] These laws vary in terms of the loans they cover, the practices they prohibit, and the methods of enforcement they permit. In addition to the mini-HOEPA laws, numerous states have laws that predate HOEPA and prohibit specific loan terms such as prepayment penalties or balloon payments. These laws function alone or alongside more comprehensive mini-HOEPA laws.

Because home mortgage default and foreclosure rates have escalated in recent years,[7] antipredatory lending measures have moved into the policy limelight. Lenders and others in the mortgage industry claim that the laws drive up the cost and reduce the availability of credit, especially to low-income borrowers. In contrast, those who endorse the laws argue that they are needed to protect vulnerable consumers and the communities in which they live.[8] They further argue that any costs are *de minimis* relative to the protection the laws offer.

Any laws that restrict loan terms and lending practices invariably have some effect on credit flows in the home mortgage market. Until recently, the nature and extent of those effects have only been speculative. The availability of loan pricing and other data now makes it possible to evaluate the impact of laws on the flow and cost of credit. This chapter reviews past studies on the impact of antipredatory lending laws and describes the results of our research, which expands on earlier studies by (1) using a more nuanced legal index; (2) examining antipredatory lending laws that predate HOEPA as well as the HOEPA analogues; (3) looking at the role of enforcement mechanisms, including assignee liability

---

4. Truth in Lending Act rules at the time did not require lenders to inform borrowers about the exact dollar amounts of their maximum possible monthly payments following rate reset (McCoy 2007).

5. Home Ownership Equity Protection Act (HOEPA) 1994. 15 U.S.C. §§ 1601, 1602(aa), 1639(a)–(b).

6. Azmy (2005).

7. By the end of 2007, approximately 21 percent of subprime adjustable-rate mortgages were past due 90 days or more (Bernanke 2008).

8. Apgar and Duda (2005); Engel (2006).

laws, on loan volumes; and (4) disaggregating antipredatory lending laws along three dimensions—coverage, restrictions, and enforcement.

Description of Antipredatory Lending Laws

Antipredatory lending laws take two forms. The older laws typically prohibit one or a few specific loan terms such as prepayment penalties.[9] The more modern laws are patterned on the federal HOEPA law. HOEPA governs "high-cost" loans, which are defined as loans that exceed one of two triggers: (1) where the APR at consummation exceeds the yield on Treasury securities of comparable maturity plus 8 percent for first-lien loans or 10 percent for subordinate lien loans, or (2) where the total points and fees exceed 8 percent of the total loan amount or $547, whichever is greater.[10] HOEPA covers, at most, 1 percent of subprime residential mortgages.[11] For that narrow set of loans, HOEPA restricts numerous lending terms and practices, including balloon terms and prepayment penalties. Lenders must also make specialized, advance disclosures to borrowers receiving HOEPA loans. HOEPA imposes liability for violations on lenders and assignees of HOEPA loans.[12]

In 1999, North Carolina passed the first mini-HOEPA law. This statute adopted the HOEPA APR trigger, but used a lower points and fees trigger and gave more extensive substantive protections than HOEPA. In short order, other states followed North Carolina's lead and enacted their own mini-HOEPA laws. Some of these laws augmented existing laws and others were states' first forays into limiting loan terms. As of 2007, more than thirty states had mini-HOEPA laws and only six states had neither mini-HOEPA laws nor laws regulating prepayment penalties or balloon clauses in home mortgages.[13]

The coverage, restriction, and enforcement provisions in state mini-HOEPA laws vary widely. Although some states have adopted the same coverage triggers as HOEPA, most set their triggers below one or both of the HOEPA triggers. Still others have some laws that apply to all mortgage loans without any triggers and

9. These laws are part of state usury laws or in state versions of the Uniform Consumer Commercial Code (Eskridge 1984; Alexander 1987; Whitman 1993).

10. HOEPA, §§ 1601 et seq. The points and fees trigger is subject to annual indexing; $547 was the trigger amount in 2007.

11. Gramlich (2007b, p. 28).

12. Board of Governors of the Federal Reserve System (2001). In general, holders of HOEPA loans "are subject to all claims and defenses . . . that could be raised against the original lender" (HOEPA §1641(d)).

13. A few states eschewed mini-HOEPA laws and instead required expanded disclosures to borrowers. Other states focused on mortgage brokers by expanding broker licensing requirements and subjecting brokers to greater regulation. Similarly, numerous cities and counties passed antipredatory lending ordinances. The city and county ordinances either are limited in scope to lenders who contract with the cities or have been preempted (Bostic and others 2008).

other laws that apply only to high-cost loans. With regard to restrictions, prohibited practices also vary widely in both quantity and quality among the states. For example, some states ban prepayment penalties altogether and others ban prepayment penalties only after five years from origination.[14]

Like the coverage and restriction provisions, state laws establish an array of different enforcement provisions from exclusive governmental enforcement to private redress by aggrieved borrowers in court. Some laws allow borrowers to bring claims against loan originators alone, and other laws also authorize assignee liability, which permits borrowers to recover against securitized trusts and other holders of notes. Available relief ranges from actual damages to civil penalties or punitive damages.[15]

Studies of Antipredatory Lending Laws

Although some states have regulated practices associated with predatory lending for decades, until recently no studies evaluated the effects of antipredatory lending laws (other than caps on interest rates) on credit flows and loan prices. That changed with the passage of North Carolina's antipredatory lending law in 1999. Since then, several studies have assessed the impact of state mini-HOEPA laws on lending patterns.

An early study by Morgan Stanley surveyed subprime branch managers and mortgage brokers across the country to learn their views on the effect of antipredatory lending laws on loan volumes. The investment bank reported that growth forecasts by respondents in states with tough laws were not significantly different from growth forecasts by respondents in less regulated states. The report observed, "One of the consistent messages we heard from our respondents was that the increased level of disclosures was boosting consumer comfort levels with subprime products and thus providing a positive impact on loan volume."[16]

Li and Ernst used a database of securitized subprime loans from January 1998 through December 2004 to study the effect of state laws on loan originations. The study ranked state laws according to the type of loans covered, points-and-fee triggers, substantive legal protections, and remedies available to borrowers. The authors conclude that, for the most part, state mini-HOEPA laws did not reduce subprime originations and did reduce the number of subprime loans with predatory terms. In addition, in all but two states with antipredatory lending laws, the

14. See, for example, Annotated Laws of Mass. ch. 183C, § 5, which bans all prepayment penalties in high-cost loans; 63 Pennsylvania Statutes § 456.511(f), which prohibits prepayment penalties in high-cost loans after five years.

15. Federal law has preempted portions of these state laws at various times for certain types of lenders and loan products; see chapter 4 by McCoy and Renuart in this volume.

16. Morgan Stanley (2002, p. 11).

nominal interest rates on home mortgages were static or dropped compared with the control states.[17]

Ho and Pennington-Cross used Home Mortgage Disclosure Act (HMDA) data to conduct a cross-border study of the impact of antipredatory lending laws on the probability of subprime applications, originations, and rejections.[18] They develop a legal index that ranked the strength of antipredatory lending laws and, using this index, compare loan volumes in adjacent states with and without antipredatory lending laws. The results are that the typical state antipredatory lending law (1) did not have an impact on the probability of originations, (2) had a small negative effect on the likelihood of applications, and (3) reduced the chances that borrowers would be rejected. In states with stronger restrictions, however, the likelihood of originations and applications dropped. State antipredatory lending laws with broad coverage increased the likelihood of subprime originations and applications.[19]

Ho and Pennington-Cross took the same approach in a study of the effect of state antipredatory lending laws on the cost of credit. They found that antipredatory lending laws that more strongly restrict lending practices modestly drive up the cost of borrowing on fixed-rate loans. The results also indicate that it is very easy for lenders to avoid coverage of most laws on adjustable-rate mortgages by designing loans in ways that reduce the reportable and the actual APR below the laws' triggers.[20]

A national study by Elliehausen, Staten, and Steinbuks (2006) used a data set that included about 22 percent of the total volume of subprime mortgages (defined as high-cost loans) made by eight large lenders from 1999 through 2004 to study the effect of antipredatory lending laws. The authors use several approaches to examine the effect of state laws on subprime originations and found that subprime originations dropped in states with antipredatory lending laws. They argue that these results reflect a supply-side phenomenon; lenders substituted loans that fell below the triggers in the new antipredatory lending laws for high-cost loans that would be subject to laws.[21]

Expanding the Field

The various studies of the new antipredatory lending laws all have limitations. This work attempts to address some of these limitations, in particular by examining

17. Li and Ernst (2006).

18. This cross-border analysis helped hold labor and housing markets constant (Ho and Pennington-Cross 2006a).

19. Ho and Pennington-Cross (2006a).

20. Ho and Pennington-Cross (2006b). Compare Gramlich (2007a, pp. 11–12), who expresses concern about the possibility of similar evasion under HOEPA and proposing lower HOEPA triggers for adjustable-rate loans than for fixed-rate loans.

21. Elliehausen, Staten, and Steinbuks (2006).

state laws that were enacted before HOEPA as well as state laws that were modeled on HOEPA. As a result we can look at the individual effects of both the old and new state laws and, in states that had older laws and newer mini-HOEPA laws, assess the effect of adding a new law to an existing regime.

Creating the Legal Index

We created a legal index by engaging in a careful textual review of every antipredatory lending statute throughout the country that was in force in 2004 or 2005. The legal indexes used in other studies were created from charts summarizing laws that had been compiled by nonprofits, trade associations, or lending industry lawyers. Our legal index is both more complete and more nuanced than earlier efforts. Because Bostic and others (2008) describe it more fully, the procedure is only sketched here. Following Ho and Pennington-Cross (2006a, 2006b), this work includes four coverage and four restriction measures. We expand, however, on these studies by adding a new dimension—enforcement mechanisms—that takes into account the potential liability of owners of loans, known as assignees, and other remedial provisions in the laws.

As appendix A describes, each law received a score for coverage, restrictions, and enforcement, with a higher score indicating a stronger law (see table 5A-1). The coverage measure takes into account the types of loans covered by the law: the broader the law's coverage, the higher the coverage score.[22] The restrictions measure takes into account the strength of each law's credit counseling provisions, restrictions on prepayment penalties and balloon payments, and restrictions on loan terms that limit or bar borrowers' access to the courts. Again, the more restrictive the law, the higher the score. The enforcement score reflects the types and strength of enforcement mechanisms allowed—that is, governmental only or also private remedies for injured borrowers. This enforcement measure makes a unique contribution. One issue that is at the center of current policy debates is whether the ultimate purchasers of mortgage notes, including securitized trusts, should be liable for wrongdoing by originators.[23] Our methodology allows us to study the scope of such assignee liability provisions and their effect on credit flows.

Each state then received a score along each measure (the lowest score was a 1), a component score for coverage, restrictions, and enforcement, and an overall score. We constructed additive and multiplicative indexes using the three component scores. Table 5A-2 lists the constructed index values for each state based on the mini-HOEPA laws in that state; Table 5A-3 reports the state-level indexes as calculated based on older antipredatory lending laws.

---

22. Among other things, the coverage score helps distinguish between older laws that cover the entire residential mortgage market from certain newer laws that only cover high-cost loans.

23. In recent years, up to 80 percent of subprime loans were securitized (Engel and McCoy 2007).

The Data

Assessing the effect of these state laws involved using 2004 and 2005 HMDA data, which captures most residential mortgage lending.[24] These data permitted us to assess (1) the probability of applying for a subprime loan relative to a prime loan, (2) the probability of originating a subprime loan relative to a prime loan, and (3) the probability that a subprime application will be rejected. For 2004 loans are subprime if lenders identified as subprime by HUD made the loans.[25] For 2005 the HUD subprime list and HMDA pricing information identified subprime loans.[26] HMDA-reported loans that had APR yield spreads of 3 percentage points or more above the comparable Treasury yields are considered subprime.

Cross-Border Analysis

Most studies of antipredatory lending laws examine the effect of laws on loan volumes and prices statewide. This approach fails to take into account intrastate variations in economic conditions that could influence credit markets. To avoid this pitfall we used a cross-border sample. Our sample included only loans from counties located on state borders where one of the two border states had an antipredatory lending law.[27]

The base model can thus be specified as:

$$Outcome_{it} = \beta^0 + \beta^1 Law_i + \sum_{j=ALFL}^{VAWV} \beta_j^2 Border_{ji} + \beta^3 Borrower_i + \beta^4 Location_i + \varepsilon_i,$$

where i and j index, respectively, the individual loans and the state border pair, *Law* reflects the presence and strength of an antipredatory lending law, *Border* indicates that loans are in border counties for the indicated pair, *Borrower* and *Location* reflect borrower and location-specific characteristics, and ε is the error term.[28]

This analysis considers various specifications of the *Law* vector. Two specifications use the combined (composite) index that aggregates scores across the three dimensions. Establishing whether index construction is important involves combined indexes that are additive and multiplicative in their construction. We also

24. We excluded states in which the antipredatory lending laws changed or took effect in the middle of the calendar year in either 2004 or 2005.

25. HUD included a lender on its subprime list where subprime loans accounted for 50 percent or more of the lender's total mortgage originations. Under that approach, lenders were free to identify themselves as subprime based either on the credit profile of their borrowers or the high-cost nature of their loans (Scheessele 1999).

26. We did not use the HMDA price information to analyze the 2004 data because of concerns about reporting and other errors in the data (Bostic and others 2008).

27. In a separate article (Bostic and others 2008) we used the same data and sampling technique; however, we took a different sample. The results using the two different samples were virtually the same.

28. For a complete discussion of these controls, see Bostic and others (2008).

disaggregate these combined indexes to determine whether and how individual components of the legal framework—that is, coverage, restrictions, and enforcement mechanisms—affect mortgage outcomes. Finally, we distinguish between state provisions in older laws and those in the newer mini-HOEPA laws.

Empirical Results

Our initial discussion of empirical results focuses on estimates of the base model. We report only the law-related variables, but all other control variable results are available from the authors on request.

Originations

Table 5-1 reports the results of estimates of how antipredatory lending laws influence the relative probability of originating a subprime loan instead of a prime loan. Estimates using the combined indexes (both additive and multiplicative) consistently suggest that older laws usually make a subprime origination more likely than prime, and the newer laws have no significant effect on the likelihood of a subprime origination (except for one result in 2004). Subsequent estimates, however, indicate that these aggregated metrics mask important influences.

First, the individual components of the legal framework turn out to be important. Fewer subprime originations exist relative to prime originations where laws are more restrictive but comparatively more subprime originations exist where laws have broader coverage or enforcement mechanisms.

Moreover, further deconstructing the indexes to distinguish between older and newer laws reveals that both older and newer laws are important. Enforcement provisions appear to be the most important consideration for the older laws. The results show that the stronger the enforcement mechanisms in the older laws, the more likely an application is to be a subprime.

Among the newer laws, laws with greater restrictions reduce the probability of a subprime origination compared to that of a prime origination. Newer laws with broader coverage are associated with a higher probability of a subprime origination relative to prime.[29] Perhaps these opposite forces explain the lack of significant results using the aggregated indexes. The restrictions results might be a supply side story, with lenders being limited in the subprime products they can offer. The coverage results—like the enforcement results for the old laws—may reflect a judgment by stronger prospective applicants who had previously stayed on the sidelines that the new laws gave them added protection against potentially abusive lenders, leading them to apply and to have their applications approved. On balance, these results are broadly consistent with those observed in earlier research.

29. In this analysis the definition of a subprime loan for purposes of calculating origination, application, and rejection probabilities remains the same whether a law's coverage is narrow or broad.

Table 5-1. *Regression Results for Originations*[a]

| | 2005 | | | | 2004 | |
| | HUD list | | HMDA price | | HUD list | |
Specification variable	Estimate	Odds ratio	Estimate	Odds ratio	Estimate	Odds ratio
Specification 1						
Old index[A]	0.009*	1.02	0.032***	1.09	0.014**	1.04
	(0.005)		(0.004)		(0.005)	
New index[A]	−0.002	0.99	0.004	1.01	−0.001	1.00
	(0.004)		(0.004)		(0.004)	
Specification 2						
Old index[M]	0.002*	1.03	0.006	1.07	0.003*	1.03
	(0.001)		(0.001)		(0.001)	
New index[M]	−0.001	0.98	0.000	1.00	−0.002*	0.97
	(0.001)		(0.001)		(0.001)	
Specification 3						
Combined restrictions	−0.053***	0.92	−0.025*	0.96	−0.031*	0.95
	(0.012)		(0.010)		(0.015)	
Combined coverage	0.047	1.09	0.045***	1.08	0.036***	1.07
	(0.010)		(0.008)		(0.010)	
Combined enforcement	0.029	1.05	0.042***	1.07	0.015	1.02
	(0.014)		(0.011)		(0.016)	
Specification 4						
Old restrictions	−0.005	0.99	0.000	1.00	−0.004	1.00
	(0.016)		(0.013)		(0.017)	
Old coverage	−0.035	0.97	0.054*	1.05	−0.003	1.00
	(0.027)		(0.022)		(0.033)	
Old enforcement	0.064***	1.07	0.049**	1.05	0.052*	1.06
	(0.020)		(0.017)		(0.025)	
New restrictions	−0.097***	0.89	−0.038*	0.96	−0.048*	0.95
	(0.019)		(0.016)		(0.024)	
New coverage	0.054***	1.09	0.037***	1.06	0.037***	1.06
	(0.011)		(0.009)		(0.010)	
New enforcement	0.041	1.05	0.020	1.02	−0.006	.099
	(0.021)		(0.018)		(0.024)	

*Significant at $p < 0.05$; **significant at $p < 0.01$; ***significant at $p < 0.001$.

A = the respective index was created using an additive methodology; M = the respective index was created using a multiplicative methodology.

a. The dependent variable is origination. Odds ratios reflect a 1 standard deviation increase in the variable. "List" refers to samples in which subprime loans were identified using the HUD-generated subprime lender list. "Price" refers to samples in which subprime loans were identified using the high-cost loan indicator in the HMDA data. Numbers in prentheses are standard errors of the coefficient estimates.

Table 5-2. *Regression Results for Rejection Probability*[a]

Specification variable	2004		2005	
	Estimate	Odds ratio	Estimate	Odds ratio
Specification 1				
Old index[A]	−0.013***	0.97	−0.004	0.99
	(0.004)		(0.003)	
New index[A]	−0.002	0.99	0.003	1.01
	(0.003)		(0.003)	
Specification 2				
Old index[M]	−0.002***	0.97	−0.001	0.99
	(0.001)		(0.001)	
New index[M]	−0.001*	0.98	0.000	0.99
	(0.001)		(0.001)	
Specification 3				
Combined restrictions	0.074***	1.13	0.098***	1.18
	(0.011)		(0.009)	
Combined coverage	−0.078***	0.87	−0.091***	0.85
	(0.007)		(0.007)	
Combined enforcement	−0.028*	0.96	−0.030*	0.95
	(0.011)		(0.010)	
Specification 4				
Old restrictions	0.041***	1.05	0.051***	1.06
	(0.013)		(0.012)	
Old coverage	−0.085***	0.93	−0.055**	0.95
	(0.024)		(0.019)	
Old enforcement	−0.023	0.98	−0.033*	0.96
	(0.018)		(0.014)	
New restrictions	0.132***	1.17	0.155***	1.20
	(0.017)		(0.013)	
New coverage	0.081***	0.88	−0.098***	0.85
	(0.007)		(0.008)	
New enforcement	−0.048**	0.95	−0.069***	0.93
	(0.018)		(0.015)	

*Significant at $p < 0.05$; **significant at $p < 0.01$; ***significant at $p < 0.001$.

A = the respective index was created using an additive methodology; M = the respective index was created using a multiplicative methodology.

a. The dependent variable is rejection. Odds ratios reflect a 1 standard deviation increase in the variable. Subprime loans were identified using the HUD-generated list of subprime lenders in both years. Numbers in parentheses are standard errors of the coefficient estimates.

Rejections

As seen in table 5-2, the combined indexes show a limited relationship with the likelihood of a subprime rejection. But, as with originations, these belie more significant effects for the individual components. Indeed, when the indexes are disaggregated and the components are considered individually, restrictions, coverage, and enforcement provisions all have significant relationships with the probability of rejection.

The effects here are opposite from, but consistent with, those observed for originations. Greater restrictions are associated with increases in the likelihood of rejection. This could arise because the restrictions limit the types of products that lenders might consider offering, which in turn limits the types of borrower profiles (for example, in terms of credit risk) that are likely to be approved. If so, then one would expect elevated rejection rates in high-restriction states after controlling for borrower profiles.

Broader coverage and tougher enforcement reduce the probability of rejection. Moreover, the coverage effects appear to be stronger than the enforcement relationships across the board. Once again, extending coverage to a wider swath of subprime loans and adopting strong enforcement mechanisms may boost the confidence of better quality borrowers who, without legal protection, would fear exploitation. If more creditworthy borrowers are entering the mix, one would expect rejection probabilities to decline.

These rejection results are robust. They are broadly consistent across the two years and are qualitatively identical for both the older and newer laws. That said, the strength of the effects is greater for the newer laws. That is not surprising because most of the newer laws contain multiple restrictions, unlike the older laws, which tended to have fewer restrictions. This suggests that the new law mechanisms may have had an important effect on underwriting policies and outcomes and on borrowers' comfort with subprime products.

Applications

The results for the probability of a subprime application versus a prime application (table 5-3) are largely statistically insignificant and inconsistent across different specifications. There are, however, some consistent results.

When the components are disaggregated, the results for coverage are consistently negative—greater coverage is associated with a lower probability that an application will be subprime and a greater probability that an application will be prime. This holds when one uses both the combined indexes or breaks the index out according to older and newer laws. The enforcement relationships are inconsistent across law type and largely insignificant when aggregated.

Interactions among the Components in the Legal Framework

So far, this analysis considered the legal framework components in isolation. These components could, however, be interacting with one another in different ways. They might be mutually reinforcing such that strength along one dimension amplifies the effects associated with another dimension. Alternatively, they could be counterbalancing, so strength in one dimension reduces the strength of the relationship for another dimension. To explore these possibilities, we esti-

Table 5-3. *Regression Results for Application Probability*[a]

Specification variable	2004		2005	
	Estimate	Odds ratio	Estimate	Odds ratio
Specification 1				
Old index[A]	−0.001	1.00	0.004	1.01
	(0.004)		(0.004)	
New index[A]	−0.015***	0.95	−0.006	0.98
	(0.004)		(0.003)	
Specification 2				
Old index[M]	0.000	1.00	0.002*	1.02
	(0.001)		(0.001)	
New index[M]	−0.004***	0.93	−0.002**	0.97
	(0.001)		(0.001)	
Specification 3				
Combined restrictions	0.002	1.00	0.018	1.03
	(0.012)		(0.010)	
Combined coverage	−0.025**	0.96	−0.005	0.99
	(0.008)		(0.008)	
Combined enforcement	−0.004	0.99	−0.024*	0.96
	(0.013)		(0.011)	
Specification 4				
Old restrictions	0.032*	1.04	0.057***	1.07
	(0.014)		(0.013)	
Old coverage	−0.126***	0.90	−0.064**	0.95
	(0.026)		(0.021)	
Old enforcement	0.065**	1.07	0.003	1.00
	(0.020)		(0.016)	
New restrictions	0.015	1.02	−0.014	0.98
	(0.019)		(0.015)	
New coverage	−0.026**	0.96	−0.002	1.00
	(0.008)		(0.008)	
New enforcement	−0.050*	0.95	−0.020	0.98
	(0.020)		(0.017)	

*Significant at $p < 0.05$; **significant at $p < 0.01$; ***significant at $p < 0.001$.

A = the respective index was created using an additive methodology; M = the respective index was created using a multiplicative methodology.

a. The dependent variable is application. Odds ratios reflect a 1 standard deviation increase in the variable. Subprime loans were identified using the HUD-generated list of subprime lenders in both years. Numbers in parentheses are standard errors of the coefficient estimates.

mated the relationships again with interaction terms between the various indexes. Table 5-4 shows the results of this exercise for regressions including each interactive term separately.

The results show few systematic interactive effects. The interaction between the coverage and restrictions index yields few significant coefficients, and where significant coefficients are observed there are reasons to have robustness concerns.

Table 5-4. *The Coefficients on the Interactive Terms*[a]

Originations	(Coverage) × (Restrictions)	(Coverage) × (Enforcement)	(Restrictions) × (Enforcement)
2004—List	0.006	0.011	0.042***
	(0.007)	(0.006)	(0.007)
2005—List	−0.018**	−0.002	0.007
	(0.006)	(0.006)	(0.006)
2005—Price	0.002	0.005	0.021***
	(0.005)	(0.005)	(0.005)
Rejections (list)			
2004	0.006	−0.029***	0.000
	(0.005)	(0.005)	(0.005)
2005	0.019***	−0.006	0.014**
	(0.004)	(0.005)	(0.004)
Applications (list)			
2004	−0.006	−0.013**	0.029***
	(0.005)	(0.005)	(0.005)
2005	−0.006	−0.002	0.016***
	(0.005)	(0.005)	(0.005)

*Significant at $p < 0.05$; **significant at $p < 0.01$; ***significant at $p < 0.001$.

a. Odds ratios reflect a 1 standard deviation increase in the variable. Each coefficient in the table was obtained by running a separate regression. Specifications in which all coefficients are included together are not shown. "List" refers to samples in which subprime loans were identified using the HUD-generated subprime lender list. "Price" refers to samples in which subprime loans were identified using the high-cost loan indicator in the HMDA data. Numbers in parentheses are standard errors of the coefficient estimates.

For example, signs differ between the significant and insignificant coefficients for originations, and similarly weak results exist for the interaction of coverage with enforcement. The originations results show nothing systematic, but the rejections and applications estimates reveal significant relationships for 2004 but not 2005.

The lone exception to this is the restrictions-enforcement interaction, which shows significant positive coefficients for both applications and originations (except for one case). In the applications case, the positive interaction suggests that enforcement mechanisms inhibit the likelihood of a subprime application less where restrictions are strong and vice versa. This suggests that there might be a limit to the cumulative effects of these provisions, perhaps because there is a finite pool of applicants whose decisions might be affected by the nature of the legal framework. A similar offset is clear in terms of originations, though the individual enforcement effect here is much weaker.

Figure 5-1. *The Impact of Law Coverage on Mortgage Outcome*

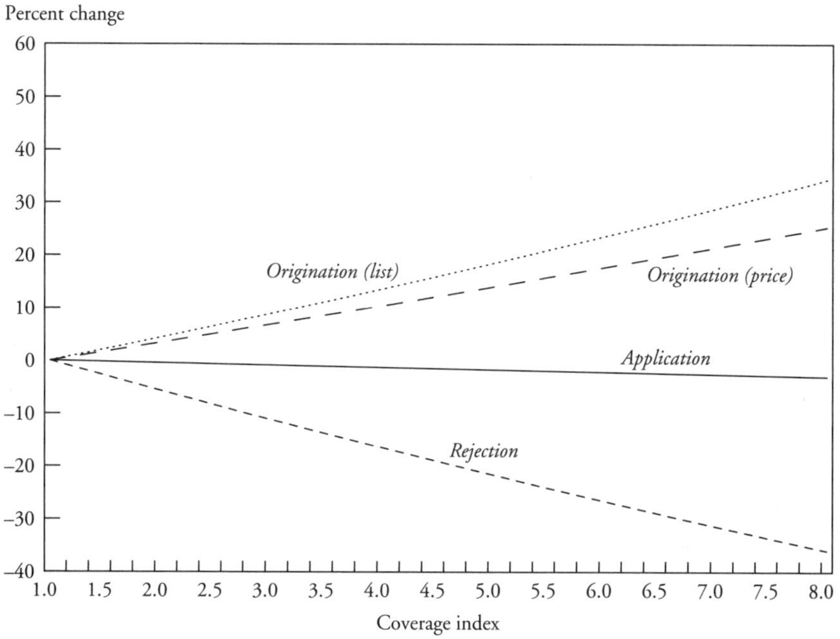

Percent change

Coverage index

Putting It Together: How Legal Framework Provisions Affect the Market

Given the many moving parts in this framework, it is perhaps more straightforward to discern the relationships graphically based on a simulation using the coefficient estimates discussed earlier.[30] Figures 5-1 through 5-3 show how our model using the 2005 combined index data predicts that applications, rejections, and originations would change as a state's score changes along one dimension. Because the results for originations are qualitatively similar when one uses the HUD list or HMDA price information to define a subprime loan, the two are discussed singly.

Figure 5-1 shows that the probability of a subprime origination increases significantly as a state law covers more loans. By contrast, regulating more loans reduces the subprime application probability only slightly, even when one compares states at the extremes of the coverage index. Finally, increasing coverage reduces the probability that a subprime application will be denied. Taken together, these suggest that the increased probability of origination as coverage increases is

---

30. Given the limited robustness of the interaction results, this discussion focuses on the coefficients obtained using specifications that omitted interactions.

Figure 5-2. *The Impact of Law Restrictions on Mortgage Outcome*

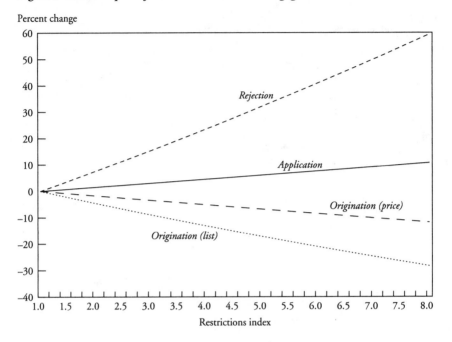

Percent change

mainly caused by a decline in the likelihood that a given application will be rejected.

For restrictions (figure 5-2), the outcomes relate to each other similarly but produce the opposite outcome. Here the probability of rejection rises considerably as a law becomes more restrictive, yet applications again move only slightly, this time increasing as restrictions increase. Originations fall, though not nearly as much as rejections increase. From this it appears that originations decline because of an increased likelihood of denial, and the slight increase in applications that occurs as restrictions increase offsets the rejection effect and mutes the overall decline in originations.

The graph for enforcement mechanisms (figure 5-3) shows somewhat smaller effects than those observed for the other two components. The probability that a subprime loan is originated rises as one moves to states with broader enforcement measures. This occurs despite the fact that subprime application probabilities fall as enforcement increases.[31] Finally, rejection likelihood declines as enforcement mechanisms increase. In considering these three trends, it appears that the appli-

---

31. Although these probabilities are generally insignificant, their estimated magnitude is large.

Figure 5-3. *The Impact of Law Enforcement Mechanisms on Mortgage Outcome*

Percent change

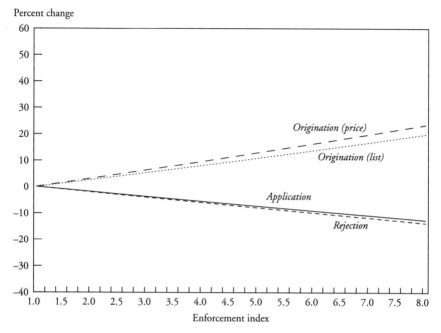

Enforcement index

cation and rejection trends offset each other, with the rejection trends prevailing such that subprime origination probabilities ultimately increase.

Summary Analysis

The results clearly indicate an important role for antipredatory lending laws and highlight the importance of disaggregating the laws to focus on the effects of their different components. The extent of coverage, restrictions, and enforcement embodied in a state's legal framework is associated with significant changes in the probability that a subprime application is rejected and a subprime loan is originated. As the individual components of the newer laws become stronger, they have different and often complementary effects on applications, originations, and rejections.

These results can be used to paint different stories with different implications. For example, better quality applicants or greater efforts by lenders to discourage people with weak credit risks from applying could explain why increased coverage is associated with lower subprime rejection probabilities. This would be a "modified lemons" story, whereby expanded coverage encourages people on the stronger end of the credit spectrum who previously avoided the subprime market to enter that market and obtain subprime loans.

Restrictions tend to increase the likelihood of rejection and hence retard originations in the subprime market. Restrictions typically limit the menu of subprime products a lender can offer and reduce the lender's ability to tailor products to the particular needs and profiles of borrowers. Borrowers who might have been served before may no longer find products for which they qualify. The higher rejection probabilities may also indicate that borrowers and lenders have not adjusted to the stricter lending standards through greater prescreening of loan customers with weak credit profiles. The increased likelihood of rejections from stronger restrictions could also be a sign, albeit an indirect one, that lenders are complying with the laws.[32]

Finally, the key result in the analysis of enforcement is that stronger enforcement mechanisms reduce subprime rejection probabilities. The overall trend for enforcement is consistent with the view that the laws affect the market through changes in rejection probabilities.

In thinking about the results for enforcement mechanisms, one or more things could be going on. On the lower end of the credit spectrum, fear of legal exposure may cause brokers and loan officers to discourage people with weaker credit from applying for subprime loans. Removing these high-risk applicants from the loan pool would reduce subprime rejection probabilities. In addition, objective standards and quantifiable damages caps may give lenders greater certainty about their legal obligations and legal exposure, making them more comfortable with originating subprime loans.

Slider Effects and Implications for the Design of New Antipredatory Lending Laws

These results have important implications for the design of antipredatory lending laws. The three major components of antipredatory lending laws—coverage, restrictions, and enforcement mechanisms—have "slider effects" in which the strength of one component offsets the negative effects of another.

To test and illustrate this, we selected seven states with newer laws featuring different combinations of weak and strong components and compared the outcomes in those states with those in Montana, which had (and still has) no antipredatory lending law. Using the 2005 data for the newer laws, we simulated how each particular state's law would affect the likelihood of originations, applications, and rejections relative to Montana.

As seen in table 5-5, for four model laws—Nevada, New Mexico, New York, and Minnesota—both the probability of a subprime application and that of a subprime rejection went down compared to Montana. In each case, moreover, the

---

32. Compare Li and Ernst (2006, pp. 11–13), who found that loans in states with mini-HOEPA laws had fewer abusive terms.

Table 5-5. Simulation of Model Laws: Percent Change Relative to Montana (with No Law)

	Nevada	Oklahoma	North Carolina	New York	Massachusetts	New Mexico	Minnesota
Component							
Coverage	Least	Least	Low-medium	Medium	Medium	Broad	Broadest
	(1.00)	(1.00)	(2.72)	(3.15)	(3.15)	(5.17)	(7.46)
Restrictions	Least	Medium	High	Medium	Highest	High	Low
	(1.00)	(3.18)	(4.27)	(2.91)	(4.82)	(4.27)	(1.55)
Enforcement mechanisms	Highest	Medium	Low	Medium	High	High	Lowest
	(3.81)	(3.11)	(2.41)	(2.76)	(3.46)	(3.46)	(1.00)
Outcome							
Origination							
List	7.6	-4.8	-4.5	4.7	-2.6	8.8	27.8
Price	9.2	2.6	4.3	9.6	8.2	16.7	22.4
Application	-5.3	-0.9	1.3	-1.5	0.1	-1.8	-2.00
Rejection	-5.7	10.4	8.4	-4.2	7.1	-8.8	-32.4

The numbers in parentheses are standard errors of the coefficient estimates.

likelihood of rejection dropped more than the likelihood of a subprime application. As a result, in these four states, the probability of a subprime origination rose. For the other three model states, rejection probabilities rose relative to Montana's, but application rates either increased or fell relative to Montana only slightly. These three states do not have a consistent signal regarding subprime origination probabilities. One could infer an increased origination likelihood (Massachusetts), no change (North Carolina),[33] and a reduced origination likelihood (Oklahoma).

What distinguishes the second group of three model laws from the four model laws that show a consistent increase in origination probability? Essentially, the second group of model laws (based on laws in Massachusetts, North Carolina, and Oklahoma) has narrower coverage than restrictions. For instance, the Oklahoma-type law has the lowest score for coverage but a medium score for restrictions, and the North Carolina-type law features low-to-medium coverage with high restrictions. The Massachusetts-type law follows a similar pattern, combining medium coverage with the highest score for restrictions. In Nevada, New Mexico, New York, and Minnesota, in comparison, the relative coverage is as strong or stronger than the restrictions.

The Effects of Strict Assignee Liability Laws

Our simulation also sheds light on the effect of assignee liability laws on flows of subprime credit, which is currently a topic of hot debate. Table 5-6 simulates the effect of adopting either of the two strictest types of assignee liability laws and compares those effects to outcomes in Montana, which has no law. Two of the model laws, patterned on laws in Nevada and Pennsylvania, impose full assignee liability with no safe harbors. The other seven model laws, patterned on the laws in New Mexico, Massachusetts, Illinois, Indiana, Maine, New Jersey, and West Virginia, create a limited safe harbor for assignees who perform due diligence and do not engage in willful violations of the law. Under those seven model laws, assignees who qualify for the safe harbor are subject only to limited claims and defenses that the borrower could raise against the lender. All other assignees are subject to full liability for all claims and defenses available against the lender.

Our simulation results show no definitive effect of assignee liability on the likelihood of subprime originations, even when the liability provisions are in their strongest form. In many instances, higher probabilities of origination relative to Montana are seen across the two definitions of subprime lending (HUD list and HMDA price); in a smaller number of cases, origination probabilities are lower than those in Montana.

---

33. Here and throughout this chapter, we evaluate North Carolina law only as of 2004 and 2005, not as of 2007, when North Carolina amended its mini-HOEPA law to strengthen it.

Table 5-6. Simulation of Assignee Liability Laws: Percent Change Relative to Montana (with No Law)

	New Mexico	Massachusetts	Illinois	Indiana	Maine	New Jersey	West Virginia	Nevada	Pennsylvania
Component									
Coverage	Broad (5.17)	Medium (3.15)	Medium-broad (4.74)	Low (2.29)	Least (1.00)	Medium (3.15)	Broad (6.6)	Least (1.00)	Least (1.00)
Restrictions	High (4.27)	Highest (4.82)	Medium (2.91)	High (4.00)	Low (1.55)	Medium-high (3.73)	Medium (2.64)	Least (1.00)	Medium (2.36)
Enforcement mechanisms	High (3.46)	High (3.46)	High (3.46)	High (3.46)	High (3.46)	High (3.46)	Medium (2.76)	Highest (3.81)	High (3.11)
Raw assignee liability score[a]	3.00	3.00	3.00	3.00	3.00	3.00	3.00	4.00	4.00
Outcome									
Origination									
List	8.8	-2.6	14.0	-2.4	3.9	2.6	22.6	7.6	-1.0
Price	16.7	8.2	17.9	6.7	7.0	10.4	23.1	9.2	4.2
Application	-1.8	-0.1	-3.5	-0.9	-3.9	-1.7	-3.4	-5.3	2.0
Rejection	-8.8	7.1	-14.7	7.0	-1.4	-0.2	-25.1	-5.7	4.8

The numbers in parentheses are the index scores for the states for each component.

a. Raw assignee liability score reports the score before being scaled down for the overall enforcement mechanism index. A raw assignee liability score of 3.00 means that assignees who exercise due diligence are subject to limited claims and defenses, whereas other assignees (plus any assignees guilty of willful violations) are subject to full liability for claims and defenses. A raw assignee liability score of 4.00 means assignees have full liability for claims and defenses, regardless of due diligence. Model laws based on states with the strongest assignee liability laws, that is, with raw scores of 4.00, are shaded in gray.

Our simulation results are based on credit flows for calendar year 2005. Given the events of 2007, when delinquencies of subprime mortgages skyrocketed and investors fled the market for subprime mortgage-backed securities, it is necessary to ask whether our results still hold or whether assignee liability laws played a role in investor flight.

Although it is too early to arrive at a definitive answer to this question, several factors suggest that the dismal performance of subprime loans in late 2006 and in 2007 and the resulting inability to value subprime mortgage-backed securities, not assignee liability provisions, were what prompted the exit. First, in the summer of 2007, investors fled the entire subprime market (and even instruments remotely tied to that market), not just in states with assignee liability laws.[34] Second, as our origination results suggest, investors invested heavily in loans from states with assignee liability laws of various strengths for several years before the subprime market collapsed. This suggests that the poor performance of subprime loans, which experienced a sharp downturn in the months preceding the market's collapse, was the precipitating factor for the implosion, not assignee liability laws. Finally, most states with assignee liability laws, such as New Mexico and West Virginia, also regulated loan terms such as prepayment penalties and balloon clauses to curtail the higher risk of default and foreclosure associated with those terms.[35]

Unanswered Questions

Our results raise as many questions as they answer. What future research avenues do these findings suggest?[36]

What Are the Implications of Referring Loan Applicants to Loans Priced below the Triggers?

Future research could clarify the meaning of our findings on the effects of restrictions in the newer laws. Stronger restrictions make a prime origination more likely relative to a subprime origination, indicating that lenders and brokers may be doing a better job of screening stronger loan candidates and referring them to loans that are not subject to the laws. What this means is not entirely clear. Our

34. See, for example, Standard and Poor's (2007), which notes that by September 12, 2007, "Wall Street firms, banks and investors had almost completely lost their appetite for nonagency mortgage-backed assets," including subprime MBS. Compare Board of Governors of the Federal Reserve System (2007), which cut the federal funds and discount rates by 50 basis points on September 18, 2007, because "the tightening of credit conditions has the potential to intensify the housing correction and to restrain economic growth more generally."

35. Quercia, Stegman, and Davis (2005, p. 25).

36. In addition to the discussion that follows, future extensions are likely to include consideration of differences in state foreclosure laws, exploration of the geographical distribution of legal frameworks, and estimation of the effects of laws according to lien status, owner-occupancy status, and refinance versus purchase loans.

results could mean that lenders and brokers referred these applicants to less expensive[37] and safer loans. Alternatively, originators may have referred applicants to risky loan products that are consciously written to evade the triggers of a particular state law. In a third scenario, irrespective of state laws, originators may have referred applicants to loan products featuring low initial interest rates with low monthly payments, but with high rate resets. This practice would have enabled lenders to underwrite loans based on lower, initial interest rates and thus increase the likelihood that applicants would qualify for loans.

Concerns about evasion arise from the fact that most of the newer antipredatory lending laws have triggers that hinge on a loan's APR or total points and fees. Any loans that fall below both triggers will escape regulation under these statutes. Most of these triggers can be gamed by writing an adjustable-rate mortgage (ARM) with a low introductory teaser rate that later adjusts to a fully indexed rate above the trigger. Currently, under the Truth in Lending Act, the APR formula for teaser-rate ARMs is a composite of the teaser rate for the introductory period and the fully indexed rate at closing for the remaining term of the loan.[38] Lengthening the introductory period and offering a low teaser rate could produce an APR for an ultimately expensive loan that nevertheless falls below the APR trigger.

During 2004 and 2005 the product mix of subprime loans shifted, raising questions about the reason for that shift. In those years hybrid ARMs and interest-only ARMs became much more prevalent relative to fixed-rate loans in the subprime market.[39] ARMs made up 74 percent of nonprime loans in 2004 and 79 percent in 2005.[40] A disproportionate number of the subprime ARMs for those years had low annual teaser rates of 4 percent or less for two years, three years, or five years.[41] Similarly, interest-only loans (many of which were subprime loans) mushroomed in 2004 and 2005.[42]

Evasion is not the only possible explanation for this shift in product mix. In 2004 and 2005 interest rates were rising and so were home prices. Lenders, believing that they could take on more risk because of home appreciation, may have marketed hybrid ARMs and interest-only ARMs products more vigorously to applicants who did not qualify for other loans.[43] That hybrid ARMs and interest-

37. We cannot measure the extent of migration to cheaper loans because both of the definitions of subprime loans used in this chapter are subject to limitations. The HUD list does not identify subprime loans at the loan level and the HMDA price test categorizes first-lien loans below the 300 bps spread—which is a relatively large spread—as prime.

38. 12 C.F.R. § 226.22 and app. J to 12 C.F.R. pt. 226.

39. Duncan (2006, p. 18); see also Avery, Brevoort, and Canner (2007, pp. 8–9) and Crews Cutts (2007, p. 13).

40. Walsh (2006, p. 5).

41. Cagan (2006, pp. 24–27); see also Cagan (2007) and FitchRatings (2006a, pp. 2–3).

42. FitchRatings (2006a, 2006b, 2006c).

43. See, for example, Pavlov and Wachter (2007, pp. 23, 27–30), stating that areas with higher concentrations of nontraditional ARMs have affordability constraints and experience faster home price appreciation during up markets.

only ARMs were offered across the country in both heavily regulated and lightly regulated states gives this explanation currency.

Without more detailed information on loans, it is unclear whether rising home prices or evasion motivated the product shift toward ARMs. Future research using loan-level data on loan type and the presence of teaser rates on loans would shed light on this issue. Research would also be helpful on the effects, both good and bad, of including more fees (such as prepayment penalties and yield spread premiums) in triggers for points and fees and of redefining the APR trigger at the fully indexed rate.

What Are the Implications of Increased Subprime Originations?

What are the policy implications of the higher probability of subprime originations that result from broader coverage? On one hand, broader coverage expands access to credit, which is generally seen as desirable. On the other hand, from a policy perspective lawmakers should be wary of writing laws that encourage consumers to enter markets rife with lax underwriting or abusive practices as the recent subprime experience shows. If a law has broad coverage but restrictions or enforcement that are overly weak, the law may give consumers false confidence that they will be shielded from abuses when they apply for subprime loans.

How Well Did Loans Perform in States Governed by the Newer Laws?

The subprime crisis raises the related question of how well loans performed in states with antipredatory lending laws relative to loans in other states. It is well known by now that the 2005, 2006, and 2007 books of subprime loans had significantly elevated rates of delinquency and default.[44] Future research is needed on the effects of state antipredatory laws on the performance of subprime loans and the associated welfare effects. Questions of interest include the following: How well did loans covered by state antipredatory lending laws perform? How well did noncovered loans in those states perform? Noncovered loans include loans originated in states with newer laws that fell below a law's triggers and loans originated in the same states that were exempt from coverage because of federal preemption. In comparison, what was the default experience of loans in states without antipredatory lending laws? Finally, in assessing performance, did it matter whether a state's mini-HOEPA law imposed underwriting standards on borrowers' ability to pay? In our canvass of state laws, some mini-HOEPA laws adopted such standards and others did not.

What Was the Effect of Federal Preemption?

National banks, federal savings associations, and their mortgage lending subsidiaries are exempt from state antipredatory lending laws and state enforcement

44. Youngblood (2006); Sabry and Schopflocher (2007, pp. 8–10); Standard and Poor's (2007).

under federal preemption orders issued by federal banking regulators under the Home Owners' Loan Act[45] and the National Bank Act.[46] In contrast, mortgage brokers and independent nondepository lenders, along with many state-chartered depository institutions and their subsidiaries,[47] must comply with most provisions in state antipredatory lending laws.[48] Although estimates vary, in 2004 and 2005, possibly 30 to 50 percent of subprime mortgage loans originated in states with mini-HOEPA laws were exempt from compliance with those laws because of federal preemption.[49]

Dual regulation creates a natural experiment for exploring the effects of different modes of regulation and their strength. During 2004 and 2005 national banks, federal savings associations, and their mortgage lending subsidiaries were subject to very few restrictions on the terms in their mortgage loans. Both types of federal depository institutions, however, did face capital regulation and periodic examinations for safety and soundness, community reinvestment, and lending discrimination. Independent nondepository lenders were exempt from those examinations but had to comply with the state laws. State banks and thrifts were often subject to both.

This scheme presents several interesting questions for exploration. What effect did federal preemption have on subprime flows of credit and why? Did the relative lack of legal restrictions on federally preempted loans affect the default risk of those loans? Could consumers discern which loans were covered by state antipredatory lending laws or did federally preempted loans receive a spillover effect from increased consumer confidence in regulated states? Is there a difference in origination rates and quality of loan performance between loans originated by national banks and federal savings associations (which have heavy federal banking

45. 12 C.F.R. § 560.2.

46. 69 *Fed. Reg.* 1904 (January 13, 2004; codified at 12 C.F.R. §§ 34.3, 34.4). Federal preemption for national banks and their operating subsidiaries did not take effect until February 12, 2004; see ibid.

47. In isolated cases, state "wild-card" laws may excuse state-chartered banks and thrifts from having to observe state mini-HOEPA laws. For instance, Georgia has a wild-card law that exempts state-chartered banks and thrifts and their subsidiaries from state anti-predatory lending laws to the same extent as national banks and federal thrifts. See, for example, Official Code of Georgia Ann. §7-6, A-12.

48. We say "most provisions" because the federal Alternative Mortgage Transactions Parity Act (AMTPA) exempts most lenders, including independent non depository lenders, from having to comply with state limitations on balloon clauses except for traditional fixed-rate, fully amortizing mortgages. A few states exercised their right to timely opt out of federal preemption under AMTPA (Renuart and Keest 2005, §§ 3.10.1, 3.10.2 at n. 679. pp. 108–13).

49. Avery, Brevoort, and Canner report that depository institutions and their subsidiaries together made 37.4 percent of all higher-priced loans reported under HMDA in 2004 and 35.8 percent in 2005. That sum rose to 40.9 percent in 2006 (2007, p. 25 and table 9). To determine the number of loans shielded by federal preemption, these sums are overinclusive because they include state depository institutions and subsidiaries that had to comply with state laws. At the same time, the sums are underinclusive because they omit loans by other nondepository lenders that were preempted from some state restrictions under AMTPA.

regulation) and their mortgage lending subsidiaries (which were lightly regulated)? Do federally preempted loans display a higher incidence of injurious loan practices and terms such as long prepayment clauses or yield spread premiums? Finally, did federally chartered depository institutions and their subsidiaries gain relative market share in regulated states?

Conclusion

This work measures the effect of state antipredatory lending laws on the flow of subprime credit. The findings are robust and sometimes counterintuitive. For example, it has long been assumed that broadening the market coverage of an antipredatory lending law would impede access to credit. Broader coverage, however, is associated with much lower probabilities that subprime loans will be rejected. As a result, expanded coverage tends to increase access to subprime credit, as do increased enforcement mechanisms. Stronger restrictions have the opposite effect, most likely by limiting the types of subprime loan products that a lender can offer.

The 2007 crisis in subprime mortgages is evidence that the subprime mortgage market is immature and in a state of flux. The subprime market of 2007 was quite different from the market of 2004 and 2005. What direction the subprime market ultimately will take is unknown, but the market that emerges out of the current situation will most likely be subject to greater controls. Some may be in the form of federal and state legislation. Others may be through new, more stringent, underwriting standards adopted by regulators, lenders, or securitizers. Whatever forms these controls take, these findings shed some light on the efficacy of different approaches.

References

Alexander, Frank S. 1987. "Mortgage Prepayment: The Trial of Common Sense." *Cornell Law Review* 72, no. 2: 288–343.

Apgar, William C., and Mark Duda. 2005. *Collateral Damage: The Municipal Impact of Today's Mortgage Foreclosure Boom.* A report prepared for the Homeownership Preservation Foundation. Minneapolis, Minnesota (www.995hope.org/content/pdf/Apgar_Duda_Study_Short_Version.pdf).

Avery, Robert B., Kenneth P. Brevoort, and Glenn B. Canner. 2007. "The 2006 HMDA Data." *Federal Reserve Bulletin* A73 (www.federalreserve.gov/pubs/bulletin/2007/pdf/hmda06 draft.pdf).

Azmy, Baher. 2005. "Squaring the Predatory Lending Circle: A Case for States as Laboratories of Experimentation." *Florida Law Review* 57, no. 2: 295–409.

Bernanke, Ben S. 2007. "Subprime Mortgage Lending and Mitigating Foreclosures." Testimony before the Committee on Financial Services, U.S. House of Representatives, September 20 (www.federalreserve.gov/newsevents/testimony/bernanke20070920a.htm).

———. 2008. "Financial Markets, the Economic Outlook, and Monetary Policy." Speech before the Women in Housing and Finance and Exchequer Club Joint Luncheon. Washington, D.C., January 10 (www.federalreserve.gov/newsevents/speech/bernanke2008 0110a.htm).

Board of Governors of the Federal Reserve System. 2001. "Truth in Lending." *Federal Register* 66, no. 245 (December 20): 65604–5622 (www.access.gpo.gov/su_docs/fedreg/a011220c. html).

———. 2007. Press Release (September 18) (www.federalreserve.gov/newsevents/press/ monetary/20070918a.htm).

Bostic, Raphael, and others. 2008. "State and Local Anti-Predatory Lending Laws: The Effects of Assignee Liability and Legal Remedies." *Journal of Economics and Business* 60, nos. 1–2: 47–66.

Cagan, Christopher L. 2006. "Mortgage Payment Reset: The Rumor and the Reality." White Paper. Santa Ana, Calif.: First American Real Estate Solutions (www.facorelogic.com/ uploadedFiles/Newsroom/Studies_and_Briefs/Studies/MPR_White_Paper_FINAL.pdf).

———. 2007. "Mortgage Payment Reset: The Issue and the Impact." Santa Ana, Calif.: First American CoreLogic, Inc. (www.facorelogic.com/uploadedFiles/Newsroom/Studies_and_ Briefs/Studies/20070048MortgagePaymentResetStudy_FINAL.pdf).

Crews Cutts, Amy. 2007. "Economic and Housing Market Outlook." Presentation to MBA National Mortgage Servicing Conference and Expo. San Diego, California, February 21 (www.mbaa.org/files/Conferences/2007/Servicing07/Tab14-FocusontheEconomy1.pdf).

Duncan, Doug. 2006. "Market Outlook: MBA Nonprime Conference" (www.mortgage bankers.org/ProfessionalDevelopment/UpcomingConferencesandEvents/Presentationsfrom PastConferencesandEvents/Non-PrimeLendingandAlternativeProductsConference.htm).

Elliehausen, Gregory, Michael Staten, and Jevgenijs Steinbuks. 2006. "The Effects of State Predatory Lending Laws on the Availability of Subprime Mortgage Credit." Monograph 38. Georgetown University Credit Research Center (www.business.gwu.edu/research/centers/ fsrp/pdf/M38.pdf).

Engel, Kathleen C. 2006. "Do Cities Have Standing? Redressing the Externalities of Predatory Lending." *Connecticut Law Review* 38, no. 3: 355–91.

Engel, Kathleen C., and Patricia A. McCoy. 2007. "Turning a Blind Eye: Wall Street Finance of Predatory Lending." *Fordham Law Review* 75, no. 4: 2039–103.

Eskridge, William. 1984. "One Hundred Years of Ineptitude: The Need for Mortgage Rules Consonant with the Economic and Psychological Dynamics of the Home Sale and Loan Transaction." *Virginia Law Review* 70, no. 6: 1083–130.

FitchRatings. 2006a. "Rating Subprime RMBS Backed by Interest-Only ARMs" (March 9).

———. 2006b. "U.S. RMBS Criteria for Subprime Interest-Only ARMS" (October 4) (www. fitchratings.com/corporate/reports/report_frame.cfm?rpt_id=292928).

———. 2006c. "U.S. Subprime RMBS in Structured Finance CDOs" (August 21) (www. fitchratings.com/corporate/reports/report_frame.cfm?rpt_id=286382&sector_flag=3& marketsector=2&detail=).

Edward M. Gramlich. 2007a. "Booms and Busts, The Case of Subprime Mortgages." Speech given at the Federal Reserve Bank of Kansas City Annual Economic Symposium. Jackson Hole, Wyoming, August 31 (www.kansascityfed.org/publicat/sympos/2007/pdf/2007.09.04. gramlich.pdf).

———. 2007b. *Subprime Mortgages: America's Latest Boom and Bust.* Washington: Urban Institute Press.

Ho, Giang, and Anthony Pennington-Cross. 2006a. "The Impact of Local Predatory Lending Laws on the Flow of Subprime Credit." *Journal of Urban Economics* 60, no. 2: 210–28.

———. 2006b. "Predatory Lending Laws and the Cost of Credit." Working Paper 2006-022A. Federal Reserve Bank of St. Louis, Research Division (http://research.stlouisfed.org/wp/ 2006/2006-022.pdf).

Li, Wei, and Keith S. Ernst. 2006. "The Best Value in the Subprime Market: State Predatory Lending Reforms." Durham, N.C.: Center for Responsible Lending (www.responsiblelending. org/pdfs/rr010-State_Effects-0206.pdf).

McCoy, Patricia A. 2007. "Rethinking Disclosure in a World of Risk-Based Pricing." *Harvard Journal on Legislation* 44, no. 1: 123–66 (http://papers.ssrn.com/sol3/papers.cfm?abstract_id= 952907).

Morgan Stanley. 2002. "Channel Check: Surprisingly Strong Subprime Growth." *Diversified Financials* (August 1) (http://butera-andrews.com/legislative-updates/directory/Media/other/ MS-SubPrime.pdf).

Pavlov, Andrey, and Susan Wachter. 2007. "Aggressive Lending and Real Estate Markets." Working Paper.

Quercia, Roberto G., Michael A. Stegman, and Walter R. Davis. 2005. "The Impact of Predatory Loan Terms on Subprime Foreclosures: The Special Case of Prepayment Penalties and Balloon Payments." University of North Carolina at Chapel Hill, Center for Community Capitalism, Kenan Institute for Private Enterprise (www.kenan-flagler.unc.edu/assets/ documents/foreclosurepaper.pdf).

Renuart, Elizabeth, and Kathleen Keest. 2005. *The Cost of Credit: Regulation and Legal Challenges.* 3rd ed. Washington: National Consumer Law Center.

Sabry, Faten, and Thomas Schopflocher. 2007. "The Subprime Meltdown: A Primer." NERA Economic Consulting (June 21) (www.nera.com/image/SEC_SubprimeSeries_Part1_ June2007_FINAL.pdf).

Scheessele, Randall. 1999. "1998 HMDA Highlights." Working Paper HF-009. U.S. Department of Housing and Urban Development, Office of Policy Development and Research.

Standard and Poor's. 2007. "A Subprime Hangover: Credit and Liquidity Concerns Cloud the Broader U.S. Mortgage Market" (September 12) (www2.standardandpoors.com/portal/site/ sp/en/us/page.article/2,1,1,0,1148448414278.html?vregion=us&vlang=en).

Walsh, Marina. 2006. "Issues and Trends in the Nonprime Market." Presented at the Nonprime Lending and Alternative Products Conference. Washington, D.C., May 22 (www. mortgagebankers.org/ProfessionalDevelopment/UpcomingConferencesandEvents/Presenta tionsfromPastConferencesandEvents/Non-PrimeLendingandAlternativeProductsConfer ence.htm).

Whitman, Dale. 1993. "Mortgage Prepayment Clauses: An Economic and Legal Analysis." *UCLA Law Review* 40, no. 4: 851–29.

Youngblood, Michael. 2006. "Explaining the Higher Default Rates of the 2005 Origination Year." *MarketPulse* (June): 1–4 (www.firstam.com/pressrelease.cfm?pr_id=1474).

Appendix A. Scoring Scheme—Index Creation

Each component is made up of various dimensions. We convert subcomponent scores to a 0–1 scale and then roll them up into a consolidated dimension score. This score is then rescaled by dividing by the component average score to ensure that the indexes are not overly representative in terms of absolute value or variance of any single subcomponent. Consider the creation of the old law coverage index for Alaska. Because Alaska's score for loan purpose was a 2 and the maximum loan purpose score is 4, Alaska's converted loan purpose value is 0.5. The same procedure yields scores of 1 for the APR trigger for a first lien, the APR trigger for subordinate liens, and the points and fees trigger subcomponents. These values sum up to 3.5 for Alaska. This sum is then divided by the average coverage value for all states (2.068627), then added to 1, resulting in Alaska's coverage index value being 2.69 (1 + 3.5 / 2.068627). The additive version takes the value of each component and adds them together (index^A). We also create a multiplicative index (index^M).

Table 5A-1. *Coding Rules for State-Level Index Creation*

Coverage dimensions	
Loan type	0 = HOEPA equivalent
	1 = law does not cover government loans
	2 = law does not cover reverse and/or open-ended loans
	3 = law does not cover business and/or construction loans
	4 = law covers all loans
APR trigger for first lien mortgages	0 = HOEPA equivalent
	1 = 7–8% plus the comparable Treasury security yield
	2 = 6–7% plus the comparable Treasury security yield
	3 = no APR trigger
APR trigger for subordinate mortgages	0 = HOEPA equivalent
	1 = 9–10% plus the comparable Treasury security yield
	2 = 8–9% plus the comparable Treasury security yield
	3 = 6–8% plus the comparable Treasury security yield
	4 = no APR trigger
Points and fees trigger	0 = HOEPA equivalent (8% of loan amount or $400)
	1 = 6–8% of the total loan amount
	2 = 5–6% of the total loan amount
	3 = less than 5% of the total loan amount
	4 = no points and fees trigger
Restrictions dimensions	
Prepayment penalties	0 = no prepayment penalty restrictions
	1 = bans all penalties 60–84 months after origination
	2 = bans all penalties 36–42 months after origination
	3 = bans all penalties 24 months after origination
	4 = bans all prepayment penalties

(continued)

Table 5A-1. *Coding Rules for State-Level Index Creation (continued)*

Balloon payments	0 = no restriction
	1 = no balloons allowed in first 7 years of loan
	2 = no balloons allowed in first 10 years of loan
	3 = no balloons allowed after 10 or more years of loan
	4 = no balloons allowed
Credit counseling requirements	0 = credit counseling not required
	1 = credit counseling recommended
	2 = credit counseling is required
Limits on judicial relief/ mandatory arbitration	0 = does not prohibit restrictions on judicial relief
	1 = limits restrictions on judicial relief
	2 = prohibits restrictions on judicial relief

Enforcement dimensions

Assignee liability	0 = no assignee liability for holders in due course
	1 = only relief against assignees is defensive
	2 = assignee liability only if no due diligence
	3 = assignees subject to limited claims and defenses
	4 = assignees are liable even if they exercise due diligence
Enforcement against originators	0 = state government enforcement only
	1 = borrower recovery limited to compensatory relief
	2 = borrower relief compensatory and punitive

Table 5A-2. *Mini-HOEPA Index*[a]

	Mini-HOEPA				
State	Coverage	Restrictions	Enforcement	Index— additive	Index— multiplicative
Alaska	1.00	1.00	1.00	3.00	1.00
Alabama	1.00	1.00	1.00	3.00	1.00
Arizona	1.00	1.00	1.00	3.00	1.00
Arkansas	2.72	3.73	3.11	9.56	31.58
California	3.15	2.36	2.41	7.93	17.95
Colorado	1.43	2.64	3.11	7.18	11.73
Connecticut	1.86	2.91	3.11	7.88	16.85
Delaware	1.00	1.00	1.00	3.00	1.00
District of Columbia	4.74	2.91	3.11	10.75	42.85
Florida	1.00	2.64	3.11	6.75	8.20
Georgia	2.72	4.00	3.11	9.83	33.89
Hawaii	1.00	1.00	1.00	3.00	1.00
Idaho	1.00	1.00	1.00	3.00	1.00
Illinois	4.74	2.91	3.46	11.11	47.69
Indiana	2.29	4.00	3.46	9.76	31.75
Iowa	1.00	1.00	1.00	3.00	1.00

(continued)

Table 5A-2. *Mini-HOEPA Index*[a] (*continued*)

	Mini-HOEPA				
State	Coverage	Restrictions	Enforcement	Index—additive	Index—multiplicative
Kansas	1.00	1.00	1.00	3.00	1.00
Kentucky	1.86	3.18	3.81	8.86	22.59
Louisiana	1.00	1.00	1.00	3.00	1.00
Maine	1.00	1.55	3.46	6.01	5.35
Maryland	2.44	1.55	2.41	6.39	9.06
Massachusetts	3.15	4.82	3.46	11.44	52.63
Michigan	6.17	1.82	1.00	8.99	11.22
Minnesota	7.46	1.55	1.00	10.01	11.54
Mississippi	1.00	1.00	1.00	3.00	1.00
Missouri	1.00	1.00	1.00	3.00	1.00
Montana	1.00	1.00	1.00	3.00	1.00
Nebraska	1.00	1.00	1.00	3.00	1.00
Nevada	1.00	1.00	3.81	5.81	3.81
New Hampshire	1.00	1.00	1.00	3.00	1.00
New Jersey	3.15	3.73	3.46	10.34	40.71
New Mexico	5.17	4.27	3.46	12.90	76.42
New York	3.15	2.91	2.76	8.82	25.32
North Carolina	2.72	4.27	2.41	9.40	28.01
North Dakota	1.00	1.00	1.00	3.00	1.00
Ohio	1.00	2.36	3.11	6.47	7.35
Oklahoma	1.00	3.18	3.11	7.29	9.90
Oregon	1.00	1.00	1.00	3.00	1.00
Pennsylvania	1.00	2.36	3.11	6.47	7.35
Rhode Island	1.00	1.00	1.00	3.00	1.00
South Carolina	1.86	3.18	2.76	7.80	16.34
South Dakota	1.00	1.00	1.00	3.00	1.00
Tennessee	1.00	1.00	1.00	3.00	1.00
Texas	1.86	2.36	3.11	7.34	13.69
Utah	2.72	3.18	1.00	6.91	8.67
Vermont	1.00	1.00	1.00	3.00	1.00
Virginia	1.00	1.00	1.00	3.00	1.00
Washington	1.00	1.00	1.00	3.00	1.00
West Virginia	6.60	2.64	2.76	12.00	48.02
Wisconsin	1.00	1.00	1.00	3.00	1.00
Wyoming	1.00	1.00	1.00	3.00	1.00
Average	2.00	2.00	2.00	6.00	13.03
Minimum	1.00	1.00	1.00	3.00	1.00
Maximum	7.46	4.82	3.81	12.90	76.42
Standard deviation	1.62	1.17	1.10	3.19	17.36

a. The designation of 1.00 for a dimension indicates either that there is no relevant law or that the existing law has little or no practical impact.

Table 5A-3. *Older Law Index*[a]

| State | Older laws (before mini-HOEPA) | | | | |
	Coverage	Restrictions	Enforcement	Index— additive	Index— multiplicative
Alabama	2.69	3.68	1.64	8.02	16.28
Alaska	2.57	3.68	3.57	9.82	33.78
Arizona	1.00	1.00	1.00	3.00	1.00
Arkansas	2.93	2.34	1.00	6.28	6.87
California	2.93	1.67	2.92	7.53	14.34
Colorado	2.45	3.68	2.92	9.06	26.40
Connecticut	2.81	2.34	1.00	6.15	6.59
Delaware	1.00	1.00	1.00	3.00	1.00
District of Columbia	2.93	2.34	2.28	7.56	15.69
Florida	1.00	1.00	1.00	3.00	1.00
Georgia	1.00	1.00	1.00	3.00	1.00
Hawaii	1.85	1.67	2.92	6.44	9.02
Idaho	2.81	2.34	3.57	8.72	23.49
Illinois	1.00	1.00	1.00	3.00	1.00
Indiana	2.93	2.34	2.92	8.20	20.09
Iowa	2.93	3.68	1.64	8.26	17.74
Kansas	2.93	3.68	3.57	10.18	38.54
Kentucky	2.57	1.67	2.92	7.17	12.57
Louisiana	2.81	1.67	1.00	5.48	4.70
Maine	2.57	3.68	2.92	9.18	27.70
Maryland	2.57	3.68	3.57	9.82	33.78
Massachusetts	1.00	1.00	1.00	3.00	1.00
Michigan	2.57	2.34	1.96	6.88	11.82
Minnesota	1.00	1.00	1.00	3.00	1.00
Mississippi	2.93	1.67	2.92	7.53	14.34
Missouri	2.81	1.67	2.92	7.41	13.75
Montana	1.00	1.00	1.00	3.00	1.00
Nebraska	2.93	1.00	1.64	5.58	4.82
Nevada	1.00	1.00	1.00	3.00	1.00
New Hampshire	1.00	1.00	1.00	3.00	1.00
New Jersey	1.00	1.00	1.00	3.00	1.00
New Mexico	2.93	3.68	3.57	10.18	38.54
New York	1.00	1.00	1.00	3.00	1.00
North Carolina	2.69	2.34	2.92	7.96	18.44
North Dakota	1.00	1.00	1.00	3.00	1.00
Ohio	2.93	1.67	2.92	7.53	14.34
Oklahoma	1.97	3.68	3.57	9.22	25.84
Oregon	1.00	1.00	1.00	3.00	1.00
Pennsylvania	1.00	1.00	1.00	3.00	1.00
Rhode Island	2.93	3.01	1.00	6.95	8.84
South Carolina	2.93	3.68	3.57	10.18	38.54
South Dakota	1.00	1.00	1.00	3.00	1.00

(continued)

Table 5A-3. *Older Law Index*ᵃ *(continued)*

State	Older laws (before mini-HOEPA)				
	Coverage	Restrictions	Enforcement	Index—additive	Index—multiplicative
Tennessee	1.00	1.00	1.00	3.00	1.00
Texas	1.00	1.00	1.00	3.00	1.00
Utah	2.81	3.68	3.57	10.06	36.95
Vermont	2.57	3.68	2.92	9.18	27.70
Virginia	2.81	1.00	3.57	7.38	10.03
Washington	1.00	1.00	1.00	3.00	1.00
West Virginia	1.00	1.00	1.00	3.00	1.00
Wisconsin	1.00	1.00	1.00	3.00	1.00
Wyoming	1.85	3.68	3.57	9.10	24.25
Average	2.00	2.00	2.00	6.00	12.09
Minimum	1.00	1.00	1.00	3.00	1.00
Maximum	2.93	3.68	3.57	10.18	38.54
Standard deviation	0.88	1.12	1.09	2.75	12.47

a. The designation 1.00 for a dimension indicates either that there is no relevant law or that the existing law has little or no practical impact.

6

Behaviorally Informed Home Mortgage Credit Regulation

MICHAEL S. BARR, SENDHIL MULLAINATHAN,
AND ELDAR SHAFIR

Choosing a mortgage is one of the biggest financial decisions an American consumer will make. Yet it can be a complicated one, especially in today's environment, where mortgages vary along several dimensions and on unique features. This complexity has raised regulatory issues. Should some features be regulated? Should product disclosure be regulated? And most basic of all, is there a rationale for regulation or will the market solve the problem? Current regulation of home mortgages is largely stuck in two competing models of regulation—disclosure and usury or product restrictions. This paper uses insights from both psychology and economics to construct a framework for understanding both models and to suggest a fundamentally new perspective.

Disclosure regulation, embodied in the Truth in Lending Act (TILA) of 1968, presumes one market failure: the market will fail to produce a clear and comparable disclosure of all product information needed by consumers. That is, TILA responds to two types of potential problems: First, firms will not reveal all information that borrowers should understand and analyze when taking out a loan. Second, firms will not reveal information in a way to facilitate comparability across products. The first concern speaks to consumer knowledge, solving the problem with information; the second speaks to consumer decisionmaking, solving the problem through coordination of terms and definitions.

Though TILA presumes one form of market failure—the lack of comparable and full disclosure—*homo economicus* is very much the intellectual basis for disclosure regulation. "Freedom of Contract" is the dominant background assumption for disclosure regulation—and the dominant intellectual paradigm more generally for the last thirty years. It relies on fully rational agents who make intelligent choices about their options. This chapter argues that a more insightful model of human behavior enriches our understanding of disclosure and that neoclassical assumptions are misplaced and in many contexts consequential. Among other topics, we discuss these facts: that the availability of data does not always lead to communication and knowledge, that understanding and intention do not necessarily lead to action, and that contextual nuances can lead to poor choices.

By contrast to disclosure regulation, usury laws, doctrines of substantive unconscionability,[1] and product restrictions start from the idea that certain prices or products are inherently unreasonable and that consumers need to be protected from making bad choices. Moreover, the presumption is that the market will not weed out such products (or may even offer them very easily).

Product regulations and related doctrines of unconscionability appear to build on a model other than *homo economicus,* yet even this framework could benefit from a richer view of human behavior. The central concerns with such laws are threefold. First, we reiterate the traditional economic argument, namely, that product restrictions may diminish access to credit or reduce innovation of financial products. Second, we argue that for certain types of individuals some legal limitations may themselves increase consumer confusion regarding what rules apply to which products and what products may be beneficial or harmful to them. Third, firms will most likely develop ways around such product restrictions, undermining the core rule, increasing costs, and confusing consumers.

At the core of the analysis in this chapter is the interaction between individual psychology and market competition. The classic model works through emphasizing the interaction between rational choice and market competition. Because rational agents choose well, firms compete to offer products that improve welfare. Because rational agents process information well, firms compete to give information that improves decision quality. The introduction of a richer psychology complicates the effect of competition. Now firms compete based on how actual individuals will respond to products in the marketplace, and actual competitive outcomes may not always and in all contexts closely align with increasing consumer welfare.

In the home mortgage market, for example, the standard model assumes that people evaluate options well and that the more options people have, the better. Firms will thus offer more options, people will pick the best ones, and competition will drive out bad options. In reality, people drown in too many options and

---

1. Claims of unconscionability are relatively rare, and until this decade plaintiff victories based on unconscionability were also relatively rare. The number of these cases and the portion won by plaintiffs have increased in the 2000s (data on file with authors).

make mistakes, often in predictable ways. Borrowers, for example, might pick the most salient dimension (lowest monthly cost) rather than focusing on the long-term cost of credit—or the fact that taxes and insurance will not be escrowed and are not included in the monthly cost. Consequently firms can and will introduce options that reflect these behaviors, and people will pick options that they themselves would find suboptimal upon further reflection and analysis, or as to which the likelihood of personal failure is much higher than they think. Consumers, moreover, are likely misled by false beliefs about regulation itself, such as whether the law requires that mortgage brokers work in the interests of borrowers; it generally does not.[2] These behavioral insights suggest that disclosure of information alone will often be insufficient to give consumers what they need to optimize their understanding, their decisionmaking, and the resulting outcomes.

This work is clearly related to the emerging literature on behaviorally informed policymaking. This literature produces novel considerations about designing and implementing regulations, including features such as framing information, setting defaults or opt-out rules, giving warnings, and explicating other strategies to alter individual behavior.[3] Although we ourselves have written about framing and defaults as policy strategies, the focus in this chapter is to embed this thinking more deeply in the logic of markets. Specifically, we rely on a framework that more directly accounts for firm incentives to respond to behaviorally motivated regulation. We understand outcomes as an equilibrium interaction between individuals with specific psychologies and firms that respond to those psychologies within specific markets. Regulation must then account for failures in this equilibrium.

This perspective produces two dimensions to consider. First, sometimes the psychological biases of individuals either help or hurt the firms they interact with; hence firms' and regulators' interests are sometimes misaligned and sometimes not. Consider the consumer who does not understand the profound effects of the compounding of interest. Such a bias would lead the individual to undersave and overborrow. Society would prefer that the individual did not have such a bias in both contexts. Firms, however, would prefer that the individual not have the bias to undersave but would be perfectly content to see the same individual overborrow. The market response to individual bias can profoundly affect regulation. For example, to boost participation in 401(k) retirement plans, the regulator faces at worst indifferent and at best positively inclined employers seeking to boost employee retention and to comply with federal pension rules. In forcing disclosure of hidden prices of credit, by contrast, the regulator faces noncooperative firms whose interests are to find ways to work around or undo interventions.

---

2. See Jackson and Burlingame (2007).

3. These strategies have been called variously "asymmetric paternalism," "libertarian paternalism," and "debiasing through law." See, for example, Camerer and others (2003); Jolls and Sunstein (2005); Thaler and Sunstein (2008).

A second implication of our equilibrium model of firms, in particular markets interacting with individuals with specific psychologies, is that the mode of regulation chosen should take account of this interaction. In particular, the regulator holds two different levers, which we describe as changing the rules and changing the scoring. When forcing disclosure of the APR, for example, the regulator effectively changes the rules of the game: what a firm must do or say. When changing liability rules, the regulator changes the way the game is scored. This distinction is important because changing the rules of the game maintains the firms' original incentives to help or hurt consumer bias, yet changing the scoring of the game can alter those incentives.

This perspective illustrates that one must be careful when transferring the insights of the most prominent example of behavioral regulation—defaults in 401(k) participation—to other examples. We suggest that changing the rules on retirement saving (introducing defaults) works well because employers' incentives generally align (or do not misalign) with regulatory efforts to guide individual choice. In other words, employers are either unaffected or hurt by an individual's propensity to undersave in 401(k) accounts. They thus will not lean against an attempt to fix that problem. In other applications, for example, where firms' incentives misalign with regulatory intent, changing the rules alone may not work well because firms may have the ability to work creatively around those rule changes. Interestingly, this logic leads to regulations (changing the scoring) that, though deeply motivated by behavioral insights, are not themselves particularly psychological in nature. We discuss specific examples of the proposed framework applied to home mortgage credit markets.

In the next section, we discuss disclosure and product regulation, the two dominant models of consumer protection in credit markets.[4] Next, we explain how behavioral insights might matter for policy, and how such insights are constrained by the realities of industrial organization. In that discussion, we develop our equilibrium model of human behavior and market reaction. Finally, we introduce our alternative, "behaviorally informed" mode of home mortgage regulation, encompassing "sticky" opt-out regimes and other strategies based on behavioral insights and market response.

The Existing Structure of Home Mortgage Credit Market Regulation

Existing home mortgage regulation encompasses disclosure regulation and product regulation, and both models miss the interaction between individual psychology and market structure.

---

4. Barr (2005).

Two Types of Disclosure Regimes

The two types of disclosure regimes are consumer-oriented disclosures and public-oriented disclosures. Consumer-oriented disclosures are designed to improve consumers' ability to shop for products and services. The theory is that information in credit markets is imperfect, firms lack sufficient incentives to coordinate to reveal comparable information, and disclosures lower the cost of acquiring more information. More information, if comparable, should help consumers negotiate better; that in turn leads to more competition and a more efficient market. TILA embodies this approach. Under the act, creditors have to reveal in a conspicuous and clear manner the APR and other key costs of credit.

A second type of regime, public-oriented disclosure, uses disclosure to reveal information more generally to the market, the general public, the media, and regulators. Such disclosures are not necessarily designed to improve consumer decisionmaking but to further enforcing other laws or to communicate social norms. For example, the Home Mortgage Disclosure Act requires creditors to reveal information publicly regarding the race, ethnicity, gender, and income of borrowers and applicants for a loan who were turned down. The underlying premise is that financial institutions should not base lending decisions on factors other than creditworthiness and that publicly revealing loan decisions helps outsiders evaluate whether creditors have in fact based their lending decisions solely on that criterion. Public disclosure of this type relies on market reactions, media reporting, consumer and community group activism, legislative oversight, engagement of financial regulators, and other public pressures to alter private sector behavior. The effectiveness of a public disclosure strategy rests not only on the ability to enforce the disclosure requirement through public remedy or private sanction but also on the other laws and social norms that the law is meant to reinforce and on the strength of the groups and institutions that informally work toward compliance with those norms.

Limits to the Effectiveness of Consumer-Oriented Disclosure Regimes

Two essential problems emerge with consumer-oriented disclosure regimes such as TILA. First, behavioral research teaches the pitfalls of relying on consumer understanding to influence consumer behavior; second, many transactions in the financial marketplace involve both complicated legal rules and complicated product structures that even financially sophisticated parties do not fully understand. Empirical evidence suggests that consumers have a hard time understanding credit disclosures, and research in behavioral economics confirms that often consumers do not act on available information. If consumers are unlikely to understand a financial transaction and in many cases are unlikely to behave fully rationally even in the face of disclosed information, then relying on disclosure alone to address information asymmetries may be an ineffectual response. Still, disclosure might be improved based on behavioral research.[5]

TILA requires disclosures to consumers regarding the cost of loans.[6] This type of disclosure seeks to remedy asymmetric information and improve market competition and efficiency through price disclosure, which would make it easier to comparison shop.[7] TILA disclosure most likely improves transparency in the market and thus efficiency, even if not all consumers understand the disclosures.[8] Yet we should be concerned not only with an efficient market in the aggregate but also with efficiency within markets serving low- and moderate-income households and with the consequences of inadequate disclosures for affected consumers. Although TILA facilitates consumer comparison shopping, in some cases too much information is given to consumers and in other cases too little. Even outside the subprime market, there is little reason to think that consumers understand most aspects of mortgage transactions.[9] Decision research suggests a need for simplicity: individuals faced with complex problems often simplify them to one or two basic decisions.[10] The need for simplicity conflicts, however, with the goal of producing comprehensive disclosures that permit consumers to comparison shop based on the real price of multiattribute loans.

In addition, borrowers may trust mortgage brokers to give them full and accurate information and to offer them the best loan product. Yet it is in the broker's interest to offer the borrower the highest rate loan that the broker can convince the borrower to accept. Brokers can earn higher yield spread premiums for placing borrowers into more expensive loans even if the borrower qualifies for a lower cost alternative. Even in competitive retail consumer markets for simple products, price dispersion can persist.[11] In home mortgage transactions, borrower understanding of complicated home mortgage terms is likely to be much lower.

---

5. See, for example, Jolls, Sunstein, and Thaler (1998); Camerer and others (2003, p. 1211, 1230–237).

6. See, for example, 12 *C.F.R.* pt. 226.17 (2001).

7. See 15 U.S.C. § 1601 (2000), which states "The Congress finds that . . . competition among the various financial institutions and other firms engaged in the extension of consumer credit would be strengthened through informed use of credit. [Furthermore, i]t is the purpose of this subchapter to assure a meaningful disclosure of credit terms so that the consumer will be able to compare more readily the various credit terms available to him. . . ." Engel and McCoy (2002, pp. 1255, 1280–281), who describe opportunities that information asymmetries provide for predatory lenders and brokers; Schwartz and Wilde (1979, pp. 630, 635): "Because more consumers will become informed if information acquisition costs are decreased, reducing these costs is thought to be the preferable response to the problem of imperfect information" (footnote omitted).

8. Schwartz and Wilde (1979, p. 630).

9. Board of Governors of the Federal Reserve System and the Department of Housing and Urban Development (1998), which notes consumers' difficulty in understanding mortgage terms with or without disclosure.

10. See, for example, Hogarth (1980, pp. 4–6); Plous (1993, pp. 107–88); Baron (2000, pp. 43–68).

11. Carlton and Perloff (2000, pp. 437–41).

Transactions for home mortgages present an even greater possibility for price differentials based on race, sophistication, willingness, and ability to shop for better terms or other factors.[12] Moreover, with credit scoring, creditors know whether borrowers qualify for less expensive loans under the lender's pricing schedules, but most borrowers do not realize this about themselves.[13]

Unfortunately, TILA is extraordinarily complex.[14] The efficacy of disclosures is diminished by inadequacies in the nature and timing of disclosures,[15] their limited effect on consumer behavior, and consumers' cognitive, emotional, and behavioral limitations. In fact, TILA disclosures may not actually be noticed, read, or understood.[16] TILA disclosures may also inundate the consumer with too much information to process.[17] Moreover, low-income and minority buyers are the least likely to shop for alternative financing arrangements,[18] and these problems are exacerbated in the subprime market.

TILA plays an important role in improving credit markets, and reforms would most likely contribute to improvements in credit markets. But the current structure of the home mortgage market, at least for those borrowing from subprime lenders, suggests that disclosure will not be enough. In addition, financial education can play a role in helping consumers understand disclosures better; however, expenditures for financial education lead to strong externalities, so it is quite difficult to induce private market participants to offer financial education to the borrowing public at anything close to the scale it would take to make a difference. Furthermore, most empirical research on financial education concludes that its effect on real outcomes is typically quite modest.[19] This may be caused by at least in part a behavioral tension, pitting intention against action, which we discuss in the section on Psychology and Industrial Organization.

Product Regulation

Alongside disclosure, governments historically have delineated the terms and conditions of some financial service products. Usury laws are the most common form

---

12. Jackson and Burlingame (2007, p. 63). Ayres (2001, p. 19–44) has documented similar price discrimination in automobile sales and other markets.

13. Credit reports and credit scores are now available to borrowers on request. See Fair and Accurate Credit Transactions Act of 2003, Pub. L. 108-159, §§ 211–12, 117 Stat. 1952, (2003): 1968–969, codified as amended at 15 U.S.C. (2003), § 1681.

14. See, for example, *Emery* v. *Am. Gen. Fin., Inc.,* 71 F. 3d 1343, 1346 (7th Cir. 1995), which describes the ineffectiveness of TILA in conveying relevant information and concludes, "so much for the Truth in Lending Act as a protection for borrowers." See also Durkin (2002, p. 201, p. 208, and table 9), who found that 75 percent of respondents either agreed somewhat or agreed strongly that TILA credit card disclosures are complicated.

15. Eskridge (1984, pp. 1128–130).

16. Renuart (2003, pp. 421, 432).

17. Landers and Rohner (1979, p. 722–25); Eskridge (1984, pp. 1133–135).

18. See, for example, Hogarth and Lee (2000).

19. Caskey (2006).

of such restrictions. In economic terms, one might argue in favor of usury laws to block the granting of credit at high interest rates because the implied default rates would pose unacceptable social externalities. The concern with usury laws is that they often result in credit constraints on poor (or even middle-income) households that could otherwise afford and benefit from credit. Usury laws may also drive lending underground to loan sharks, precluding the possibility of effective consumer protection regulation.

Another type of product regulation excludes certain types of loan terms or sales practices. Such restrictions often have two intertwined motivations. On one hand, restrictions on loan terms can enhance price disclosure and competition by focusing borrowers and creditors on the price of credit rather than on other features of the loan that consumers may ill understand. On the other hand, product restrictions may be thought of as a substantive judgment that certain loan terms are inherently unreasonable. In either event, product restrictions are based on the notion that consumers cannot fully understand or act in their own best interests in the face of confusing terms or transactions or deceptive sales practices to promote these unreasonable terms; moreover, in this view, competition alone is insufficient to drive out such practices.

For example, Congress enacted the Home Ownership Equity Protection Act (HOEPA) in 1994 to respond to unscrupulous lending practices in the subprime home equity mortgage market.[20] For some high-cost loans, HOEPA imposes restrictions on certain contract provisions, requires enhanced disclosures, and enhances remedies for violations. In addition to product regulation, HOEPA requires, directly and indirectly, enhanced disclosures for borrowers facing high-cost loans. Directly, HOEPA enhances disclosure by requiring creditors to disclose mortgage terms three days before closing. Indirectly, HOEPA product restrictions ought to drive more of the cost of the loan into the APR because lenders cannot use the prohibited mortgage terms to cover costs. With more of the cost of the mortgage reflected in the APR, it should be easier for consumers to understand the costs of the loan and go through effective comparison shopping. Creditors would then tend to compete more on price and less on other factors, which consumers have difficulty evaluating. Product regulation could, then, under some circumstances, enhance the effectiveness of disclosure regimes.

HOEPA, however, is decidedly underinclusive: it is designed to curb abusive practices at the fringe of lending rather than overcome broader failures. Moreover, as a practical matter, HOEPA's record has been mixed at best.[21] In response, a HUD-Treasury report proposed a four-part approach to curbing predatory lending in June 2000.[22] Quite recently, the Federal Reserve Board unveiled major

20. Home Ownership and Equity Protection Act of 1994, Pub. L. 103-325, § 151, 108 Stat. 2190 (1994): codified at 15 U.S.C. (2000), § 1601.
21. See, for example, HUD-Treasury Report (2000).
22. See HUD-Treasury Report (2000). See also Barr (2005).

changes to its HOEPA and TILA rules.[23] Many other improvements to abusive practice regulation are desirable, and may now be forthcoming given the fallout from the subprime mortgage lending crisis. Congress is currently considering antipredatory lending legislation.[24]

In addition to the federal regulatory landscape, many states have passed new antipredatory lending laws or enhanced existing ones.[25] Many of these laws are modeled on the federal HOEPA legislation, but increase coverage, enhance restrictions, or bolster enforcement.[26] A vigorous debate exists about whether these state laws diminish access to credit and harm consumers or diminish access to credit that ought not to have been provided and thus increase consumer welfare. Bostic and others (2007) find that the broader coverage of these laws tends to increase subprime origination, but increased restrictions and enforcement tend to diminish such originations. The empirical debate about the scope and effectiveness of these provisions is likely to continue.

In principle, overly prescriptive product regulations can diminish financial access and harm product competition and innovation that might serve low-income households. Governments may easily err by restricting products that would be advantageous or creating new consumer confusion through complicated rules regarding product regulation. Financial markets change rapidly, and firms can easily innovate in ways that are not anticipated by government regulators. Such innovations could better serve consumers than government-imposed product regulations, or conversely such innovations could help firms evade government regulations to the detriment of consumers. It is difficult to know in advance how market innovations will interrelate with product regulations, but for many reasons government regulators may not be able to keep up with these changes. The trade-offs inherent in product regulation ought to be considered, as should alternative forms of regulation.

Psychology and Industrial Organization

With the background on home mortgage regulation having been established, the chapter turns next to the particular dynamic between individual behavior and industrial organization in that market. Recent behavioral research promises to enrich our understanding of the tensions outlined above, by providing a more nuanced and faithful rendition of the psychological and organizational facts that characterize people's relevant behaviors. We first proceed briefly to consider some

23. See Federal Reserve Board, Final Rule Amending Regulation Z, 12 CFR Part 226 (July 14, 2008); Summary of Findings: Consumer Testing of Mortgage Broker Disclosures, submitted to the Board of Governors of the Federal Reserve System, July 10, 2008; Federal Reserve Board, Proposed Rule Amending Regulation Z, 12 CFR Part 226 (June 14, 2007), Federal Register 72, No. 114: 32948; Design and Testing of Effective Truth in Lending Disclosures, Submitted to the Board of Governors of the Federal Reserve System, May 16, 2007.

24. See, for example, Mortgage Reform and Anti-Predatory Lending Act of 2007, H.R. 3915, 110 Cong. 1 sess.

25. Ho and Pennington-Cross (2006); Li and Ernst (2006); Bostic and others (2007).

26. Bostic and others (2007).

of the major insights and then turn to the industrial organization of the mortgage market as it relates to these behavioral patterns. We then develop a model of the interaction, and illustrate how it should affect regulatory choice.

A Deeper Look at Insights from Behavioral Research

How firms will respond to regulation is bound to depend on people's perceptions and behaviors that firms react to in marketing and in offering products and services. Understanding such behaviors promises to give a clearer picture of the contour of market forces and of the problems regulation is attempting to solve.

Behavioral research paints a picture of the average citizen quite different from that typically envisioned in economic policy circles, with significant implications for policy design and implementation. The classical, rational agent model assumes actors with well-ordered preferences and calibrated judgments who are well informed, maximize their self-interested well-being via tangible rewards, and make coherent and insightful plans, which they pursue with efficiency and self-control. In contrast, behavioral research finds people are quite different: their preferences are malleable, their judgment prone to predictable heuristics and biases, their interests often neither selfish nor material, and their plans and behaviors often more context dependent than planned and calculating. What is notable about the emerging behavioral picture is that it paints people as not merely often confused and error-prone but driven by tendencies that are systematic and predictable, yet profoundly different from those typically envisioned by the rational model. A better understanding of such tendencies, appropriately applied, promises to yield more successful policies. In the words of John Maurice Clark almost 100 years ago, "The economist [policy analyst] may attempt to ignore psychology, but it is sheer impossibility for him to ignore human nature. . . . If the economist [policy analyst] borrows his conception of man from the psychologist, his constructive work may have some chance of remaining purely economic in character. But if he does not, he will not thereby avoid psychology. Rather, he will force himself to make his own, and it will be bad psychology."

Consider, for example, such central notions as decisional conflict, information, learning, and planning. Each plays an important role in influencing behavior but deviates in important ways from what is typically assumed by the normative account.

DECISIONAL CONFLICT. People's preferences are typically constructed, not merely revealed, during the decisionmaking process, and the construction of preferences is influenced by the nature and the context of the decision, with important implications. Consider, for example, the role of decisional conflict. Because preferences need to be constructed, choices can be hard to make. People often look for a good reason, a compelling rationale, for choosing one option over another. At times, compelling rationales are easy to articulate; at other times no easy rationale presents itself, which can make the conflict between options hard to resolve. This can prove aversive, and can lead people to postpone decisions or to choose a default option, generating preference patterns that are fundamentally different from those predicted by classical accounts based on value maximization. According to the classical analysis, each option is assigned a subjective value, or utility, and the decisionmaker proceeds to choose the option assigned the highest utility. Such analysis does not anticipate decisional conflict, and it assumes that having more alternatives is a good thing since the more options there are, the more likely the consumer is to find one that satisfies her utility function.

Instead, a proliferation of alternatives can dissuade consumers from making what might otherwise be a favorable choice. As choice becomes difficult, decisions are deferred, often indefinitely.[27] This has been documented in decisions ranging from the choice of jams in upscale grocery stores[28] to decisions to apply for loans equal to roughly a third of one's income,[29] to participation in retirement savings plans, which drops as the number of fund options offered increases.[30] Furthermore, the tendency to refrain from making a choice gives an uncanny advantage to the default, or the perceived status quo. This has been observed in several naturally occurring "experiments," for example, in the context of insurance decisions, when New Jersey and Pennsylvania both introduced the option of a limited right to sue, entitling automobile drivers to lower insurance rates. The two states differed in what was offered as the default option: New Jersey motorists needed to acquire the full right to sue (transaction costs were minimal: a signature), whereas in Pennsylvania the full right to sue was the default, which could then be forfeited in favor of the limited alternative. Only about 20 percent of New Jersey drivers chose to acquire the full right to sue, whereas approximately 75 percent of Pennsylvania drivers chose to retain it, which had substantial financial repercussions.[31] A second naturally occurring experiment was recently observed in Europeans' decisions regarding being potential organ donors.[32] In some European nations drivers are by default organ donors unless they elect not to be; in other, comparable European nations they are by default not donors unless they choose to be. Observed rates of organ donors are almost 98 percent in the former nations and about 15 percent in the latter, a remarkable difference given the low transaction costs and the significance of the decision.

Such patterns suggests that minor contextual changes can alter what consumers choose in ways that are unlikely to relate to their ultimate utility. Of course, the fact that consumers are influenced by conflict and context need not immediately imply that choices ought to be taken away or even that the number of available alterna-

27. Tversky and Shafir (1992); Shafir, Simonson, and Tversky (1993); Iyengar and Lepper (2000).

28. Iyengar and Lepper (2000).

29. Bertrand and others (2007).

30. Iyengar, Huberman, and Jiang (2004).

31. Johnson and others (1993).

32. Johnson and Goldstein (2003).

tives ought to be restricted. It does suggest, however, that a proliferation of alternatives needs to be considered with care rather than seen as an obvious advantage. It also suggests that the choice of a default outcome, for example, rather than a mere formality that can be effortlessly changed, needs to be chosen thoughtfully because it acquires a privileged status. In effect, when a large array of options, or the status quo, is inappropriately handled (intentionally or not), this can lead to substantial decrement in consumers' welfare. A proliferation of complicated decisions in the mortgage market, for example, can lead to quite bad outcomes for borrowers.

OTHER CONTEXTUAL FACTORS: IDENTITIES AND ACCOUNTS. A variety of contextual factors can influence decisionmaking, among them identity salience and mental accounts. People derive their identity in large part from the social groups to which they belong,[33] and identity salience and stereotyping have been shown to affect various behaviors, including resistance to persuasion,[34] reactions to advertisements,[35] hypothetical choices between items,[36] and the rating of consumer products,[37] and it thus has implications for consumers' decisions. In particular, people targeted by negative stereotypes are more likely to mistrust other people's motives,[38] fear rejection, and experience stereotype threat—the fear of confirming a negative stereotype about their own group.[39] Adkins and Ozanne (2005) argue that when low-literacy consumers accept the low-literacy stigma, they perceive market interactions as more risky, engage in less extended problem solving, limit their social exposure, and experience greater stress. In one study, low-socioeconomic-status students performed worse than high-status students when the test was presented as a measure of intellectual ability, but performance was comparable when the test was not seen as pertaining to intellectual measures.[40]

Several other behavioral factors can influence the outcome of consumer decisions in ways that standard analysis is likely to miss. People often are weak at predicting their future tastes or at learning from past experience,[41] and their choices can be influenced by anticipated regret,[42] by costs already incurred,[43] and by effects of sequencing and of temporal separation, where high discount rates for future as compared to present outcomes can yield dynamically inconsistent preferences.[44] Contrary to standard assumptions, the psychological carriers of value are perceived

33. Turner (1987).
34. Kelley (1955).
35. Forehand, Deshpandé, and Reed (2002).
36. Benjamin, Choi, and Strickland (2006); LeBoeuf, Shafir, and Belyavsky (2008).
37. Reed (2004).
38. Crocker and others (1991); Mendoza-Denton and others (2002); Shelton and Richeson (2005); see also Cohen, Steele, and Ross (1999).
39. Steele (1997); Aronson (2002); Walton and Cohen (2007).
40. Croizet and Claire (1998).
41. Kahneman (1994).
42. Bell (1982).
43. Arkes and Blumer (1985); Gourville and Soman (1998).
44. Loewenstein and Elster (1992); Loewenstein and Thaler (1989).

gains and losses rather than anticipated final states of wealth, and attitudes toward risk tend to shift from risk aversion in the face of gains to risk seeking for what appear as losses.[45] Moreover, people are loss averse; that is, the loss associated with giving up a good is substantially greater than the utility associated with obtaining it.[46] This, in turn, leads to reluctance to depart from the status quo because things to be renounced are valued more highly than comparable gains.[47]

People use intuitive mental accounting schemes in which they compartmentalize wealth and spending into distinct budget categories such as savings, rent, and entertainment, and into separate mental accounts such as current income, assets, and future income.[48] Contrary to standard fungibility assumptions, people exhibit different degrees of willingness to spend from various accounts, yielding consumption patterns that are sensitive to labels, overly dependent on current income, and often problematic, such as saving at a low interest rate while borrowing at a higher rate at the same time.[49]

Common to these patterns is the highly "local" and context-dependent nature of consumer decisions. Standard thinking envisions preferences that are largely impervious to minor contextual nuances. In contrast, people's choices are heavily context-dependent, with the option chosen not infrequently being one that would have been forgone had the context differed by just a little, and often in rather trivial ways. What this means is that people's choices are often at the mercy of chance forces as well as of intentional manipulation, which merits careful consideration particularly in contexts with potentially serious consequences.

KNOWLEDGE, ATTENTION, AND INTENTION. A standard assumption is that consumers are attentive, knowledgeable, and typically able to avail themselves of important information. Instead, consumers across a wide range of income and education levels often do not understand or are unaware of options, program rules, benefits, and opportunities. Surveys show that fewer than one-fifth of investors (in stocks, bonds, funds, or other securities) can be considered financially literate,[50] and similar findings describe the understanding shown by pension plan participants.[51] Indeed, even older beneficiaries often do not know what kind of pension they are set to receive or what mix of stocks and bonds they own.

Cognitive load, the amount of information attended to, has been shown to affect performance in a great variety of tasks. To the extent that consumers find themselves in situations that are unfamiliar, distracting, tense, or even stigmatizing (say, applying for a loan), all of which tend to consume cognitive and emo-

---

45. Kahneman and Tversky (1979).
46. Tversky and Kahneman (1991).
47. Samuelson and Zeckhauser (1988); Knetsch (1989).
48. Thaler (1985, 1992).
49. Ausubel (1991).
50. Alexander, Jones, and Nigro (1998).
51. Schultz (1995).

tional resources, fewer resources will remain available to process information relevant to the decision at hand. As a result, decisions may become even more dependent on situational cues and irrelevant considerations. This is observed, for example, in studies of low-literacy consumers, who apparently struggle with trade-offs between effort and accuracy, are overly dependent on peripheral cues in product advertising and packaging, and show systematic withdrawal from market interactions.[52]

More generally, information cannot be equated with knowledge. People often do not fully process imminently available data because of limitations in attention, understanding, perceived relevance, or misremembering. Program designers often do not appreciate this, having been trained to think that people will know what is important and knowable.

An important theme in behavioral research with profound consequences for thinking about policy is the systematic discrepancy between intention and action, which is essentially assumed away in analyses of rational behavior. Knowing what is the right thing to do, even intending to do it, often does not bring about the intended action. Even when intentions are genuine and strong, self-control problems, poor planning, lack of attention, and forgetting can all intervene. On the flip side and for similar reasons, actions may be taken that were genuinely unintended, thus violating the notion of revealed preference. A degree of self-knowledge in turn leads people to take precautions against such tendencies, which can lead to unintended consequences when policies are designed with different creatures in mind.

CHANNEL FACTORS. The pressures exerted by situational factors can constitute restraining forces hard to overcome or can create inducing forces that can be harnessed to great effect. In contrast with massive interventions that often prove ineffectual, seemingly minor situational changes can have a large impact. Kurt Lewin, who coined the term "channel factors,"[53] suggests that certain behaviors can be facilitated by opening a channel, whereas other behaviors can be blocked by closing a channel. Leventhal, Singer, and Jones (1965) document an illustrative example of a channel factor: their subjects received persuasive communications about the risks of tetanus and the value of inoculation, and were then invited to go to the campus infirmary for a tetanus shot. Follow-up surveys showed that the communication was effective in changing beliefs and attitudes. Nonetheless, only 3 percent actually took the step of getting themselves inoculated compared with 28 percent of those who received the same communication but were also given a map of the campus with the infirmary circled and urged to decide on a particular time and route to get them there. Along these lines, Koehler and Poon (2005) argue that people's predictions of their future behavior overweight the

---

52. Adkins and Ozanne (2005).
53. Lewin (1951).

strength of their current intentions and underweight contextual factors that influence the likelihood that those intentions will translate into action. This can generate systematically misguided plans among consumers who, reassured by their good intentions, proceed to put themselves in situations that are powerful enough to make them act and choose otherwise.

Behavioral research highlights a simple fact that is both terribly trivial and extremely profound: people choose between, act toward, and exercise judgment about not things in the world but those things as they are mentally represented. And the relationship between extensional outcome and internal representation is rarely one to one. Instead, options are construed, elaborated, and contextually interpreted in ways that are both systematic and consequential.

Framing, context effects, and channel factors are some of the features of the construal process with important policy implications. The take-up of a program, for example, will depend on whether it is construed as the default or as a departure from the status quo, whether others are thought to have adopted it, or whether it requires what is perceived as a difficult choice from among an array of alternatives or, instead, appears like an easy choice.

The Promise of Behavioral Regulation

Recent work on savings has shown the promise of behavioral regulation—regulation that is motivated directly by specific psychological insights. Research suggests that individual choices regarding saving are profoundly affected by psychology: mental accounting, anchoring, endowment effects, and other psychological constructs and frames make a big difference to outcomes. Recent policy innovations have exploited the power of defaults. Default rules, for example, are critical in determining whether and how much individuals will save. By using default rules, governments might encourage welfare-enhancing behavior without prohibiting other market choices. If employers are required to enroll workers in automatic retirement plans unless the worker affirmatively opts out of participating, enrollment rates will be higher and net savings may increase.

Behavioral principles have figured prominently in recent attempts at constructive policy applications. Save More Tomorrow (SMaRT), a program intended to increase retirement savings, deposits money into savings out of future salary raises rather than out of current income, with the added proviso that one can withdraw from the program at any time. It has relied on fundamental behavioral insights—future discounting, nominal loss aversion, and status quo bias—to generate substantial increases in retirement savings and has been adopted by many employers, affecting the lives of millions in the United States and abroad. Attention has been focused on the ways in which retirement savings plans can be made automatic to increase participation and savings rates.[54]

---

54. Thaler and Benartzi (2004); Benartzi and Thaler (forthcoming); Iwry and John (2006).

Similar types of policies can be pursued across a range of financial products and services that reach low-income households. By further extension from the retirement literature, employers could be required to deposit worker income checks directly into a low-cost bank account with an automatic savings plan unless the employee opts out of the arrangement. Governments could make tax refund and benefit payments through direct deposit into a safe and affordable bank account with savings features, again unless the beneficiary opts out.[55]

Our starting point, however, is that opt-out rules and other such examples seem to be limited in their scope of application. Consider the common opt-out experience of signing a rental car contract. Individuals actively opt out of many features of a rental contract but do so almost automatically: "Initial here, here, and here." Although opting out may be effective in the lack of a strong market pressure, it is far too easily overcome by the firm that interacts directly with the consumer. This raises the more basic question: what would behavioral regulation look like in a richer context, where we consider the ability of the firm to respond to this regulation (and potentially undo or magnify it)?

Industrial Organization: How Market Forces Can Undermine or Reinforce Behaviorally Informed Regulation

In principle, market forces help push private sector actors to offer the best products at the lowest prices. The theory, however, depends crucially on assumptions of rationality. In the classic economic model, the setup is this: free competition for the provision of goods and services to consumers who obtain full information, understand the information they receive, and act based on that full information. Market actors are restrained from peddling welfare-reducing products by consumers who will demand better. In practice, as we have seen, in some contexts the market has produced products and services that are suboptimal. It is easier to see why market forces may sometimes not produce optimal products and services once one relaxes the assumptions underlying the classic model.

Returning to the opt-out regulation, the presumption is that individuals fail to maximize their own utility because of temporal inconsistency—they would like to save but fail to do so. Opt-out regulation eases this problem by facilitating savings even among those who do nothing (perhaps because of procrastination). What are firm (employer) incentives in this case? Employers appear to be largely indifferent or perhaps even motivated to decrease the bias against savings.[56] This incentive is crucial.

55. Barr (2007).

56. This is largely because of the existing regulatory framework—pension regulation gives employers at least some incentive to enroll lower-income individuals in 401(k) programs. Absent this, it is likely that firms would be happy to discourage enrollment because they often must pay the match for these individuals. Even with the incentive the pension structure creates far from perfect alignment of public and private interests in enrolling workers. This point is interesting because it suggests that even defaults in savings work only because some other regulation changed the scoring of the game.

Table 6-1. *The Firm and the Individual*

Behavioral fallibility	Market-neutral or wants to overcome consumer fallibility	Market exploits consumer fallibility
Consumers misunderstand compounding	Consumers misunderstand compounding in *savings* → Banks would like to *reduce* this to increase savings base	Consumers misunderstand compounding in *borrowing* → Banks would like to *exploit* this to increase borrowing
Consumers procrastinate	Consumers procrastinate in signing up for EITC → Tax filing companies would like to *reduce* this so as to increase number of customers	Consumers procrastinate in returning rebates → Retailers would like to *exploit* this to increase revenues

EITC = earned income tax credit.

Consider another case. As has been argued elsewhere,[57] in some markets firms have incentives to confound consumers. In posting prices, for example, firms have strong market and private incentives to hide certain prices. If consumers sort into those who understand complicated offers and those who do not, it is difficult for firms to compete by offering the most transparent products if such products are less profitable; consumers who understand bad deals already avoid them and will shun the new offer and consumers who do not understand them and go for the new, better offer will just lower profits for the firm.[58] This result—that transparency does not always pay off for firms once one recognizes that people are fallible and easily misled—illustrates how firms sometimes have strong incentives to exacerbate psychological biases. Regulation in this case faces a much more difficult challenge than in the savings situation.

This distinction is central to our framework and is illustrated in table 6-1. In some cases, the market is either neutral or wants to overcome consumer fallibility. In other cases, the market would like to exploit or exaggerate consumer fallibility. For example, when consumers misunderstand compounding of interest in the context of saving, banks have incentives to reduce this misunderstanding so that they can increase their deposits. When consumers misunderstand compounding in the context of borrowing, lenders have little incentive to remove this misunderstanding. It could decrease the debts they are able to issue.[59] When consumers procrastinate in signing up for the earned income tax credit (EITC) and hence in filing at all for taxes, private tax preparation firms have incentives to help remove this procrastination to increase their customer base. When consumers

57. Laibson, Repetto, and Tobacman (1998).
58. Laibson, Repetto, and Tobacman (1998).
59. This stylized example abstracts from collection issues.

Table 6-2. *Changing the Game*

Rules	Set the defaults in 401(k) savings
	Opt-out rule for organ donation
Scoring	Penalties for 401(k) enrollment, top heavy with high-salary employees
	Grants to states that enroll organ donors

procrastinate in returning rebates (but make retail purchases as if they are going to get a rebate), retailers benefit. Note the parallelism here in the examples: firm incentives to alleviate or exploit a bias are not an intrinsic feature of the bias itself. Instead, they are a feature of how the bias plays itself out in that particular market structure.

In the consumer credit market, one worries that many firm-individual interactions are in the second category: firms seeking to exploit rather than alleviate bias. If true, this raises the concern of overextrapolating from the 401(k) defaults example to credit products. To the extent that 401(k) defaults work because optimal behavior is largely aligned with market incentives, other areas such as credit markets might be more difficult to regulate with mere defaults. Furthermore, if the credit market is dominated by "low-road" firms offering opaque products that prey on human weakness, it is more likely that regulators of such a market will be captured by the regulated entities and permit the bad behavior to continue, that market forces will defeat any positive defaults set, and that low-road players will continue to dominate. Many observers believe that the credit markets today are in fact dominated by such low-road firms[60] and that formerly "high-road" players have come to adopt the sharp practices of their low-road competitors. If government policymakers want to use defaults in such contexts, they might need to deploy "stickier" defaults or more aggressive policy options.

Table 6-2 illustrates a conceptual approach to the issue of regulatory choice. The regulator can either change the rules of the game or change the scoring of the game.[61] Setting a default is an example of changing the rules of the game. Disclosure regulation also fits this case as well. Specifically, regulators change the rules of the game when they attempt to change the nature of firm–individual interactions, when the regulation attempts to affect what can be said, offered, or done. Changing the scoring of the game, by contrast, changes the payoffs a firm will receive for particular outcomes. Pension regulation that penalizes firms whose 401(k) plan enrollment is top-heavy with high-paid executives is an example of how firms are given incentives to enroll low-income individuals without setting particular rules on how this is done.

---

60. See, for example, Bar-Gill (2004); Mann (2007).

61. We do not mean to suggest that this binary framework encompasses all possible regulatory solutions. We merely deploy the binary model to illustrate how individual psychology and firm incentives interact with regulatory choice.

Table 6-3. *Behaviorally Informed Regulation*

Item	Market-neutral or wants to overcome consumer fallibility	Market exploits consumer fallibility
Rules	Public education on saving Direct deposit and auto-save Licensing	Opt-out mortgage system Information debiasing on debt
Scoring	Tax incentives for savings vehicles for the poor	Penalties to make the opt-out system sticky Ex post liability standard for truth in lending Broker fiduciary duty or changing compensation (yield spread premiums)

Table 6-3 puts these two different dimensions together, illustrating that regulatory choice should be analyzed according to the market's stance toward human fallibility. As the discussion that follows illustrates, policies in the top-right-hand corner face a particular challenge. Changing the rules of the game alone will be difficult when firms are highly motivated to find work-arounds and to exploit human fallibility. As such, when we suggest opt-out policies in mortgages, the challenge will be to find ways to make these starting positions sticky, so that firms do not simply undo their default nature. In our judgment, both achieving a good default and figuring out how to make it work require separating low-road from high-road firms and making it profitable for high-road firms to offer the default product.[62] For that to work, the default must be sufficiently attractive to consumers based on behavioral research and sufficiently profitable for high-road firms to succeed in offering it; further, penalties for deviations from the default must be sufficiently costly that the default is sticky even in the face of market pressures from low-road firms. It may be that in some credit markets low-road firms have become so dominant that sticky defaults will be ineffectual. Moreover, achieving such a default is likely to be more costly than making defaults work when market incentives align, not least because the costs associated with the stickiness of the default involve deadweight losses given that there will be those for whom deviating from the default is optimal. These losses would need to be weighed against the losses from the current system as well as against losses from alternative approaches such as disclosure or product regulation. Nonetheless, we believe it is worth exploring whether such sticky defaults can help to alter the underlying dynamics of the home mortgage market.

Behaviorally Informed Home Mortgage Regulation

In what follows, we discuss the specific application of these forces of individual psychology and firm incentives to mortgage markets. The default example is just

---

62. For a related concept, see Kennedy (2005).

one of a set of examples of potential regulatory interventions based on our conceptual framework. In this chapter, we explore four ideas: an ex post standard for truth in lending, a requirement of full information disclosure to borrowers, a "sticky" opt-out mortgage system, and restructuring the relationship between borrowers and brokers. Given the complexities involved, this chapter does not champion specific policies. Instead, it illustrates how a behaviorally informed regulatory analysis would lead to a deeper understanding of the costs and benefits of each policy.

Ex Post Standards-Based Truth in Lending

Optimal disclosure will not occur in all markets simply through competition alone. Competition under a range of plausible scenarios will not necessarily generate psychologically informative and actionable disclosure[63] as the current crisis in the subprime mortgage sector suggests may have occurred. If competition does not produce informative disclosure, disclosure regulation might be necessary. But simply because disclosure regulation is needed does not mean it will work. Regulating disclosure appropriately is difficult and requires substantial psychological sophistication by regulators.

A behavioral perspective could focus on improving disclosures themselves. For example, such a perspective would suggest that simply adding information is unlikely to work. The goal of disclosure should be to improve the quality of information about contract terms in meaningful ways. The goal of disclosure, furthermore, probably ought not to be to improve the quality of decisions solely by changing the intentionality of the consumer, as tempting as that might seem at first glance. But there is much evidence that focusing on intentionality may be misplaced. For example, if people are overconfident about their ability to repay, disclosure policy should probably not require firms to tell people about their overconfidence and try to convince them to take a smaller loan because such policies will generally fail. Disclosure policies that are effective depend on presenting a frame that is well understood and actually conveys salient information that would help the decisionmaker act optimally. It is possible, for example, that information about the frequency of losses from a particular product might help ("2 out of 10 borrowers who take this kind of loan default"), but proper framing is quite difficult to achieve.

Even if regulators were sophisticated, it is difficult to determine what constitutes neutral, purely informative regulation and difficult to enforce that frame given that it may vary across situations. It is too difficult to determine all the ways in which frames can confound consumers. What is confusing in a frame is highly context specific, depending on subtle nuances of presentation and what other information is being presented. It is difficult to gauge what the inferred

---

63. Contrast Laibson, Repetto, and Tobacman (1998) with Grossman and Hart (1980).

underlying messages are. The goals of disclosure rules, moreover, are easily evaded. Sellers can undermine whatever regulatory disclosure regime is established, in some contexts simply by complying with it: "Here's the disclosure form I'm supposed to give you; just sign here." In addition, with rules-based ex ante disclosure requirements such as TILA, firms (the discloser) move last, after the rule is set up, and whatever gave the discloser incentives to confuse consumers remains in the face of the regulation.

We propose that policymakers consider shifting from relying solely on a rules-based, ex ante regulatory structure for disclosure embodied in TILA toward integrating an ex post, standards-based disclosure requirement as well. This type of policy intervention would correspond to a change in scoring, in the lower right of table 6-3. In essence, courts, or an expert agency, would determine whether the disclosure would, under common understanding, effectively communicate the key terms of the mortgage to the typical borrower. This approach would be similar to ex post determinations of reasonableness of disclaimers of warranties in sales contracts under Uniform Commercial Code (UCC) 2-316.[64]

The debate over whether standards or rules should be preferred is long-standing.[65] Law and economics scholars have used transaction-cost economics to argue that the higher cost of articulating rules ex ante is worthwhile when many people engage in the activity being regulated, multiplying the transaction costs of ex post determinations.[66] Kaplow suggests that the cost of rulemaking will be higher ex ante than the cost of developing a standard, but that standards generate higher ex post costs because of uncertainty and other factors.[67] A standard might have advantages over a rule if the rule is easy to evade, however, and a rule can become stale over time because it is not easily adapted to changing market conditions. Yet translating transaction-cost theory into application is difficult because it is hard to measure the costs and benefits of alternative rules and standards formulations.

In our judgment, establishing a new ex post version of truth in lending based on the reasonable-person standard rather than relying solely on fixed disclosure rules might permit innovation—both in products themselves and in strategies of disclosure—while minimizing rule evasion. An ex post standard with sufficient teeth could change the incentives of firms to confuse; such a standard would also make it difficult to evade. Under the current approach, creditors can easily evade TILA, not by failing to comply with its actual terms but by making the required disclosures regarding the terms effectively useless in the context of the borrowing decision. Given the malleability of people's decisions and the myriad ways in

---

64. See White and Summers (1995).

65. See, for example, Kennedy (1976, pp. 1685, 1688); Schlag (1985, p. 379, pp. 382–83); Rose (1988, p. 577); Radin (1989, p. 781); Schauer (1991, pp. 149–55); Kaplow (1992, p. 557); Posner (1997, pp. 101–07).

66. See, for example, Kaplow (1992, p. 562–63). But see also Rose (1988); Posner (1997).

67. Kaplow (1992, p. 562–63).

which specific details of how a loan is presented can affect consumer decisions, there is enough freedom, given any ex ante rules, to present loan information in a way that alters consumer decisionmaking. TILA does not block a creditor, for example, from introducing a more salient term ("lower monthly cost!") to compete with the APR for borrowers' attention. Under a standards approach, lenders could not plead compliance with TILA as a defense; rather, the question would be one of objective reasonableness: whether the lender meaningfully conveyed the information required for a typical consumer to make a reasonable judgment about the loan. Standards would also lower the cost of specification ex ante. Clarity of contract is hard to specify ex ante but much easier to verify ex post.

Although TILA has significant shortcomings, we do not propose abandoning it. Rather, TILA would remain, with whatever useful modifications to it might be gleaned from understanding consumers' emotions, thought processes, and behaviors.[68] A modified and improved TILA would still be important in permitting comparison shopping among mortgage products, one of its two central goals. But some of the pressure on TILA to induce firms to reveal information that would promote better consumer understanding would be shifted to the ex post standard proposed here.

Of course, such an approach would have significant costs. These costs vary significantly depending on how the concept is implemented. For example, introducing an important role for the generalist courts in assessing compliance with this new ex post disclosure standard—a much more open-ended analysis than currently conducted by the courts in assessing compliance with TILA—might conflict with the role of specialist bank regulators in developing disclosure policies. Moreover, litigation over the reasonableness standard is likely to be costly, at least in the first instance. To limit the costs associated with our approach, the liability exposure associated with the ex post determination of reasonableness could be significantly confined. For example, one could provide that the ex post standard for reasonableness of disclosure might provide a (partial) defense to payment in foreclosure or bankruptcy, rather than permitting affirmative suits for rescission or cure based on violations of the standard, or tort suits based on gross deviations from it.[69] One might further minimize such costs by turning to the banking agencies to articulate the standard, develop safe harbors, provide "no action" letters regarding reasonable disclosures, and enforce the provision through agency actions or fines, rather than relying on courts and private suits.

Regardless of the particular form of enforcement, the uncertainty in enforcing the standard ex post would itself impose costs regarding the appropriate form of

68. See Federal Reserve Board, Final Rule Amending Regulation Z, 12 CFR Part 226 (July 14, 2008); Summary of Findings: Consumer Testing of Mortgage Broker Disclosures, submitted to the Board of Governors of the Federal Reserve System, July 10, 2008; Federal Reserve Board, Proposed Rule Amending Regulation Z, 12 CFR Part 226 (June 14, 2007), Federal Register 72, No. 114: 32948; Design and Testing of Effective Truth in Lending Disclosures, Submitted to the Board of Governors of the Federal Reserve System, May 16, 2007.

69. For a related concept, see Pottow (2007), who suggests ex post liability for substantively "reckless lending."

disclosure. Perhaps more seriously uncertainty regarding how to disclose novel or innovative mortgage products might deter innovation in developing the mortgage products themselves, not just the disclosures. The additional costs of compliance with a disclosure standard might reduce lenders' willingness to develop new mortgage products designed to reach lower-income or minority borrowers who might not be served by the firms' "plain vanilla" products. The lack of clear rules might also increase consumer confusion about how to compare innovative mortgage products to each other even while it increases consumer understanding of the particular mortgage products. Even if one couples the advantages of TILA for mortgage comparisons with the advantages of an ex post standard for disclosure in promoting clarity, the net result may simply be greater confusion for everyone with respect to cross-loan comparisons, given market complexity. That is, if consumer confusion results mostly from firm obfuscation, then our proposal will most likely help a good deal; by contrast, if consumer confusion results mostly from market complexity in product innovation, then our proposal is unlikely to make a major difference.

Despite the shortcomings of an ex post standard for truth in lending, we believe that such an approach is worth pursuing. The limits of the existing ex ante rules have become all too apparent, and we believe that an ex post standard may help to correct for many of these deficiencies. The precise contours of liability for failure to disclose reasonably are not essential to the design, and weighing the costs and benefits of different methods of implementation is beyond the scope of what we hope to do in introducing the idea in this chapter.

Full Information Disclosure

Although further research and experimentation are appropriate, it may be that consumers have false background assumptions regarding what brokers and creditors reveal to them about their borrowing status and about regulation of the mortgage market itself. What if consumers believe the following:

> Creditors reveal all information about me and the loan products I am qualified to receive. Brokers work for me in finding me the best loan for my purposes, and lenders offer me the best loans for which I qualify. I must be qualified for the loan I have been offered, or the lender would not have validated the choice by offering me the loan. Being qualified for a loan means that the lender thinks that I can repay the loan. Why else would they lend me the money? Moreover, the government tightly regulates home mortgages; they make the lender give me all these legal forms. Surely the government must regulate all aspects of this transaction.

In reality, the government does not regulate as the borrower believes and the lender does not necessarily behave as the borrower hopes. Moreover, with the advent of nationwide credit reporting systems and refinement of credit scoring and modeling, the creditor and broker know information about the borrower that the borrower does not necessarily know about himself, including not just his credit score but also his likely performance regarding a particular set of loan products. Creditors will know whether the borrower could qualify for a better, cheaper loan as well as the likelihood that the borrower will meet his obligations under the existing mortgage or become delinquent, refinance, default, or go into foreclosure.

Given the consumer's probably false background assumptions and the reality of asymmetric information favoring the lender and broker, we suggest that creditors be required to reveal favorable information to the borrower at the time of the mortgage loan offer, including disclosure of the borrower's credit score and the borrower's qualifications for the lender's products. Brokers would be required to reveal the wholesale rate sheet pricing for loans for which the applicant qualifies. Such an approach corresponds to using the debiasing information given in the top right of table 6-3.

The goal of these disclosures would be to put pressure on creditors and brokers to be honest in their dealings with applicants. The additional information might improve comparison shopping and perhaps outcomes. Of course, revealing such information would also reduce broker and creditor profit margins. But if the classic market competition story relies on full information and assumes rational behavior based on understanding, one could view this proposal as simply attempting to remove market frictions from information failures and move the market competition model more toward its ideal. Full information disclosure does have its downsides, among them the fact that the disclosure may be too weak to change market dynamics, and that the disclosure itself may increase the often misplaced bond of trust between brokers and borrowers, leading potentially to worse outcomes. The disclosure may increase information overload and simply be ignored. Still, full information disclosure is worth consideration as a method to correct for information asymmetries in the mortgage market.

An Opt-Out Mortgage Product

Even though the causes of the mortgage crisis are myriad, a central problem was that many borrowers took out loans that they did not understand and could not afford. Brokers and lenders offered loans that looked much less expensive than they really were because of low initial monthly payments and hidden, costly features. Families commonly make mistakes in taking out home mortgages because they are misled by broker sales tactics, misunderstand the complicated terms and financial trade-offs in mortgages, wrongly forecast their own behavior, and misperceive their risks of borrowing. How many homeowners really understand how the teaser rate, introductory rate, and reset rate relate to the London interbank offered rate plus some specified margin, or can judge whether the prepayment penalty will offset the gains from the teaser rate?

Disclosure along the lines we suggest might help. By altering the rules of the game of disclosure and altering the scoring for seeking to evade proper disclosure, such approaches may be sufficient to reduce the worst outcomes; however, if market pressures and consumer confusion are sufficiently strong, such disclosure may not be enough. Moreover, if market complexity is sufficiently disruptive to consumer choice, product regulation might be appropriate. For example, barring prepayment penalties could reduce lock-in to bad mortgages, or barring short-term bullet ARMs and balloon payments could reduce refinance pressure; in both cases, more of the cost of the loan would be pushed into interest rates and competition could focus on price. Price competition would benefit consumers, and consumers would be more likely to understand the terms on which lenders are competing. Product regulation would also reduce cognitive and emotional pressures for bad decisionmaking. As we note in the section on regulation, however, product regulation may stifle beneficial innovation and the government may simply get it wrong.

For that reason, we propose what we call a "sticky" opt-out mortgage system to help anchor consumer decisionmaking among the range of potentially confusing choices. An opt-out system would fall, in terms of stringency, somewhere between product regulation and disclosure. Under the proposal, legislation would be enacted requiring firms to offer an opt-out home mortgage product. An opt-out product regulation corresponds to changing the rules of the game, in the top right of table 6-3. In this model, lenders would be required to offer eligible borrowers a standard mortgage (or set of mortgages) such as a fixed-rate, self-amortizing 30-year mortgage loan, according to reasonable underwriting standards. Lenders would be free to charge whatever interest rate they wanted on the loan and, subject to several constraints, could offer whatever other loan products they wanted. Borrowers would get the standard mortgage(s) offered, unless they chose to opt out in favor of another option, after honest and comprehensible disclosures from brokers or lenders about the risks of the alternative mortgages. An opt-out mortgage system would mean borrowers would be more likely to get straightforward loans they could understand.

But a plain vanilla opt-out policy is likely to be inadequate. We return to our equilibrium model of firm incentives and individual psychology. Unlike the savings context, where market incentives align well with policies to overcome behavioral biases, in the context of credit markets, firms often have an incentive to hide the true costs of borrowing. Lenders may seek to extract surplus from borrowers because of asymmetric information about future income or default probabilities,[70] and borrowers may be unable to distinguish among complex loan products and act optimally based on such an understanding.[71]

---

70. Musto (2007).
71. See, for example, Ausubel (1991).

Given the strong market pressures to deviate from the offer, more would be required than a simple opt-out to render the default sticky enough to make a difference in outcomes. Deviation from the offer would require heightened disclosures and additional legal exposure for lenders to make the default sticky. Under this plan, lenders would have stronger incentives to provide meaningful disclosures to those whom they convince to opt out, because they would face increased costs if the loans did not work out. That is, we need to change the scoring of the game. For example, under one approach, if default occurs when a borrower opts out, the borrower could raise the lack of reasonable disclosure as a defense to bankruptcy or foreclosure. Using an objective reasonableness standard akin to that used for warranty analysis under the UCC, if the court determined that the disclosure would not effectively communicate the key terms and risks of the mortgage to the typical borrower, the court could modify or rescind the loan contract. In another approach, rather than relying on courts, the banking agencies could impose fines for unreasonable disclosures. The precise nature of the stickiness required and the trade-offs involved in imposing these costs on lenders would need to be explored in greater detail, but in principle a sticky opt-out policy could effectively leverage the behavioral insight that framing matters with the industrial organization insight that credit market incentives work against a pure opt-out policy.

An opt-out mortgage system with stickiness might provide several benefits over the current market outcomes. A plain vanilla set of mortgages would be easier to compare across mortgage offers. Consumers are likely to understand the key terms and features of such standard products better than they would alternative mortgage products. Once the alternative products are introduced, the consumer would be made aware that the alternatives represent deviations from the default, and the creditors themselves would be required to make heightened disclosures about the risks of the loan product for the borrower, subject to legal sanction (to be determined) in the event of failure to reasonably comply with the disclosure requirements. Consumers may be less likely to make mistakes. The approach would allow lenders to continue to develop new kinds of mortgages, but only when they can explain the key terms and risks clearly to borrowers.

Moreover, requiring the default to be offered plus requiring heightened disclosures and increased legal exposure for deviations may help make high-road lending more profitable than low-road lending. If offering an opt-out mortgage product helps split the market between high- and low-road firms and rewards the former, the market may shift (back) toward firms that offer home mortgage products that better serve borrowers. For this to work effectively, the default—and the efforts to make the default sticky—would need to distinguish the typical good loan, benefiting both lender and borrower, from a wide range of bad loans: for example, those that benefit the lender (taking fees that exceed default costs) but harm the borrower; those that benefit the borrower (duping the lender and escaping high foreclosure/bankruptcy costs) but harm the lender; and those that harm the borrower and lender but benefit third parties (brokers taking fees on loans likely to fail).

Costs will be associated with requiring an opt-out home mortgage. For example, the sticky defaults may not be sticky enough, given market pressures. Implementing the measure may be costly, thus reducing overall access to home mortgage lending. There may be too many cases in which alternative products are optimal, so that the default product is in essence incorrect and comes to be seen as such. The default would then matter less over time, and forcing firms and consumers to go through the process of deviating from it would become increasingly just another burden (like existing disclosure paperwork) along the road to getting a home mortgage loan.

One could somewhat improve these outcomes in a variety of ways. For example, smart defaults could be based on key borrower characteristics such as income and age. With a handful of key facts, an optimal default might be offered to particular borrowers. Smart defaults might reduce error costs associated with the proposal; however, smart defaults could add to consumer confusion because of too many choices. Another approach would be to build in periodic required reviews of the defaults so that the opt-out product stays current with our knowledge of outcomes in the home mortgage market. Firms might be required to conduct survey research on the effectiveness of disclosures and research could lead the banking agencies to develop safe harbors for reasonable disclosures.

Restructure the Relationship between Brokers and Borrowers

An alternative approach to addressing the problem of market incentives to exploit behavioral biases would be to focus directly on the relationship between brokers and borrowers. Mortgage brokers dominate the subprime market. Brokers are compensated for getting borrowers to pay higher rates than those for which the borrower would qualify. Such yield spread premiums are used widely.[72] In loans with yield spread premiums, unlike other loans, there is wide dispersion in prices paid to mortgage brokers. As Howell Jackson has shown, within the group of borrowers paying yield spread premiums, African Americans paid $474 more for their loans and Hispanics $590 more than white borrowers; thus, even if minority and white borrowers could qualify for the same rate, in practice minority borrowers are likely to pay much more.[73]

---

72. See Jackson and Burlingame (2007, p. 127). Although in principle yield spread premiums could permit lenders legitimately to pass on the cost of a mortgage broker fee to a cash-strapped borrower in the form of a higher interest rate rather than in the form of a cash payment, the evidence suggests that yield spread premiums are in fact used to compensate brokers for getting borrowers to accept higher interest rates.

73. Jackson and Burlingame (2007, p. 125); see also Guttentag (2000, p. 8).

Brokers cannot be monitored sufficiently by borrowers.[74] We are dubious that additional disclosures would help borrowers to be better monitors,[75] in part because disclosures about brokers may reinforce borrower trust in them. Disclosing conflicts of interest may paradoxically increase consumer trust.[76] For example, if the broker is required to tell the borrower that the broker works for himself, not in the interest of the borrower, the borrower's trust in the broker may increase. After all, the broker is being honest with her! Moreover, evidence from the subprime mortgage crisis suggests that, in theory, creditors and investors have incentives to monitor brokers, but they do not do so effectively.

One could alter the incentives of creditors and investors to monitor or directly regulate mortgage brokers. The ex post disclosure standard we suggest might have a salutary effect by making it harder to evade disclosure duties. Moreover, in addition to licensing requirements that may increase regulator and public scrutiny of broker practices, we also believe it is worth considering treating mortgage brokers as fiduciaries to borrowers, similar to the requirements for investment advisers under the Investment Advisors Act. This would, of course, require vast changes to the brokerage market, including to the ways in which mortgage brokers are compensated and by whom. We would need to shift from a lender-compensation system to a borrower-compensation system, and we would need a regulatory system and resources to police the fiduciary duty. An interim step with much lower costs, and potentially significant benefits, would be to ban yield spread premiums. Banning YSPs could reduce broker abuses by eliminating a strong incentive for brokers to seek out higher-cost loans for customers.

Conclusion

Existing regulations fail to take account of advances in behavioral research about how people think and act. Existing regulations based on the rational actor model have significant shortcomings. Our understanding of how human beings perceive and act based on regulatory and market "facts" in the world suggests an alternative approach. Behaviorally informed regulation would take account of the importance of framing and defaults, of the gap between information and understanding, and intention and action as well as of decisional conflict and other psychological factors affecting how people behave. At the same time, behaviorally informed regulation should take into account not only behavioral insights about individuals but also economic insights about markets. Markets can be shown to systematically favor overcoming behavioral biases in some contexts and to

74. Jackson and Burlingame (2007).
75. See, for example, FTC (2007).
76. Cain, Lowenstein, and Moore (2005).

systematically favor exploiting those biases in other contexts. A central illustration of this distinction is the contrast between the market for saving and the market for borrowing—in which the same human failing in understanding and acting on the important concept of compound interest leads to opposite market reactions in the two contexts.

In our model outcomes are an equilibrium interaction between individuals with specific psychologies and firms that respond to those psychologies within specific markets. Regulation must then account for the social welfare failures in this equilibrium. Taking both individuals and industrial organization into account seriously suggests the need for a range of market-context-specific policy options, including changing both the rules of the game and its scoring. We have sketched here what some of these policy options might be, although we have not defended them as optimal. In particular, the focus is on an ex post, standards-based truth in lending law, a requirement of full disclosure of information favorable to the borrower, a "sticky" opt-out mortgage system, and restructuring the relationship between brokers and borrowers. Further work will be required to explore whether these alternative approaches might merit enactment.

References

Adkins, N., and J. Ozanne. 2005. "The Low Literate Consumer." *Journal of Consumer Research* 32, no. 1: 93–105.

Alexander, G., J. Jones, and P. Nigro. 1998. "Mutual Fund Shareholders: Characteristics, Investor Knowledge, and Sources of Information." *Financial Services Review* 7, no. 4: 301–16.

Arkes, H. R., and C. Blumer. 1985. "The Psychology of Sunk Cost." *Organizational Behavior and Human Decision Processes* 35, no. 1: 124–40.

Aronson, J. M., ed. 2002. *Improving Academic Achievement: Impact of Psychological Factors in Education.* San Diego, Calif.: Academic Press.

Ausubel, L. M. 1991. "The Failure of Competition in the Credit Card Market." *American Economic Review* (March): 50–81.

Ayres, I. 2001. *Pervasive Prejudice? Unconventional Evidence of Race and Gender Discrimination.* University of Chicago Press.

Bar-Gill, O. 2004. "Seduction by Plastic." *Northwestern University Law Review* 98 no. 4: 1373–434.

Baron, J. 2000. *Thinking and Deciding.* 3rd ed. Cambridge University Press.

Barr, M. S. 2005. "Credit Where It Counts." *New York University Law Review* 80, no. 2: 513–652.

———. 2007. "An Inclusive, Progressive National Savings and Financial Services Policy." *Harvard Law and Policy Review* 1, no. 1: 161–84.

Bell, D. E. 1982. "Regret in Decisionmaking under Uncertainty." *Operations Research* 30, no. 5: 961–81.

Benartzi, S., and R. Thaler. 2001. "Naive Diversification Strategies in Defined Contribution Saving Plans." *American Economic Review* 91, no. 1: 79–98.

Benartzi, S., and R. H. Thaler. Forthcoming. "Heuristics and Biases in Retirement Savings Behavior." *Journal of Economic Perspectives.*

Benjamin, D. J., J. J. Choi, and J. Strickland. 2006. "Social Identity and Preferences." Working Paper 13309. Cambridge, Mass.: National Bureau of Economic Research (issued August 2007, rev. April 13, 2008).

Bertrand, M., and others. 2007. "What's Psychology Worth? A Field Experiment in the Consumer Credit Market." Discussion Paper 918. Yale University Economic Growth Center (www.econ.yale.edu/~egcenter/).

Board of Governors of the Federal Reserve System and the Department of Housing and Urban Development. 1998. "Joint Report to the Congress Concerning Reform to the Truth in Lending Act and the Real Estate Settlement Procedures Act" (www.federalreserve.gov/boarddocs/RptCongress/tila.pdf).

Bostic, Raphael, and others. 2007. *State and Local Anti-Predatory Lending Laws: The Effect of Legal Enforcement Mechanisms* (http://papers.ssrn.com/sol3/papers.cfm?abstract_id=1005423).

Cain, D. M., G. Lowenstein, and D. A. Moore. 2005. "The Dirt on Coming Clean: Perverse Effects of Disclosing Conflicts of Interest." *Journal of Legal Studies* 34, no. 1: 1–25.

Camerer, C. and others. 2003. "Regulation for Conservatives: Behavioral Economics and the Case for 'Asymmetric Paternalism.'" *University of Pennsylvania Law Review* 151, no. 3: 1211, 1230–37.

Carlton, Dennis, and Jeffrey Perloff. 2000. *Modern Industrial Organization.* 3rd ed. Reading, Mass.: Addison-Wesley.

Caskey, John. 2006. "Can Personal Financial Management Education Promote Asset Accumulation by the Poor?" Policy Brief 2006-PB-06. Indianapolis, Ind.: Networks Financial Institute (March).

Cohen, G. L., C. M. Steele, and L. D. Ross. 1999. "The Mentor's Dilemma: Providing Critical Feedback across the Racial Divide." *Personality and Social Psychology Bulletin* 25, no. 10: 1302–318.

Crocker, J., and others. 1991. "Social Stigma: The Affective Consequences of Attributional Ambiguity." *Journal of Personality and Social Psychology* 60, no. 2: 218–28.

Croizet, J. C., and T. Claire. 1998. "Extending the Concept of Stereotype Threat to Social Class: The Intellectual Underperformance of Students from Low Socioeconomic Backgrounds." *Personality and Social Psychology Bulletin* 24, no. 6:588–94.

Durkin, Thomas A. 2002. "Consumers and Credit Disclosures: Credit Cards and Credit Insurance." *Federal Reserve Bulletin* 88, no. 4: 201–14.

Engel, Kathleen C., and Patricia A. McCoy. 2002. "A Tale of Three Markets: The Law and Economics of Predatory Lending." *Texas Law Review* 80, no. 6: 1255–382.

Eskridge, William. 1984. "One Hundred Years of Ineptitude: The Need for Mortgage Rules Consonant with the Economic and Psychological Dynamics of the Home Sale and Loan Transaction." *Virginia Law Review* 70, no. 6: 1083–130.

Forehand, M. R., R. Deshpandé, and A. Reed, III. 2002. "Identity Salience and the Influence of Differential Activation of the Social Self-Schema on Advertising Response." *Journal of Applied Psychology* 87, no. 6: 1086–099.

Federal Trade Commission (FTC). 2007. "Improving Consumer Mortgage Disclosures: An Empirical Assessment of Current and Prototype Disclosure Forms." Bureau of Economics Staff Report (www.ftc.gov/be/workshops/mortgage/articles/lackopappalardo2007.pdf).

Gabaix, X., and D. Laibson. 2006. "Shrouded Attributes, Consumer Myopia, and Information Suppression in Competitive Markets." *Quarterly Journal of Economics* 121, no. 2: 505–40.

Gourville, J. T., and D. Soman. 1998. "Payment Depreciation: The Effects of Temporally Separating Payments from Consumption." *Journal of Consumer Research* 25, no. 1: 160–74.

Grossman, S. J., and O. D. Hart. 1980. "Disclosure Laws and Takeover Bids." *Journal of Finance* 35, no. 2: 323–34.

Guttentag, Jack. 2000. "Another View of Predatory Lending." Working Paper 01-23-B. University of Pennsylvania, Wharton Financial Institutions Center (http://fic.wharton.upenn.edu/fic/papers/01/0123.pdf).

Ho, Giang, and Anthony Pennington-Cross. 2006a. "The Impact of Local Predatory Lending Laws on the Flow of Subprime Credit." *Journal of Urban Economics* 60, no. 2: 210–28.

Hogarth, Jeanne M., and Jinkook Lee. 2000. "Consumer Information for Home Mortgages: Who, What, How Much, and What Else?" *Financial Services Review* 9, no. 3: 277–93.

Hogarth, Robin M. 1980. *Judgment and Choice: The Psychology of Decision.* New York: John Wiley.

Huber, J., J. W. Payne, and C. Puto. 1982. "Adding Asymmetrically Dominated Alternatives: Violations of Regularity and the Similarity Hypothesis." *Journal of Consumer Research* 9, no. 1: 90–98.

HUD-Treasury 2000. "Curbing Predatory Home Mortgage Lending." U.S. Department of Housing and Urban Development and U.S. Department of the Treasury (June).

Iwry, M. J., and D. C. John. 2006. "Pursuing Universal Retirement Security through Automatic IRAs." Working Draft (February 12) (www.heritage.org/research/socialsecurity/upload/95858_1.pdf).

Iyengar, S. S., G. Huberman, and W. Jiang. 2004. "How Much Choice is Too Much? Determinants of Individual Contributions in 401k Retirement Plans." In *Pension Design and Structure: New Lessons from Behavioral Finance,* edited by O. S. Mitchell and S. Utkus, pp. 83–95. Oxford University Press.

Iyengar, S. S., and M. R. Lepper. 2000. "When Choice Is Demotivating: Can One Desire Too Much of a Good Thing?" *Journal of Personality and Social Psychology* 79, no. 9: 995–1006.

Jackson, H. E., and L. Burlingame. 2007. "Kickbacks or Compensation: The Case of Yield Spread Premiums." *Stanford Journal of Law, Business and Finance* 12: 289–361.

Jolls, C., and C. R. Sunstein. 2005. "Debiasing through Law." 2005. University of Chicago Law and Economics, Olin Working Paper 225. Harvard Law and Economics Discussion Paper (http://ssrn.com/abstract=590929).

Jolls, Christine, Cass R. Sunstein, and Richard Thaler. 1998. "A Behavioral Approach to Law and Economics." *Stanford Law Review* 50, no. 5: 1471–550.

Johnson, E. J., and D. Goldstein. 2003. "Do Defaults Save Lives?" *Science* 302, no. 5649: 1338–339.

Johnson, E. J., and others. 1993. "Framing, Probability, Distortions, and Insurance Decisions." *Journal of Risk and Uncertainty* 7, no. 1: 35–51.

Kahneman, D. 1994. "New Challenges to the Rationality Assumption." *Journal of Institutional and Theoretical Economics* 150: 18–36.

Kahneman, D., and A. Tversky. 1979. "Prospect Theory: An Analysis of Decisions under Risk." *Econometrica* 47, no. 2: 263–91.

Kaplow, Louis. 1992. "Rules versus Standards: An Economic Analysis." *Duke Law Journal* 42, no. 3: 557–629.

Kelley, H. H. 1955. "The Two Functions of Reference Groups." In *Readings in Social Psychology,* 2nd ed., edited by G. E. Swanson, T. M. Newcomb, and E. L. Hartley, pp. 410–14. New York: Holt.

Kennedy, Duncan. 1976. "Form and Substance in Private Law Adjudication." *Harvard Law Review* 89, no. 8: 1685–778.

———. 2005. "Cost-Benefit Analysis of Debtor Protection Rules in Subprime Market Default Situations." In *Building Assets, Building Credit,* edited by Nicolas Retsinas and Eric Belsky, pp. 266–82. Brookings.

Knetsch, J. L. 1989. "The Endowment Effect and Evidence of Nonreversible Indifference Curves." *American Economic Review* 79, no. 5: 1277–284.

Koehler, D. J., and C. S. K. Poon. 2005. "Self-Predictions Overweight Strength of Current Intentions." *Journal of Experimental Social Psychology* 42, no. 4, 517–24.

Laibson, D., A. Repetto, and J. Tobacman. 1998. "Self-Control and Saving for Retirement." *Brookings Papers on Economic Activity* 1: 91–196.

Landers, Jonathan M., and Ralph J. Rohner. 1979. "A Functional Analysis of Truth in Lending." *UCLA Law Review* 26, no. 4: 711–52.

LeBoeuf, R. A., and E. Shafir. 2006. "The Long and Short of It: Physical Anchoring Effects." *Journal of Behavioral Decision Making* 19, no. 4: 393–406.

Leventhal, H., R. Singer, and S. Jones. 1965. "Effects of Fear and Specificity of Recommendation upon Attitudes and Behavior." *Journal of Personality and Social Psychology* 2, no. 1: 20–29.

Lewin, K. 1951. *Field Theory in Social Science.* New York: Harper and Row.

Li, W., and K. S. Ernst. 2006. "The Best Value in the Subprime Market: State Predatory Lending Reforms." Durham, N.C.: Center for Responsible Lending (www.responsiblelending.org/pdfs/rr010-State_Effects-0206.pdf).

Loewenstein, G., and J. Elster, eds. 1992. *Choice over Time.* New York: Russell Sage Foundation.

Loewenstein, G., and R. Thaler. 1989. "Anomalies: Intertemporal Choice." *Journal of Economic Perspectives* 3, no. 4: 181–93.

Mann, Ronald. 2007. "Bankruptcy Reform and the Sweat Box of Credit Card Debt." *University of Illinois Law Review*, no. 1: 375–403.

Mendoza-Denton, R., and others. 2002. "Sensitivity to Status-Based Rejection: Implications for African American Students' College Experience." *Journal of Personality and Social Psychology* 83, no. 4: 896–918.

Musto, David K. 2007. "Victimizing the Borrowers: Predatory Lending's Role in the Subprime Mortgage Crisis." Wharton Working Paper. Published February 20, 2008, on Knowledge@Wharton (http://knowledge.wharton.upenn.edu/article.cfm?articleid=1901).

Posner, Eric A. 1997. "Standards, Rules, and Social Norms." *Harvard Journal of Law and Public Policy* 21, no. 1: 101–17.

Pottow, J. A. E. 2007. "Private Liability for Reckless Consumer Lending." *University of Illinois Law Review* 2007, no. 1: 405–65.

Plous, Scott. 1993. *The Psychology of Judgment and Decision Making.* New York: McGraw-Hill.

Radin, Margaret Jane. 1989. "Reconsidering the Rule of Law." *Boston University Law Review* 69, no. 4: 781–819.

Reed, A., II. 2004. "Activating the Self-Importance of Consumer Selves: Exploring Identity Salience Effects on Judgments." *Journal of Consumer Research* 31, no. 2: 286–95.

Renuart, Elizabeth. 2003. "Comment, Toward One Competitive and Fair Mortgage Market: Suggested Reforms in a Tale of Three Markets Point in the Right Direction." *Texas Law Review* 82, no 2: 421–38.

Rose, Carol M. 1988. "Crystals and Mud in Property Law." *Stanford Law Review* 40, no. 3: 577–610.

Samuelson, W., and R. Zeckhauser. 1988. "Status Quo Bias in Decisionmaking." *Journal of Risk and Uncertainty* 1, no. 1: 7–59.

Schauer, Frederick. 1991. *Playing by the Rules: A Philosophical Examination of Rule-Based Decision-Making in Law and in Life.* Oxford University Press.

Schlag, Pierre. 1985. "Rules and Standards." *UCLA Law Review* 33, no. 2: 379–430.

Schultz, C. 1995. "Wages and Employment in a Repeated Game with Revenue Fluctuations." Discussion Paper 95-01. University of Copenhagen, Department of Economics.

Schwartz, Alan, and Louis L. Wilde. 1979. "Intervening in Markets on the Basis of Imperfect Information: A Legal and Economic Analysis." *University of Pennsylvania Law Review* 127, no. 3: 630–82.

Shafir, E., and R. A. LeBoeuf. 2002. "Rationality." *Annual Review of Psychology* 53: 491–517.

Shafir, E., I. Simonson, and A. Tversky. 1993. "Reason-Based Choice." *Cognition* 49, no. 1: 11–36.

Shelton, J. N., and J. A. Richeson. 2005. "Intergroup Contact and Pluralistic Ignorance." *Journal of Personality and Social Psychology* 88, no, 1: 91–107.

Simonson, I. 1989. "Choice Based on Reasons: The Case of Attraction and Compromise Effects." *Journal of Consumer Research* 16 (September): 158–74.

Simonson, I., and A. Tversky. 1992. "Choice in Context: Tradeoff Contrast and Extremeness Aversion." *Journal of Marketing Research* 29 (August): 281–95.

Steele, C. M. 1997. "A Threat in the Air: How Stereotypes Shape Intellectual Identity and Performance." *American Psychologist* 52, no. 6: 613–29.

Thaler, R. H. 1985. "Mental Accounting and Consumer Choice." *Marketing Science* 4, no. 3: 199–214.

———. 1992. *The Winner's Curse.* New York: W. W. Norton.

Thaler, R. H., and S. Benartzi, 2004. "Save More Tomorrow: Using Behavioral Economics to Increase Employee Savings." *Journal of Political Economy* 112, no. 1 (pt. 2): S164–S187.

Thaler, R. H., and Sunstein, C. R. 2008. *Nudge: Improving Decisions about Health, Wealth, and Happiness.* Yale University Press.

Turner, J. C. 1987. *Rediscovering the Social Group: A Self-Categorization Theory.* Oxford, U.K.: Basil Blackwell.

Tversky, A., and D. Kahneman. 1991. "Loss Aversion in Riskless Choice: A Reference Dependent Model." *Quarterly Journal of Economics* 106, no. 4: 1039–061.

Tversky, A., and E. Shafir. 1992. "Choice under Conflict: The Dynamics of Deferred Decision." *Psychological Science* 3, no. 6: 358–61.

Walton, G. M., and G. L. Cohen. 2007. "A Question of Belonging: Race, Social Fit, and Achievement." *Journal of Personality and Social Psychology* 92, no. 1: 82–96.

White, J. J., and R. S. Summers. 1995. *Uniform Commercial Code.* 4th ed. Practitioner Treatise Series. St. Paul, Minn.: West Publishing.

7

Interventions in Mortgage Default: Policies and Practices to Prevent Home Loss and Lower Costs

AMY CREWS CUTTS AND WILLIAM A. MERRILL

The implosion of the subprime market in early 2007 and subsequent deterioration of the prime market in 2008 caused by the rapid rise in mortgage defaults resulted in significant media and political focus on saving homeowners from foreclosure and the possible loss of their home. Although the default problem in the prime segment of the market is less severe, the issues related to keeping borrowers in their homes affect all market segments, not just subprime loans. In particular, what do we know about defaults and what causes them? Is there an ideal cost-benefit time frame for the foreclosure process? What are the costs of foreclosure? Where will the next gains in default servicing come from to maximize the potential for borrowers to keep their homes?

This chapter examines these issues, focusing on the prime side of the market and in particular prime conventional (that is, not government insured) and conforming (meeting the underwriting guidelines of Freddie Mac or Fannie Mae)

The authors are grateful to Jimmy Cheng, Shawn Connell, Steven Geyer, Nathaniel Hoover, Sandy Sweeney, and Robin Toothman for their research assistance, and Bob Kimble and Calvin Schnure for their valuable comments. Any remaining errors or omissions are ours.

loans. It also considers some aspects of the subprime and Alt-A segments of the mortgage market.[1]

The primary issue is one of incentives: if the borrower values the home and if the benefits of continued ownership exceed the costs, then her interests align with those of the lender. The servicer is an agent of the investor, and to align his incentives with those of the investor, he is compensated for delivering favorable results for the investor, namely maximizing the timely repayment of the debt as agreed to in the mortgage contract. But when the borrower is in financial distress, her motivation or capacity to carry the debt typically has been diminished, thus raising the risk she will default on the mortgage, an outcome that both the home-owner and lender would like to avoid.

Time is of the essence at this point because costs for all parties increase over time. The steady rise in costs drives two of our principal findings. First, the earlier the discussions between the borrower and the servicer on workout plans, the greater the chances that the borrower will be able to retain ownership, because the plan can be put into place before costs rise prohibitively to the point of unafford-ability to the borrower. Second, once the loan is referred to foreclosure, starting the legal process by which the lender makes a claim on the mortgage collateral, there appears to be an optimal time frame for the state-defined legal foreclosure process. If the timeline is too short, there may be insufficient time for a borrower to recover and save the home from foreclosure. If the timeline is too long, the bor-rower's incentives are compromised by costs that continue to rise, ultimately reducing the chances that a borrower will successfully avoid foreclosure and thereby increasing costs to financial institutions.

Many borrowers never speak with servicers, despite the persistent efforts of ser-vicers to reach them by phone, by letter, or by e-mail, and the longer they wait to do so, the less likely they are to recover from their problems and keep their homes. Short-term repayment plans are effective when the delinquency is minor and the repayment of arrearages occurs over a few months, but loan modifications, even though imposing nontrivial costs on lenders, are more successful when the delin-quency problem is more severe.

The foreclosure process varies widely across states. Based on data from Freddie Mac in 2007, the foreclosure process lasts an average of 355 days between the due

---

1. The subprime segment of the market is often defined as mortgage loans made to borrowers with blemished credit, which is sometimes interpreted to mean those with FICO® credit bureau scores below 620, loans originated by a lender who specializes in subprime loans, loans with a high coupon interest rate (the current Home Mortgage Disclosure Act reporting requirement is one such example of the interest rate definition), or by loan product, such as a 2/28 ARM or 3/27 ARM loan. The Alt-A segment is usually defined by loans that have prime or near prime credit (credit scores above 620), but for various reasons have no or limited documentation of income or assets as might occur with a self-employed borrower. It can also denote loans with nontraditional features such as interest-only or negative-amortization payments.

date of the last payment made and the loss of the home at the foreclosure sale, but ranged from 248 to 598 days. The costs of foreclosure rise significantly with the length of the foreclosure timeline, by as much as 12 percent for every 50 days added to the timeline. Perhaps more important, the likelihood a borrower will reinstate her loan out of foreclosure falls as the length of time in the legal foreclosure process increases; by our estimates, states with excessively long legislated foreclosure timelines could increase the probability of successful reinstatement of delinquent borrowers by 3 to 9 percentage points by shortening their statutory timelines to match the national median timeline.

Studies of Foreclosure and Foreclosure Cost

Because of the rapid rise in delinquencies across the United States that started in 2006, investors and their servicing agents are trying to avoid an equally rapid rise in losses. The economic incentives are aligned to keep the borrower in the home if possible; mortgage investors make the most money when the mortgage contract is paid on time according to the contract terms. Generally speaking, borrowers who can afford the mortgage payments will make the payments even if they owe more than the property is worth because the value of the housing services (the dividend value of rent) is high, the cost to their credit rating from default is substantial, sale of the home or default realizes the loss on the home, keeping the home preserves the option of future gains in the property's value, and the cost of moving is nontrivial. These incentives are well documented in the economics literature.[2]

With the obvious gains in loss mitigation/foreclosure avoidance practices and servicing operations already widely adopted,[3] attention has shifted to new and more challenging methods for reducing losses. Some of the common tactics now include using risk-model-based calling campaigns, pre-reset solicitation of borrowers with performing adjustable-rate mortgages (ARMs), partnering with nonprofit counseling groups and local housing authorities on borrower outreach, using vendors for in-person contact at the borrower's home, reducing net proceeds requirements on short sales, and allowing more aggressive modifications to loan terms.

Because of the very large costs of foreclosures in dollars and in human terms on the borrower, the servicer, the lender investor, and the community, discussions of how best to apply private and public resources to the current crisis are timely.

---

2. See, for example, Kau and Keenan (1995); Deng, Quigley, and Van Order (2000) and references cited therein; Lacour-Little (2004), and Cutts and Green (2005).

3. Lacour-Little (2000); Cutts and Green (2005).

Ironically, we have been here before as an industry and a country, as highlighted by Bridewell in 1938:[4]

> The present deplorable state of mortgage and foreclosure law is probably due to the persistent desire of the courts and legislatures to better the position of the helpless borrower against the supposed greed of the money-lender. Recent enactment of moratoria and anti-deficiency judgment laws is the most modern demonstration of this desire to protect the mortgage borrower. But to this judicial and legislative tendency to favor the mortgagor has attached the law of diminishing returns. The resulting waste of money and time has checkmated any benefit derived by the mortgagor. Instead of safeguarding the mortgagor, many of the existing procedures have saddled him with additional charges or made more unfavorable the terms of his mortgage loan.

He goes on to document the unnecessary costs added by lengthy foreclosure proceedings that do little to assist distressed borrowers but increase costs on credit-worthy borrowers as lenders try to protect against losses. He estimates that if ". . . $55, the approximate average cost of foreclosure in states in the first group [efficient, low-cost foreclosure states], is sufficient to cover the cost of foreclosure, it appears that during the last 10 years approximately $70,000,000 has been spent unnecessarily because foreclosure proceedings in all states were not as simple, inexpensive, and expeditious as in states in that group."[5] Assuming the same distribution of costs today and similar numbers of foreclosures as in 1928–1938, these excess costs would be equivalent to roughly $650 million today.[6] Many things have changed for the better in mortgage lending, servicing, and foreclosure processes since Bridewell's study, but as this chapter discusses, many issues that concerned him remain the same today.

More recently, Pence (2001, 2006) investigated the costs of different state foreclosure laws on the availability of mortgage credit. Corroborating one of Bridewell's worries, she has found in the 2006 study ". . . that loan sizes are 3 to 7 percent smaller in defaulter-friendly states; this result suggests that defaulter-friendly laws impose material costs on borrowers at the time of origination."[7]

Other recent studies have investigated the costs of the legal structure of state foreclosure laws. For example, Wood (1997) documents that states with judicial foreclosure proceedings took an average of five months longer than nonjudicial states, and Wilson (1995) finds that the judicial foreclosure process greatly increased costs to investors, implying the (five-month) delay in judicial states raises time-dependent costs by 5 percent of the loan balance. Pennington-Cross (2003)

---

4. Bridewell (1938, p. 545).
5. Bridewell (1938, pp. 551–52).
6. Inflated using the Consumer Price Index (CPI): urban consumer, all items price index for December 1947 through December 2007.
7. Pence (2006, p. 177).

finds that houses in judicial foreclosure states sold for 4 percent less than those in statutory foreclosure states, presumably because of greater depreciation during the longer foreclosure process.

Clauretie (1989) and Clauretie and Herzog (1990) looked at losses to primary mortgage insurance companies in the 1980s. Clauretie (1989) summarizes the primary conclusions of both studies as ". . . because a judicial procedure and a statutory right of redemption lengthen the foreclosure process and delay the liquidation of the property, losses are greater in states which require the former and grant the latter. A prohibition on deficiency judgments precludes any amelioration of these losses."

The most recent study of the costs of foreclosure, Hayre and Saraf (2008), looks at Asset Backed Securities (ABS) and Mortgage Backed Securities (MBS)[8] data from LoanPerformance[9] to estimate discounts on home values brought by the type of property transfer (short sale, foreclosure, or real-estate owned [REO]), loss severities based on age of the loan and loan amount, lien status, state foreclosure regulations, and the effects of other related characteristics of the loan or borrower, such as the presence of mortgage insurance or bankruptcy declarations. This study notes that on average states that have a statutory or "power-of-sale" foreclosure process take 11 months and states with judicial foreclosure proceedings take 14 months between the last payment made by the borrower and the foreclosure sale (excluding postsale redemption periods). It further notes that Vermont and Connecticut, states with "strict foreclosure" processes, take the longest, with an average time of 16 months, and that associated legal fees for the foreclosure process are much higher in judicial foreclosure states.

These studies show that different state and federal approaches to foreclosure have risks: policies that may appear to be more or less borrower-friendly, or in the words of Pence, "defaulter-friendly," can turn out to be the opposite by imposing greater costs on borrowers either at default or at origination. This chapter examines both new trends in foreclosure avoidance tactics by lender investors and the structure of state laws and how they affect not only costs to the industry but also the likelihood that delinquent borrowers will ultimately remain in their homes.

8. Mortgage-backed securities are a type of security instrument in which the cash flows from borrower payments on the underlying mortgage loans are passed on to security investors. While MBS can mean the class of all such securities, the label "MBS" or "private-label MBS" distinguishes these securities from those issued by Freddie Mac, Fannie Mae, and Ginnie Mae, which provide a guarantee to investors that they will receive not only the passthrough of borrower payments but also full payment of principal if the borrower on an underlying loan should default. When used together with ABS, the term MBS denotes that the security contains loans that are considered prime investment grade whereas asset-backed securities contain loans that the market investors deem to be non-prime investment quality on some dimension. Typically ABS are marketed as subprime or Alt-A, depending on the characteristics of the loans in the security.

9. LoanPerformance is a division of First American CoreLogic, Inc.

The Vocabulary of Loan Servicing

Mortgage loan servicing has its own vocabulary, and it is worth defining some terms relevant to this analysis at the outset to avoid confusion.[10]

Servicer: Classified as a debt collector in legal terms, the servicer is the agent who collects payments from the borrower and passes on principal and interest to the investor, taxes to the local government, insurance premiums to the homeowner's insurance company, and mortgage insurance premiums to the mortgage insurer and who reports borrower payment status to the investor and credit reporting bureaus. This agent has a direct relationship with the borrower and, because of this relationship, is who many borrowers mistakenly think is the lender behind their loan. But servicing rights are bought and sold independently of who owns the loan, and by law under the Real Estate Settlement Procedures Act (RESPA), borrowers are notified when the servicing rights on their loans are transferred. This misunderstanding is more common among loans originated by mortgage brokers.

Investor: The creditor agent who holds the credit risk on the loan and who takes a loss on a defaulted loan. It could be the original lender or an investor who acquired the loan by purchasing it on the secondary market. Borrowers rarely know who the investors behind their loans are unless they ask the servicer or are in foreclosure.

Default: A breach of any of the terms of the mortgage contract, but most often is associated with missed monthly payments.

Foreclosure: The legal process by which the property backing a mortgage is liquidated to help pay off the mortgage debt and any additional costs, such as legal fees and escrow advances, accrued through delinquency. In the vast majority of cases the foreclosure proceeds fall short of the total amount due. The foreclosure process concludes at the foreclosure sale when the borrower's right of title is terminated. The borrower may still have right of possession if the state has a post-foreclosure sale "right of redemption" provision.

Workout: A negotiated plan to avoid home loss through foreclosure. Home retention workouts are used when the borrower has both a desire to keep the home and the capacity to carry payments under the workout plan. These workouts include repayment plans, a contracted plan to make up past due amounts; forbearance, a defined period where no or only partial payments are required followed by a repayment plan to make up the arrearage; and loan modifications, a permanent altering of one or more of the loan terms. Voluntary home-loss workouts avoid foreclosure but the borrower gives up the home. These are deed-in-lieu

---

10. Cutts and Green (2005) outline the alternatives to borrowers in greater detail and summarize the economics of the default option for borrowers and recent innovations in defaulted loan servicing. See also Lacour-Little (2000) for a discussion of the evolution of technology used in the mortgage industry.

transfers, in which the borrower essentially gives the investor the keys and title to terminate the debt, and short sales, where the lender agrees to accept proceeds from the sale of the home to a third party even though the sales price is less than the principal, accrued interest, and other expenses owed.

Foreclosure Alternative: Foreclosure alternative (see also Workout) is a term of art in the servicing industry that means any alternative to the legal taking of the home through the foreclosure process that terminates in a foreclosure sale. People outside of loan servicing often interpret the term to mean only home-retention workouts. Our study uses it in the former, broader sense unless otherwise indicated.

REO: Real estate owned, the term given to properties that become owned by the investor at the foreclosure sale. This term is sometimes used more broadly to indicate any collateral property owned by the investor, whether obtained by fore-closure or a deed-in-lieu transfer.

Redemption: A period of time during which no additional costs can be accrued by the borrower in foreclosure, essentially a stipulated time-out. The borrower can redeem the home out of redemption by paying all principal, interest, taxes, and other costs owed before the expiration of the period. In the six postforeclosure-sale redemption states where the redemption period is longer than 60 days (Colorado until January 2008, Kansas, Michigan, Minnesota, South Dakota, and Wyoming), the borrower retains the right of occupancy but loses title. The investor gains the title but has no rights of possession such as the right to enter the property even to make repairs or to preserve the property unless invited by the borrower or as required by local ordinances (such as for lawn maintenance). Many other states also have postsale redemption provisions if certain foreclosure processes are used, and some have a redemption period before the foreclosure sale.

DDLPI: Due date of the last paid installment, the term used by Freddie Mac for the onset of the delinquency. Under the commonly used Mortgage Bankers Association's (MBA) definition, a loan is said to be 30 days late (or delinquent) when the next payment due date is reached after a payment is missed, but because interest is paid in arrears for the previous month, the DDLPI is a more accurate start point and is calculated as 60 days for that loan. For example, if a payment is due and paid on June 1 but the borrower fails to make a payment in July, the borrower will be counted as 30 days delinquent under the MBA definition on July 31, but the DDLPI will be 60 days counted from the June 1 due date of the last payment.

Cure: A loan is said to cure when all past-due amounts are paid in full by the borrower. The borrower may have fully reinstated the loan, thus returning it to full active status, or the borrower may have paid off the loan and past-due amounts by selling the home in a regular market transaction or by refinancing the mortgage.

Fail: In the context of this chapter, a loan is said to fail when the borrower loses the home through foreclosure sale, deed-in-lieu transfer, or short sale or the lender takes a charge-off.[11]

Recent Findings on the Importance of Early Intervention

In all foreclosure alternatives—whether for home retention or when the borrower voluntarily gives up the home—the borrower must talk with the servicer. Loans that self-cure quickly without intervention from the servicer are not of much concern, but borrowers who have no contact with their servicers are missing out on the many effective options available for foreclosure avoidance, not only hurting themselves but also increasing investor costs.

Borrower Contact

Contacting the financial institution that services your mortgage may seem a simple task to many, but a 2005 groundbreaking survey of delinquent Freddie Mac borrowers by Roper and Freddie Mac has found many substantial barriers to this important communication.[12]

Specifically, the survey reveals that on the effectiveness of servicer outreach, 75 percent of the delinquent borrowers who responded to the survey said they remembered being contacted by their loan servicer by letter or phone. A substantial percentage, however, gave a variety of reasons for neglecting to follow up with their servicers to discuss workout options. For example, 28 percent said there was no reason to talk to their servicers or that their servicers could not help them; 17 percent said they could take care of their payment problems without any help; and 7 percent said they did not call because they did not have enough money to make the payment. Another 6 percent cited embarrassment, 5 percent didn't respond out of fear, and 5 percent said they did not know whom to call.

The survey also looks at what could be done to improve borrower outreach. On this topic, 61 percent of late-paying borrowers said they were unaware of the variety of workout options that could help them overcome short-term financial difficulties, and 92 percent said that they would have spoken with their loan servicers had they known these options were available to them.

Roper and Freddie Mac conducted a second survey in 2007 to see if the collective industry and media efforts to educate the public about foreclosure alternatives had been successful in increasing awareness.[13] The good news is that across

11. In a charge-off, the lender writes off the debt as a loss; however, the borrower is still liable for the debt owed at the time of the charge-off and the property lien remains in effect. Charge-offs are usually associated with a property problem such as fire damage or other hazard on the property.

12. See www.Freddiemac.com/news/archives/corporate/2005/20051212_ropersurvey.html for more information on the first Freddie Mac–Roper survey.

13. See www.freddiemac.com/news/archives/corporate/2008/20080131_07ropersurvey.html for more information on the 2007 Roper survey.

the board improvements were noted, but 57 percent of late-paying borrowers still did not know that their lenders might offer alternatives to help them avoid fore-closure and 33 percent claimed there was no reason to call or there was nothing the servicer could do to help them. Among the 2007 survey respondents, 86 percent recalled their servicers having tried to reach them and 75 percent of respondents in turn reached out to their lenders.[14]

Given the results from the Roper-Freddie Mac surveys, we decided to look at the reported contact information from Freddie Mac's electronic default reporting (EDR) data—by contact we mean that the servicer and the borrower had at least one reciprocal conversation regarding the loan delinquency.[15] Although the contact field is not required, and thus may underreport successful servicer contact with borrowers, the performance of borrowers and the corresponding contact rates are quite striking in table 7-1. In data from September 2005 through August 2007, Freddie Mac servicers reported a no-contact rate of 53.3 percent of all loans that went to foreclosure sale and became REO in Freddie Mac's portfolio. This represents a missed opportunity for more than half of all borrowers that lost their home through foreclosure during that period to work together with their servicers and investors to try and avoid the loss of their home.

The contact rate is lower on the total delinquent loan population because of the significant cure rate out of the 30-day delinquency population without servicer intervention: many borrowers that miss one payment do so out of very temporary financial stress, a pending home sale, or forgetfulness, and thus can reinstate without servicer intervention. As the time in delinquency increases, however, so does the hurdle the borrower has to overcome to reinstate the loan and the importance of calling the servicer.

The mortgage industry has made a significant effort on borrower education and outreach, and media attention on recent mortgage industry issues has highlighted options available if borrowers call their servicers. An encouraging trend in the more recent data shows rising reciprocal contact rates across the board. Contact rates on loans going to REO increased slightly by 0.7 percentage points and contact rates on loans that cure out of foreclosure were up by 25 percentage points over the two years between the surveys.

From a foreclosure avoidance perspective, it is distressing that more than 50 percent of borrowers who lose their homes to foreclosure do so without ever speaking to a servicer. Whether they do so out of despair, fear, or embarrassment,

14. Some of the more creative servicers mail prepaid disposable cell phones with the servicer's number programmed in to delinquent borrowers. Others send calling cards worth $5 or $10, and still others offer cash payments or entry into a prize drawing if the borrower returns the servicer's call.

15. The EDR is an automated process, whereby servicers send delinquency data to Freddie Mac for investor reporting purposes. Servicers are contractually required by investors to call or send letters to delinquent borrowers by a certain date following the onset of delinquency. Many servicers begin these activities before that date.

Table 7-1. *Servicer-Borrower Communication Rates among Delinquent Loans,*
2005–07
Percent

Contact rates for delinquent loans observed in the fifteen months before December 2006[a]

Loan outcome	Contact rate
Active or closed	13.4
Active or closed that was previously at least 90 days delinquent	32.4
Active or closed that was previously at least 120 days delinquent	33.2
Active or closed that was previously in foreclosure	29.9
Foreclosure sale (REO)	46.4

Contact rates for delinquent loans observed from January to September 2007

Loan outcome	Contact rate
Active or closed	28.9
Active or closed that was previously at least 90 days delinquent	55.9
Active or closed that was previously at least 120 days delinquent	58.5
Active or closed that was previously in foreclosure	54.8
Foreclosure sale (REO)	47.2

Source: Authors' estimations based on a sample of delinquent loans that were reinstated or terminated between September 2005 and September 2007.

REO = real-estate owned.

a. "Contact" means the servicer and the borrower had reciprocal communication regarding the status of the loan. Servicers attempt to contact borrowers through a variety of means including letters, phone calls, and other means to initiate communication with the borrower. Many borrowers avoid the servicer's attempts to reach them or are not occupants at the mortgage property and are otherwise unreachable.

as the Roper-Freddie Mac survey indicates, or some other reason, the bottom line is that these borrowers lose out on any opportunity to try to keep their home, incur tremendous psychological and economic costs for their family, and cause losses to servicers, investors, neighbors, and their community.[16]

Default Counseling

Preorigination homebuyer counseling is an effective way to help ensure that first-time homebuyers remain long-term homeowners, particularly when the counseling is in one-on-one or classroom settings; there has been only limited success with telephone or other noninteractive settings.[17] Counseling has, however, limitations on its long-term effectiveness in assisting borrowers who enter

16. What we do not know from the population of noncontact borrowers that lost their homes through foreclosure is how many of these borrowers simply walked away from the property, perhaps because it was really an investment property and not owner-occupied or there was some element of fraud, and how many were true hardships on homeowner families.

17. Hirad and Zorn (2002).

delinquency. Fields and others (2007) find that "even among those who received prepurchase counseling and education from well established NeighborWorks Organizations (NWOs) there is little awareness about the post-purchase services or foreclosure intervention assistance that are available."[18]

Default counseling is a rapidly growing opportunity to help borrowers with delinquency and assist them generally through financial hardship. In the 2005 Roper-Freddie Mac Survey, many borrowers reported that they felt no need to contact their servicer, but 74 percent of the delinquent borrowers would be likely to talk to a counseling agency if that option were available. Collins (2007a) finds that ". . . counselors report many borrowers fail to seek help or communicate with their lender when alternatives to foreclosure are appropriate, largely due to [the] borrower's high level of stress and anxiety."[19]

These studies demonstrate the obstacles for reciprocal contact between servicers and borrowers and a possible solution to improve the contact rate through default counseling. Using a trusted, reputable, and experienced nonprofit default counselor enables servicers to increase their contact rate and creates a new source for workout activity. For borrowers who use a trusted third-party intermediary to discuss holistic debt management, focusing on the secured debt, this is an opportunity to not only reinstate their mortgage but also manage their other financial problems, including other credit delinquencies, over the long term.

The CCCS–Freddie Mac Default Counseling Program Pilot

In cooperation with its two counseling partners, Consumer Credit Counseling Service of San Francisco, Inc., and Consumer Credit Counseling Service of Greater Atlanta, Inc., Freddie Mac published best practices for default counseling, including the concept that "first contact is the best contact." The focus is on seeking all reasons leading to the default, discussing all debts at once with a focus on the mortgage and reduction in consumer debt, educating the borrower on all options, and building a solid communication process with servicers all in the first contact with the borrower.[20]

Freddie Mac began its counseling efforts in 2005 with small pilots to gauge the effectiveness of default counseling and to work through the operational process across four business partners: the investor, the servicer, the counseling agency, and the borrower. The main operational goals to monitor were contact rate with the borrower, the cure rate (pay off or reinstate the loan), and the redefault/recidivism rate of closed workouts after a counseling session. The initial target solicitations were borrowers meeting the U.S. Department of Housing and

---

18. Fields et al. (2007, p. 17).
19. Collins (2007a, p. 1).
20. The full document can be found at www.freddiemac.com/learn/counselor/pdfs/bp_hc.pdf.

Urban Development's (HUD's) affordable housing goals[21] who were at least 45 days delinquent and who had not communicated with their servicer about their delinquency. Servicers removed any borrowers from the pilot who declared bankruptcy, independently reinstated, or recently contacted the servicer. The screening minimized any confusion to the borrower should contact come from multiple organizations. This provided a focus on helping no-contact affordable borrowers and on lifting borrower contact rates.

Given the large difference in results in the Hirad and Zorn (2002) study on prepurchase homeownership counseling showing that in-person counseling was far superior to other, noninteractive means, Freddie Mac was particularly interested in outcomes from the pilot program using phone counseling versus in-person counseling. After reviewing preliminary results, Freddie Mac ended the in-person default counseling program and focused solely on phone counseling for delinquent borrowers. This decision was driven by the inability of in-person counseling to support a wide geographic area, a high rate of appointment cancellations by borrowers (approaching 50 percent), lower volume capacity of local ground-based counselors compared with national call-center counseling groups, and the reduced benefit to the investor through fewer delinquency resolutions given the additional cost to support the in-person counseling group. This pilot program has expanded to an operational baseline program for Freddie Mac, with new servicers being added and ever-increasing numbers of loans processed in this successful partnership with the two CCCS organizations.

Other studies corroborate the Freddie Mac findings. Collins (2007b) finds in a small sample of borrowers in mortgage default that face-to-face counseling was more effective than telephone counseling, but that this difference largely went away when time in counseling was considered. Ding, Quercia, and Ratcliffe (forthcoming) find significant benefit from delinquency counseling on failure rates; in particular, ". . . well-timed, situation appropriate counseling, even over the phone, effectively increases the curing probability of delinquent borrowers." And Quercia, Cowan, and Moreno (2004) find "with regard to the rate of recidivism, about one quarter of borrowers who avoided foreclosure reported being delinquent again 12 months after program intervention, and about one third were delinquent again after 36 months. Households that did not receive an assistance loan as part of the intervention had a higher incidence of recidivism over time, about 45 percent."[22]

---

21. By federal law, Freddie Mac and Fannie Mae are subject to several affordable housing goals targeting underserved borrower groups and neighborhoods. These goals are set by HUD and require that certain percentages of the housing units financed by the two companies satisfy the goal requirements. More on the goal specifics can be found at www.freddiemac.com/corporate/about/policy/faq_affordability.html.

22. Quercia, Cowan, and Moreno (2004, p. 1).

Performance of Default Counselors and Counseled Borrowers

Since the spring of 2005 when Freddie Mac began the default counseling outreach program, 44,266 solicitations have been mailed to its delinquent borrowers. From these mailings and the counselors' outbound calls to the borrowers, the counselors have contacted 11,693 borrowers, creating a contact rate among borrowers that had not previously talked to their servicers of 26.4 percent of the solicitations.

The counselors are effective at working with borrowers to resolve the situation either through a counseling session on personal finances or simply a short conversation to motivate the borrower to self-cure. Of the 11,693 borrowers contacted, 6,099 cured either through reinstating the loan or by paying it off and an additional 282 applied for a workout, indicating a 54.5 percent borrower contact to cure or workout rate. The remaining borrowers are either still in a delinquent status or have lost the home through a foreclosure sale.

The final benchmark is the longer-term effectiveness of a counseling session completed through the counseling agency, with the premise that the financial counseling session and the financial documentation process increase borrowers' ability to resolve future financially stressful situations on their own or even avoid them altogether through prudent expense management. Among the reinstated loans in the pilot program, 18.7 percent of this population went 60 days delinquent after reinstating through the counseling program. The recidivism rate over a similar period of time on workouts for borrowers qualifying under HUD goals and not receiving counseling is 25.0 percent. Because neither population has reached the peak redefault rate of approximately three years, the recidivism rate of both populations will need further scrutiny over time; the initial results, however, are striking and economically relevant.

To continue building on the success of the initial default counseling programs, the next phases of default counseling should be to (1) continue to train and build a larger population of qualified default counselors; (2) build better technology to track data, increase efficient communication with servicers and investors, assist counselors with financial analysis, and eventually allow counselors to negotiate workouts themselves;[23] (3) strengthen the relationship between local housing authorities, servicers, and reputable nonprofits; (4) create a workout that is structured with future counseling; and (5) examine the possibility of building workout options directly into the mortgage contract that do not create a moral hazard problem. The industry also should investigate the possibility that the best long-term solution may reside at origination. As loans are originated, providing default counseling, educating borrowers on workout options and gathering better borrower contact data such as cell phone numbers and e-mail addresses as part of the loan

---

23. Servicers cannot abdicate their contractual servicing responsibilities so the degree to which counselors can assist with the workout approval may be limited in practice.

documentation and closing process would enable homeownership preservation to be part of where it is the most successful—early in the process.

Early Intervention

Working with borrowers early in delinquency serves two benefits, creating a motivated and educated borrower to partner with and lowering delinquent arrearages, which offers more opportunities for a successful workout. Repayment plans are the most frequent workout chosen by Freddie Mac servicers, with more than 37,000 completed in 2006. A repayment plan spreads the delinquent arrearage over a calculated period of time and is added to the current monthly payment. In a simple example, if the borrower has a monthly payment of $1,000 and is one payment delinquent, the servicer can structure a repayment plan where a borrower pays $1,200 per month for five months and thus becomes current. Because repayment plans are easy to implement, are easy to explain to the borrower, and do not change any of the formal terms of the mortgage contract, they are often tried as the first step in the workout process.[24]

The success of repayment plans varies by the stage of delinquency, when the plan starts, and how long the plan is in place to reach the reinstatement. Repays with less arrearage and shorter timelines are much more likely to reinstate or pay off than those with higher arrearage and longer plans. The economics of the higher cure rate among shorter repayment plans is that borrowers who have the capacity to make up the arrearage in a few payments most likely have greater ability to weather a financial setback; those who require a longer timeline to get current, all else equal, are more likely to be at their financial limit, and a loan modification is probably a better option.

Table 7-2 demonstrates the effectiveness of repayment plans based on the stage of delinquency at the start of the plan. Repayment plans that start when the borrower is 30 days delinquent and due for two payments (the missed payment and the current installment) are significantly more successful than repayment plans that start when the borrower is 90 days or more delinquent and due for four or more payments. The cure rate among loans that are only 30 days delinquent is just under 60 percent, but that rate falls to less than 30 percent if they are three or more payments behind at the onset of the plan. Moreover, among repayment plans for borrowers with only one missed payment, the redefault rate (the share

24. An important benefit of repayment or forbearance plans is that they do not trigger any accounting losses for the investor that are not already recorded by the delinquency status of the loan. Any change to the mortgage contract such as through a loan modification changes the accounting treatment of the loan and can trigger an immediate loss in the investor's financial statements that may be larger than the actual realized losses over time. In addition, borrowers can also engage in multiple repayment plans over time. Repayment plans normally do not result in the acceleration (removal) of a securitized loan out of a security, while generally a loan modification would require that the loan be removed under the terms of the security trust.

Table 7-2. *Share of Loans in Repayment Plans That Redefault
by the End of the Repayment Plan*
Percent

	Status at end	
Status at the start of repayment plan	Redefaulted[a]	Cured[b]
30 days late, due for 2 payments	44.11	55.89
60 days late, due for 3 payments	60.47	39.53
90+ days late, due for 4+ payments	71.03	28.97

Source: Authors' estimations on a sample of Freddie Mac loans that had a repayment plan that ended in
years 2000–06.
a. "Redefaulted" means the loan was 30 days or more late as of the end of the repayment plan.
b. A loan is cured if it ends the repayment plan and all past-due arrearages have been paid in full; the
loan may be reinstated or paid off.

of loans that once again become delinquent by 30 days or more) is a bit more than
44 percent, but it jumps to more than 70 percent if they get to be 90 days or more
late before starting the repayment plan.

We looked also at data on the length of time the repayment plan lasted and the
cure rate among loans that started a repay plan at a certain level of delinquency.
Most loans that will cure out of a repayment plan do so within the first six months,
and repayment plans of three months or less are the most successful, as shown in
figure 7-1. For all loans in a particular delinquency status at the start of the plan,
we plot the marginal cure rate by when the plan ended.[25]

Among the nearly 56 percent of loans 30 days delinquent at the start of the
plan that will ultimately cure, more than three-quarters have fully reinstated by
month 3 and a little more than half of 60-day delinquent loans in repayment plans
that will cure do so in a three-month or shorter plan. Repayment plans are effective when used early in the delinquency and within reasonable time frames. If the
borrower is outside these parameters, a loan modification may be a more effective
long-term solution.

Loan Modifications

Loan modifications are an effective tool for foreclosure avoidance in later stages
of delinquency and are used increasingly in the current rising default environment. To illustrate the effect of loan modifications on a borrower's monthly payment obligation, imagine a borrower who is 36 months into his 30-year fixed-
rate loan with monthly interest rate r and who has missed six principal, p, and
interest, i, payments along with associated monthly escrows for taxes, T, and

25. The rate is the number of cured loans in that length of repayment plan divided by all loans that
entered a repayment plan at that level of delinquency; that is, the denominator is constant over time.

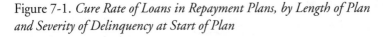

Figure 7-1. *Cure Rate of Loans in Repayment Plans, by Length of Plan and Severity of Delinquency at Start of Plan*

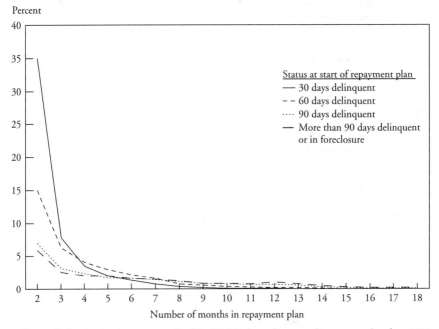

Source: Authors' estimations on a sample of Freddie Mac loans that entered repayment plans from 2000 to 2006, with performance measured through August 2007.

insurance, I. His total principal balance is given by P_{30} (he last made a payment in month 30) and his arrearages equal

$$(1) \qquad \sum_{j=31}^{36} \left(i_j + T_j + I_j + f_j \right),$$

where f are any fees relating to legal fees or other associated costs, but not late fees or the cost of the loan modification.[26] The simplest form of a loan modification places the delinquent arrearage into the unpaid principal balance and reamortizes the loan over the remaining term, and the borrower's payments will increase from the original payment. Investors and servicers may also extend the term past the original maturity, for example, by extending the amortization from the remaining term to a new full maturity term of 30 years or even to a 40-year term or reduce

26. The taxes and insurance arrearages may differ from this simple calculation; because taxes and insurance fees can change over a year and are paid out in lump sums, the escrow account may need to be replenished by more or less than the simple sum of the missed escrow contributions. The servicer would conduct a full escrow analysis when underwriting the loan modification.

the interest rate to lower the new monthly payment based on the borrower's financial capacity. Letting M_{new} denote the modified months to maturity, t denote the month in which the last payment was made, m equal the number of missed payments, and r_{new} be the new interest rate, the modified loan payment becomes

$$(2) \qquad x_{new} = \frac{r_{new}\left[P_t + \sum_{j=1}^{m}\left(i_j + T_j + I_j + f_j\right)\right]\left(1+r_{new}\right)^{M_{new}}}{\left(1+r_{new}\right)^{M_{new}} - 1},$$

based on the standard amortization function.[27]

Continuing the example, suppose the loan principal was $150,000 originally, and the note rate was 7 percent annually (0.565 percent monthly), making the borrower's total monthly $p + i$ payments equal to $998. At the point of delinquency his outstanding principal balance would be $145,091 and the interest arrearages would sum to $5,078 (only the simple interest portion, calculated at 0.0565 percent times $145,982 at $846 per month, is added to arrearages). Because tax and insurance escrows would be depleted by now, they will also have to be included in the arrearage amount. If we assume property taxes and insurance run at 3 percent of the original unpaid principal balance (UPB) annually, then at least half of this annual amount ($2,250) would have to be added to bring the escrow account current, thus increasing his total arrearage to $7,328. For simplicity we assume no additional fees in this example. Under the first loan modification structure of adding arrearages and reamortizing over the remaining term of 27 years (324 payments), his new $p+i$ payment would be $1,048 per month. Under the longer amortization option of a 40-year term, his new $p+i$ payment would be $947 per month, $50 less than his original payment in our simplified example. Monthly tax and insurance escrow would be added to this amount.[28]

There is also the option to lower the note rate depending on the reason for the default, the borrower's cash flow situation, and his future income potential. Many people are surprised to learn that loan modifications usually increase the borrower's payments unless specifically structured to lower the payment. However, a loan modification results in a smaller payment than the borrower would make under a repayment plan: a 12-month repayment plan would have added $673 a month to our example borrower's payment for a year, a 67 percent increase from his original $p+i$ payment, compared with $50 a month under a modification with the original maturity date.

27. A very good and short primer on the amortization function along with a simple calculator written by Bret Whissel is available at http://www.bretwhissel.net/amortization/moreamort.html.

28. If the servicer does not already handle escrow payments for taxes and insurance, these should be added to the payment under the loan modification terms. Tax liens and force-placed insurance caused by failure to pay these items can delay or defeat a loan modification or other workout option.

Figure 7-2. *Average Cumulative Incidence of Failure among Loans in Foreclosure, by Whether Loan Was Modified after Foreclosure Referral*[a]

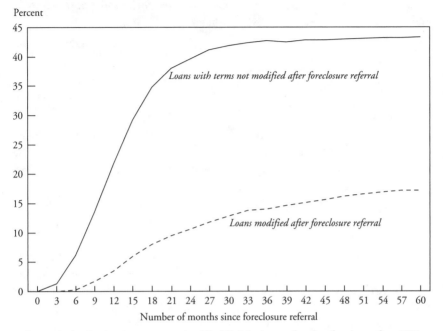

Percent

Loans with terms not modified after foreclosure referral

Loans modified after foreclosure referral

Number of months since foreclosure referral

Source: Authors' estimations on a sample of Freddie Mac loans referred to foreclosure from 2001 to 2006, with performance measured through June 2007.

a. "Failure" means home loss through foreclosure sale, deed-in-lieu transfer, or short sale.

The performance of Freddie Mac's portfolio of modified loans shows a high degree of successful outcomes, measured by low failure rates. Between 1995 and 2000, Freddie Mac completed 15,834 loan modifications, of which just 20 percent ended up failing (foreclosure sale, short sale, or deed-in-lieu) after twenty quarters of observation. More recently, Freddie Mac loan modifications have been performing better than those before 2001 because of high home price appreciation and very low interest rates since 2003, and the 2006 book of loan modifications is the best yet, driven in part by high volumes of well-performing Hurricane Katrina loan modifications. However, deteriorating economic and housing market conditions in many areas of the country will erode these successes going forward.

Figure 7-2 shows the performance of loans referred to foreclosure (the legal process of foreclosure was started) between 2001 and 2006 and their subsequent performance by whether the loan was modified after the referral. The fail rates of loans that were modified and those that were not differ dramatically: cumulatively 17 percent by the end of 60 months for modified loans versus 43 percent for non-modified loans. Given the previously stated statistics on noncontact of borrowers, it is reasonable to assume that more than half of these non-modified loan borrowers did not receive the option of a loan modification because they did not talk to their servicer. Fail rates among modified loans peak at about two years after the modification occurs, with additional failures beyond that time occurring less and less frequently; this can be seen in figure 7-2, where the steepness of the curves lessens after 24 months. Cutts and Green (2005) also find that borrowers who had previously had a loan modification but were again in default were significantly less likely to fail than those who had not previously been through a loan modification, perhaps because of the borrower's willingness to work with the servicers to reach a positive resolution.

With a five-year performance success rate of close to 80 percent, loan modifications are a successful tool for foreclosure avoidance. The cost and complexity of a loan modification, such as state recording fees on large arrearage, notary signatures, income and expense documentation, mailing costs, and potential tax consequences, create significant barriers to an otherwise good option for borrowers who do not qualify for repayment plans or who would have payment terms too burdensome under a repayment plan to be feasible. As a matter of public policy, investors, government officials, and consumer groups may find value to revisit the accounting, as well as federal, state, and local laws affecting loan modifications to make them more affordable for investors and borrowers, and to look for potential incentives to offset the economic cost of capital from a modification for investors such as credit on HUD Affordable Housing Goals or Federal Community Reinvestment Act goals. Such actions could help clear the way for more loan modifications and greater success in sustaining homeownership.

Increasing delinquency volume coupled with intense media and consumer advocate positioning on increasing loan modifications will increase the pressure on investors and servicers to reduce the underwriting standards on loan modifications. The trade-off is an increase in the recidivism rate, a likely increase in the failure rate among modified loans, and higher losses for all parties involved. For example, Freddie Mac guidelines have traditionally looked for a 20 percent free cash-flow buffer (after expenses) when underwriting a borrower for a loan modification. This income cushion helps with unexpected expenses, variance in income, and positions the borrower for a greater level of success on the loan modification; more modifications could be done if this limit were lowered to 19 percent or 15 percent, but each step down adds to the risk of failure. But the plethora of new mortgage products pushing borrowers into distress and the risk of adding new REO inventories into markets with falling home values may tip the balance toward different thresholds in the hopes of lowering overall credit losses. Investors and servicers will continually evaluate the best options for executing loan workouts in the current environment, but as a society we have to accept that none of the answers is easy or obvious.

Impediments to a Loan Modification

When an investor lowers the note rate below the original coupon rate or changes other terms of the mortgage contract, the investor incurs a troubled debt restructuring (TDR) loss that it must record as an immediate accounting loss when the loan is modified because of the decreased present value of the income stream.[29] The investor also takes an economic loss on its use of capital, a component of which, in the prime market, is using the original prime interest rate to modify a borrower with delinquent credit history inclusive of the ongoing default (that is, a subprime credit borrower), when this capital could be used to fund a new prime and presumably performing loan.

A second component is the present value of sustaining the loan versus foreclosing. This consists of the expected lower collateral value of the property net of sales costs plus any proceeds from credit enhancements (such as borrower-paid mortgage insurance [MI] or investor-paid pool MI) minus the loss on the loan. In some cases the investor can be made whole if the loan goes to REO but might suffer an expected economic loss from completing the loan modification. Thus, properly structured home-retention workout options may result in borrowers' keeping their homes, but they usually result in a loss for investors through the subsidy for a subprime borrower at a prime (or lower) rate and other real and opportunity costs, and sometimes these losses are greater than the loss they would take if the investor forced the foreclosure.

Last, under private label mortgage-backed and related security trust agreements (that is, any mortgage-backed security not issued by Freddie Mac, Fannie Mae, or Ginnie Mae), the ability to modify a loan may be severely limited. Some of these securities, particularly collateralized debt obligations (CDOs), are structured to protect investors in certain tranches from default risk; a loan modification affects their income from the security and strict interpretation of the trust agreement would not allow it. The Securities and Exchange Commission (SEC) and other regulators, Congress, and industry groups are looking at options to allow more borrowers with loans in these securities to avoid foreclosure.

A Shifting Paradigm in Loan Performance

The subprime sector historically was a minor part of the overall mortgage market, focusing on serving credit-blemished borrowers in need of refinancing. According to the National Delinquency Survey results,[30] subprime loans made up less

---

29. If you look at the financial statements of any mortgage investor, you will find a line item for TDRs from the execution of loan modifications. The Statement of Financial Accounting Standards No. 15 (FASB 15) is the accounting rule that governs the loss calculations from loan modifications in financial statements.

30. Mortgage Bankers Association (2007).

than 2.5 percent of the outstanding loans from 1998 (when they started survey-ing this information) to 2000. In 2001, the share of subprime loans started to grow, making up 2.7 percent of loans in 2001, 8.4 percent by the end of 2003, and 13.7 percent by the end of 2006. The growth of Alt-A lending was just as extreme. According to Inside Mortgage Finance (2007), subprime loans made up 5.5 percent of the dollars of new single-family loans originated in 2001, and Alt-A loans were 2.4 percent. For 2006, International Mortgage Finance reported that subprime originations accounted for 20.1 percent of the single-family mortgage market and Alt-A loans made up another 13.3 percent. These figures are not consistent with the "niche" market definitions most people associate with the subprime and Alt-A segments, and their rapid growth has radically changed the performance of the market overall.

The widespread degradation of underwriting standards in the subprime and Alt-A segments of the market, in which documented capacity to repay the loan was not considered and downpayment requirements were largely waived, in com-bination with declining home values in many markets, is behind the rapid rise in foreclosures in 2006–08. For example, the number of low- or no-income docu-mentation loans originated in the subprime segment grew from less than 30 per-cent in 2001 in the LoanPerformance securities database to over 50 percent among 2006 loans. In the Alt-A segment, the share in 2006 topped 80 percent.

Because capacity to repay was not considered in the underwriting decision of these loans, many of borrowers took out loans that they could not afford, which is vividly evident in cohort trend analysis. In figure 7-3, we evaluate the perfor-mance of loans as they age monthly by origination year using data from the Loan-Performance securities database. Figure 7-3a shows cumulative 60-day delin-quency rates for Alt-A and subprime loans for origination years 2002–07, and the maximum level of prime 60-day delinquency rates in the shaded area at the bot-tom of each chart for reference.

Loans originated in 2002 came after the 2001 recession, but the loss of jobs continued throughout 2002 even with economic recovery. This weakness led to higher cumulative default rates than among loans originated in 2003, which were underwritten with 45-year lows in interest rates, rising home values, and a strong economy, leading to superior performance at each month of season-ing. Loans originated in 2007 show the worst performance. While the 2007 loans are more severely affected by falling home prices and a weakening econ-omy as they have not added any equity since origination, the large share of early-payment defaults, loans that become delinquent on the first or second payment, points more to reduced underwriting standards and perhaps increased fraud. Prime loan performance shows the same pattern by origina-tion cohort; however, the scale is one-fourteenth that of the subprime chart, as shown by the height of the gray bar marked at 2.5 percent at the bottom of the subprime and Alt-A charts.

Figure 7-3a. *Cumulative Incidence of 60-Day and Worse Delinquency among Nonprime First Lien Mortgage Loans as a Share of Loans Originated, by Origination Year*[a]

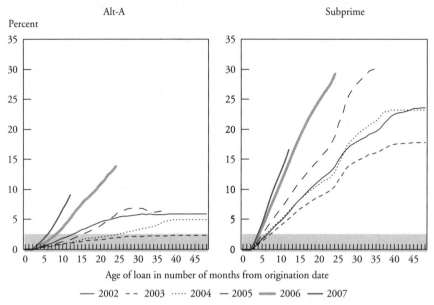

Alt-A   Subprime

Age of loan in number of months from origination date

—— 2002   – – 2003   ····· 2004   — 2005   ▬▬ 2006   —— 2007

Source: Authors' estimations based on First American CoreLogic's LoanPerformance ABS securities database.

a. Shaded area represents the range of default rates for prime loans.

In figure 7-3b, the exercise is repeated, but this time examining the fail rate of loans, that is, loans that go through a deed-in-lieu transfer or foreclosure sale to become REO properties. Given the pattern in the 60-day delinquency rates, this pattern is expected. Loans are failing, however, at a higher rate than those that came before. For example, comparing the 60-day delinquency rate of subprime loans in figure 7-3a at 12 months of seasoning to the REO rate of subprime loans at month 24, based on the 2002–04 loan cohorts we would expect to see a fail rate of roughly 25 percent. The 2006 book is failing at a rate that exceeds 50 percent. Among Alt-A loans we would expect a fail rate of roughly 25–30 percent (2003–04 cohorts' average fail rate), but 2006 loans are failing at a rate of more than 60 percent.

Combining the higher transition rates into REO from delinquency, the higher delinquency rates among the 2006 and 2007 loan cohorts, and the higher shares of loans serviced among the nonprime segments, the effect of these market segments on the broader housing market is larger than at any previous time. Even if interest rates remain constant, as home values continue to fall in many areas of

Figure 7-3b. *Cumulative Incidence of REO among Nonprime First Lien Mortgage Loans as a Share of Loans Originated, by Origination Year*[a]

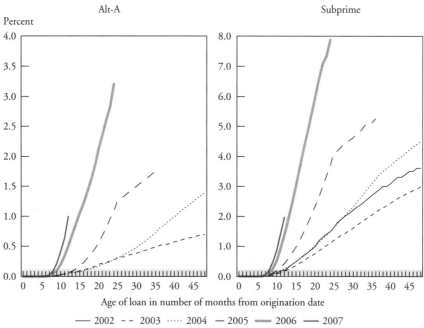

Source: Authors' estimations based on First American CoreLogic's LoanPerformance ABS securities database.

REO = real-estate owned.

a. Shaded area represents the estimated range of REO rates for prime loans based on REO transition rates from 60-day delinquencies in Cutts and Green (2005) and the 60-day delinquency rates in figure 3a.

the country through 2008 and likely 2009 and perhaps even later, more borrowers will see their opportunity for refinancing into a more affordable loan product erode and investors will struggle to contain rising disposition times and credit losses.

Default Options and Triggers

Negative equity alone rarely causes default because borrowers also enjoy a stream of dividend-like payments in the form of shelter services in addition to the potential for capital gains that they give up if they exercise the default or "put" option in the mortgage contract. A negative economic shock affecting the borrower's capacity to pay the mortgage when there is positive equity is rarely sufficient to cause default severe enough to lead to foreclosure. The borrower will simply sell the home if there is enough equity. Thus, the investor in the mortgage debt will only see a default option exercised when it is well out of the money on the deal.

But what causes the economic shock? Are all shocks the same with respect to the borrower's likelihood of home loss?

Generally, local economic conditions and changes in underwriting standards over time affect the performance of loans as they age. More restrictive underwriting standards will diminish and delay the incidence of delinquency, yet local recessions will slow home sales and depress prices, increase unemployment, and thus increase the incidence and move up the timing of delinquency relative to stronger economic conditions. Falling mortgage rates will lead to faster prepayments and drive down delinquency rates as borrowers refinance their way out of potential problems. Rising interest rates increase delinquency rates by causing payment shocks at the reset date for adjustable-rate mortgages and reduce the ability of borrowers to afford a fixed-rate refinance. Tightened underwriting standards, although having the benefits listed, also limit a borrower's ability to refinance out of financial stress or delinquency.

According to Freddie Mac data, prime credit borrowers get into serious mortgage delinquency primarily because of income shocks, excessive obligations, and health-related problems. Because data are hard to obtain, differences in the likelihood of home loss conditional on the trigger event have not been explored. In table 7-3 we examine a sample of Freddie Mac loans that went delinquent between 2001 and 2006 and were underwritten for a workout using Freddie Mac's Workout Prospector® system, and among borrowers who were approved for a loan modification, we record the incidence of subsequent home loss given the primary reason cited by borrowers for their mortgage problems.

Income loss is the primary reason for mortgage delinquency at 41.8 percent for delinquent borrowers, but the incidence of home loss after a loan was modified among borrowers citing this reason is the third highest at 18.5 percent. But not all income loss is the same. Job loss is harder to overcome than business failure, which may be, in part, because of a longer lead time (the business owner knows his or her business is failing long before the doors are shut) or networks (the business owner may be able to find employment with a prior client), or curtailment of income (which may be a cutback in hours or salary or loss of secondary job) because the borrower still has income with which to negotiate a workout.

Borrowers who cite marital difficulties as the primary reason for the delinquency lose the home to foreclosure at a rate of nearly 22 percent, the highest fail rate among major delinquency causes. This is a result of both the financial stress of divorce and, often, the unwillingness of the borrower and co-borrower to cooperate with the lender, because that would require cooperation with one another, a rare event during divorce proceedings. Although extreme financial hardships not related to a drop in income are fodder for newspaper stories on foreclosure (the

Table 7-3. *Reasons for Default and the Credit Performance of Modified Loans*
Percent

Mortgage hardship reason	Share of delinquent loans citing reason[a]	Fail rate among modified loans[b]
Loss of income	41.8	18.5
Unemployment	17.4	19.7
Curtailment of income	22.0	17.9
Business failure	2.3	15.6
Death or illness in the family	23.2	17.6
Extreme financial stress other than loss of income	14.4	14.4
Excessive obligation	11.5	15.0
Extreme hardship	2.5	12.7
Payment adjustment	0.4	14.3
Marital difficulties	7.6	21.8
Property problem or casualty loss	1.9	4.7
Inability to sell or rent property	1.3	23.7
Employment transfer or military service	0.8	21.1
All other reasons[c]	9.0	9.5

Source: Authors' calculations based on a sample of Freddie Mac loans that went delinquent between 2001 and 2006 and were evaluated using the Workout Prospector® system.

a. Among loans in which the borrower is successfully contacted by the servicer and is underwritten for a workout.

b. Among loans that were modified after being underwritten by Workout Prospector®, the incidence of home loss through foreclosure sale, deed-in-lieu transfer, or charge-off.

c. The category "all other reasons" includes property abandonment, environment or energy costs, incarceration, payment disputes, fraud, servicing problems, borrower noncontact, and simply "other" reasons.

"too much debt" stories), these borrowers have a relatively low fail rate of 14.4 percent in this sample.

Borrowers with multiple delinquent debts can be thoughtful about cash flow and the implications of paying debt late. For example, a borrower may choose to pay a home equity line of credit (HELOC) loan first, knowing the credit line would be shut down if they were delinquent, compared with their first mortgage, which could take more than a year in foreclosure. The lower loss-of-home rate on excessive debt obligations in table 7-3 shows that these borrowers have a greater propensity to resolve the situation than borrowers experiencing negative (and possibility unexpected) impacts to their income capacity. Through the work of servicers to restructure debt payments, many of these borrowers can negotiate a workout if they have the income capacity and willingness to carry new payments. Borrowers attempting to avoid foreclosure by themselves (self-cure), however, are having more difficulty because recent vintage (2006–07) loans have a higher incidence of negative equity (making it hard for homeowners to sell the property or refinance) and the large inventory of homes for sale (increasing competition and lengthening sale times). These two factors reduce borrowers' ability to resolve the delinquency on their own and increase reliance on workouts from a servicer.

The Foreclosure Process and the Costs of Foreclosure to Investors

Emphasis on loss mitigation began in earnest in the mid- and late 1990s, driven in part by the development of automated underwriting systems and default models that could be used to underwrite workout options for delinquent borrowers based on their current financial situation. These tools allowed servicers to identify borrowers most at risk of worsening delinquency and those that have the financial capacity to handle a loan workout.[31]

As outlined in Cutts and Green (2005), default occurs whenever any term of the mortgage contract is violated, but the term is most often associated with nonpayment. Most investors offer servicers financial and reputation incentives or apply penalties to align their interests with those of the investors, which means minimizing the incidence of foreclosure—that is, negotiating a workout plan to keep the borrowers in their homes or, if a home-retention workout is not possible, completing a foreclosure alternative such as a short sale or deed-in-lieu transfer.[32] For example, some of the incentives Freddie Mac pays servicers are $500 for each successful repayment plan completed, $800 for each approved loan modification executed, $275 for each deed-in-lieu of foreclosure negotiated,[33] and $2,200 for each short sale executed.[34] Fannie Mae offers servicers $400 for each repayment plan and $700 for a loan modification. Fannie Mae incentive payments for short sales (preforeclosure sales) range from $1,000 to $1,500 and payments for deeds-in-lieu of foreclosure are $1,000.[35]

---

31. See Comeau and Cordell (1998); Cutts and Green (2005).

32. A deed-in-lieu transfer occurs when the borrower voluntarily gives the home to the investor in exchange for the debt obligation. A short sale is when the investor agrees to take proceeds from the sale of the home in exchange for the debt obligation even though the principal amount due exceeds the sale proceeds. See USFN (2007) for an overview of state foreclosure processes and Freddie Mac, Fannie Mae, Federal Housing Administration, and Veterans Administration policies regarding foreclosure execution, foreclosure alternative procedures, and other policies on servicing delinquent loans.

33. To aid in negotiating deed-in-lieu transfer agreements, investors will allow servicers under certain conditions to offer borrowers "cash-for-keys" payments to help cover moving expenses, and the investor will reimburse the servicer for the advance of these payments.

34. These payment amounts are effective August 1, 2008. Prior to that date, compensation amounts were 50 percent lower. See http://www.freddiemac.com/news/archives/servicing/2008/20080731_servicers.html for an overview on these payments. See also Freddie Mac's Seller/Servicer Guide at www.freddiemac.com/singlefamily/# for the most up-to-date policies on Freddie Mac loans.

35. See Fannie Mae Press Release on changes to the compensation paid to servicers at www.fanniemae.com/newsreleases/2008/4439.jhtml;jsessionid=44POQJFMFNLBJJ2FQSHSFGA?p=Media&s=News+Releases. See USFN (2007) for an overview of Fannie Mae's policies regarding incentives for servicers to negotiate foreclosure alternatives. See also Fannie Mae's Seller/Servicer Guide at www.efanniemae.com/sf/guides/ssg/index.jsp for the most up-to-date policies on Fannie Mae loans.

In addition to the workout incentives for servicers, Freddie Mac monitors servicer performance through its Performance Profiles, with the greatest weighting on 1) the number of workouts closed versus the number of loans that proceed to REO and 2) the diligent management of foreclosure timelines per state law.[36] Freddie Mac recognizes high-performing servicers annually in mortgage trade magazines and gives them additional financial compensation. In addition, servicers can be monetarily penalized for failure to report default data, out-of-standard foreclosure timelines, reduced credit enhancement recoveries, and ultimately may face repurchase of the loan for nonprudent servicing of the loan.

The Foreclosure Process

Once a borrower has breached a term of the mortgage contract, the investor can seek enforcement of his or her right to claim the collateral in exchange of the debt through the foreclosure process. If there is no alternative to foreclosure either because the borrower is unable to meet the financial requirements of a workout or the servicer is unable to contact the borrower, the servicer seeks to minimize the time until the property is sold at foreclosure sale according to the governing state statutes on foreclosure. A common misconception is that borrowers lose their homes when foreclosure starts, when in fact the legal process averages almost one year since the borrower's last payment, and many borrowers are able to reinstate their loans out of foreclosure and keep their homes.

Foreclosure starts with the filing of the first legal action in foreclosure, usually a Notice of Default, Substitution of Trustee, or similar document filed with the county in which the property is located. The foreclosure sale (sometimes called a sheriff's sale) is the event where borrowers lose their title right to the property—monies from the sale are used toward paying off the debt owed to the loan investor. The investor sets the minimum price or bid for the foreclosure sale, and if no bids are submitted above that bid, the title conveys to the investor in exchange for the debt. In most states the purchaser of a property gains possession at the foreclosure sale; however, in seven states (Colorado,[37] Kansas, Michigan, Minnesota, New Mexico, South Dakota, and Wyoming), borrowers have a right of redemption for a defined period of time of at least 30 days after foreclosure sale, during which time they can continue to live in the home but no additional interest or fees can be assessed to the debt. Borrowers can claim their homes out of redemption by paying the full principal amount owed, arrearages for interest accumulated, legal and court fees, taxes, and other expenses incurred by the investor

---

36. More information on Freddie Mac's Performance Profiles and Servicer Incentives can be found at www.freddiemac.com/service/msp/.

37. Colorado changed its foreclosure process so that after January 2008 the redemption period would fall before the foreclosure sale. The redemption period was after the foreclosure sale in that state for all periods covered by our data.

from the point of the DDLPI through the foreclosure sale or the start of the redemption period according to state law. Two other states have postsale redemption periods: in New Jersey it is ten days following the sale; North Dakota has a right of redemption that is the lesser of six months after the filing of the Summons and Complaint (first legal action in the state's foreclosure process) or 60 days from the foreclosure sale (we assume this translates into a postsale redemption period of 60 days for our analysis, but could be shorter or longer in practice depending on the efficiency of the foreclosure process).

Freddie Mac and other mortgage investors have policies regarding when to refer the loan to foreclosure, that is, when to send the files to foreclosure attorneys to begin the legal process of foreclosure. This can in theory be as soon as the mortgage contract is breached, but in practice is usually several months after the default occurs. In table 7-4 we highlight Freddie Mac's timeline for servicing a delinquent loan up to the point of foreclosure referral. This timeline assumes that the servicer makes every reasonable attempt to reach the borrower and that either there is no borrower contact or the borrower and servicer are unable to negotiate a workout option. Servicers continue to pursue foreclosure avoidance and workout activity with the borrower all the way through the foreclosure process, including up to the foreclosure sale. It is entirely possible that the foreclosure is stopped on the steps of the courthouse immediately before the foreclosure sale. Different investors may have different requirements for how long the servicer should attempt loss mitigation/foreclosure avoidance before referring a loan to foreclosure. If the borrower can negotiate a home-retention workout such as a repayment plan or loan modification, then the foreclosure referral may be delayed as long as the contracted terms of the plan are met. The table assumes that no such delays occur, and thus represents the minimum time until the loan is referred to foreclosure.

The foreclosure process is a well-defined stipulated legal process in all 54 states and territories where Freddie Mac conducts business. Table 7-5 highlights the most common foreclosure method, the legal events in the process, the timelines for each event, and average timeline from the due date of the last payment made by the borrower to the date of the foreclosure sale for loans on properties in the statutorily shortest and longest foreclosure timeline states, Tennessee and Maine, respectively. Table 7-6 contains the timeline information for all 50 states and the District of Columbia.[38] In general, states follow one of two methods for their foreclosure process. A judicial foreclosure involves a judge or court official who presides over the case, and a statutory or power of sale foreclosure allows a trustee or

---

38. The original version of this study, available at www.jchs.harvard.edu/publications/finance/ understanding_consumer_credit/papers/index.html, contains detailed information on each state's foreclosure timeline (as in table 7-5) in addition to the timelines given in table 7-7. As states pass new legislation relating to foreclosure process, these timelines may not reflect current practices.

Table 7-4. *Freddie Mac Preforeclosure Steps for Delinquent Mortgage Loans as Specified in Seller/Servicer Guide*[a]

		Expected optimal time[b]	
Step	Description of steps before foreclosure referral	Days in step	Total days since DDLPI
1	Notify Freddie Mac (the investor) that borrower is "30 days late," measured as 60 days after the due date of last paid installment (DDLPI).	60	
2	Servicers send breach letter to borrowers notifying them that they are in default on their mortgage or deed of trust and that if full payment is not made within 30 days, the servicer will begin enforcement of investor's rights under contract including foreclosure.	15	
3	Servicer initiates call campaign to delinquent borrower and works on loss mitigation efforts through workout options when contact with borrower is made. Most servicers will initiate call campaigns starting at day 10 of the delinquency (40 days past DDLPI).	75	
4	Loan is now referred to an attorney licensed in the property state to begin the legal foreclosure process. Borrower is 4 payments late with 5 total payments due, and 150 days have passed since the due date of last payment.		
	Total time elapsed from due date of last payment to foreclosure referral		**150**

Source: Freddie Mac.

a. Standard across all states and territories.

b. Freddie Mac provides cash and other incentives to servicers to try to negotiate home-retention workout options with the borrower. If a workout plan is successfully negotiated, the foreclosure process is delayed or suspended, and the timeline in this table does not reflect these delays.

investor to proceed without a court hearing but in accordance with state law, including recurring publication notices. The simple (unweighted) average time between foreclosure referral and foreclosure sale based only on state legislated timelines is 120 days, and the average redemption period is 103 days for the nine states that have postsale redemption. Many states have a confirmation of foreclosure sale provision during which the buyer of the home at the foreclosure sale takes title and has rights of entry to the property and can begin eviction if it has not already taken place, but the new owner of the property cannot market the home for sale until the foreclosure has been confirmed; this process is expected to take 27 days on average assuming no delays. Adding in the prereferral timeline according to Freddie Mac's guidelines brings the average expected foreclosure

Table 7-5. *Freddie Mac Analysis of Expected Optimal Statutory Timeline for Foreclosure: Shortest and Longest Timeline States*[a]

| | | | Expected optimal statutory timeline | | | | | |
| | | | | | Number of days in postsale | | | |
State and foreclosure type[c]	Step	Description of step[b]	Days in step after FCL referral	Total days FCL since referral to sale	Redemption period	Confirmation period	Total days from DDLPI to finalized FCL sale including postsale redemption period	Actual average time from DDLPI to finalized FCL sale/ possession[b]
Maine Judicial	1	Foreclosure referral: attorney sends FDCPA letter with contact information	3					
	2	Title work	5					
	3	**Complaint is filed**	1					
	4	Sheriff is appointed and completes service of process	30					
	5	Response or answer period	20					
	6	Judgment	30					
	7	Redemption (90 days)	90					
	8	Publication of sale, 3 consecutive weeks with first publication not less than 30 days before sale	30					
	9	Foreclosure sale		209	none	none	359	598
Tennessee Statutory	1	Foreclosure referral: attorney sends FDCPA letter with contact information	3					
	2	**Title work and substitution of trustee is filed**	5					
	3	Publication of sale, 3 times for a period covering at least 20 days	25					
	4	Foreclosure sale		33	none	27	183	248
All states average[c]			120	120	103	27	292	355

Sources: Freddie Mac; authors' interpretation of state statutes. This is not intended to be exhaustive, and the authors cannot guarantee the information is accurate or suitable for any particular purpose. Many states provide for both statutory and judicial foreclosure options; the most commonly used option is presented in this table. See also USFN (2007).

DDLPI = due date of last paid installment; FCL = foreclosure; FDCPA = Fair Debt Collection Practices Act; REO = real-estate owned.

a. First legal action against the borrower is in bold. Steps before first legal action are required, but there is no statutory limitation on the number of days these steps should take. We allow 8 days in nearly all states for legal processing prior to the first legal action.

b. Authors' estimations based on a sample of Freddie Mac REO property acquisitions in 2007.

c. National average is calculated as simple average over number of states; redemption and confirmation periods are averages over states that have these provisions.

Table 7-6. *Share of Foreclosure Sales in which Properties Are Acquired by Third-Party Purchasers*
Percent

State[a]	Foreclosure sales to third parties[b]	State[a]	Foreclosure sales to third parties[b]
Alabama	14.9	*Montana*	*30.0*
Alaska	*25.0*	Nebraska	15.5
Arizona	15.5	Nevada	13.5
Arkansas	17.3	New Hampshire	22.5
California	16.6	**New Jersey**	**28.8**
Colorado	**4.9**	***New Mexico***	***8.5***
Connecticut	38.6	New York	19.5
District of Columbia	*50.0*	North Carolina	22.2
Delaware	*75.0*	***North Dakota***	***17.6***
Florida	15.3	Ohio	12.5
Georgia	15.7	Oklahoma	19.2
Hawaii	*20.0*	Oregon	39.2
Idaho	24.5	Pennsylvania	14.4
Illinois	14.9	*Puerto Rico*	*20.0*
Indiana	8.4	*Rhode Island*	*15.4*
Iowa	9.3	South Carolina	20.2
Kansas	**10.3**	***South Dakota***	***16.2***
Kentucky	15.1	Tennessee	19.4
Louisiana	16.7	Texas	12.6
Maine	*14.3*	Utah	46.4
Maryland	34.9	*Vermont*	*0.0*
Massachusetts	18.1	Virginia	25.4
Michigan	**2.3**	Washington	40.0
Minnesota	**1.8**	West Virginia	9.8
Mississippi	8.5	Wisconsin	19.7
Missouri	11.8	***Wyoming***	***0.0***
Total[c]	13.2	Redemption states	3.90
		Nonredemption states	16.3

Source: Authors' estimations based on a sample of Freddie Mac loans that went to foreclosure sale before September 2007.

a. States with post-foreclosure-sale redemption periods are in bold; states in which fewer than 50 foreclosure sales were observed are in italics.

b. Third-party purchaser is any agent who bids on a property at foreclosure sale who is not affiliated with the lender or investor that brought the foreclosure action.

c. Average weighted by number of sales.

Table 7-7. Freddie Mac Analysis of Expected Optimal Statutory Timeline for Foreclosure, by State

State	Foreclosure type	Total days since FCL referral to sale	Number of days in postsale		Total days from DDLPI to finalized FCL sale including postsale redemption period[a]	Actual average time from DDLPI to finalized FCL sale (days)[b]	Actual average cost from DDLPI to FCL sale relative to U.S. average (percent)[c]
			Redemption period	Confirmation period			
Alabama	S	36	none	none	186	291	49
Alaska	S	43	none	none	193	387	106
Arizona	S	98	none	none	248	253	68
Arkansas	S	41	none	none	191	281	63
California	S	116	none	none	266	268	171
Colorado	S	78	75	none	303	339	101
Connecticut	J	157	none	none	287	319	156
Delaware	J	139	none	30	319	402	125
District of Columbia	S	38	none	none	188	n.a.	n.a.
Florida	J	131	none	10	291	326	96
Georgia	S	47	none	none	197	241	69
Hawaii	S	128	none	30	308	n.a.	n.a.
Idaho	S	128	none	none	278	395	80
Illinois	J	265	none	none	415	398	112
Indiana	J	180	none	none	330	402	87
Iowa	J	312	none	none	462	458	113
Kansas	J	110	90	none	350	410	76
Kentucky	J	130	none	none	280	420	86
Louisiana	J	99	none	none	249	476	89
Maine	J	209	none	none	359	598	135

Maryland	S	39	none	60	249	274	65
Massachusetts	S	70	none	none	220	263	142
Michigan	S	38	180	none	368	380	70
Minnesota	S	53	180	none	383	425	82
Mississippi	S	38	none	none	188	367	58
Missouri	S	38	none	none	188	217	51
Montana	S	129	none	none	279	356	98
Nebraska	J	122	none	none	272	278	82
Nevada	S	120	none	none	270	283	118
New Hampshire	J	38	none	none	188	229	122
New Jersey	J	270	10	none	420	436	224
New Mexico	J	155	30	none	335	426	86
New York	J	280	none	none	430	392	118
North Carolina	S	89	none	10	249	281	72
North Dakota	J	140	60	none	350	422	76
Ohio	J	193	none	30	372	480	107
Oklahoma	J	159	none	30	339	452	94
Oregon	S	128	none	none	278	369	104
Pennsylvania	J	171	none	none	321	453	110
Rhode Island	S	59	none	none	209	251	146
South Carolina	J	170	none	30	350	336	80
South Dakota	J	110	180	none	440	503	85
Tennessee	S	33	none	none	183	248	57
Texas	S	42	none	none	192	254	93
Utah	S	129	none	none	279	303	89
Vermont	J	290	none	none	440	446	114
Virginia	S	36	none	none	186	213	63
Washington	S	128	none	none	278	299	98

(continued)

Table 7-7. *Freddie Mac Analysis of Expected Optimal Statutory Timeline for Foreclosure, by State (continued)*

State	Foreclosure type	Total days since FCL referral to sale	Number of days in postsale		Total days from DDLPI to finalized FCL sale including postsale redemption period[a]	Actual average time from DDLPI to finalized FCL sale (days)[b]	Actual average cost from DDLPI to FCL sale relative to U.S. average (percent)[c]
			Redemption period	Confirmation period			
West Virginia	S	38	none	none	188	277	44
Wisconsin	J	260	none	14	424	458	140
Wyoming	S	53	120	none	323	342	69
U.S average[d]		120	103	27	292	355	100

Sources: Freddie Mac; authors' interpretation of state statutes. This is not intended to be exhaustive and the authors cannot guarantee the information is accurate or suitable for any particular purpose. Many states provide for both statutory (S) and judicial (J) foreclosure options; the most commonly used option is presented in this table. See also USFN (2007).

DDLPI = due date of last paid installment; FCL = foreclosure; n.a. = not available.

a. Includes the 150 days recommended by Freddie Mac between DDLPI and foreclosure referral from table 7-2. Includes postsale redemption and confirmation periods. "Finalized sale" means that the sale has been confirmed and the lender has full title, right of entry, right of eviction, and right of sale.

b. Authors' estimations based on a sample of Freddie Mac REO property acquisitions before September 30, 2007. Includes postsale redemption and confirmation periods. "Finalized sale" means that the sale has been confirmed and the lender has full title, right of entry, right of eviction, and right of sale.

c. Authors' estimations based on a sample of Freddie Mac REO property dispositions before September 30, 2007. A value of 100 percent means that the average preforeclosure cost in that state is equal to the national average cost. Costs include interest expenses before foreclosure sale.

d. National average is calculated as simple average over number of states; redemption and confirmation periods are averages over states that have these provisions.

timeline to 292 days between DDLPI and finalized foreclosure sale/investor possession.[39] The average actual time across all states between the due date of the last paid mortgage installment and the foreclosure sale is almost one year, at an average 355 days.

The timeline in table 7-7 assumes that the foreclosure attorneys working on the investor's and servicer's behalf execute the foreclosure with maximum efficiency but that each step in the process takes the full time allotted for the minimum time required under state law. Delays throughout the foreclosure process are often caused by backlogs in the court system, bankruptcy filings by borrowers, or borrowers who contest the foreclosure. But importantly the foreclosure process can be delayed or suspended at any time before the foreclosure sale to accommodate a workout deal with the borrower. If the borrower fails to meet the terms of contract on a home-retention workout, the foreclosure process resumes, usually at the point in the process at which it was suspended. We would thus expect actual average foreclosure timelines to exceed expected optimal foreclosure times by a significant amount, and indeed this is the case in nearly all states.

Once the property goes to foreclosure sale the investor sets the minimum bid on the property. To minimize expected losses to the investor, from an economic standpoint, this bid should approximately equal the present discounted market value of the property based on expectations of the length of time needed to market the home in current conditions net of expected marketing expenses, real-estate agent commissions, and maintenance and repair costs. If no third-party purchaser offers the minimum bid, the investor "wins" the property at the sale and it becomes real estate owned on the investor's books.

Up to this point the investor has already incurred significant costs and still faces large costs in disposing of the property.

The Costs of Foreclosure to Investors

Figure 7-4 breaks out the average gross costs of foreclosure by the time in the process in which they are incurred; these are only as represented by Freddie Mac's experience as an investor in conventional, conforming prime mortgages. Gross costs are all expenses incurred by the investor and any losses taken on the unpaid principal balance when the property is sold. Any proceeds from credit enhancements such as primary mortgage insurance would be netted out against these values to calculate the total net loss to the investor; the total cost to the industry, however, is best represented by the gross value. Costs incurred before the foreclosure sale are "prefore-

---

39. In postsale redemption period states we include the redemption in the timeline. In those states borrowers have the right of occupancy until the redemption period expires or they voluntarily give up the right. Thus we count it as part of the preforeclosure timeline and mark the end of the timeline as when the investor has full rights of possession. Similarly we add in the confirmation period for states that have a foreclosure sale confirmation period because this marks the full transfer of property rights from the borrower to the investor.

Figure 7-4. *Composition of Average Total Costs to a Mortgage Investor*[a]

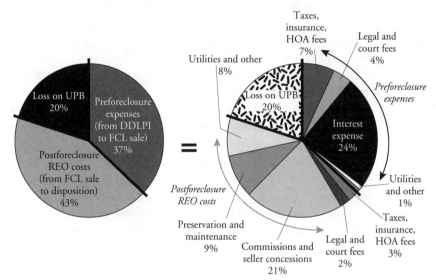

Source: Authors' estimations based on a sample of recent Freddie Mac property dispositions.
DDLPI = due date of last paid installment; FCL = foreclosure; HOA = homeowners association; UPB = unpaid principal balance.
a. Costs incurred during postsale redemption period are added to preforeclosure costs since they are incurred before investor possession. Costs include loss on unpaid principal balance of REO properties among prime conventional conforming loans. Percentages may not sum to 100 because of rounding.

closure" costs and are calculated from the due date of the last payment made by the borrower to the date of possession, either the foreclosure sale date or the date the postsale redemption period ends and the investor takes possession of the property. All costs incurred after the date of possession are "postforeclosure REO" costs.

PREFORECLOSURE COSTS. Preforeclosure costs account for 37 percent of the total gross losses to the investor, and among these preforeclosure costs, accumulated interest accounts for 66 percent and local property taxes, insurance, and homeowners' association (HOA)/condo fees account for 21 percent of the expenses up to the foreclosure sale and possession. The 10 percent share of preforeclosure costs marked as legal and court fees includes expenses for publication of foreclosure notices of sale; court, sheriff, and auctioneer's fees; attorney's fees; and title-search and title-insurance-related fees.[40] The preforeclosure interest expense in figure 7-4 is the accrued interest arrearages since the DDLPI and includes the explicit interest expenses from the interest passed through to investors

40. The notice of publication requirements are dictated by state law and local foreclosure statutes; these regulations govern the type of publication that is acceptable (often the widest circulation print newspaper in the county or city), the size of the notice, and the information contained in the notice. For example, the *Washington Post* is the publication most commonly used in the Washington, D.C.,

in mortgage-backed securities issued by Freddie Mac and Fannie Mae (F&F), as long as the mortgage is held in that security; generally speaking, loans are pulled from these securities when the loan is modified or the property goes to foreclosure sale. Investors in F&F securities are promised the timely payment of principal and interest from a loan as long as the loan is in the security, regardless of whether the borrower has made such payments to the servicer (and thus to F&F). Before December 2007, Freddie Mac and Fannie Mae would remove a loan from a security when the loan was referred to foreclosure, thus paying the security investor the full amount of the loan principal due under the guarantees given by Freddie Mac and Fannie Mae.[41] At that point, the explicit interest expense became an implicit cost of capital expense to Freddie Mac or Fannie Mae until the property was sold out of REO inventory or the loan was reinstated or was paid off. For Freddie Mac and Fannie Mae securities after December 2007, a loan remains in the pool until the foreclosure sale or a loan modification is executed, and the security investors are then paid the principal amount of their investment; thus interest arrearages are explicit costs for the servicer or F&F until the foreclosure sale.[42] Ginnie Mae security issuers (lenders) generally can buy a loan that is in a delinquent status for at least 90 days out of the security at market value and hold it in their portfolio. The investor receives a payout from Ginnie Mae if the market value is below par, and the lender receives a mortgage insurance payout from the government program guaranteeing the loan.[43] For all other whole-loan or private-label securities investors, the interest expense is an explicit cost to servicers until the property is sold out of REO Inventory. The servicer is then reimbursed out of proceeds from the property sale.

POSTFORECLOSURE REO EXPENSES. In figure 7-4, among postforeclosure REO expenses, which account for 43 percent of the gross losses on prime conventional, conforming loans, the largest component is the sum of commissions paid to the listing agent and concessions paid to the buyer at closing (for example, seller contribution toward closing costs). The next largest component comes from preservation, maintenance, and improvement costs.

The investor has to prepare the home for listing, including making any capital improvements necessary to bring the home to habitable condition, such as reinstalling plumbing and appliances, painting and reroofing, and making other significant repairs; maintaining the property to all local ordinances with lawn care, winterization where necessary, cleaning of the home, and other mainte-

metro area for publishing foreclosure notices from the Virginia and Maryland suburbs and D.C.; depending on the county in which the property is located, these notices can run from 1 to 2 column inches of print to more than 4 column inches.

41. See www.freddiemac.com/news/archives/mbs/2007/20071210_pc_change.html.

42. For more information on Ginnie Mae securities, see www.ginniemae.gov/guide/pdf/chap15.pdf.

43. Ginnie Mae securities loans from the Federal Housing Administration, Department of Veterans Affairs, and other government agency mortgage insurance programs.

nance chores; and paying local property taxes and fees, HOA and condo fees, and utilities.[44] Borrowers often do extensive damage to a property before losing it through foreclosure, such as removing all copper pipes and appliances, destroying walls and windows, and stopping drains and running faucets to create flooding. This raises the cost to the investor to repair the damage and lengthens the time to market. REO property disposition timelines and commission incentives depend on the condition of the property when it is acquired by the lender, the neighborhood's characteristics, and the economic conditions of the local area.

LOSS ON UPB. The last major expense shown in figure 7-4 is the loss taken on the unpaid principal balance (UPB) because of the negative equity position of the borrower. On average, these losses currently account for a little more than 20 percent of the total costs of foreclosure for prime conventional, conforming mortgages. The expected worsening of the REO rates and falling home prices in 2008 and 2009 will likely push this share much higher.

The mission of homeownership preservation and the avoidance of the cost of REO are motivation for the investor to encourage servicers to offer both retention and nonretention workouts (mentioned earlier) and measure servicer performance against expected benchmarks. But additional costs to society come from a foreclosure beyond the losses suffered by loan investors and borrowers that place additional value on loss mitigation and foreclosure prevention. For example, a concentration of REO properties in a neighborhood depresses the prices of all homes in it and increases the time it takes to dispose of any one property. Within one neighborhood, for example, "Accounting for both the foreclosure costs paid for by City and County agencies, and the impact of foreclosures on area property values, a foreclosure on this block could impose direct costs on local government agencies totaling more than $34,000 and indirect effects on nearby property owners (in the form of reduced property values and home equity) of as much as an additional $220,000."[45]

In the subprime and Alt-A market segments, preforeclosure costs excluding interest expenses (which depend on the effective interest rate) are likely to be similar to those of Freddie Mac because these are largely driven by statutory requirements in each state. To the extent, however, that borrowers in these segments had lower initial equity, had no or negative amortization because of the structure of the mortgage, and were disproportionately located in areas or in price ranges with rapidly falling home values, REO costs and the loss on UPB could be higher than represented by Freddie Mac's experience.

---

44. According to Hayre and Saraf (2008), if the property has private mortgage insurance (PMI), the contract with the insurer usually requires that before a claim can be submitted the home must be in similar condition to when the policy was taken out. This prevents the servicer/investor from neglecting the property to the detriment of the insurer.

45. Apgar, Duda, and Gorey (2005).

Foreclosure and REO processes are expensive for investors, with foreclosure costs being driven by state legal requirements and REO costs driven by preservation and maintenance costs, sales commissions, and seller concessions along with the loss on UPB. Currently, there is a policy debate about delaying the foreclosure process to stimulate more loss mitigation activities and the cost of the foreclosure process (that is, legal and court fees) being a barrier to a borrower's reinstating the loan or qualifying for a workout. In the analysis of preforeclosure costs, just 11 percent of preforeclosure process costs are legal and court-related expenses and the remaining 89 percent are all costs that the borrower would incur as part of continued homeownership, such as property taxes, HOA fees, insurance, utilities, maintenance, and interest.

Ironically, the securitization of mortgages in the secondary market, which attracted global capital and led to a strong supply of low-cost mortgage funds, is now impeding the ability of borrowers to get relief when it is economically correct to offer it. At the beginning of the subprime market problems in early 2007, many subprime servicers claimed they were unable to help borrowers because the security trust agreements under SEC rules did not allow them to alter the terms of the loans in the securities. The SEC has since come back with an interpretation of the rule that expressly allows the issuer to do a loan modification when the borrower is in imminent danger of losing the home through foreclosure. The current foreclosure crisis has revealed that some state and federal laws and regulatory policies negatively alter the economics of loan modifications or other foreclosure alternatives, generally as a result of unintended outcomes from policies enacted in a different economic climate.

Policymakers, investors, servicers, and borrowers face many challenges in minimizing the incidence of home loss through foreclosure. Among them is the tension between too little time in the foreclosure process such that some borrowers are unable to recover from mild setbacks before they lose the home but investors minimize preforeclosure time-related costs, and too much time in the foreclosure process such that the borrower is encouraged to take the option of free rent until the home is lost at the foreclosure sale while investor costs rise rapidly.

The Sweet Spot of Foreclosure Timelines and Borrower Reinstatement

State foreclosure processes fall into two broad categories, statutory power of sale, where the process is outside of the courtroom, and judicial, where a judge presides over the process. These two methods create timeline differences between foreclosure referral to an attorney (first legal action) and the foreclosure sale (loss of property). Table 7-7 lists the foreclosure method for each state. In general, statutory states require less process, fewer associated legal fees, and shorter timelines to foreclosure sale and are less expensive for the investor and any borrower receiving a workout or reinstating the loan. The average expected timeline based on legislated

Figure 7-5. *Preforeclosure Sale Costs and Expected Time between Date of Foreclosure Referral and Date of Foreclosure Sale*[a]

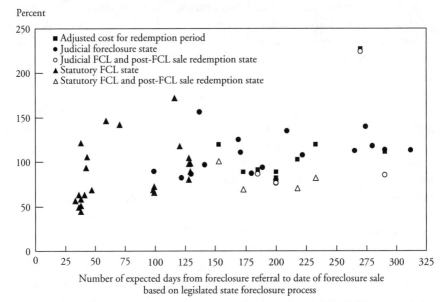

Percent

Number of expected days from foreclosure referral to date of foreclosure sale
based on legislated state foreclosure process

■ Adjusted cost for redemption period
● Judicial foreclosure state
○ Judicial FCL and post-FCL sale redemption state
▲ Statutory FCL state
△ Statutory FCL and post-FCL sale redemption state

Source: Authors' estimations on a sample of Freddie Mac loans that went to foreclosure sale before September 30, 2007.

DDLPI = due date of last paid installment; FCL = foreclosure.

a. Preforeclosure sale costs are costs incurred by servicer and investor from DDLPI to date of foreclosure sale. Adjusted cost for redemption period adds in interest cost of capital during postsale redemption period in the nine states that have them.

legal process from referral to finalized foreclosure sale and possession is 206 days in judicial foreclosure states compared with an average of 93 days in statutory foreclosure process states. Actual timelines in statutory process states currently are almost four months faster, at 149 days compared with 272 days, than those in judicial foreclosure states.[46]

TIME VERSUS COSTS. The longer the time between referral and foreclosure sale, the higher the costs to the investor and the higher the hurdle for a borrower trying to reinstate a loan through a workout. In figure 7-5 we show the relationship between the actual average time from DDLPI to the foreclosure sale and the associated preforeclosure costs relative to the average preforeclosure costs based on Freddie Mac's experience with conventional, conforming mortgages. States that have a statutory judicial process are marked by triangles and states that have a judi-

46. Expected statutory foreclosure and actual timelines are inclusive of the postsale redemption and confirmation periods but do not include the time spent in delinquency before the foreclosure referral (for example, the minimum 150 days from DDLPI to foreclosure referral during which Freddie Mac requires servicers to attempt borrower contact and foreclosure avoidance efforts).

cial foreclosure process are marked by dots. Nine states have a postsale redemption period and are indicated by their state foreclosure process indicator but in white instead of black. This scatter diagram clearly shows that states with a judicial process have longer foreclosure timelines and are more expensive to investors (and hence to borrowers trying to keep their homes) than those with a statutory process.

The postsale redemption states do not allow the investors/servicers to continue to add interest arrearages during the redemption period, thus in effect suppressing borrowers' costs at the expense of investors. One could argue that investors have an implicit cost of interest in any home they have in REO inventory in a nonredemption state as well. In redemption states, however, investors have title but no right of entry and thus are unlikely to be able to sell the home to third parties, as they too would not have full rights of possession until the redemption period ends and would also face redemption risk on their investment. If we add back the interest expenses as an opportunity cost of capital accruing during the redemption period, the costs of redemption states move more in line with those nonredemption states that have similar overall timelines, as shown in figure 7-5 by square markers.

Bridewell (1938) finds similar differences between judicial and statutory foreclosure states at that time. He splits states into three groups: (1) where foreclosure costs were low (less than $100) and foreclosure timelines short (three months or less); (2) where the cost of foreclosure was high (more than $100) and timelines long (more than three months); and (3) where not only foreclosure costs were high and timelines long but also the states had postsale redemption periods of six months or more. The foreclosure cost experiences of the Home Owner's Loan Corporation revealed that average costs in the first group ran roughly $55; in the latter two groups it was approximately $155. Nearly all of the states in the latter two groups in his study were judicial foreclosure states. Even in 1938, the relationship of longer foreclosure timelines with higher foreclosure costs (and thus higher borrower reinstatement costs) was known.

REDEMPTION. The inability of the investor or third-party purchaser to obtain full rights of possession in postsale redemption states has a profound effect on the market for properties at foreclosure sale. In a sample of foreclosure sales recorded through September 2007, bids by third-party purchasers successfully "won" Freddie Mac properties at foreclosure sale in a little more than 16 percent of sales in nonredemption states, but they purchased only 3.9 percent of properties offered in the seven postsale redemption states (as shown in table 7-6 on page 233). Restricting the data to only those states with at least 50 observed foreclosure sales over this period (39 in all), the highest third-party sales ratio was in Utah at 46.4 percent. The redemption states have the lowest ratio, with Minnesota at 1.8 percent, followed closely by Michigan at 2.3 percent and Colorado at 4.9 percent. The next lowest ratio, and the lowest among nonredemption states, was 8.4 percent in Indiana.

In Freddie Mac's recent experience, the percentage of borrowers that actually redeem their properties out of redemption is nontrivial, at roughly 17 percent, and a little more than 50 percent of these redemptions are in the final 45 days of the redemption period in the four states with redemption periods of 120 days or more (Michigan, Minnesota, South Dakota, and Wyoming). The share of properties redeemed out of foreclosure, however, declined from 2004 through 2006, especially in Michigan and Minnesota, two states experiencing continued economic stress. Fewer borrowers are redeeming or are capable of redeeming their property after the foreclosure sale. As this benefit to the borrower continues to decline, the cost to the investor increases.

Many consumer advocates have argued for longer foreclosure timelines or delays in starting the foreclosure process, and many argue that the legal costs are particularly onerous on borrowers trying to reinstate their loans. We saw earlier that the majority of the costs in the foreclosure process are interest arrearage (65 percent of preforeclosure expenses) and taxes and insurance (combined 19 percent of preforeclosure expenses), all of which are present on a performing loan. The legal costs of the foreclosure, although additive to the arrears, are a minority share (11 percent of preforeclosure costs) of the costs to the borrower, but certainly pose a greater constraint on borrowers in states with long judicial foreclosure processes as legal costs are higher in those states.

But the borrower's incentives also change with the length of the foreclosure timeline. Once the first legal action is filed, borrowers are in real danger of losing their homes. This encourages borrowers who have the means to act quickly to reinstate their loans. Long timelines between the start of first legal action and finalized foreclosure sale, however, lessen the incentive to reinstate. Nearly 70 percent of all loan reinstatements, once a loan has gone to foreclosure referral, happen in the first three months following referral, and the higher the cure rate within the first three months, the higher the overall cure rate. Tables 7-8 through 7-10 show these relationships.

Preforeclosure costs (table 7-8) are influenced by the actual time between DDLPI and finalized foreclosure sale, home price growth in the past year, whether a state is covered by judicial process, and the average depreciation rates of REO properties from the appraised values. Postsale redemption periods reduce explicit preforeclosure costs that would be charged to the borrower to redeem the house out of foreclosure, but this is through the mandated moratorium on interest charges; once those excluded charges are added back in for the redemption period (see squares on figure 7-5), the additional costs imposed by long postsale redemption periods are positive and significant.[47] Separating out the days in foreclosure

---

47. In a postsale redemption period, like a presale redemption period, a borrower is not adding additional interest charges. From an investor's perspective, the only difference between a pre- and postsale redemption period is that he or she has taken title but still have no rights to the property. If

by whether the state has a judicial or statutory foreclosure process shows that only the judicial states have a statistically strong relationship between longer time and higher costs.

If one looks at the three-month cure rate (table 7-9) or total cure rate (not shown in tables), or the ratio of the three-month cure rate to the total cure rate out of foreclosure (table 7-10), the time in foreclosure and the cumulative home price growth over the past five years matter, as does whether a state has a redemption period, and judicial states have a powerful negative effect on cure rates, primarily by extending foreclosure timelines.

Figure 7-6 shows data from Freddie Mac's recent experience in a theoretical chart of a cost-benefit type trade-off in foreclosure timelines. Ideally we would like to compare the marginal cost of a day in the preforeclosure process with the marginal benefit in dollars or some other constant measure and estimate the best timeline for the foreclosure process. But no such measure exists, or at least one that would be reasonable to estimate with any data set known or available to us. Instead we draw the relationship among statutory time in foreclosure and costs and time and cure rate in figure 7-6 as a theoretical exercise.[48] If the statutory foreclosure timeline of long-timeline states (those above, say, the 75th percentile of 155 days between foreclosure referral and sale, equating to roughly 300 total days with Freddie Mac's recommended 150 days of loss mitigation preforeclosure referral and 389 days in actual experience) were shortened to a time closer to the median statutory time, near 120 days or so (putting total days between DDLPI and foreclosure sale at roughly 270 days) as we have shown in the figure, the share of loans that would cure out of foreclosure is likely to rise significantly (by 3 to 9 percentage points based on the simple linear regressions in table 7-9) and to reduce costs to both investors and borrowers by 6 to 12 percent relative to the national average for every 50 days the timeline is reduced (table 7-8).

Although it is tempting to argue on the basis of recent experience and the strong linear relationships among costs, cure rates, and foreclosure time that all states should shorten their timelines, this may not be advisable across the board, especially for short timeline states. Recent experience with fast home price appreciation may be masking a nonlinear relationship between too little time in foreclosure and the cure rate of loans. For example, Virginia, which has the second

---

Freddie Mac or Fannie Mae is the investor, it will be passing along interest payments to securities holders during the presale redemption but the loan will have been pulled from a security when the foreclosure sale occurred (or before) and direct interest costs are no longer incurred by F&F. They have to fund the asset somehow, however, and because they have no rights of possession, the interest cost should be counted as part of the costs for a postsale redemption period for funding the REO property.

48. This timeline is just the legal process of foreclosure and does not include Freddie Mac's policy of the servicer's attempting loss mitigation before the foreclosure referral. If this time were added in, the timelines would be 150 days longer than the statutory timelines.

Table 7-8. *Total Preforeclosure Costs in State Relative to National Average Preforeclosure Costs*[a]

Item	Model 1	Model 2	Model 3	Model 4	Model 5	Model 6	Model 7a	Model 7b	Model 8a[b]	Model 8b[b]
Total days between DDLPI and FCL sale (in 100s)	0.126** (2.37)	0.145* (3.05)	0.133* (2.65)	0.130** (1.92)		0.154* (3.62)	0.162* (3.64)	0.168* (3.81)	0.163* (3.69)	0.170* (3.95)
One-year nominal home price growth (percent) ending 2Q 2007		-0.040* (-3.60)	-0.040* (-3.58)	-0.039* (-3.50)	-0.039* (-3.50)	-0.043* (-4.35)	-0.043* (-4.36)	-0.442* (-4.47)	-0.042* (-4.28)	-0.044* (-4.53)
State has post-FCL sale redemption period			0.098 (0.88)							
State has a judicial foreclosure process				0.038 (0.32)						
Judicial foreclosure state: Total days from DDLPI and FCL sale					0.136** (2.37)					
Statutory foreclosure state: Total days from DDLPI and FCL sale					0.126 (1.58)					
Number of days in postforeclosure sale redemption period							-0.001 (-0.63)		-0.002* (-2.83)	

	(1)	(2)	(3)	(4)	(5)	(6)	(7)	(8)	(9)	(10)
Number of days in postforeclosure sale redemption or confirmation period								−0.001 (−1.14)		−0.003* (−3.36)
Average percent depreciation of REO properties in state from original appraised value						−1.519* (−3.61)	−1.524* (−3.59)	−1.537* (−3.66)	−1.505* (−3.57)	−1.537* (−3.75)
Constant	0.555** (2.86)	0.573* (3.31)	0.600* (3.41)	0.610* (2.93)	0.623* (2.63)	0.889* (5.02)	0.874* (4.86)	0.867* (4.88)	0.863* (4.82)	0.866* (5.00)
Number of observations	49	49	49	49	49	49	49	49	49	49
R squared	0.107	0.303	0.315	0.304	0.304	0.459	0.464	0.475	0.478	0.509
Adjusted R squared	0.088	0.273	0.269	0.258	0.258	0.423	0.415	0.427	0.430	0.464

Source: Authors' estimations on a sample of Freddie Mac REO property dispositions from January 1, 2007 to September 30, 2007.

Note: DDLPI = due date of last paid installment; FCL = foreclosure; REO = real-estate owned; t-values are in parentheses under coefficients.

*Significant at the 1 percent level; **significant at the 5 percent level.

a. Preforeclosure costs are all costs incurred by investor and servicer before the foreclosure sale. In postforeclosure sale redemption states, costs include any expenses incurred during the redemption period except interest expenses incurred in redemption.

b. Same as model 7 except that the interest arrears from the postsale redemption period are subtracted from preforeclosure costs in the 9 states with these periods.

Table 7-9. Cure Rate in the First Three Months following Foreclosure Referral[a]

Item	Model 1a	Model 1b	Model 2	Model 2b	Model 3a	Model 3b	Model 4a	Model 4b	Model 5a	Model 5b
Total average actual days between DDLPI and FCL sale (in 100s)	-0.031** (-2.35)		-0.015*** (-1.90)		-0.004 (-0.36)		-0.015*** (-1.91)		-0.016*** (-1.98)	
Total expected days between FCL referral and FCL sale based on state laws (in 100s)		-0.026* (-2.77)		-0.022* (-2.81)		0.017 (-1.50)		-0.023*** (-2.88)		-0.026* (-3.11)
Five-year cumulative nominal home price growth ending 2Q 2007			0.148* (4.34)	0.150* (4.64)	0.143* (4.25)	0.146* (4.44)	0.138* (3.29)	0.133* (3.30)	0.153* (4.33)	0.161* (4.86)
State has a judicial foreclosure process					-0.028 (-1.51)	-0.760 (0.45)				
Average percent depreciation of REO properties in state from original appraised value							-0.036 (-0.38)	-0.068 (-0.75)		
Number of days in postforeclosure sale redemption period									0.010 (0.63)	0.020 (1.32)
Constant	0.320* (9.72)	0.283* (18.04)	0.236* (6.91)	0.214* (10.85)	0.211* (5.64)	0.214* (10.77)	0.249* (5.18)	0.239* (6.29)	0.236* (6.86)	0.212* (10.74)
Number of observations	49	49	49	49	49	49	49	49	49	49
R squared	0.105	0.141	0.365	0.415	0.395	0.422	0.367	0.422	0.370	0.437
Adjusted R squared	0.086	0.122	0.337	0.389	0.355	0.384	0.324	0.383	0.328	0.399

Source: Authors' estimations on a sample of Freddie Mac loans that entered foreclosure in 2006 with performance measured through September 2007.

Note: DDLPI = due date of last paid installment; FCL = foreclosure; REO = real-estate owned.

*Significant at the 1 percent level; **significant at the 5 percent level; ***significant at the 10 percent level.

a. "Cure" is defined as a loan that fully reinstates or is paid off before the foreclosure sale. t-values in parentheses under coefficients.

Table 7-10. *Ratio of Cure Rate in First Three Months of Foreclosure to Total Cure Rate*[a]

Item	Model 1a	Model 1b	Model 2a	Model 2b	Model 3a	Model 3b	Model 4a	Model 4b	Model 5a	Model 5b
Total days between DDLPI and FCL sale (in 100s)	-0.053* (-5.45)		-0.051* (-5.34)		-0.054* (-5.35)		-0.032** (-2.49)		-0.055* (-5.66)	
Total expected days between FCL referral and FCL sale based on state laws (in 100s)		-0.050* (-4.49)		-0.051* (-4.76)		-0.057* (-5.45)		-0.027** (-1.93)		-0.059* (-5.33)
Nominal home price growth over year ending June 2007 (percent)			-0.004*** (-1.80)	-0.006 (-2.42)	-0.004* (-1.79)	-0.006 (-2.48)	-0.005** (-2.10)	-0.005** (-2.53)	-0.004 (-1.68)	-0.005 (-2.37)
State has post-FCL sale redemption period					0.019 (0.87)	0.033 (1.39)				
State has a judicial foreclosure process							0.046** (-2.03)	-0.055** (-2.40)		
Number of days in postforeclosure sale redemption period									0.028 (1.59)	0.039 (2.06)
Constant	0.880* (24.85)	0.765* (41.55)	0.882* (25.48)	0.778* (42.44)	0.888* (25.18)	0.781* (42.66)	0.838* (21.01)	0.769* (43.09)	0.891* (25.83)	0.782* (43.85)
Number of observations	49	49	49	49	49	49	49	49	49	49
R squared	0.388	0.300	0.428	0.379	0.438	0.405	0.476	0.450	0.459	0.433
Adjusted R squared	0.375	0.2854	0.403	0.3522	0.400	0.3649	0.441	0.4131	0.422	0.3947

Source: Authors' estimations on a sample of Freddie Mac loans that entered foreclosure in 2006 with performance measured through September 2007.

Note: DDLPI = due date of last paid installment; FCL = foreclosure; REO = real-estate owned.

*Significant at the 1 percent level; **significant at the 5 percent level; ***significant at the 10 percent level.

a. "Cure" is defined as a loan that fully reinstates or is paid off before the foreclosure sale. *t*-values in parentheses under coefficients.

Figure 7-6. *Theoretical Share of Loans That Cure out of Foreclosure and Total Foreclosure Costs, by State Statutory Foreclosure Timeline*[a]

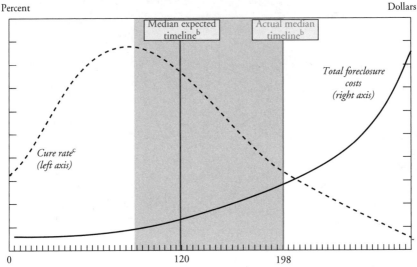

a. The crossing of the cure rate line and the foreclosure costs line is simply a coincidence and does not indicate an optimal timeline; the lines reflect different scales. Length and position of section with rising cure rate are unknown.

b. Timeline less Freddie Mac 150 days prereferral period. Actual timeline as of 2007.

c. Share of loans that fully reinstate after foreclosure referral.

fastest statutory foreclosure timeline but the fastest actual timeline, has also experienced very fast home price appreciation and job growth over the five years ending in 2006, particularly in its northern counties near Washington, D.C. With home values now falling, especially in the outer suburbs of the D.C. area, Virginia's foreclosure timeline could be too fast and could reduce some borrowers' ability to avoid the loss of their homes once the legal foreclosure process has begun.

The shaded area in figure 7-6 shows the potential sweet spot of ideal foreclosure timelines: short enough to give borrowers a strong incentive to cure out of foreclosure if they have the means and long enough to allow those who have a reasonable chance of economic recovery a chance to avoid the loss of their homes. What happens in truth to the left of that section is unknown at this time; that is, we do not know how short a timeline is too short, causing too low a cure rate. But we do know from empirical evidence that lengthy legal foreclosure timelines reduce the chances a borrower will keep his or her home.

From the earlier discussion, many of the costs to the borrower during the pre-foreclosure process are taxes and hazard insurance advanced by the servicer; these and all other costs increase over time and make it more difficult for a borrower to reinstate or qualify for a workout. Given that most foreclosure avoidance happens near the beginning of the legal foreclosure process (after referral to an attorney) coupled with the continual rise in costs as the foreclosure process ages, the time at the beginning of the foreclosure process should be a main focus for workouts. As a matter of policy, states may wish to consider the length of the foreclosure process, inclusive of redemption, and its negative impact on the borrower's ability to avoid foreclosure sale resulting from higher costs, and the possible feedback effects created through further pressure on home values. Colorado could be used as a case study by looking at the incidence of third-party sales after January 1, 2008, when it moved its redemption period prior to the foreclosure sale. Other considerations might be property tax forgiveness or tax workout plans to accommodate mortgage loan workouts that might avoid foreclosure, or equity protection plans that might entice new homebuyers into a community by minimizing their risk of declining home values such as the program started in the late 1990s in Syracuse, N.Y.[49]

Conclusion

It is highly likely that the current delinquency environment will become increasingly difficult in both volume and transition over the next few years, say 2008–10. There are several reasons for this, the primary drivers being limited home equity on recent origination years (2006 and 2007), new products with limited documentation of borrower ability to pay (Alt-A), falling house prices, and a worsening economic and employment situation. Public policymakers and the servicing industry need to prepare for this further deterioration on the overall economy, the financial condition or failure of industry players, and the operation capacity of the servicing platforms.

On prime loans, loss of income remains the primary reason for default because the interruption in the borrower's income stream is happening in a society where consumer-driven spending is a priority over savings. Of all the material reasons for default on prime loans, divorce remains the one cause with the highest failure rate on completed modifications, most likely driven by borrower behavior during that situation. But rapidly falling home values may cause some borrowers with the capacity to carry the mortgage debt to default if the negative equity position hits a trigger threshold, significantly tipping the balance in favor of the put option.

The importance of early contact and workout intervention is very clear, with the demonstrated success of such workouts within the first months of delin-

---

49. See Caplin and others (2007) for a description of this program.

quency. Helped by a lower accrued delinquent arrearage and a cooperative and income-qualifying borrower, this combination is a strong indicator of success. Repayment plans started late in delinquency or set for a long period of time have a much lower chance of success, driven by the large arrearage. Contact rate is a critical factor in the ability of a servicer to partner with a borrower to complete a workout. With 52 percent of foreclosure sales lacking reciprocal borrower contact, this is a significant missed opportunity to help homeownership preservation.

Default credit counseling is proving to be a valuable new element in foreclosure prevention, but the availability of the service is low relative to the need, which is growing fast. Public policymakers may wish to consider methods or programs to help borrowers overcome their fear, acknowledge the situation, and educate them on all their foreclosure avoidance options.

With the rapid rise in foreclosures following a long period of very few foreclosures, along with the increased focus and scrutiny of government officials and consumer groups, it is interesting to review the long-standing and well-defined foreclosure processes and costs at the state level. The average timeline from last payment to loss of property is one year, and significant opportunities for workout options exist once borrower contact is achieved. The significant costs to the borrower of the foreclosure process are delinquent interest, taxes, and insurance, but not legal costs as many advocates allege. These significant costs are present on all performing loans and exist when the loan is not in foreclosure.

A sweet spot for the optimal time in foreclosure likely exists within a statutory timeline of 120 days (the current national median, and equivalent to 270 days after adding in 150 days for prereferral loss mitigation activities by servicers through workouts) in which the borrower's incentives are aligned with a high probability of curing out of the foreclosure and keeping the preforeclosure costs to the investor contained. States with short foreclosure timelines may want to lengthen the preforeclosure process if, given experiences in this current environment with falling home values and unstable credit markets, they find too many borrowers unable to recover from relatively short and mild financial problems before they lose the home to foreclosure. States with long foreclosure timelines may find that they could increase the number of borrowers who successfully reinstate their loans by shortening the timelines, reducing arrearages, and providing motivation for acting early to work with servicers on foreclosure alternatives.

The human cost of the current foreclosure crisis is extraordinary, and the industry costs are staggering. Thoughtful and informed discussions about how to best help borrowers keep their homes is needed, and borrowers, investors, servicers, and communities all bear costs when a family loses a home to foreclosure. We have presented what we believe is information not previously discussed in the default and foreclosure literature, and more important, that sheds light on industry trends, borrower behavior, and the role of time in both helping and hurting a borrower's chance of home retention.

References

Apgar, William C., Mark Duda, and Rochelle Nawrocki Gorey. 2005. "The Municipal Cost of Foreclosures: A Chicago Case Study." Paper prepared for the Homeownership Preservation Foundation, Minneapolis, Minnesota. Housing Finance Policy Research Paper 2005-1 (www.995hope.org/content/pdf/Apgar_Duda_Study_Full_Version.pdf).

Bridewell, David. 1938. "The Effect of Defective Mortgage Laws on Home Financing." *Law and Contemporary Problems* no. 5: 545–63.

Caplin, Andrew, and others. 2007. "Home Equity Insurance: A Pilot Project." Working Paper. Yale School of Management, International Center for Finance.

Clauretie, Terrence M. 1989. "State Foreclosure Laws, Risk Shifting, and the PMI Industry." *Journal of Risk and Insurance* 56, no. 3: 544–54.

Clauretie, Terrence M., and Thomas Herzog. 1990. "The Effect of State Foreclosure Laws on Loan Losses: Evidence from the Mortgage Insurance Industry." *Journal of Money, Credit and Banking* 22, no. 2: 221–33.

Collins, J. Michael. 2007a. "Lessons from the Front Lines: Counselor Perspectives on Default Interventions." Report prepared for the Homeownership Preservation Initiative (HOPI), PolicyLab Consulting Group, LLC White Paper (October 29).

Collins, J. Michael. 2007b. "Exploring the Design of Financial Counseling for Mortgage Borrowers in Default." *Journal of Family and Economic Issues* 28, no. 2: 207–26.

Comeau, Phil, and Larry Cordell. 1998. "Case Study: Beating the Odds. Loss Mitigation Scores Helped Wells Fargo Save Resources, Assist Borrowers in Avoiding Foreclosure." *Servicing Management* (June): 70.

Cutts, Amy Crews, and Richard K. Green. 2005. "Innovative Servicing Technology: Smart Enough to Keep People in Their Houses?" In *Building Assets, Building Credit: Creating Wealth in Low Income Communities,* edited by Nicolas Retsinas and Eric Belsky, pp. 348–77. Brookings.

Deng, Yong Heng, John Quigley, and Robert Van Order. 2000. "Mortgage Terminations, Heterogeneity, and the Exercise of Mortgage Options." *Econometrica* 68, no. 2: 275–307.

Ding, Lei, Roberto G. Quercia, and Janneke Ratcliffe. Forthcoming. "Post-Purchase Counseling and Default Resolutions among Low- and Moderate-Income Borrowers." *Journal of Real Estate Research.*

Fields, Desirée, Kimberly Libman, Susan Saegert, Hélène Clark, and Fran Justa. 2007. "Understanding Responses to the Threat of Foreclosure among Low-Income Homeowners." New York: Center for Human Environments, Graduate Center of the City University of New York.

Hayre, Lakhbir S., and Manish Saraf. 2008. "A Loss Severity Model for Residential Mortgages." Citigroup Global Markets Fixed-Income Research Report (January 22).

Hirad, Abdighani, and Peter M. Zorn. 2002. "Pre-Purchase Homeownership Counseling: A Little Knowledge Is a Good Thing." In *Low-Income Homeownership: Examining the Unexamined Goal,* edited by Nicolas Retsinas and Eric Belsky, pp. 146–74. Brookings.

Inside Mortgage Finance. 2007. *The 2007 Mortgage Market Statistical Annual,* vol.1. Bethesda, Md.

Kau, James, and D. C. Keenan. 1995. "An Overview of Option-Theoretic Pricing of Mortgages." *Journal of Housing Research* 6, no. 2: 217–44.

Lacour-Little, Michael. 2000. "The Evolving Role of Technology in Mortgage Finance." *Journal of Housing Research* 11, no. 2: 173–205.

———. 2004. "Equity Dilution: An Alternative Perspective on Mortgage Default." *Real Estate Economics* 32, no. 3: 359–84.

Mortgage Bankers Association. 2007. "National Delinquency Survey Q207." Washington.

Pence, Karen. 2001. "Essays on Government Policy and Household Financial Decisions." Ph.D. dissertation, University of Wisconsin.

———. 2006. "Foreclosing on Opportunity: State Laws and Mortgage Credit." *Review of Economics and Statistics* 88, no. 1: 177–82.

Pennington-Cross, Anthony. 2003. "Subprime and Prime Mortgages: Loss Distributions." Working Paper 03-1. Office of Federal Housing Enterprise Oversight.

Quercia, Roberto G., Spencer Cowan, and Ana Moreno. 2004. "The Cost-Effectiveness of Community-Based Foreclosure Prevention." Working Paper BABC 04-18. Harvard University Joint Center for Housing Studies (JCHS) (http://www.jchs.harvard.edu/publications/finance/babc/babc_04-18.pdf).

USFN. 2007. *The National Mortgage Servicer's Reference Directory.* 24th ed. Tustin, Calif.: USFN (U.S. Foreclosure Network).

Wilson, Donald G. 1995. "Residential Loss Severity in California: 1992–2005." *Journal of Fixed Income* 5, no. 3: 15–48.

Wood, Claudia. 1997. "The Impact of Mortgage Foreclosure Laws on Secondary Market Loan Losses." Ph.D. dissertation, Cornell University.

8

Looking beyond Our Shores: Consumer Protection Regulation Lessons from the United Kingdom

ELAINE KEMPSON

C redit regulation in the United Kingdom has been undergoing substantial reform in the past three years. This chapter reviews these reforms and discusses how they take account of criticisms of previous regulatory regimes. It draws out some of the strengths and weaknesses of current regulation from a consumer's perspective. In doing so, there is a need to distinguish between mortgages and other forms of consumer credit because there are two quite different regulatory regimes for the conduct of business, including consumer protection. The chapter is restricted to retail markets and does not cover prudential regulation.

Mortgage Regulation

Since October 31, 2004, all mortgage lending has been fully regulated by the Financial Services Authority (FSA) through its mortgage Conduct of Business Rules.[1] This includes all subprime as well as prime mortgages and also all intermediaries that sell mortgages to the public.

The FSA is a relatively new regulatory body and was set up under the Financial Services and Markets Act 2000 with four statutory objectives covering market confidence, public awareness, consumer protection, and reduction of finan-

---

1. See www.hm-treasury.gov.uk/documents/financial_services/mortgages/fin_mort_reglend.cfm.

cial crime. It now covers all retail and wholesale financial markets, with the single exception of unsecured consumer credit.[2]

At the time that the FSA was set up, mortgages were still covered by a self-regulatory regime through the Mortgage Code. This had been introduced for prime lenders in 1997 and for intermediaries in 1998. Some 98 percent of lenders and more than 20,000 intermediaries signed up to the code, but there was still evidence of bad practice and noncompliance.[3] When the FSA was established as the single regulator, covering all aspects of financial services, consideration was also given to bringing aspects of conduct of business subject to self-regulation within its framework.

An independent review for HM Treasury[4] recognized that the Mortgage Code had delivered a number of consumer benefits but was not "a sufficiently strong regime for service standards for mortgages" because "mortgages involve a long-term commitment and for many consumers represent their largest financial undertaking." It therefore recommended that only a statutory regulatory regime for mortgages, including intermediaries as well as lenders, offered sufficient protection to consumers. Consumer groups supported this conclusion as did the bulk of the mortgage industry, including the Council of Mortgage Lenders (their trade body).[5]

Under the new regime, lenders and intermediaries have to be authorized to carry out business and must comply with the FSA's *Conduct of Business Rules*. This rule book is wide-ranging and more than 300 pages in length. It covers sale and advice standards; preapplication disclosure; disclosure at the offer stage, start of contract, and after sale; equity release advising and selling standards; equity release product disclosure; APRs (and total cost of credit); responsible lending; charges (including early settlement and arrears charges); and the handling of arrears and possessions. Some of the important changes it introduced are described in the following paragraphs.

Consumers must receive clear presale information about mortgage terms, conditions, and costs in a standard "key facts" format to enable them to shop around more easily. This includes information about the firm itself (its charges and the range of products on which it is authorized to give advice) as well as a document setting out the adviser's understanding of the borrower's needs and intentions, full details of the product being recommended, the fees involved (including any redemption fees likely to be incurred by settling an existing mortgage early), and any insurance or investment products being sold alongside the mortgage.

---

2. In addition, although retail banking is regulated by the FSA, in practice the powers to regulate the conduct of business in this area are currently switched off and devolved to the Banking Code— self-regulation by the industry—which is described in the section on unsecured consumer credit.

3. HM Treasury (1999).

4. HM Treasury (2000); see paragraph 3.17.

5. Council of Mortgage Lenders (2001).

Where firms give advice, they must ensure that they offer the consumer a suitable mortgage product. This involves completing a very detailed "fact find" of the consumer's personal circumstances, income, and financial commitments.

Price information (including the APR) in any mortgage advertising and marketing material must be clear, and any advantageous features of products quoted in advertising must be balanced by a description of any associated drawbacks.

Both lenders and advisers have to consider the affordability of any mortgage that they identify for individual consumers. Again, this involves completing a detailed fact find of the consumer's personal circumstances, income, and financial commitments.

Lenders must put in place measures to help borrowers in arrears on their mortgage, having a sale shortfall, or facing repossession. This includes having a written policy to make reasonable efforts to reach an agreement with the customer; adopting a reasonable approach over time, including setting up a payment plan; where payment plans break down, giving consideration to allowing the borrower to remain in possession to effect a sale; and repossessing the property only when all other reasonable attempts to resolve the position have failed.

Lifetime mortgages (a form of equity release or home equity loan) are subject to additional disclosure requirements because of the higher risks associated with these products.

Mortgage borrowers have access to an independent dispute resolution service, the Financial Ombudsman Service (FOS), and to the Financial Services Compensation Scheme (FSCS). These services are free to consumers and paid for by a levy on the industry.

In general, the rules do not distinguish subprime lending from other forms of residential mortgages. So firms involved with subprime mortgages need to comply with all the standard rules. That said, some of the standard rules are likely to have increased relevance for subprime mortgages, and in the current climate it is worth spelling some of these out. For example,

—Subprime advertising referring to paying off unsecured debts must include a specific risk warning (MCOB 3.6.13R(2)).

—Advertising targeted at subprime borrowers must include an APR (MCOB 3.6.17R).

—Where the APR in a promotion will vary depending on the consumer's circumstances, the promotion must include a risk statement encouraging the customer to seek a personalized illustration (MCOB 3.6.25R).

—If the intermediary can charge a fee for advising or arranging, as is often the case for subprime business, any promotion must disclose this (MCOB 3.6.27R).

—A firm specializing only in subprime business will not be able to describe itself as either covering the "whole of market" or "independent" (MCOB 4.3.4R).

—Where debt consolidation is a main purpose of any mortgage, advisers have added obligations when they are recommending the most suitable product (MCOB 4.7.6R).

—Mortgage lenders must report to the FSA quarterly on the level of advances they have made to consumers with an impaired credit history.

Supervision of Mortgage Lending

FSA supervision of firms takes a risk-based approach and uses two main methods: assessing risk in individual firms, and thematic supervision, which assesses risk across a range of firms within a particular market or industry sector.[6] This has included major reviews of the mortgage market generally as well as specific reviews of, for example, the subprime market and self-certification of income.[7]

This work has shown that some significant shortcomings still exist in the behavior of firms that sell and advise on mortgages. Despite this, there is general consensus that bringing mortgages within the regulatory framework of the FSA has delivered higher levels of consumer protection.

Regulation of Unsecured Consumer Credit

As noted previously, unsecured consumer credit is the only area of retail financial services that the FSA does not cover. Indeed, regulation in this area is much less straightforward and has aspects to be commended and ones that are not.

After many years of waiting,[8] the legislation covering unsecured credit was recently revised by the Consumer Credit Act 2006, which updates, but does not entirely supersede, the Consumer Credit Act 1974. Both pieces of legislation (as with almost all legislation in the United Kingdom) are enabling, with most of the detail set out in a set of specific regulations laid under them and precise interpretations often being set through case law. The 2006 Act covers all forms of consumer credit, including payday lending, which was not previously covered.

This Act and the regulations laid to bring it into force have already introduced three important changes: the licensing regime for lenders has been tightened, a new "unfair relationship" test protects consumers from abuses in the market, and consumer credit has been brought within the remit of the FOS. Each of these is discussed more fully below.

---

6. See www.fsa.gov.uk/pages/About/What/thematic for the major thematic work plan for 2007 and 2008.

7. See www.fsa.gov.uk/.

8. There had been many changes in the regulations under the 1974 Act during this period and, as time went on, there was a need to consolidate these. Two things slowed this down: the prolonged gestation of a new European Consumer Credit Directive and the need for parliamentary time for primary legislation. Indeed, one Bill fell because a general election was called and time had to be found in a busy legislative program to reintroduce the Bill and, effectively, start again.

Credit Licenses

To lend in the United Kingdom, a company needs to hold a consumer credit license, which is issued by the Office of Fair Trading (OFT), the consumer and competition authority and a nonministerial government department established by statute in 1973. Local trading standards officers (employed by local authorities, not the OFT) investigate alleged breaches of licenses and report to the OFT, which is responsible for enforcement. In the past the licensing regime was heavily criticized, not least by trading standards officers, for the ease of obtaining a license, the very low likelihood that a license would be rescinded even when lenders have engaged in criminal activities, and the fact that individuals who had lost a license were able to find their way around the rules and obtain a new license, enabling them to start a new lending business.[9] Concern has been growing about the activities of unlicensed lenders and the failure to take action against them.

Since April 2008, the licensing regime has been tightened considerably. The OFT has an enhanced ability to ensure applicants are fit to hold a license and to monitor their ongoing conduct. They also have stronger powers to investigate suspected cases of misconduct and to apply a wide range of sanctions when lenders breach the terms of their license, including fines of up to £50,000 (about $100,000) or the suspension of credit licenses; previously the only sanction was to revoke the license. The OFT recently put out two consultation papers on the proposed licensing regime. The first covers the factors it will consider when assessing whether or not a consumer credit license holder or an applicant is fit to hold a license and how it will exercise its powers to impose requirements on license holders.[10] The second consultation covers key factors the OFT will consider when assessing whether or not to impose a financial penalty on a license holder who has failed to comply with a requirement imposed on it and sets out the factors it will consider when assessing the amount of any penalty it will impose. The final guidance was published in January 2008.[11]

The new legislation does not address the issue of illegal (unlicensed) lending, but in 2004 the government established two pilot schemes, in Glasgow and Birmingham, to tackle this problem. In these two cities, specially trained trading standards officers working with the police identified 200 "loan sharks" (unlicensed lenders) and shut down loan books worth more than £3 million (about $6 million). An evaluation of the pilots concluded that they had been effective and represented good value for the money.[12] Consequently, the government has allocated £3 million (about $6 million) to enable the pilot scheme to be rolled out across Britain,

9. Kempson and Whyley (1999).
10. Office of Fair Trading (2007).
11. www.oft.gov.uk/shared_oft/business_leaflets/credit_licences/oft969.pdf.
12. Ellison and Collard (2007).

by expanding the geographical coverage of the existing two teams and establishing six new ones.

Unfair Credit Bargains

Consumer credit legislation has for some time sought to protect consumers against extortionate credit bargains, but the 1974 Act defined this narrowly and primarily in terms of charges. It did not, however, set a usury level, although the Moneylenders Act 1927 (which it replaced) stated that an interest rate of more than 48 percent was prima facie excessive. It was widely acknowledged that the extortionate credit provisions of the 1974 Act did not work as intended for two main reasons. First, it defined "extortionate" too narrowly and was interpreted as referring to basic charges, while many of the market abuses related to wider terms and conditions. Second, the legislation relied on individual consumers to apply to a court to have the terms of their agreement reviewed, and very few did. The OFT has estimated that between 1977 and 1989 only 23 cases went to the courts. Although this has been challenged as an underestimate, it is unlikely that more than a few hundred cases have reached the courts in the 30 years since the provisions were enacted.[13] Consequently, research has shown that the great majority of judges had no personal experience of such cases and almost no case law to guide them should they get one. It is not, therefore, surprising to find that many did not feel competent to form judgments in this area.[14] Moreover, class actions cannot be brought in the United Kingdom, and so even in the small number of cases where judges found that credit terms were extortionate, only the individual plaintiff benefited and the defendant continued to lend to others on the same terms.[15]

The 2006 Act sought to tackle these problems by introducing an "unfair relationship" test that replaces the extortionate credit bargain provision in the 1974 Act. This test is considerably wider and allows a court to consider all the relevant circumstances of a credit relationship to determine its fairness, including: any of the terms of the credit agreement and any related agreement; the way in which the creditor has exercised or enforced any of its rights; and "any other thing done by or on behalf of the creditor either before or after the making of the agreement or any related agreement."

The Act itself does not define an unfair relationship beyond setting out in general terms these broad classes of factors that can give rise to unfairness. The OFT has, however, issued guidance for firms, indicating the sort of factors that are likely

13. Kempson and Whyley (1999).
14. Ellison and Collard (2007).
15. There is, however, provision for a small number of nominated bodies to initiate a "super-complaint" under the Enterprise Act 2002, which may result in a full inquiry by the Competition Commission. Two recent cases resulted in investigation of the charges on credit and store cards and of lending terms and practices in the subprime home credit industry. Both resulted in lenders as a whole having to take remedial action.

to inform its enforcement action.[16] It will, however, be for the courts to determine what is unfair to a borrower.

The intentionally broad scope of this test therefore gives sweeping powers to the courts to examine every aspect of a credit relationship, not just the written terms of any credit agreement. The provisions apply to all new agreements made on or after April 6, 2007, and any existing agreements that continue beyond April 6, 2008. It is therefore too early to tell how well they are working, although they have received a warm welcome by the major consumer bodies.

Supervision of Compliance with Consumer Credit Legislation

Responsibility for supervising compliance with consumer credit legislation lies with the OFT through the credit licensing regime. As indicated earlier, this was somewhat circumscribed by the 1974 legislation, added to which there were complaints that the OFT did not use the powers it had at its disposal. The new licensing arrangements give the OFT much wider powers and a broader range of sanctions. It remains to be seen how this will operate in practice, but it is still likely to fall short of the mortgage supervision exercised by the FSA.

Self-Regulation of Unsecured Consumer Credit

Perhaps because of past failures in supervising compliance with consumer credit legislation, consumer credit lending in the United Kingdom is also subject to self-regulation through the Banking Code[17] and the Finance and Leasing Association (FLA) Lending Code.[18]

The Banking Code is sponsored by three trade associations: the British Bankers Association (representing banks), the Building Societies Association (representing the mutual building societies, most of which of do not offer unsecured credit), and the Association of Payment Clearing Systems (APACS, representing credit card issuers). The first Code came into effect in March 1991, and the eighth edition was published in March 2008. All retail banks and building societies that offer consumer credit and credit card issuers in the United Kingdom are signatories of the Banking Code and between them cover 63 percent of unsecured lending. Companies that have signed up to the FLA Lending Code include those that offer consumer and car finance, including store cards and in-store finance. The association has 53 companies in membership, which between them cover 30 percent of unsecured lending in the United Kingdom. Many of these specialize in the subprime market. In other words, less than 10 percent of unsecured lending is not covered by either Code. For the most part, this will be mail order and traditional subprime

16. Office of Fair Trading. Unfair relationships: OFT guidance. 2006. www.oft.gov.uk/shared_oft/business_leaflets/enterprise_act/oft854.pdf.
17. See www.bankingcode.org.uk.
18. See www.tlr.ltd.uk/fla/lendingcode.aspx. The FLA is the trade body for consumer credit companies.

lenders such as home credit companies and pawnbrokers (who have their own self-regulatory regimes, although these fall short of the Banking and FLA Codes).

Broadly speaking, the content of these two codes is similar. Both have sections on marketing and advertising, on responsible lending, and on dealing with customers in financial difficulty. Both place requirements on lenders with regard to dealing with customers in financial difficulty, and these have been the subject of extensive consultation with independent, not-for-profit debt advisers. The Banking Code also has a separate section covering credit cards. The key difference lies in the fact that the Banking Code is accompanied by detailed *Guidance for Subscribers,* which provides details of how they are expected to interpret and implement the Code.[19]

In contrast, the procedures for revising the content of the two codes are rather different, with Banking Code procedures being rather more rigorous than those of the FLA Lending Code. The Banking Code is subject to independent review every three years (previously every two years). An independent reviewer is appointed who takes written evidence from a broad range of stakeholders and, following one or more roundtables, recommends changes to the Code and Guidance.[20] The three sponsoring bodies consider the report, issue a public response, and amend the Code and Guidance accordingly.[21] In theory the Code sponsors can ignore the recommendations of the Code reviewer. In practice they accept the great majority of them. One of the areas where recommendations have not been implemented in full relates to responsible lending.

Supervision of Compliance with the Codes

The Banking Code has an independent compliance monitoring body, the Banking Code Standards Board (BCSB).[22] The board itself includes the chief executives of the three sponsoring bodies, but independent nonexecutives are in the majority and the chair is drawn from these independents. It has an executive whose primary role is to assess compliance with the Code. This is done through a range of methods that are very similar to those used by the FSA in monitoring compliance by mortgage lenders. All subscribers are required to file a detailed annual statement of compliance. In addition, BCSB staff undertake general compliance monitoring and themed investigations. Both involve visits to subscribers, scrutiny of files, and sitting in while staff do their jobs, including taking calls from the public. In addition, themed reviews use mystery shopping. General reports are produced on themed reviews and are available through the BCSB website. See, for example, the 2007 review of credit assessment.[23]

19. www.bankingcode.org.uk/libraryhome.htm.
20. www.bba.org.uk/content/1/c4/47/59/Full_Kempson_review1.pdf.
21. www.bba.org.uk/content/1/c4/47/61/Subscribers_response.pdf.
22. www.bankingcode.org.uk/home.htm.
23. www.bankingcode.org.uk/wpdocs/Credit%20assessment%20themed%20review.doc.

Detailed discussions are held with Code subscribers who are not fully compliant, with a view to putting things right. Serious breaches are referred to the disciplinary committee of the board members (with independents in the majority), which has an independent chair who does not sit on the board. There is a right of appeal to the full board. The BCSB does not have the power to fine, but it can require a subscriber to compensate customers. It can also "name and shame," which is a very powerful sanction because breaching your own code of practice is seen as worse than breaching an externally imposed rule. See, for example, the disciplining of Capital One for breach of the code sections prohibiting mailing credit card cheques to people likely to be in financial difficulty.[24] Very serious breaches would result in the expulsion of a subscriber from the Code.

The Banking Code regime is, therefore, as rigorous as that applied by the FSA. Indeed, the review of self-regulation conducted for the Treasury described it as "an exemplar"[25] and said that, unlike mortgages, conduct of business in the area of retail banking (including unsecured credit offered by subscribers) should continue to be subject to self-regulation under the Banking Code. It was not, therefore, brought under full regulation by the FSA.

In contrast, compliance monitoring of the FLA Lending Code is less extensive and until recently has been primarily based on complaints received and annual compliance statements from subscribers. Part of the explanation for this lies in the nature of the subscribers. In contrast to the Banking Code, which has a relatively few large subscribing institutions, the FLA Lending Code has a large number of small institutions in membership. It is overseen by a Lending Code Group (with independent members in the majority), and the compliance regime has recently been strengthened by visits undertaken by the chair of the Group, a second group member, and the FLA compliance officer. As with the Banking Code, detailed discussions are held with Code subscribers who are not fully compliant to improve procedures and practices. Serious breaches are referred to the Lending Code Group for subscribers to explain their procedures and proposals for improvement. The ultimate sanction is expulsion from the Code and there are plans to establish a Disciplinary Committee of the FLA Board to carry out this function.[26]

The Financial Ombudsman Service

The FOS, like the FSA, was set up under the Financial Services and Markets Act 2000 and was formed in 2001 from a merger of seven ombudsman schemes covering specific aspects of financial services.

24. www.bankingcode.org.uk/press/BCSB%20-%20Capital%20One%20Press%20Release%20%20FINAL%20071106.doc.

25. www.publications.parliament.uk/pa/cm109899/cmselect/cmtreasy/73/73ap13htm.

26. See www.fla.org.uk/downloads/download.asp?Ref=4357&hash=fa12c724b96a2cbb59a694269ea539f9.

The FOS was set up to resolve individual disputes between consumers and financial services firms "fairly, reasonably, quickly and informally." It covers all retail financial firms that are regulated by the FSA and deals with all complaints about activities regulated by the FSA, including selling mortgages, accepting deposits, selling insurance policies, and selling or advising on investment products. Since 2007 it has also handled all complaints about consumer credit, bringing in 60,000 businesses that had never before been subject to an ombudsman scheme; previously it could only deal with credit offered by regulated firms (principally the banks). The service is free to consumers and informal in nature.

Complaints are handled first by the Customer Contact Division, where consumers can discuss the matter and be advised whether or not their complaint falls within the jurisdiction of the FOS. If the complaint is within jurisdiction and remains unresolved, the case is passed to an adjudicator for assessment and investigation. Cases may be resolved through mediation and/or by formal adjudication. Complainants or firms can ask for their case to be referred to an ombudsman if they are dissatisfied with the assessment or adjudication issued by an adjudicator. Disputed cases may also be referred directly to an ombudsman by an adjudicator.

The approach taken by adjudicators and ombudsmen when looking at cases is to decide what is fair and reasonable in the circumstances of each particular case. This includes taking into account relevant law, codes of practice, and regulatory rules and guidance. If the evidence is contradictory, or the two sides of the story do not tally, they make decisions on the basis of what they believe is most likely to have happened on the balance of probability. Although the ombudsman service is not bound by legal precedent, adjudicators and ombudsmen aim to be consistent in the approach they take to particular types of complaints. Decisions are binding on firms, although consumers who do not accept the decision they receive may take their case to the courts.

If the FOS upholds a complaint, it can require the firm at fault to make appropriate redress to the complainant. The aim is to put complainants back into the financial position that they would have been in had the situation giving rise to the complaint not occurred.

In 2006–07, the FOS received 627,814 inquiries, half of which were about endowment-backed mortgages. In total, adjudicators took on 94,392 new cases, 46,134 of which related to endowment mortgages. Just 1,755 were about other types of mortgages and secured or unsecured loans, and 2,731 were about credit cards. This, of course, predates full coverage of consumer credit by the FOS. Three-quarters of all new cases were initiated by consumers themselves, the remainder by bodies acting on their behalf.[27]

An independent review of the FOS concluded that it provided a high-quality and accessible service that was fair and reasonable in both the decisions it made

27. Financial Ombudsman Service (2007).

and the procedures it followed.[28] A second review was commissioned in 2007 to look, specifically, at accessibility and transparency of the FOS.[29]

Strengths and Weaknesses of the Current System

Recent changes have led to much more wide-ranging and robust statutory regulation of both mortgages and unsecured credit. This goes far beyond requirements for information disclosure and provides extensive consumer protection, both when and after they purchase products. Mortgage regulation is currently more extensive than that of consumer credit, which is supplemented by self-regulation. That may change when the Consumer Credit Act 2006 is implemented in full.

At present, self-regulation plays an important part in providing full consumer protection in responsible lending and dealing with customers in financial difficulty (both of which are covered by the FSA conduct of business rules for mortgages). This is not necessarily a weakness, however, because self-regulation has proved itself able to respond more quickly to abuses in the marketplace than full regulation. Because self-regulation involves a mutual acceptance of the need to conform to mutually agreed norms of behavior, it has also driven up standards across the industry. Companies are expected to comply with the spirit, not the letter, of the Banking Code or FLA Lending Code. A key weakness is that only 63 percent of unsecured lending is covered by a rigorous code and compliance monitoring that approaches the level for mortgages; 30 percent is covered by a less detailed but still rigorous code, but one where compliance monitoring is weaker, and just under 10 percent of lending is not covered by adequate self-regulation at all. Because this sector specializes in small loans to people on low incomes, it means that many vulnerable consumers have inadequate protection.

A key omission from the regulatory framework is that there is nothing similar to the U.S. Community Re-investment Act or Home Mortgage Disclosure Act, although there have been various calls for CRA-like legislation. In general, there is little evidence of redlining and geographical discrimination, although that is not to say that everyone has access to mortgages and credit. Instead debates center on providing access to affordable consumer credit, and a Financial Inclusion Taskforce has been set up by Treasury ministers to oversee work in this area, reporting annually to ministers and, through them, to Parliament.

Legislation alone is not sufficient to ensure consumer protection; compliance needs to be monitored and enforced. Compliance monitoring by statutory regulators is, undoubtedly, far more extensive for mortgages than it is for unsecured credit, which has primarily been undertaken through self-regulation. In the past the OFT has had limited powers and has been slow to use them. Even the new

28. Kempson, Collard, and Moore (2004).
29. Hunt (2007).

credit license regime that was introduced in 2008 is likely to fall well short of the supervision of mortgages by the FSA. Mindful of this shortcoming, the banking industry has put in place a robust system of compliance monitoring of the Banking Code that mirrors the procedures of the FSA. Other consumer credit companies, through the FLA, are also tightening the way that compliance with their Lending Code is monitored and enforced. Together this ensures that most firms do act responsibly in their dealings with their customers. Self-regulation does not, however, include the power to fine or to remove the right of a company to trade. The maximum penalty is naming and shaming and expelling a firm from membership of the Banking or Lending Code. In practice, though, this is seldom needed and the real value of self-regulation is the way that firms approach it. BCSB compliance officers, for example, achieve a great deal through informal negotiation with firms to ensure that policies and procedures are fully compliant with the Banking Code. The overwhelming majority of firms feel a strong pressure not to breach their own mutually agreed rules.

Compliance monitoring, especially for unsecured credit, is a complex system that requires memoranda of understanding between the main players to avoid overregulation (and double jeopardy) and underregulation. It is open to criticism for its complexity, resulting in periodic calls for consumer credit also to be brought within the remit of the FSA. In time that seems the most likely outcome.

Finally, until very recently, the only means of redress for consumers with extortionate credit agreements was individually through the courts, and very few cases had been brought. Bringing consumer credit into the remit of the FOS should mark an important improvement in consumer redress. But without provision for class actions through the courts, there are limits on wider benefits deriving from individual complaints. Input from the FOS to the independent review of the Banking Code has brought about substantial changes to its provisions. And the super-complaints brought by consumer bodies, under the Enterprise Act 2002, that have resulted in an inquiry by the Competition Commission have also tackled market abuses. But neither has the direct impact of a class action.

References

Council of Mortgage Lenders. 2001. "CML Responds to Treasury Announcement on Mortgage Regulation." Press release, October 26.

Ellison, A., and S. Collard. 2007. "Evaluation of the Illegal Money Lending Pilots." London: Department for Trade and Industry (DTI) (www.pfrc.bris.ac.uk/publications/credit_debt/Reports/Illegal%20lending%20pilot%20evaluation.pdf).

Financial Ombudsman Service (FOS). 2007. "Annual Review 2006/07." London (www.financialombudsman.org.uk/publications/ar07/index.html).

HM Treasury. 1999. "Financial Services Regulation Report 3 1998/99 (Appendix 9), Memorandum from the Council of Mortgage Lenders" (www.publications.parliament.uk/pa/cm199899/cmselect/cmtreasy/73/73ap13.htm).

———. 2000. "Cracking the Codes for Customers." Banking Services Consumer Codes Review Group.

Hunt, D. 2008. "An Agenda for Accessibility and Excellence in the Financial Ombudsman Service." Financial Ombudsman Service (www.thehuntreview.org.uk/updates/FOS_Report.pdf).

Kempson, E., and C. Whyley. 1999. "Extortionate Credit in the UK: A Report to the DTI." London: Department for Trade and Industry (www.pfrc.bris.ac.uk/Reports/Extortionate%20Credit%20in%20the%20UK.pdf).

Kempson, E., S. Collard, and N. Moore. 2004. "Fair and Reasonable: An Independent Assessment of the Financial Ombudsman Service." Bristol: University of Bristol Personal Finance Research Centre (www.pfrc.bris.ac.uk/Reports/Financial_Ombudsman_Service.pdf).

Office of Fair Trading (OFT). 2007. "Consumer Credit Licensing: General Guidance for Licensees and Applicants. Draft Guidance on Fitness and Requirements—Consultation Document." London (www.oft.gov.uk/shared_oft/consultations/oft920con.pdf).

Contributors

Michael S. Barr
University of Michigan

Eric S. Belsky
Harvard University

Raphael W. Bostic
University of Southern California

Shawn Cole
Harvard University

Amy Crews Cutts
Freddie Mac

Kathleen C. Engel
Cleveland State University

Ren S. Essene
Harvard University

Elaine Kempson
University of Bristol

Patricia A. McCoy
University of Connecticut

William A. Merrill
Wells Fargo Home Mortgage

Sendhil Mullainathan
Harvard University

Anthony Pennington-Cross
Marquette University

Elizabeth Renuart
National Consumer Law Center

Nicolas P. Retsinas
Harvard University

Edna R. Sawady
Market Innovations Inc.

Eldar Shafir
Princeton University

Jennifer Tescher
*Center for Financial Services
   Innovation*

John Thompson
H&R Block

Peter Tufano
Harvard University

Susan M. Wachter
University of Pennsylvania

Index